Novembver 3-8, 2013
Chicago, IL, USA

Association for Computing Machinery

Advancing Computing as a Science & Profession

SIGUCCS'13

Proceedings of the ACM Annual Conference on

Special Interest Group on University and College Computing Services

Sponsored by:

ACM SIGUCCS

Supported by:

Bomgar, Cherwell Software, Taskstream, TopHat, Unidesk, & Mozy

**Association for
Computing Machinery**

Advancing Computing as a Science & Profession

The Association for Computing Machinery
2 Penn Plaza, Suite 701
New York, New York 10121-0701

Notice to Past Authors of ACM-Published Articles
ACM intends to create a complete electronic archive of all articles and/or other material previously published by ACM. If you have written a work that has been previously published by ACM in any journal or conference proceedings prior to 1978, or any SIG Newsletter at any time, and you do NOT want this work to appear in the ACM Digital Library, please inform permissions@acm.org, stating the title of the work, the author(s), and where and when published.

ISBN: 978-1-4503-2318-5 (Digital)

ISBN: 978-1-4503-2682-7 (Print)

Additional copies may be ordered prepaid from:

ACM Order Department
PO Box 30777
New York, NY 10087-0777, USA

Phone: 1-800-342-6626 (USA and Canada)
+1-212-626-0500 (Global)
Fax: +1-212-944-1318
E-mail: acmhelp@acm.org
Hours of Operation: 8:30 am – 4:30 pm ET

Printed in the USA

Conference Chair's Welcome

Welcome to the 2013 SIGUCCS Management Symposium and Services & Support Conference!

Welcome to the 50th anniversary of SIGUCCS!

It's hard not to be excited about this event. We have a lot to celebrate. The conference is located in a fantastic city; rich in art, architecture, music, and food. We are celebrating our third year as a combined conference. And, most importantly, we are making history as we celebrate the 50th anniversary of SIGUCCS.

SIGUCCS has meant so much to me and I am thrilled to have this opportunity to give back to this organization. When I attended my first SIGUCCS conference, I was a fresh-faced newcomer, just entering the world of user services. That first conference opened my eyes to new opportunities, new adventures, and new contacts. At that first conference, I made friends with people in similar positions to mine from all around the country and have kept those friendships going for sixteen years. And each time I attend a SIGUCCS conference, I add a dozen or so new SIGUCCS friends into that fold.

If this is your first (or second) SIGUCCS, take this opportunity to not only attend sessions, but to also meet people. Connections can be the most significant takeaway from this week. These are the people that you can email when you are having problems. These are the people that you can email to ask "How are you handling this situation?" We are all in the same boat in supporting information technology; we just work at different institutions. Our schools may be competing for students, but as IT professionals, we all just want to make our campuses the best possible place for the students that end up there. We can all REACH NEW HEIGHTS by sharing our experiences, both formally and informally at this conference.

Putting this conference together is a team effort. I want to extend a special thanks to the SIGUCCS 2013 Core Committee, all of whom have been working on this together for over a year. I have enjoyed working with all of you and getting to know all of you a little better. I count each of you as very special SIGUCCS friends! I also want to thank the many that volunteered to help out in various ways throughout the planning stages; from the track chairs and readers who have made our program special, to those that coordinate some unique part of the conference. Each of you has done a fantastic job and I commend you. Next, I want to extend a deep gratitude to the presenters, without whom this conference would not be possible. And finally, I want to thank all the attendees. Each and every one of you is important to the makeup of the conference and has something to contribute.

And remember, even if you don't make it to the top of Willis Tower this week, we can all REACH NEW HEIGHTS right here at the conference.

Lisa Brown
SIGUCCS'13 Conference Chair

Program Chairs' Welcome

As Service and Support Program Co-Chairs, it is our distinct pleasure to welcome you to SIGUCCS 2013 in downtown Chicago. This year's conference will draw attendance from Higher Education IT professionals across the nation and abroad.

This November, we will be afforded an excellent opportunity to meet with peers at formal and informal events, share experiences, and create an opportunity for networking, collaboration and the building of relationships that remain valuable all year long.

Our Service and Support conference program is rich with informative and inspiring sessions, engaging plenary speakers, and many opportunities to engage with seasoned professionals.

As you plan your session attendance, feel free to select topics from any of the tracks. Our newest track, Career Development, builds on enthusiasm present in some of the 2012 sessions regarding personal and professional development in our industry.

Don't miss the poster sessions on Thursday afternoon, featuring communication award winners, our conference vendors, SIGUCCS' program information, and selected authors.

We would especially like to thank the authors, track chairs, and readers. Many hours of work have gone into each paper and presentation. The quality of our program depends upon the tireless efforts of these volunteers!

The SIGUCCS Conferences have been invaluable and enriching for both of us and we hope to bring you the same experience at the 2013 Conference. Please take advantage of all that the conference and Chicago has to offer.

Laurie Fox
SIGUCCS'13 Program Co-Chair

Jean Tagliamonte
SIGUCCS'13 Program Co-Chair

Table of Contents

Session 4

Session 5

Session 6

Session 7

Session 8

Session 9

Author Index

SIGUCCS 2013 Conference Organization

General Chair: Lisa Brown *(University of Rochester)*

Program Chairs: Laurie Fox *(SUNY Geneseo)*
Jean Tagliamonte *(Vassar College)*

Local Arrangements Chair: Melissa Doernte *(DePaul University)*

Publicity Chair: Jody Gardei *(Ferris State University)*

Treasurer: Allan Chen *(Menlo College)*

Registration Chair: Kristin Dietiker *(University of Washington)*

Program Committee: Blake Adams *(University of West Georgia)*
Ben Arnold *(University of Northern Iowa)*
Miranda Carney-Morris *(Lewis & Clark College)*
Allan Chen *(Menlo College)*
Michael Cooper *(West Virginia University)*
Kelly McLaughlin *(Hobart and William Smith Colleges)*
Jean Ross *(Vassar College)*
Brett Williams *(University of Wyoming)*

Additional reviewers:

Vijay Anand	Bob Haring-Smith
Sandra Bury	Kristi Evans Lenz
Steven Fife	Patti Mitch
Kathy Fletcher	Trevor Murphy
Lucas Friedrichsen	Darin Phelps
Larry French	Cheryl Stahler
Chad Fust	Frances Carr Versace
	Brett Williams

SIGUCCS 2013 Sponsor & Supporters

Sponsor:

Supporters:

A Centralized Storage System with Automated Data Tiering for Private Cloud Environment

Mikifumi Shikida
Research Center for
Advanced Computing
Infrastructure
Japan Advanced Institute of
Science and Technology
Nomi, Ishikawa, Japan
shikida@jaist.ac.jp

Hiroaki Nakano
Research Center for
Advanced Computing
Infrastructure
Japan Advanced Institute of
Science and Technology
Nomi, Ishikawa, Japan
nhiroaki@jaist.ac.jp

Shuichi Kozaka
Research Center for
Advanced Computing
Infrastructure
Japan Advanced Institute of
Science and Technology
Nomi, Ishikawa, Japan
kosaka@jaist.ac.jp

Masato Mato
Research Center for
Advanced Computing
Infrastructure
Japan Advanced Institute of
Science and Technology
Nomi, Ishikawa, Japan
masato-m@jaist.ac.jp

Satoshi Uda
Research Center for
Advanced Computing
Infrastructure
Japan Advanced Institute of
Science and Technology
Nomi, Ishikawa, Japan
zin@jaist.ac.jp

ABSTRACT

This paper describes a new centralized storage system with automated data tiering for use in the private cloud environment of the authors' institute. There are various purposes for a user's activity in the private cloud environment. Both a high-speed storage server and high capacity storage server were needed in the previous implementation. The users could not easily handle their files because they needed to distinguish between their file servers. The new system has both high-speed storage on SSD drives and high capacity storage on SAS drives. Users can save their files on a high-speed volume. The system automatically moves access-less data to lower cost SAS drives. It provides high-speed and low cost storage services at a low power consumption. It has also improved the convenience for users.

Categories and Subject Descriptors

K.6.4 [**Computing Milieux**]: Management of Computing and Information Systems System Management [Centralization/decentralization]; H.3.2 [**Information Storage and Retrieval**]: Information Storage; C.5.5 [**Computer Systems Organization**]: Computer System Implementation Servers

General Terms

Design, Performance

SIGUCCS'13, November 3–8, 2013, Chicago, IL, USA.
Copyright is held by the owner/author(s). Publication rights licensed to ACM.
ACM 978-1-4503-2318-5/13/11 ...$15.00.
http://dx.doi.org/10.1145/2504776.2504809.

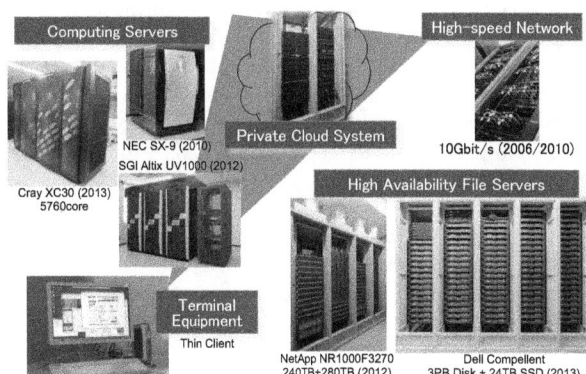

Figure 1: The overview of our computing infrastructure

Keywords

Storage System, Data Tiering, Private Cloud System

1. INTRODUCTION

Cloud computing is now more widely used for large-scale services. Our institute was established in 1990. We designed our computing environment as a centralized system since its foundation. Users can connect to their desktop environment on our server from anywhere on campus using our system.

We provided large-scale file servers for users' storage of their desktop environments on our private cloud system[4]. The storage systems provide the most fundamental services in our computing infrastructure. They are available 24 hours a day and 7 days a week. Thus, we need servers that have a large capacity of storage, operate at a high speed, and have high availability.

We had previously introduced two types of servers to provide both high-speed access and large capacity. The total cost of these systems was expensive, and space utilization was insufficient, because users do not regularly access most of their files. They could not move the files to the archive area since we could not provide a convenient way to move them.

In this paper, we describe our new centralized storage service for our private cloud environment. Since the system has an automated data tiering feature, the system can automatically and more efficiently move data between the high-speed SSD drives and the lower cost SAS drives. We also discuss the advantages of using this system as the private cloud system in our institute.

2. OUR COMPUTING INFRASTRUCTURE

In this section, we describe the computing infrastructure in our national institute, Japan Advanced Institute of Science and Technology (JAIST in short). JAIST encompasses only three graduate schools. Our users consist of about 1,000 students and 500 staff. Almost all the graduate students and most of the faculty members in our graduate schools use our computing infrastructure all day long to study and advance their world-class research. That is the reason why we must provide our fundamental services 24 hours a day and 7 days a week.

2.1 JAIST Computing Infrastructure

Figure 1 shows an overview of our computing infrastructure. We designed our computing environment from the beginning to be a centralized system[3]. Each user has a thin client as a terminal equipment on his/her desk. Users can connect to their desktop environments on the high-speed application servers. We provide both UNIX and Windows servers as application servers. All of the users' data are stored in file servers, although roaming profiles are copied to local storage temporally. We have to provide much storage capacity because they have no disk drive in the clients. We also provide several types of high-performance parallel computing servers. Some of students and researchers in school of material science make large-scale simulations of physics and chemistry running with more than 5,000 CPUs in several weeks. This is another reason that we have to provide much space in the storage. All of them are connected by high-speed and reliable duplicated network system[2], as shown in Figure 2.

In these ways, the file servers can be used for various purposes such as to provide documents on desktops and for large-scale data created on the high-performance computing servers. The storage systems provide the most fundamental services in our computing infrastructure.

2.2 The History of Storage Systems in Our Campus

In this section, we present the history of our storage systems. We list most of the primary file servers in Tables 1, 2, 3, and 4. All of the systems are leased for four years.

2.2.1 Early 1990s - Centralized File Servers for UNIX Workstations

Table 1 lists the storage systems that we introduced in the early 1990s. In those days, all of the students used a UNIX workstation created by Sun Microsystems. We centralized all of the storage for the workstations, such as the users' home directories and application folders. They could use any workstation in any room on campus to access their files. This

Table 1: Storage systems in early 1990s

Year	Company	System	Capacity	Type
1992	Fujixerox (AUSPEX)	Argoss9450	20GB	H
1993	Fujixerox (AUSPEX)	Argoss9450	40GB	H
1996	Sony	NEWS-7000	100GB	H
1997	Sun	Enterprise5000	230GB	H
1997	Sony	NEWS-7600 PetaServe	1000GB	A

cloud-like storage service was very convenient. However, they encountered major problems when there was a network or server failure.

2.2.2 Around 2000 - High Availability Clusters

Table 2: Storage systems around 2000

Year	Campany	System (HA software)	Capacity	Type
1997	Sony	NEWS-7900 (Veritas FirstWatch)	200GB	H
1999	Sun	Enterprise3500 (SunCluster)	800GB	H
2000	Sun	Enterprise4500 (SunCluster)	2TB	H
2001	NetApp /Fujitsu	NR1000 300 (ONTAP)	3TB	H
2001	Hitachi	HP9000V DF400 (MC/ServiceGuard)	3.3TB	H
2001	Fujitsu	GP7000S 22R	4.6TB	A
2002	Hitachi	H9000V L3000 (MC/ServiceGuard)	2.8TB	H

Data storage is the most fundamental service in our computing infrastructure. All of the systems stop when there is a failure on the storage system. We needed higher availability so that the system could be used at any time. Therefore, we introduced the HA cluster servers listed in Table 2 as our storage systems.

2.2.3 The late 2000s - NAS Head for NFS and CIFS Accesses

Table 3: Storage systems in the late 2000s

Year	Company	System	Capacity Physical (User)	Type
2004	Fujitsu	PRIMEPOWER 650	35TB	H
2005	NetApp/Fujitsu	NR1000 F540	64TB	H
2005	NetApp/Fujitsu	NR1000 R200	107TB	A
2008	SGI/ONStor	IS4500F + Bobcat	260TB (100TB)	H
2009	DELL/NEC	EqualLogic (CLUSTERPRO)	243TB (150TB)	H
2009	DDN	S2A9900	1.2PB	A

Table 3 lists the storage systems we introduced in the late 2000s. Most of the users used worked on Windows PCs at that time. They needed to access their files using the CIFS protocol. Our systems could serve files with both the NFS and CIFS protocols, and the users could access any file using both protocols.

2.2.4 2010s - Current systems

Table 4 shows our current storage systems.

2.3 Two Types of Storage Services

Our storage service is used for various purposes, and it is roughly distinguished into two types. One of them is for fre-

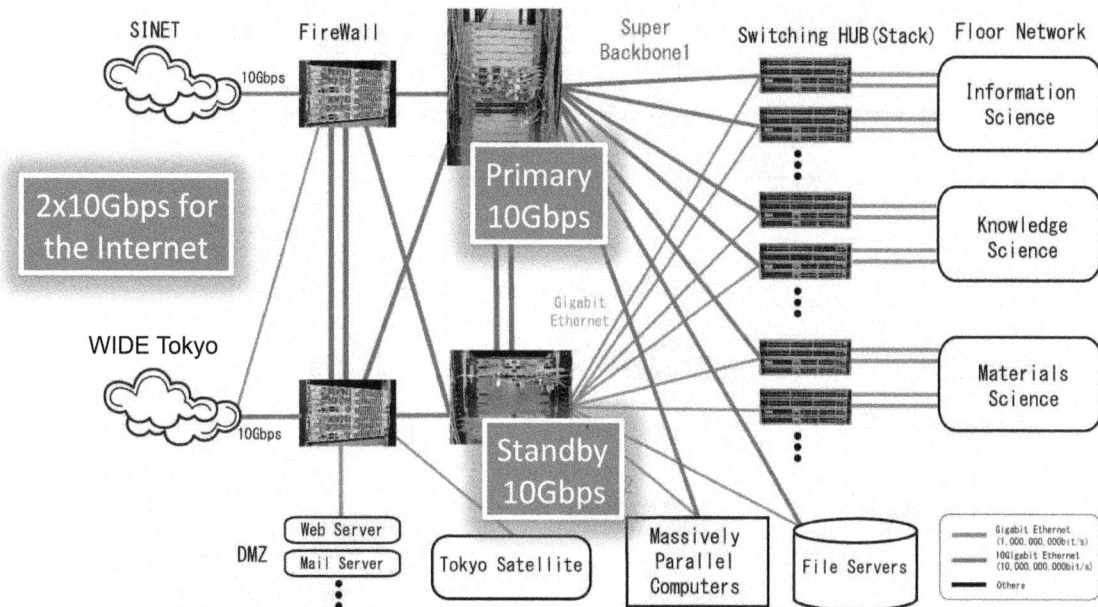

Figure 2: The network in our campus

Table 4: Current storage systems

Year	Campany	System	Capacity *Physical* (User)	Type
2012	NetApp/Fujitsu	NR1000 F3270	520TB (250TB)	H
2013	DELL	Compellent	3PB (1.2PB)	H/A

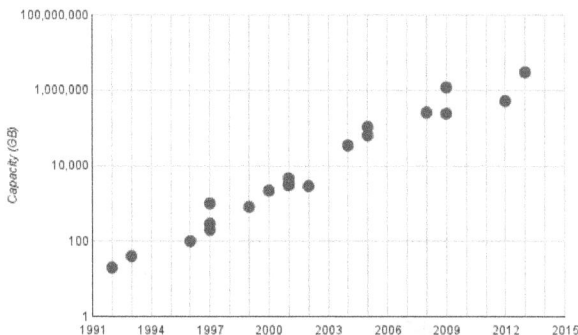

Figure 3: The capacity of each system

quently accessed files such as the users' desktop documents, and the other one is for the archived files, which they do not access for long periods of time.

We provide two types of systems for the two types of services, "high-speed servers" and "archive servers". The high-speed servers are configured using high-speed, reliable and expensive parts. The archive servers are not suitable for high-speed file access because their parts are not expensive, but they have a large capacity. These types of systems are shown as "H" and "A" in Tables 1, 2, 3, and 4.

We had to replace the last two systems from Y2009 in Table 3 earlier this year. The DELL/NEC server is a high-speed server and the DDN S2A9900 is an archive server.

2.4 Requirements for Storage System

We already mentioned that we designed centralized storage systems. The users can access any file from anywhere using any protocol. The systems are high-speed and highly available and have a large capacity.

The total amount of users' files has increased over the years. Figure 3 shows the exponential increase in capacity of our systems. Their power consumption has also been increased. However, reducing costs is one of the most important issues in JAIST. Having several different systems is ineffective at meeting this issue. Each server has space independently, although all of the files in one system are effectively stored. Users do not need to access all of their files using the high-speed access, because they do not access most of documents for long periods of time. The users should not be saving their minimally used files on the expensive high-speed server. They should move them to the archive server, but we could not provide a convenient way to move them.

3. OUR NEW STORAGE SYSTEM WITH AUTOMATED DATA TIERING

We describe our new storage system in this section.

3.1 The Overview of New Storage System

Figure 4 shows an overview of our new storage system. There are three pairs of storage array controllers. They are duplicated in case of hardware failures. All of the disk chassis are connected to one of the controllers, and the total capacity is over 3 PB. The drives are not high-speed, because the disk drives are connected using a Near-line SAS interface. However, we also use 24-TB solid state disk drives (SSD in short), which we can access at very high-speed.

This system serves the users' files using NFS and CIFS protocols. We include five pairs of duplicated NAS heads for load balancing. All of the NAS heads are connected to all of the disk array controllers by using duplicated Fibre channel switches. The NAS heads use Samba software on Solaris systems. This type of NAS head is not very fast, but

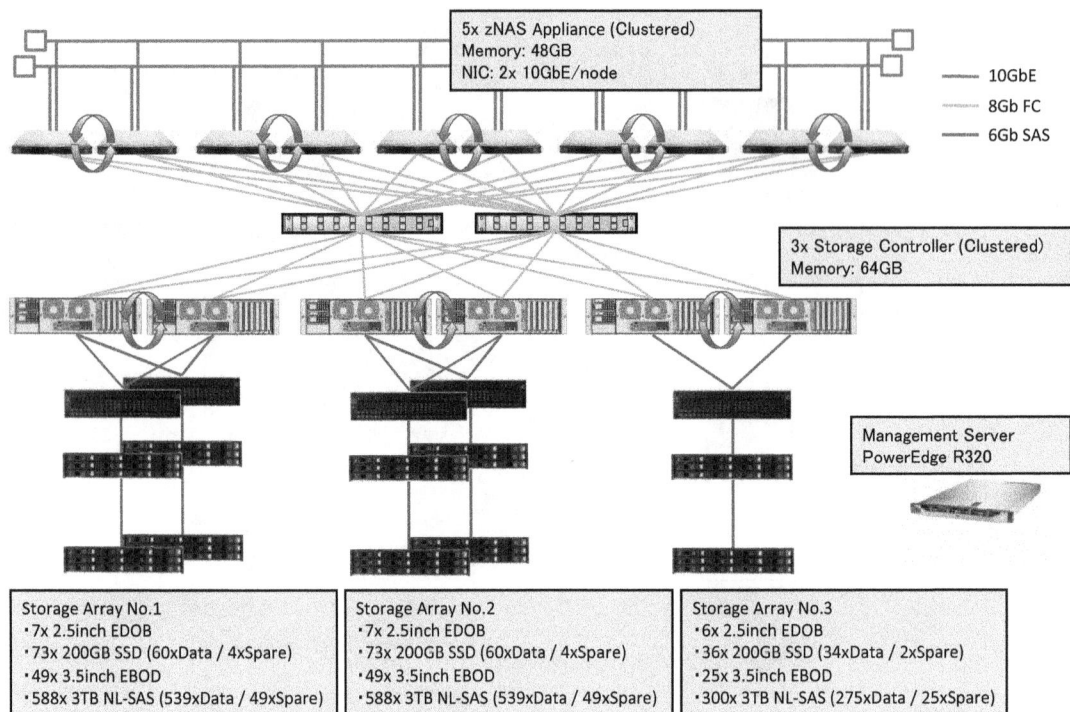

Figure 4: The overview of new storage system

3.2 Automated Data Tiering

Our system contains two types of disk drives. One of them is a Near-line SAS disk and the other is solid state disk. Users want to place their files on an SSD drive because this SSD drive is much faster than a standard disk drive. However, the SSD drive is only 24 TB, which is less than 1% of the total capacity.

The array controller has a feature for automated data tiering. Users can write their files on the fastest disk drives. The area is appropriately named "Tier 1". The frequency of access to each block is calculated. The data blocks that are not accessed for over two weeks, are migrated to "Tier 2" on the slower disk drives. In the opposite way, the data blocks that are more regularly accessed are migrated from Tier 2 to Tier 1. This migration process is executed every night. In this way, the users can access their files faster, and we can thus reduce the costs for high-speed disk drives.

3.3 Types of Services on New Storage System

We also provide two types of storage services: high-speed and archive. Users require high-speed access when using a high-speed service. However, high-speed access is not needed for the archive volumes. An SSD drive should be used only for high-speed volumes. We configured the archive volumes only on only Tier 2, which is on the hard disk drives. This means no tiering occurs for the archive volumes. The system has another migration mechanism between RAID1 and RAID5/6. RAID1 is faster than RAID5/6, but it needs a lot of space. RAID5/6 effectively uses its allocated space, but access is not very fast. Users can write archiving files

on RAID1 blocks, and the files will move to the RAID5/6 blocks after a few weeks.

4. DISCUSSION

In this section, we describe the discussion of our storage system.

4.1 Performance of the Storage System

We measured the performance of our system using the SPECsfs2008 benchmark[1]. The results from SPECsfs2008 _nfs.v3 showed there were 60,000 Ops/Sec for a high-speed volume, which uses SSD drives. However, the results for SPECsfs2008_nfs.v3 also showed there were 10,000 Ops/Sec for an archive volume. This volume uses the RAID6 blocks on the SAS hard disk drives. This is the slowest condition in this system.

We cannot compare these results with ones from another system, because we did not use enough resources for this benchmark. The SPECsfs2008_nfs.v3 of a high-speed volume goes beyond 110,000 Ops/Sec when we use more resources for this benchmark.

4.2 Cost of Storage Systems

Our previous systems corresponding to this system were DELL EqualLogic and DDN S2A9900 listed in Table 3. The monthly lease fees for these systems are approximately 5,300,000 and 3,200,000 JPY. The monthly lease fee of the new system is approximately 6,100,000 JPY. This fee is expensive for only one system, because the capacity is very large. It is 30% less than the total fee of the previous systems, although the capacity is twice the total of the previous systems.

The disk drives in the system are slow and inexpensive. There are fewer drives than the previous systems because

the compatibility of the CIFS protocol is better than for an appliance server, such as in our Y2012 system listed in Table 4.

the size of each one is large. This means that the power consumption of this system is reduced.

4.3 Usability

The users of the previous systems had to distinguish between their files in order to store them into a high-speed volume or an archive volume. This was inconvenient for the users. That is the main reason why the utilization rate of the archive volume was relatively small.

They do not need to move their files to the archive volume on our new system. They just leave their files in the document folders, and then, the system will automatically move them into the archive volume, but the users will still see them in their document folders. This is a friendly interface.

In other words, users have extraordinarily wide space to use on the high-speed volume.

4.4 Policy of Data Tiering

The policy of data tiering is very important for this system. We can control the period for moving access-less data to slower storage. Users can access them faster when the period is longer. However, this policy uses more SSD drives. We also can control the period for moving data back to faster storage. We can also choose RAID 1, 5, or 6 for each storage area. RAID1 is faster, but it takes up a lot of space. Each setting influences the performance of each volume, and thus, it is hard to find the best settings.

5. CONCLUSION

In this paper, we described our centralized storage system with automated data tiering for our private cloud environment. There are various reasons for a user's activity in the private cloud environment. Both high-speed storage servers and high capacity storage servers were needed in the previous system. This was very costly and inconvenient for the users. The new system has both high-speed storage on SSD drives and high capacity storage on SAS drives. Users can save their files on the high-speed volume. The system automatically moves access-less data to the lower cost SAS drives. It provides high-speed and low cost storage services at a low power consumption, and has also improved the level of convenience for users.

In our future work, we will investigate the users' file access patterns to attempt to find the best configuration for this system.

6. REFERENCES

[1] S. P. E. Corporation. SPECsfs2008 User's Guide. http://www.spec.org/sfs2008/docs/usersguide.pdf, 2008.

[2] M. Shikida, Y. Inoguchi, S. Miwa, Y. Tan, and T. Matsuzawa. The Design Method of Large-scale High Availability Servers (in Japanese). In *Symposium on Distributed Systems, Internet and Operation Technology*, pages 57–62. Information Processing Society of Japan, Feb. 2001.

[3] M. Shikida, Y. Inoguchi, Y. Tan, and T. Matsuzawa. Efficient Management Techniques for Large-scale Distributed Systems (in Japanese). In *Symposium on Distributed Systems, Internet and Operation Technology*, pages 75–80. Information Processing Society of Japan, Feb. 1999.

[4] M. Shikida, K. Miyashita, M. Ueno, and S. Uda. An Evaluation of Private Cloud System for Desktop Environments. In *In proceedings of the 40th annual ACM SIGUCCS conference*, pages 131–134, 2012.

Lion Taming: Desktop Management of Apple Devices

Nik Varrone
SUNY Geneseo
1 College Circle
Geneseo, NY 14454
1-585-245-5577
varrone@geneseo.edu

Shawn Plummer
SUNY Geneseo
1 College Circle
Geneseo, NY 14454
1-585-245-5577
plummer@geneseo.edu

ABSTRACT
As Apple devices have become more popular on our campus, management is a greater necessity. SUNY Geneseo's desktop management of Apple devices has evolved from treating them as individual, personal devices to deployment built, domain bound, remotely accessible, and profile manager controlled computers. We will demonstrate how we use Apple Profile Manager, Netinstall, and other tools to tame our Apple desktop deployment.

Categories and Subject Descriptors
C.5.3 [Computer System Implementation]: Microcomputers – *Microprocessors, Personal Computers, Portable Devices, Workstations.*

K.3.1 [Computers and Education]: Computer Uses in Education – *Collaborative Learning, Computer-assisted Instruction (CAI), Computer-managed instruction (CMI), Distance Learning.*

General Terms
Management, Documentation, Standardization.

Keywords
Mac OS X, Desktop Management, Wireless.

1. INTRODUCTION
Macs used to be easy to manage. There wasn't too many of them in the average organization and there'll work too many requirements for their use.

However, as the years have rolled on the requirements of an organization, the percentage of Mac users, and ease-of-use has changed. It is no longer workable in a large organization to have Macs that are not managed and a part of the campus directory.

In the past 5 years the Macs used by faculty and staff at SUNY Geneseo have been transformed from isolated computers with local accounts that were largely configured and maintained manually. to active directory bound, centrally managed, easily deployable, capable of making Kerberized connections to network resources.

With the introduction of college owned and Personal iOS devices a mobile device management solution was also required to bring these devices under control.

Doing that is not as bad as it all sounds.

2. INSTITUTION INFORMATION
SUNY Geneseo is a public liberal arts college of about 5,200 students and 1000 faculty and staff. CIT as a department has four divisions (Information Systems, Instructional Technologies, Systems & Networking and User Services) and 29 professional staff members. We have a centralized IT structure, supporting all the academic and administrative departments on campus. Additional support is provided to the campus by CIT's fleet of roughly 75 student employees.

All campus academic buildings have nearly full wireless coverage and since the fall of 2007 all incoming freshmen are required to have a laptop computer meeting the minimum specifications of our mandatory notebook program.

3. HISTORY
3.1 The old ways A.K.A Sneaker Netting your way to victory
We all know the old way of making changes on a user's computer. When you need to make a change you must make an appointment with your user to manually perform the work. Users can call a helpdesk that will attempt to solve the problem remotely either by talking through the problem or making a remote desktop connection.

3.2 Labs
The early driver for change in the old ways came from our computer labs. The nature of lab management makes it ideal to develop and utilize tools that allow you to make a change in one place and then apply that change to an array of computers. At this time most of the work was done with Active directory (AD) bound Macs controlled through Apple's work group manager and remotely accessed through Apple Remote Desktop.

3.3 Deployment

Deployment was accomplished with a mix of cloned hard drive images, NetRestores, and Apple Remote Desktop often running from the mac server. Again, this was only usually done on Lab computers.

3.4 A Need for Change

As the demands of computer support change a new option is needed. In many environments the method of Mac support has fallen behind PCs in the ability to remotely control and administer those computers. There's no reason that Mac support should continue to function the way computer support was handled in the 90s. Macs, like their PC counterparts, should run enterprise-level systems that allow the IT department to more efficiently handle the administration and remote control of those computers.

4. WHAT DOES APPLE PROVIDE

4.1 Netinstall

NetInstall is Apple's deployment tool. Macs can boot to a default network deployment environment by holding down the N key. You can also select the startup disk from the Startup Disk system preference pane. The Mac will restart and load an image from the server. Images are created using the built in System Image Utility and uploaded to a share specified on the Server App. Files are shared over FTP and HTTP. Several types exist including NetBoot, NetRestore, and Netinstall.

NetBoot hosts an image on the server of a complete operating system. A computer can boot this image over the network and run. Generally this is used for hardware testing or kiosk type machines.

NetRestore is used to put a fully configured image on a target computer much in the same way that ghost functions. Our lab admins often use the NetRestore

NetInstall is a package based deployment system. Net installs can be easily built by supplying an installation file from the App Store and creating a small workflow. Using the Customize Package Selection Action default applications can be selected for the deployment while others can be listed as optional and enabled by a student worker. NetInstalls are very modular and can be deployed to a variety of devices as long as they are supported by the version of Mac OS being deployed..

4.2 Open Directory

This is Apple's implementation of LDAP which performs a variety of functions that include identification, authentication, and client management. Binding a mac to Open Directory in addition to Active Directory is a part of the Golden Triangle of Mac Management.

Historically Binding a Mac to both Active Directory and Open Directory, allowed you to use user authentication of your Active Directory and Mac Management tools of OS X server. Profile Manager has largely obsoleted this need. You do not need to bind a mac to both directory services to leverage the features of the latest version OS X Server. Open directory is still used by OS X server to store some information about client computers, but binding your desktop Macs to an Open Directory server is less necessary than it used to be.

4.3 Active Directory Binding

Macs, including the servers, can be bound to Microsoft Active Directory. This is one of the first projects that was undertaken to "modernize" Macs. Once bound to a domain, authentication gets much easier to manage and password control policies can be applied. Users are usually very receptive to the practice as once they are bound they have one less password to deal with. Gone are the days when a user is uncertain if they should use their "mac password" or their "email password" in a given dialogue box. Once a mac has been domain bound it will also be given a kerberos ticket at login and can use kerberized services. Access to the file server, printing, and even email can all be made through kerberos making it much simpler for the user to connect to these services.

Existing local accounts used by the customer have to be migrated to a mobile account to take full advantage of binding their macs to the directory. This was done via the means of a few terminal commands and a shell script. The old user account is first deleted leaving the home directory in place. It is then renewed to avoid any home directory naming conflicts. The customer logs in to create the new mobile account. Finally the shell script we devised is run. It is an interactive script that prompts the technician for the old , now renamed, home directory and the new destination directory. Ownership of the old home directory is given to the new mobile account user and files are moved with the mv command.

4.4 Profile Manager

Apple's web based policy tool, added in Lion Server, provides both a user portal to add devices to the profile manager and an Administrator interface. In the administrator interface you can define a variety of client behaviors for both Macs and iOS devices. Profile manager can create profiles which can control many settings on Mac OS X and iOS devices that can be applied to users, groups, devices, and device groups. Users and groups can come from your Active Directory if your server is bound to AD. A wide variety of preferences from general settings, network connections, certificates, energy savings, and more can be handled through profile manager. What can't be configured with one of the many predefined payloads can be controlled through the Custom Settings payload. Once a profile is saved it is pushed through the Apple Push Service and can get to clients almost anywhere they have a network connection. This makes the service ideal for working with faculty who have irregular working hours.

In the user portal, clients can sign up their devices for management. Once they have done so they can log back into the system for remotely lock or wipe their devices. They can also, if the administrator has allowed it, remove their device from management.

4.5 Apple Remote Desktop & Task Manager

Apple Remote Desktop 3 (ARD) has been out since 2004 and allows you to remotely administer Mac computers through a variety of methods. ARD allows the admin to remotely monitor and control configured Macs. Admins can begin remote support sessions, query host computers, monitor a host of computers simultaneously, perform file management, install software, and even perform terminal commands. Most importantly, especially in an educational environment, there is a task server component and jobs that need to be pushed to more irregularly connected client workstations will wait on the task server until the desired client has become available.

4.6 Software Update

Akin to Microsoft WSUS server the Software Update server downloads software updates to the Mac server so that a client can download updates locally rather than having to go to Apple. Either all updates can be downloaded from Apple and be immediately available for clients to install or administrators can manually choose updates to download and selectively enable them. Using the software update service dramatically improves download time for updates and inbound networking traffic when connected the campus network. It also reduces use of your campus internet connection which you network administrator will likely thank you for.

4.7 Caching

The caching server caches both Software Updates AND App Store purchases. Clients do not need to be configured to connect to the Caching server and will connect to it automatically although clients have to share the same IP behind a NAT thus making it almost unusable in an enterprise environment.

5. IMPLEMENTATION AND TRAINING

Trials are attempted first to be certain that the service can be effectively used by colleagues. Student workers assist in the testing process. Additional time must be taken to present solutions to management and colleagues. Further time must be set aside for documentation. Additional time must be set aside during initial implementation to assist colleagues with any new process.

6. USE CASES

6.1 WPA2-Enterprise settings & Wi-fi at the login window

More and more apple devices are coming without a physical Ethernet port. For campuses with WPA2-Enterprise networks this is proving to be quite a headache as it becomes difficult to get a Mac on a wireless network without user credentials. Having Profile Manager manage your wireless network settings can alleviate some of this headache. Profile manager can push out your Radius server certificates so users are not prompted to accept them, it also can set the mac to pass whatever credentials a user enters in the login window to the wireless network for authentication.

For deployment setups this article may prove useful http://afp548.com/2013/03/06/automatically-enable-wifi-at-login-window/ . We have found that WPA2-Enterprise settings that require a username and password can still prove difficult. If your network policy also requires that machines use the current user's credentials to login rather than one set of credentials used across all macs you may run into issues with the Mac switching credentials.

6.2 Printer Management

Instead of managing printers by touching client computers printers can be added to Profile Manager profiles and distributed. This saves a great deal of time for desktop support technicians who would otherwise need to manually install the printers on each of their client workstations. Unfortunately printers that need to be managed on client workstations must be first added to the Profile Manager server. Additionally, removing a printer from the printer list is not reflected in the Profile Manager and an experienced technician will have to go into the database to manually remove old printers before new ones can be added.

6.3 NetInstall

A well crafted deployment can save a great deal of effort by desktop support technicians preparing new computers and greatly decrease the turn around time for rebuilding an existing computer. Packages that can be deployed via ARD can also be used in a NetInstall. By configuring a custom set of packages to be deployed a technician can hand off a deployment to a student worker, freeing up the technician to work on other tasks.

7. BACKING IT UP

Our profile manager database now has lots of useful configuration information in it, so backing it up is of greater importance.

While you can hook up an external drive to your Mac OS X server and enable Time Machine. This is not always possible in a enterprise environment and it also does not address the needs of restoring one individual portion of the device manager application rather than an entire restore of the server. Doing some sort of scripted backup of the database is recommended.

At the simplest level you can simply back up the database by running pg_dumpall against the database. Note, there are actually two databases on 10.8, one whose data resides at '/Library/Server/PostgreSQL For Server Services/Data' and one with data in '/Library/Server/PostgreSQL/Data'. You can see their socket directory by running `ps -ef | grep postgres`

```
osxserver1:~ root# ps -ef | grep postgres

 216  113   1  0 2:25PM ??     0:00.08
/Applications/Server.app/Contents/ServerRoot
/usr/bin/postgres_real -D
/Library/Server/PostgreSQL For Server
Services/Data -c listen_addresses= -c
log_connections=on -c
log_directory=/Library/Logs/PostgreSQL -c
log_filename=PostgreSQL_Server_Services.log
-c log_line_prefix=%t -c log_lock_waits=on -
c log_statement=ddl -c logging_collector=on
-c
unix_socket_directory=/Library/Server/Postgr
eSQL For Server Services/Socket -c
unix_socket_group=_postgres -c
unix_socket_permissions=0770

 216  120   1  0 2:25PM ??     0:00.08
/Applications/Server.app/Contents/ServerRoot
/usr/bin/postgres_real -D
/Library/Server/PostgreSQL/Data -c
listen_addresses=127.0.0.1,::1 -c
log_connections=on -c
log_directory=/Library/Logs/PostgreSQL -c
log_filename=PostgreSQL.log -c
log_line_prefix=%t -c log_lock_waits=on -c
log_statement=ddl -c logging_collector=on -c
unix_socket_directory=/private/var/pgsql_soc
ket -c unix_socket_group=_postgres -c
unix_socket_permissions=0770
```

The 'unix_socket_directory=' is what we need to know to connect to the database from the command line. We will pass '/Library/Server/PostgreSQL\ For\ Server\ Services/Socket/' to our pg_dumpall command. The command to back up the database will look like this:

```
pg_dumpall --username=_postgres --
host=/Library/Server/PostgreSQL\ For\
Server\ Services/Socket/
```

OS X ships by default with postgres 9.1 client tools in /usr/bin. Those are what we get by default if we just run pg_dumpall and we will get an error like this: 'server version: 9.2.1; pg_dumpall version: 9.1.5'

Server.app for 10.8 comes with a newer version of postgres (9.2.1) so we need to be sure to use the version of pg_dumpall included with server.app:

```
/Applications/Server.app/Contents/ServerRoot
/usr/bin/pg_dumpall --username=_postgres --
host=/Library/Server/PostgreSQL\        For\
Server\        Services/Socket/        --
file=backup.dumpall
```

We now have a backup of the database! It would be much more helpful to have a backup for each database rather than one file that has all the databases in it. It would also be nice if we had a script we could run on schedule. Create a script with the following info to make a script you can run on a schedule and create backups of the server's databases.

```
#!/bin/sh
PSQL=/Applications/Server.app/Contents/Serve
rRoot/usr/bin/psql

DUMP=/Applications/Server.app/Contents/Serve
rRoot/usr/bin/pg_dump

DUMPALL=/Applications/Server.app/Contents/Se
rverRoot/usr/bin/pg_dumpall

PREFIX=`date +%j`

BACKUP_DIR=/var/root/pgsqlbackups

HOST="/Library/Server/PostgreSQL\        For\
Server\ Services/Socket/"

USERNAME=_postgres


Databases="$PSQL -tq -U $USERNAME -h $HOST -
d template1 -c 'select datname from
pg_database'"
renice 19 $$


echo Backup started ...
echo "Backing up global info ..."
eval $DUMPALL -U $USERNAME -h $HOST -g >
/$BACKUP_DIR/$PREFIX.global
for db in `eval $Databases`
do
 case $db in
  template0)
   echo "Not backing up template0 because it
should never be restored"
   ;;
  *)
   echo "time: `date +%H%M%S` - Backup of
$db in progress ..."
   eval $DUMP -F c -U $USERNAME -h $HOST $db
> /$BACKUP_DIR/$PREFIX.$db
   wait
   chmod o-r /$BACKUP_DIR/$PREFIX.$db
```

```
   echo "time: `date +%H%M%S` - Backup of
$db finished ..."
   ;;
 esac
done


echo Backup finished ...


# Now vacuum the database to avoid
"catastrophic data loss"
echo
echo Analyzing Databases ...
eval /usr/bin/vacuumdb -a -z -U $USERNAME -h
$HOST
```

8. LIMITATIONS

Apple is "Not for enterprise" - This is a common theme when talking about working with Apps in an enterprise environment. I feel that this is a misconception which may come from the fact that Apple does not promote its server enterprise features as well as it does its consumer level product offerings. However it does occasionally feel as if it were true because of what seems like major lapses in its server side offerings. Some of the profile manager options get close but can't do as advertised. For example when defining a default exchange connection for iOS devices documentation says that certain fields can be left blank. However, when attempting to save the setting an error will not let the admin proceed until the fields that would be best left blank need to be filled in before proceeding. It is not entirely clear what options to set and often tasks feel like they are more reverse engineering assignments rather than desktop management.

One issue of particular annoyance is struggling with making ARD lists centralized on a network so they can be managed from a variety of workstations and by a number of users. Colleagues are more likely to use a new system if that system is easily available to them out of the gate rather than to have to climb uphill by configuring a set of users. Thankfully 3rd party tools as described in the next section are of invaluable assistance in filling in those gaps.

A major source of frustration for Mac Admins is the limitations of Apple hardware. Apple for many years offered a rack mountable server called the XServe. They discontinued the last XServe in 2011 and have not released a new one since 2009. Only being able to virtualize OS X on Apple hardware compounds this problem. This leaves the MacPro, which also has not seen an update in over 2 years and is not suited to being placed in a datacenter, and the Mac Mini which does not have enough expansion to properly virtualize many instances of OS X. Ideally, Apple would either release a new XServe or allow it's software to be virtualized onto rack mountable hardware. However, as any Apple fan knows, one can wait a long long time for Apple to release something. Here again, 3rd party solutions can ride into the rescue to handle some of the more load intensive tasks.

While many of apple's services are excellent they are not always perfect. While the current implementation of SMB is good it has been more flawed in the past and gives some trouble to domain bound macs which makes it seem like the tech is trying to find a square peg in a round hole. Macs will occasionally "fall off" the domain and need to be rebound. Further, not all of the features in the AD binding panel can always be implemented. In 10.7 Lion network administrative groups could not be set from the client. Additionally for many years the default user shell could not be set and would be overwritten from the setting in AD even though it's been explicitly set on the client.

9. ALTERNATIVES AND ADDONS

9.1 Munki

Munki provides a set of tools to manage software installation and removal from registered Macs. The Munki tools allow you to create "manifests" lists of software to be installed on machines based on how they are registered with the munki server. The software resides on a web server. Any web server will do, either one you already have or you can use OS X's built in server. You then can update the packages on the central server and your Macs registered with Munki will update their software packages accordingly. The most difficult part of a Munki installation is probably going to be getting Munki distributed and configured on all your Macs. http://code.google.com/p/munki/

9.2 CreateOSXinstallPkg

A script at http://managingosx.wordpress.com/2012/07/25/son-of-installlion-pkg/ will create a custom Lion or Mountain Lion installer. This installer can contain some packages to be installed along with the OS.

9.3 DeployStudio

DeployStudio is a set of tools to help automate the deployment of Macs. It uses Apple's built in NetInstall and NetBoot functionality and allows for the automation of post installation tasks such as naming the mac or joining it to your Active Directory with a specific name. It can also make a deployment more interactive then what Apple provides.

9.4 Alteris

A management suite for both Macs and PCs that includes asset management, imaging, package delivery, and helpdesk management. - http://www.symantec.com/configuration-management

9.5 Casper Suite

The Casper Suite, from Jamf, is yet another management solution similar to those above which offers a total management solution. The Casper Suite can do everything Alteris does but adds the features of remote desktop, usage management, and license management. http://www.jamfsoftware.com/products/casper-suite

10. ACKNOWLEDGMENTS

Our thanks to Susan Chichester, Chief Information Officer and Director of Computing and Information Technology and Laurie Fox Assistant Director and Manager the User Services group of for their support and funding of our conference travel. Thanks should also go to the Penn State Mac Admins (http://macadmins.psu.edu/) group and conference which is a great source of info for anyone who works with macs Thank you to everyone who contributed to this paper with ideas and proofreading talents.

11. REFERENCES

1. Deployment Guide: iOS 6 in Education

2. http://en.wikipedia.org/wiki/Apple_Remote_Desktop

3. http://www.afp548.com/2013/03/06/automatically-enable-wifi-at-login-window/

4. http://www.brianmadden.com/blogs/jackmadden/archive/2013/04/30/apple-wwdc-is-coming-up-soon-get-prepared-with-this-guided-history-of-ios-management-features.aspx

5. OS X Lion Server Essentials: Using and Supporting OS Lion Server

6. Solutions for Systems Management: Tools for managing Large-scale deployments of Mac computers in education

7. *Setting up a demonstration Munki Server* http://code.google.com/p/munki/wiki/DemonstrationSetup

Elevating Your Career and Making a Difference: The SIGUCCS Mentoring Program

Karen McRitchie
SIGUCCS Board
Secretary
karen.mcritchie@gmail.com

Beth Rugg
Ithaca College
953 Danby Rd
Ithaca, NY 14850
(607) 274-7349
erugg@ithaca.edu

Dan Herrick
Colorado State University
1301 Campus Delivery, Glover 218
Fort Collins, CO
(970) 491-3131
dan.herrick@colostate.edu

Brian Allen
Hennepin Technical College
13100 College View Drive
Eden Prairie, MN 55347
(952) 995-1626
brian.allen@hennepintech.edu

Mark Zocher
University of San Diego
5998 Alcalá Park
San Diego, CA 92110
(619) 260-6805
mzocher@sandiego.edu

Christine L. Vucinich
Duke University
334 Blackwell Street, Suite 1100
Durham, NC 27701
(919) 613-3782
clv4@duke.edu

ABSTRACT

Need help defining your goals, identifying strengths or just need a sounding board for new ideas? Are you a seasoned member who can share resources and experience? Come to this session to learn about SIGUCCS' newest membership benefit: a formal mentoring program. Established in fall 2012, this program gives SIGUCCS members the opportunity to define and achieve their personal and/or professional development goals in a safe partnership. This presentation will discuss the first year program guidelines, outcomes and implementation strategies such as: forming an advisory committee and pairing interested mentees and mentors. These outcomes include success stories and lessons learned, as well as how to get involved in 2014.

Categories and Subject Descriptors

K.7.m [**Computing Profession**]: Miscellaneous – *codes of good practice*

General Terms

Performance, Human Factors, Standardization

Keywords

Mentoring, Program, Structure, Mentors, Mentees

1. INTRODUCTION

SIGUCCS is committed to providing professional development opportunities for its members. Historically, this has been achieved through the annual conference, email mailing lists, discussions, webinars, and pre and post conference workshops. Since the SIGUCCS community is composed of young professionals, mid-level managers and senior decision-makers, establishing a formal

mentoring program within SIGUCCS made sense. In 2012, this program was established. This paper details the structure, design and pilot year of this program.

2. VALUE OF MENTORING

Mentoring is a learning collaboration between two individuals. It can either be formal or informal but usually involves personal development, sharing and goal setting. The focus of a professional mentoring relationship is on the mentee's career and psychosocial needs. Mentoring provides insight into issues and allows for the sharing of expertise, values, skills, and perspectives in a professional context. Mentors function as a catalyst, an agent that provokes a reaction that might not otherwise have taken place or speeds up a possible future reaction. Mentors are typically outside the mentee's organization and are able to provide objective feedback.

Research has documented the following benefits of career mentoring relationships:

- Enhanced career development and advancement of the mentee
- Enhanced compensation for the mentee
- Enhanced career satisfaction for both the mentee and the mentor
- Increased employee retention for the organization supporting the mentoring program

3. PROGRAM DEVELOPMENT

Many IT professionals recognize the importance of mentoring and yet it appears that formal mentoring programs are limited. In recent SIGUCCS conferences, this need (and gap) was a topic of many conversations. In 2012, the SIGUCCS Board decided to do something about this gap; and proposed a formal program to the membership. A draft proposal was written and the idea was discussed at the 2012 annual conference in Memphis. Formal mentoring was discussed at the Management Symposium during the "Hot Topics" session, at a DISCUSSIT session in the Service and Support conference, during the poster session and at a "Birds of a Feather" session (BOF) during the Service and Support conference. An advisory team was formed. This committee was committed to launching the program and helping the professional development coordinator manage the program. The team planned to meet on a regular basis using Google Hangouts. The initial focus was on creating a request process for prospective mentees and mentors.

3.1 Advisory Committee

The formation of the advisory team was unexpected and proved to be vital to the program's success. Members of the advisory team brought unique perspectives and commitment to the success of the program that could not be achieved by a sole volunteer professional coordinator. The team had great ideas that were much easier to implement since there were more people to delegate tasks and responsibilities to. The creation and formation of the team also allowed additional leadership opportunities for members within the SIGUCCS community outside of Board positions and conference positions. It provided one more way people could be involved in something they cared about. Over time, the advisory team became a very cohesive group providing oversight for the program and helping each other.

3.2 Program Timeline

The advisory team formed in November 2012. Between November and December, the team defined, created and publicized the request process. The mentor/mentee request forms were available to SIGUCCS membership during December. Near the end of December, the advisory team paired mentors and mentees together. This pairing was communicated to the participants. A virtual orientation session was held in January 2013. Participants were encouraged to set goals and schedule a monthly meeting to work towards those goals. This phase of the program, the real heart of the program, lasts from mid-January until November. The program ends in November 2013 for these initial pairings. Participants can request to continue with the program either with the current pairing or with someone new or the pairing can discontinue. A recognition celebration will take place at the annual conference in November and a new session will be announced in November 2013 and take place from January 2014 to the Fall 2014 conference. Since it is a voluntary commitment, the advisory team felt it was important to set clear expectations. A mid-year evaluation was conducted in early May and monthly hangouts are available to participants.

3.3 Focus and Philosophy

The advisory team had to decide who the program was for, the mentees or the mentors. This focus helped guide us when pairing participants. We decided the initial focus was on mentees and their requests. Since we did not know how many people would be interested in the program, we committed to finding a mentor for every mentee request even if we had to do additional recruitment. We also decided, not to pair people together just to make the numbers work; but instead pair participants based on goals and skills.

The advisory team discussed limiting the number of pairings in order to ensure success. The advisory team also made sure that the mentors had other mentors to turn to – this was accomplished by scheduling a monthly hangout with only mentors. Since mentors might not be able to answer every question or meet every need, the advisory team thought it would be helpful if mentors could turn to other mentors for support.

The advisory team also discussed the length of the program and decided the program would typically run from January through the annual conference, generally in October or November. This time frame allows for participants to establish and achieve discrete goals and develop a mentoring relationship without feeling trapped in the relationship. This time frame also allows SIGUCCS to continually re-evaluate the program and meet new mentoring requests. Current participants can request to continue in the program.

3.4 Success Criteria

Defining success is difficult when it comes to human relationships. The advisory team decided that interest and outcomes would be the basis for success. Numbers of participants would not determine success but feedback from participants would. Did the mentees achieve their goals? Was the experience for both the mentors and mentees beneficial? Did the pairs continue to meet throughout the duration of the program? Did the mentors and mentees participate in the monthly touch base sessions?

The team built regular touch points into the schedule so that there were opportunities to discuss problems that might arise. Every advisory team member provided oversight to two or three mentoring pairs. The advisory team did not assume that every pairing would be successful and wanted to make sure problems could be identified before individuals were disappointed. Each advisory team member reaches out to these pairs on a regular basis.

4. IMPLEMENTATION STRATEGIES

For the implementation, the team focused on creating mentee/mentor pairings that made sense, developing a structure that provided regular communication opportunities with the advisory team and provided focus topics for each month. This focus helped give the program substance and take advantage of the enthusiasm that accompanies any new idea.

4.1 Mentoring Request Form

The advisory team decided to have Mentees and Mentors fill out the same web form. The advisory team created a detailed form that would take time to complete. The advisory team felt that someone who wanted to be mentored needed to take the program seriously and be committed to investing time into the mentoring relationship. By filling out this form, the advisory team hoped to be able to gauge commitment.

Both mentees and mentors were asked specific questions:

1. title
2. position
3. years at institution
4. years in IT field
5. management strengths
6. management areas for improvement
7. technical strengths
8. technical areas for improvement
9. why they were interested in the program
10. plans for career growth

Twenty-six (26) people completed the request form in a reflective manner. Two people even joined SIGUCCS just to participate in this program. Most importantly, we had the information we needed to make pairing decisions.

The advisory team analyzed each request to determine who should be paired together. Each advisory team member took two or three mentee requests and reviewed the mentor request forms to find a match. Individual advisory team members made recommendations about the top three mentor matches for each mentee. The advisory team met as a group and discussed each pairing in detail. From that exercise every mentee was paired with a mentor. There was no need to solicit additional mentors.

Some participants requested being both a mentor and a mentee. The advisory team discussed this and in two cases, allowed that to happen. However, in hindsight it has made the monthly mentor hangouts problematic since there are two people who might attend who are also mentees.

The advisory team discussed whether to allow "late mentee requests." In the end, we did not, but encouraged these participants to apply for the next session. The advisory team made this decision because the program had an explicit structure and timeline and all of the mentor volunteers had been paired with a mentee.

Participants (via the form) and advisory team members could suggest other people they thought would be a good participant, so that the advisory team could solicit their involvement if needed. In the end, we didn't need to contact those individuals.

4.2 Publicity for Program

Once the form was complete and publicly available, two notices were sent to the open SIGUCCS list and the SIGUCCS membership email list about this opportunity. Individuals had three weeks to complete the form. Several individuals became members of SIGUCCS in order to participate in this program.

4.3 Pairing

Twenty-six (26) people wanted to participate in the program. Fourteen (14) participants expressed interest serving as a mentor, and thirteen (13) participants expressed interest in the mentee role. Some participants wanted to be both a mentor and a mentee. The advisory team met in real time, via video conference, to discuss the pairings and develop good mentor/mentee matches. We were able to match thirteen (13) mentors with thirteen (13) mentees. Four (4) members of the advisory team also participated in the program, two (2) as mentors and two (2) as mentees.

4.4 Google Site

Initially we worked with shared documents (via email and cloud based collaborative documents). We found that we needed a central website. The advisory team identified the following needs for the website:

- distribute general information about the program to participants
- provide a calendar of program events
- act as a file repository
- provide a directory of participants
- host a discussion board
- post announcements about the program

To simplify the technical work, we elected to use a content management system as the program's web site. Because the team had already used other Google cloud services, the group elected to use a Google Site (implemented at Colorado State University), in part due to the purported ease of integrating other Google cloud services into the Site structure.

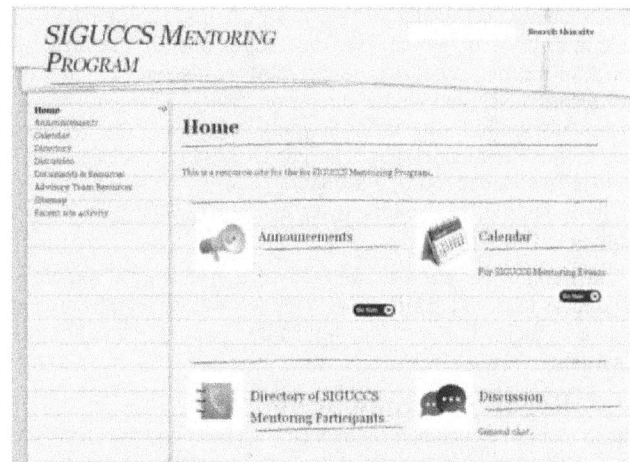

Figure 1: Mentoring Google Website

Google sites allows users to integrate a calendar and shared documents directly into the Site itself. The advisory team found this to be relatively easy, although as is the case with content management systems in general, it is not as flexible as a personally created web site. The tradeoff of flexibility versus ease of use was deemed acceptable.

One advantage to Google sites is the availability of advanced sharing options. We are able to share the site with only our programs' participants, and by enabling page-level sharing, we can share only certain parts of the site with the advisory team, thus reducing the need for a separate website to host restricted material.

4.5 Orientation Webinar

Providing an orientation to the program was important. The participants had various levels of experience with mentoring and the advisory team wanted to ensure that all teams would be successful, regardless of their mentoring experience level.

The advisory team provided a printable mentoring guide with basic mentoring resources. This guide helped define the program and set expectations for the mentees and mentors and provided resources for questions, goals, and a place to record notes from individual mentoring sessions.

The orientation webinar was scheduled so that all of the mentees and mentors could participate. The webinar outlined steps for the teams such as making the first contact, taking time to get to know each other, and discussing of desired outcomes. The advisory team recommended that every mentee/mentor pair take the Strengthfinder 2.0 survey to help understand strengths. The advisory team also recommended the book "Its Okay To Be The Boss" by Bruce Tulgan as a reference for some basic management skills.

During the webinar, the advisory team provided discussion questions for the mentor and mentee to discuss during the initial interview to try and minimize awkwardness. These questions involved expectations, motivations and challenges.

The advisory team then provided a guide for the teams to set up goals for their mentor relationship. We used the S.M.A.R.T. goals formula: specific, measurable, attainable, relevant, and timely. The advisory team provided strategies to help the teams establish their relationships. The advisory team wanted the teams to have regular meetings/check-ins, be able to provide timely support, and to make sure that successes were celebrated.

Each mentor and mentee was given a journal to record notes and action steps. The journal provides each partner a place to keep track of meetings and tasks so that they are not forgotten as well as record notes and future discussion topics. The journal was especially useful for the teams that only had formal meetings once per month. The journal pages included a 3-2-1 reflection space (3 things you learned today, 2 actions or changes you will make and 1 thing you will never forget) for reinforcing what was learned during the meeting.

At the end of the webinar, we responded to individual questions and ideas to get the partnerships started as well as introducing the teams to their advisor so they had an immediate resource for any questions.

4.6 Regular Communication

Each mentor/mentee pair set up their own meeting times but were strongly encouraged to meet at least once a month. The pairs used a variety of communication methods including email, phone and video conferences (using Google Hangouts) to find the mix that worked best for busy schedules and time zone differences.

Regular communication meetings were set up for our advisory team twice a month during November, December and January and once a month thereafter. The meetings focused on planning for the next month and touching base.

The advisory team established a monthly video conference for mentees only and mentors only. The advisory team thought it was important for peers to be able to gather, get to know one another and learn from each other's experiences. An advisory team member facilitates each hangout, sends out reminders and determines a focus topic. The topics have included setting goals, evaluations and managing work transitions.

4.7 Recognition

Recognition is an important part of any professional development program. The mentees and mentors have made a commitment to each other and this program and have devoted significant to it. The advisory team decided to get everyone together at the annual conference in Chicago in 2013. This reception will take place on Tuesday night before the Service and Support conference starts when the highest number of mentees/mentors might be there. The plans have not been finalized but the advisory team is hoping to celebrate with a pizza party. This may be the first time the mentees and mentors meet each other face to face.

The advisory team will purchase pins for the participants to be worn throughout the conference. This pin will recognize their accomplishment and publicize the program. A budget was not set aside for this purpose, so the team is working with/dependent on the SIGUCCS Board to fund these ideas.

5. FIRST YEAR OUTCOMES

Evaluation of the SIGUCCS Mentoring program has been informal, with Google hangouts and regular communication among the advisory team and members, and formal, with surveys sent to participants' mid-year and upon completion of the program. The information gathered is used to evaluate the program's success help the advisory team make any necessary adjustments moving forward.

5.1 Evaluation Results

Complete evaluation results will be shared during the presentation at the SIGUCCS 2013 Conference. The mid-term evaluations gave us very positive information and a baseline for comparison. The only change made to the program at the mid-point will be the

establishment of email lists for mentors and mentees. Other changes will wait until the new session.

According to the survey, the orientation webinar was attended by 80% of the participants and was positively received. Participants felt that it was a good way to get the program started and to answer questions. The mentor guide was rated excellent and very good by almost all of the teams. Participants perceived different value levels with different sections of the guide depending on previous mentoring experiences.

Only about 50% of the participants were able to attend the monthly Google Hangout sessions. The comments were positive by those who were able to participate. Reasons for not attending ranged from scheduling issues to social media sites blocked on campus. The advisory team may want to rethink group chats and Google hangouts and use GoToMeeting or another tool that is not considered "social media."

Overall, the frequency of contact between the mentors and mentees varied from weekly to monthly, but all of the teams expressed that they could call on each other at any time outside the scheduled meeting time. The teams used email, video, phone and chat for their communications. 100% of the participants would recommend the program to others!

Success Stories

There were many great comments shared during the evaluation:

- "It's been a great experience, sharing knowledge and setting some goals, happy to see that we created some goals which have been completed."

- "There are different ways to engage in advisory/mentoring roles. An earlier mentor of mine took a "friendly" approach. My current mentor is more...like a colleague and fellow professional. Both work."

- "It has been a good experience, sometimes I feel like I should be doing more, however I think we are on track and doing well. I don't want to seem too pushy, yet I want to make sure that my mentee is getting enough from this program. Regular contact is also important...we talk each week and I think that having that regular communication helps the partnership succeed."

When the teams were asked to share what was exciting about the partnership, they expressed:

- "I would say the synergy. I like that in helping my mentee come up with ideas that have prompted ideas for me to try in my own environment."

- "Ah hah moments. Hearing about the successes and building a friendship when there are days that are just about venting and not necessarily "the goal"."

- "Affecting change and see its results from the week of the conference until present day. The combination of good advice, a safe place to vent and my determination to overcome the challenges has been rewarding and exciting."

5.2 Lessons Learned

A few of the ideas shared by the participants will be used in the next year's program to improve communication. One idea was to include a first meeting agenda in the Mentor Guide to provide some structure to the first time that the partners talked. Another idea was to have some more ongoing communication between the advisory team and the mentoring pairs as many could not attend the Google Hangout sessions. It was expressed that we might have an email list for mentors and another for the mentees, so they could communicate with the others in the program. Overall the ideas were things we can easily incorporate into the next program.

The mentoring program was goal-focused and we encouraged the mentoring teams to create goals using the S.M.A.R.T process (specific, measureable, attainable, relevant and time-bound). This process was a learning experience for both members of the mentoring team and allowed mentees to start thinking of their goals in a more formal way. Setting goals also helped the mentor/mentee measure the success of the relationship. Some of the teams had very informal goals and we want to allow for variability regarding team goals next year.

The advisory team predicted a lot of entry level interest in the program, but that idea did not hold true. The advisory team thought new IT professionals and new managers would be interested in the program. However, many experienced professionals and managers wanted to be mentored. It is important for the advisory team not to focus the program only on the inexperienced, but realize that experienced people can gain much from a mentoring relationship as well.

5.3 Technology

Technology is key to collaborating with colleagues at a distance and to the success of mentoring partnerships. The advisory team felt that the technology options available, particularly video conferencing, played a key role in strengthening mentoring partnerships and allowing flexible collaboration among advisory team members.

The advisory team found that video conferences were an excellent method for real-time team meetings; we did brainstorming sessions, project assignments, planning, and evaluations. The ability to share and collaborate on documents necessitated a cloud-based system. A definitive and shared calendar system was also helpful in coordinating meetings and events. Finally, a website to integrate some of the above technologies, as well as provide general information, was necessary.

We primarily used Google cloud services: Drive (a.k.a. Documents), Calendar, Sites, and Hangout for most of the above technical services. However, the initial kick off seminar used Cisco GoToWebinar. In general, Google cloud services integrate well (and the "free" price tag is helpful.) The exceptions may be when team members use Google Apps services, or multiple Google accounts for different services, so workarounds were needed to allow members access to certain services. Authentication to the restricted Google Site was reported to be a problem for some individuals, but it was solved when they were invited using the email address associated with their Google account (whether Gmail or a Google Apps address.)

Google's desktop video conference technology, Google Hangout, is integrated with Google's social media offering, Google Plus. Hangout is best suited for personal and informal settings, so it works very well for the one-on-one mentoring sessions. It accommodates up to 10 participants. Fortunately for our program, we did not have more than 10 participants at our Google Hangout, but as the program grows, a business-class solution will be needed.

Figure 2: Google Hangout Screen Capture

We consistently had issues with participants not able to see Hangout invitations. We determined that the best way to distribute an invitation to a Hangout was to obtain the direct link to the Hangout and email it to participants. Google Calendar has the ability to embed a Hangout invitation in the calendar entry, but only when members viewed the calendar directly from the Google Calendar interface, and not within the embedded calendar in the website. In addition, one participant reported that social media is blocked at the workplace and thus Hangout is not accessible. One participant used Google Apps but the site administrator had not enabled Google Plus, so the Hangout option was not available until the site administrator deliberately enabled it.

Email is still the most heavily used communication and collaboration tool, partly due to its universal nature, and it is what the advisory team primarily used. There were no significant technical issues with email use.

6. GETTING INVOLVED

This mentoring program will continue in 2014. SIGUCCS members will receive an email notification about how to apply to be a mentor and mentee after SIGUCCS 2013 in Chicago. Anyone who is interested in participating and has questions can learn more about this program by attending the session on this paper during the Service and Support conference, attending the Poster session or emailing one of the committee members directly.

7. CONCLUSION

To date, the program has been very successful. The mentees and mentors seem to appreciate the opportunity. A few have changed jobs, received a promotion or already achieved the goals they set in January 2013. Each pairing is unique and has unique goals. How frequently each pairing communicates and what they "do" together vary greatly. But, overall, the feedback has been positive.

The implementation and robust structure of this program is only possible because of the role the advisory team plays. If fewer people were involved, it wouldn't be possible to provide the touch points and focus that we are currently providing for the program. The advisory team itself has become a very cohesive unit.

We believe this program has filled a gap for our membership. Several participants joined SIGUCCS to take advantage of the program. The size has been very manageable for the pilot year.

We also have a structure in place to handle more requests in the future. We won't be able to do a complete evaluation until November 2013, but the advisory team is optimistic that we have developed a sustainable program for the future.

8. ACKNOWLEDGEMENTS

Many thanks to the advisory team: Brian Allen, Dana Pfeifer, Dan Herrick, Karen McRitchie, Beth Rugg, Christine Vucinich, and Mark Zocher. Without you, this wouldn't be possible and not nearly as much fun.

9. REFERENCES

[1] Educause Mentoring website, http://www.educause.edu/careers/special-topic-programs/mentoring

[2] Mentor Mentee Request Form, http://bit.ly/SIGUCCSMentor

[3] SIGUCCS Mentoring website, https://sites.google.com/a/rams.colostate.edu/siguccs-mentoring-project/home/advisory-team-resources

[4] SIGUCCS Mentoring Orientation PowerPoint, https://docs.google.com/viewer?a=v&pid=sites&srcid=cmFt cy5jb2xvc3RhdGUuZWR1fHNpZ3VjY3MtbWVudG9yaW5 nLXByb2plY3R8R8Z3g6OWMzMjEyM2EzYzY3ODQ5

[5] SIGUCCS Mentoring Guide, https://docs.google.com/viewer?a=v&pid=sites&srcid=cmFt cy5jb2xvc3RhdGUuZWR1fHNpZ3VjY3MtbWVudG9yaW5 nLXByb2plY3R8R8Z3g6MzdjMTE1YTA5ZWQ3NTcwZQ

[6] Roth, Tom. 2007. Strengthfinder 2.0. Gallup Press.

[7] Tulgan, Bruce. 2007. It's Okay To Be The Boss. Harpur Collins.

Strategification, Synergizing Efficiencies, and Meetingitis: What your bosses _really_ do.

Robert Howard
Armstrong Atlantic State University
11935 Abercorn Street
Savannah, GA 31419
1-912-509-0050
robert.howard@armstrong.edu

ABSTRACT

Once upon a time, most people in a technical leadership role held some sort of functional Information Technology (IT) expertise. Somewhere along the path to manager, director, or Chief Information Officer (CIO), many of us became meeting loving idiots. Well, not really idiots, but losing touch with the daily realities of front line service could make it seem that way.

Here is your opportunity to get a glimpse into the various checkpoints along the management path and the sort of competencies that must be developed—by design or experience— and how this competency development impacts everyone in the organization. What do you gain along the way? What do you lose? How can you stay connected with all levels of the organization and the institution?

This paper will also give you a glimpse into how you can connect with your universities' missions in whatever role you hold. We will talk plainly of what exactly is the point of strategy, missions, visions, and the challenges facing the modern university and how that impacts YOU.

You can hear from someone who worked from the front lines to a CIO role across three universities, and we can discuss that path and you can ask questions relating to your own experiences and career path.

Categories and Subject Descriptors

K.7.1 [**The Computing Profession**]: Occupations

General Terms

Management, Performance.

Keywords

Career path, university, career planning, mentor.

1. INTRODUCTION

This paper hopes to give practical counsel to members of the IT world who would aspire to the CIO role. We will discuss how impact to the organization changes across varying management levels and selections of competencies needed for sustained career growth and personal fulfillment.

2. IMPACT

From the front lines of customer service to the datacenter to the boardroom, each position has its ability to contribute to and impact the fulfillment of the mission of the organization, corporation or institution.

Early in one's career, the impact is typically limited in scope. However, success leads to promotions where potential for contribution and impact increases. Consider a helpdesk employee who is a very important face to your customer. They impact at an individual level, which is important; however with the volume of interactions, there will always be dissatisfied clients.

Consider a system administrator: their job is to keep a system and service functioning within specifications. Presuming (and this may be a stretch) the service was satisfactory upon implementation, they have satisfied customers until services under their care fail through their actions (e.g., patches or upgrades) or some system failure. "Through 2015, 80% of outages impacting mission-critical services will be caused by people and process issues, and more than 50% of those outages will be caused by change/configuration/release integration and hand-off issues." [3]

As we move into management, the opportunity for impact increases from projects, processes, people, units, and ultimately organizations. A manager who must now care for the services must also deliberate her human capital considerations. Does the staff have the skills to meet current demands? What about future needs?

At the top of the IT organization, the CIO must balance services, relationships, competing needs for resources as well as developing leaders and providing them the opportunity to advance to reach their potential. At the macro level, the goal remains that the sum of the services and resources is focused on assisting the institution to reach its goals through the cost-effective use of technology. As of 2011 it is estimated that IT downtime costs across North America and Europe totaled $26.5B in lost revenues [5].

Especially within the higher education vertical, the author has observed that many times people have been promoted to a management position based on technical acumen rather than the ability to manage or lead an organization. Many times those skills are not directly translatable and new sets of skills are required for continued success.

2.1 Power, Authority and Influence

As we address the competencies of leadership, let us clarify a misperception that going higher in the organizational chart means more power. Yes, there is more positional power that comes with certain positions; however, exercising authority can be complicated and cost more than the benefit it yields. Essentially, power is the ability to act upon your will despite others' wishes. Authority means that there is a likelihood that your commands will be carried out by a given group of persons. Influence is when you get to moderate decisions based on some value you bring to a situation (e.g., money, expertise, resources, etc.) [4].

A police officer has the power to make an arrest, and a doctor has the authority to prescribe medicine and be reasonably assured that the pharmacist will comply. Based on his or her expertise, the doctor only influences the patient; the patient (except in extreme cases) retains the control in the encounter.

Clearly in the IT realm, power would be used only in matters that have grave consequences such as a regulatory violation (e.g. HIPAA, FERPA, PCI, etc). Authority will be held typically within one's own organization, but one will wield influence over a much broader constituency. Confusing when to use each will weaken one's position and effectiveness, especially if the use is viewed as self-serving to the leader. [2]

A moral leader who tends to be goal-oriented with regard to mutually agreeable terms and who takes care of his or her staff will be able to use authority and influence to better outcomes and better morale. [6]

3. STRATEGY

Often we speak of "strategy" as a broad based descriptor without a clear definition of what we mean. Based on Cameron & Quinn's *Diagnosing and Changing Organizational Culture* [1], strategy is the sum of the planning and execution of actions taken to modify or retain processes and organizational culture in order to achieve desired results.

They recommend analyzing the current situation, identifying the desired results, analyzing the organizational culture and processes that are in place with the current situation (figure 1), and then developing the strategy on how to modify or retain those elements to gain the desired outcome (figure 2)

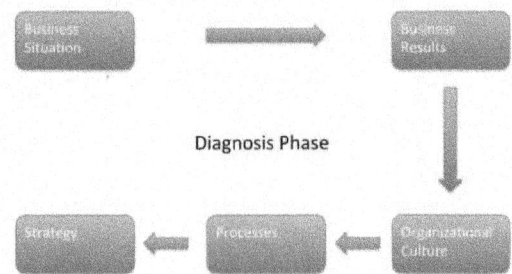

Figure 1: Organizational planning model: diagnosis phase

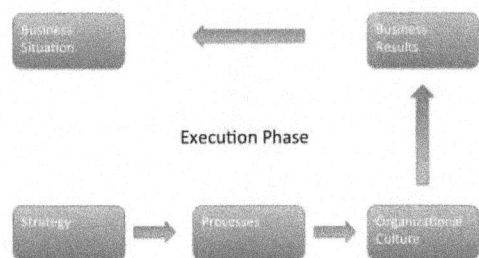

Figure 2: Organizational planning model: execution phase

4. EMBRACE CONFLICT

Many leaders attempt to avoid conflict; however, conflict is inevitable when there are competing values and scarce resources. Keep in mind that conflict is inevitable, but combat is not. Allowing, even mining for, conflict will lead to better decisions provided the conflicts are related to tasks rather than interpersonal [9]. It is essential to find a superordinate goal that everyone can agree upon to focus the conflict away from personal win-loss scenarios. As research shows task-oriented conflict can lead to better decisions, this puts an imperative for leaders to value diversity in groups to ensure multiple perspectives are represented [7].

5. LEADING CHANGE

Approximately 58% of strategy deployments succeed; 40% of technology changes succeed; and 30% of process re-engineering efforts succeed to meet original goals stated [10]. Facing these bleak statistics, along with the reality that these endeavors will be encountered every 3-5 years based on many technology lifecycles, leaders at every level should endeavor to understand the components of successful change to maximize the chance for meeting objectives.

Harvard business professor John Kotter attributes the dire success rates to a lack of focus on the people systems. He describes 8 steps to mastering change efforts.

Kotter's Eight Steps

1) Sense of Urgency
2) Guiding Coalition
3) Create a Vision
4) Communicate the Vision
5) Empower Others to Act
6) Short term Wins
7) Consolidate like Efforts
8) Institutionalize Gains

[8]

6. CONCLUSIONS

Leadership at any level is capitalizing one's ability to impact and add value to the organization. The higher up the organizational ladder one climbs, pressures increase to develop new competencies to enjoy continued success. One should understand that these new competencies generally come at a price of losing some specific technical knowledge. However, the broader impact, especially as it comes to developing other leaders is quite rewarding. The lifecycle of most technologies is under ten years, which means that the technology leader will not likely be remembered for successfully implementing specific systems. The legacy for the CIO is general institutional or corporate success and most importantly developing talent to help create new generations of leaders.

7. REFERENCES

[1] Cameron, K., & Quinn, R. (2005). *Diagnosing and changing organizational culture*. (2nd ed.). John Wiley & Sons. New York, NY.

[2] Christie, A., Barling, J., & Turner, N. (2011). Pseudo-transformational leadership: Model specification and outcomes. *Journal of Applied Social Psychology*, *41*(12), 2943-2984. doi: 10.1111/j.1559-1816.2011.00858.x

[3] Colville, R., & Spafford, G. (2010). Top seven considerations for configuration management for virtual and cloud infrastructures. Retrieved from Gartner database.

[4] Grimes, A. J. (1978). Authority, power, influence, and social control: A theoretical synthesis. *The Academy of Managment Review*, *3*(4), 724-735. Retrieved from http://www.jstor.org/stable/257928

[5] Harris, C. (2011, May 24). *IT downtime costs $26.5 billion in lost revenue*. Retrieved from http://www.informationweek.com/storage/disaster-recovery/it-downtime-costs-265-billion-in-lost-re/229625441

[6] House, R. J., & Mitchell, T. R. (1997). Path-goal theory of leadership. In R. P. Vecchio, (Ed.), *Leadership: Understanding the dynamics of power and influence in organizations* (pp. 259-273). Notre Dame, IN: University of Notre Dame Press.

[7] Jehn, K., Northcraft, G., & Neale, M. (1999). Why differences make a difference: A field study of diversity, conflict and performance in workgroups. *Administrative Science Quarterly*, *44*(4), 741-763. doi: 10.2307/2667054

[8] Kotter, J. P. (1995). Leading Change: Why Transformation Efforts Fail. *Harvard Business Review OnPoint* (March-April), 1-10.

[9] Simons, T., & Peterson, R. (2000). Task conflict and relationship conflict in top management teams: The pivotal role of intragroup trust. *Journal of Applied Psychology*, *85*(1), 102-111.

[10] Smith, M. (2002). Success rates for different types of organizational change. *Performance Improvement*, *41*(1), 26-33.

Adventures in Change Management:
Getting Everyone on the Same Page

Greg Stauffer
University of Colorado Boulder
Campus Box 313
Boulder, CO 80309
+1 303-735-1608
greg.stauffer@colorado.edu

Rochelle Scott
University of Colorado Boulder
Campus Box 313
Boulder, CO 80309
+1 303-492-8177
rochelle.scott@colorado.edu

ABSTRACT

Not so long ago at the University of Colorado Boulder the impacts of daily changes to enterprise services weren't understood by the Office of Information Technology's (OIT) own operations staff, much less the faculty, staff, or students they affected. This resulted in changes that were not well coordinated or communicated. As a result, campus constituents didn't know whether service outages were planned or unplanned contributing to a loss in faith of the services and the people who provided them.

However, a change process driven by ITIL processes, a website that gives visibility to changes within the organization, a comprehensive communication plan, and regular change advisory board meetings have transformed the process of changing services and communicating their impacts. Now changes to enterprise services at CU-Boulder have visibility to the entire organization, impacts and dependencies are understood, communication to faculty, staff and students is coordinated, and surprises and unintended consequences are minimized.

Categories and Subject Descriptors

K.6.1 [**Management of Computing and Information Systems**]: Project and People Management – *Training.*

General Terms

Management, Documentation, Reliability.

Keywords

Service Maintenance, ITIL, Communication, Change Advisory Board, Website, Customer Support.

1. INTRODUCTION

1.1 University of Colorado Boulder Overview

As the flagship university of the state of Colorado, CU-Boulder is a dynamic community of scholars and learners situated on one of the most spectacular college campuses in the country. As one of 34 U.S. public institutions belonging to the prestigious Association of American Universities (AAU) – and the only member in the Rocky Mountain region – we have a proud tradition of academic excellence. This includes five Nobel laureates and more than 50 members of prestigious academic academies. CU-Boulder enrolls approximately 30,000 on-campus degree-seeking students each fall and offers approximately 3,600 courses in 150 fields of study, in arts and sciences, business, education, engineering, environmental design, journalism, law, and music.

1.2 Office of Information Technology Overview

The Office of Information Technology (OIT) is the primary provider of IT services and support on the CU-Boulder campus with services for telephony, networking, digital media and computing. OIT also provides training for the effective use of technology, oversight for campus IT security, call-in and walk-in computer support, and support and services to further the teaching, learning and research mission of the CU-Boulder campus.

OIT employs approximately 180 full-time employees and also works with a group of campus IT representatives--called Computer Support Representatives or CSRS. CSRs range from professional IT staff to administrative assistants and at least one is appointed from each department, school and college to relay pertinent IT support information. At any one time there are approximately 350 CSRs serving as IT liaisons for the campus.

2. BACKGROUND

Until three years ago, OIT had no formal process for making changes to services or communicating about these changes. Often changes were only brought to light if someone who was involved in making the change notified an OIT communication professional. When others in the organization weren't notified of a service change, the effects of one change often had unintended consequences for other services.

For instance, the temporary pause of a registry update process could delay the creation of new accounts for incoming students, faculty, and staff. Often these effects were only noticed when a campus constituent contacted OIT with questions about why their account hadn't been created within the expected timeframe. If the pause of the registry update wasn't made known to the rest of OIT, support staff were often sent on a wild goose change to understand why accounts weren't being created as expected. As you could imagine, this contributed to inefficient case processing and poor customer service.

Because service changes were brought to light so inconsistently within OIT, no communication process was established for communicating the changes that did come to light, which resulted in inconsistent communication of changes. Most changes required the communicator to start from scratch and essentially interview the change implementer about the timing, the execution, and the customer impact of the change (outage, degradation, or no impact to customers).

This inconsistency resulted in instances where the customer impact wasn't fully communicated because the implementer didn't either realize it or the communicator didn't learn about it. This would result in increased customer support calls, which would lead to follow up clarification messages or retractions. For example, a primary Unix server upgrade was scheduled. OIT communicated the event and the downtime. It wasn't communicated that users would have to accept the public key again as a result of the upgrade. This caused confusion, calls to the IT Service Center, and follow up messages.

3. ROOTS OF CHANGE
3.1 ITIL as a Change Driver
The leadership at the highest levels recognized the importance of IT on campus and how disruptive changes were to teaching, learning, and research. Given these challenges, the OIT leadership team was able to find answers in the Information Technology Infrastructure Library (ITIL) framework.

Starting in 2007, leaders within the organization started actively learning about ITIL and created a plan for the organization to adopt ITIL best practices. The OIT leadership team, with support from CU-Boulder's administration, decided to hire Hewlett Packard to perform an assessment of our organization and provide recommendations about how to adopt ITIL best practices. A series of meetings were scheduled with key staff from OIT and with stakeholders from across campus including the CSRs. OIT learned from that assessment that a change management process would be very beneficial for us.

3.2 Identifying a Change Management Process Owner
To start getting a handle on changes, we created a role for a Change Management Process Owner. This was instrumental for getting a process off the ground. We identified a person already in our organization who had experience in creating and managing processes, and these new responsibilities fit perfectly into his existing job.

3.3 Service Catalog: Foundation to Change Process
The next step was to create a basic service catalog. This was key to wrapping our minds around what services we actually have that could be impacted by changes. This would allow our organization to get on the same page about what we provide and what we are

responsible for. A team was created from across the organization to tackle this challenge. They met regularly to work on the catalog and it was an enlightening process. They recorded lots of services, diverse in nature, even some that should be retired. The catalog now serves as the foundation of the change process and has influenced our website, and even the structure of our organization.

3.4 Maintenance Windows: Establishing Service Expectations
The creation of a service catalog presented the organization with an opportunity to establish service maintenance windows so that customers could come to expect that a service might be down for maintenance during an established day and time on a consistent basis. Maintenance windows weren't established for all services, but primarily for critical teaching and learning, and business tools such as the campus online learning environment and the email and calendaring service. The timeframe of the maintenance windows attempted to strike a balance between low customer demand upon a service and support personnel availability.

The maintenance windows not only created expectations around the availability of a service, but also how in-window and out-of-window maintenance would be communicated to campus. For instance, in-window maintenance on the campus Microsoft Exchange service would be preceded by notices to campus no less than 24 hours in advance. And maintenance that was conducted outside the window was to be communicated to the campus no less than five business days in advance.

4. TOOLS OF CHANGE
4.1 Change Management Site: Recording Changes
With a change manager, service catalog, and service maintenance windows established, OIT was set to start recording change requests. Unfortunately there wasn't a solid technology solution in place to support a change management process. The ticketing system used at that time, Supportworks, didn't have any functionality that could be utilized and OIT was just beginning an initiative to replace it with a proper IT Service Management tool. To keep the ball rolling, OIT created an online interim solution that would be tailored to the initial process and could be modified as the process evolved.

OIT used the open-source content management system Drupal—which was already in use for OIT's main website—as a platform to build a website dedicated to Change Management. The website has a form for staff members to submit change requests. The form collects change date, duration, type, risk, services affected, impact, approach, and implementer.

The goal is to have change requests submitted at least a week in advance of the change. Emergency changes are designated as such within the change form.

Change requests are then displayed in a list that can be filtered by date, disposition (Proposed, Reviewed, Completed, Cancelled), change type (standard, low risk, medium risk, high risk), and emergency (yes or no).

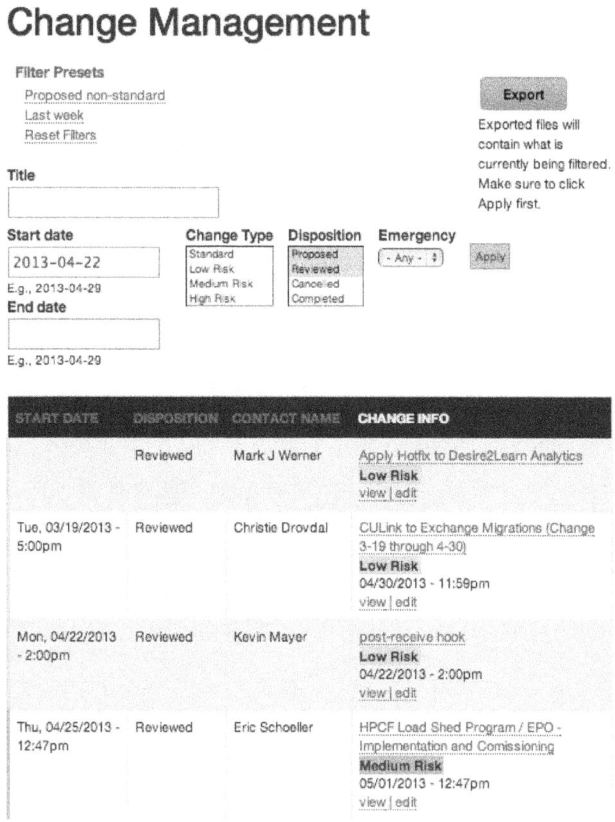

Change Management

Filter Presets
Proposed non-standard
Last week
Reset Filters

Title

Start date
2013-04-22
E.g., 2013-04-29

End date

E.g., 2013-04-29

Export

Exported files will contain what is currently being filtered. Make sure to click Apply first.

Change Type
Standard
Low Risk
Medium Risk
High Risk

Disposition
Proposed
Reviewed
Canceled
Completed

Emergency
- Any - ▾

Apply

START DATE	DISPOSITION	CONTACT NAME	CHANGE INFO
	Reviewed	Mark J Werner	Apply Hotfix to Desire2Learn Analytics **Low Risk** view | edit
Tue, 03/19/2013 - 5:00pm	Reviewed	Christie Drovdal	CULink to Exchange Migrations (Change 3-19 through 4-30) **Low Risk** 04/30/2013 - 11:59pm view | edit
Mon, 04/22/2013 - 2:00pm	Reviewed	Kevin Mayer	post-receive hook **Low Risk** 04/22/2013 - 2:00pm view | edit
Thu, 04/25/2013 - 12:47pm	Reviewed	Eric Schoeller	HPCF Load Shed Program / EPO - Implementation and Comissioning **Medium Risk** 05/01/2013 - 12:47pm view | edit

Figure 1. Change Management Website.

4.2 Change Advisory Board: Change Coordination

Since the organization had invested in ITIL v.3 certification training for staff, many of the senior staff and managers were able to share the common language and work toward the goal of implementing a basic change process. This included the formation of an informal change advisory board (CAB) to review the proposed changes. The CAB is comprised of OIT's change manager, service managers, those who implement the changes, communications representatives, and directors in the areas of security, operations, enterprise services, communications and support.

A crucial step toward adoption of a regularly observed change process was the establishment of weekly CAB meetings. These meetings were formed to ensure that the modification to IT services (including the launch of new services) was transparent, effectively coordinated, and implemented with minimal risk to existing IT services. Anyone with an interest is welcome to attend the meetings and those with a stake in the changes proposed or planned are expected to attend meetings of the CAB. And for those who can't attend the meetings, minutes are archived in the Change Management wiki pages.

In order to have positive outcomes for communication, it was important for the Communication unit to be present at the change advisory board table. This not only allowed the Communication unit to stay informed about changes, but also provide feedback about lead times and customer impacts.

4.3 Service Alerts: One-Stop for All Service Changes

Having one place for the definitive record of all service changes has been critical to successfully communicating to campus. This change form as we call it has visibility to everyone within OIT and changes within the site can be viewed and also be updated by anyone. The change reports ideally include customer impacts which are then relayed to campus customers.

The information in the change reports is then used to draft all campus communication about the change. Over time we have trained the campus that the Service Alerts section of our website is the one-stop location for information about all service impacting events whether they are planned or unplanned.

These Service Alerts include a description of the change, the impact to customers, the timeframe (day and time), service name and if applicable, the impacted campus buildings (generally for network outages). A Service Alerts box pops up in the top right corner of every OIT webpage when there is an alert with immediate impact (a current service outage or upcoming maintenance). The Service Alerts are also archived so someone can see all the alerts for the past year. And if someone wants the alerts to be pushed to them, they can sign up for an RSS feed of the alerts.

All other channel messages about a specific change point back to the Service Alert for more information. These additional channels include the campus portal, emails to CSRs, service login pages, campus news digests and OIT's social media channels. We also publish the Service Alerts on customer support interfaces such as a login page for desktop support requests and a monitor in our call center.

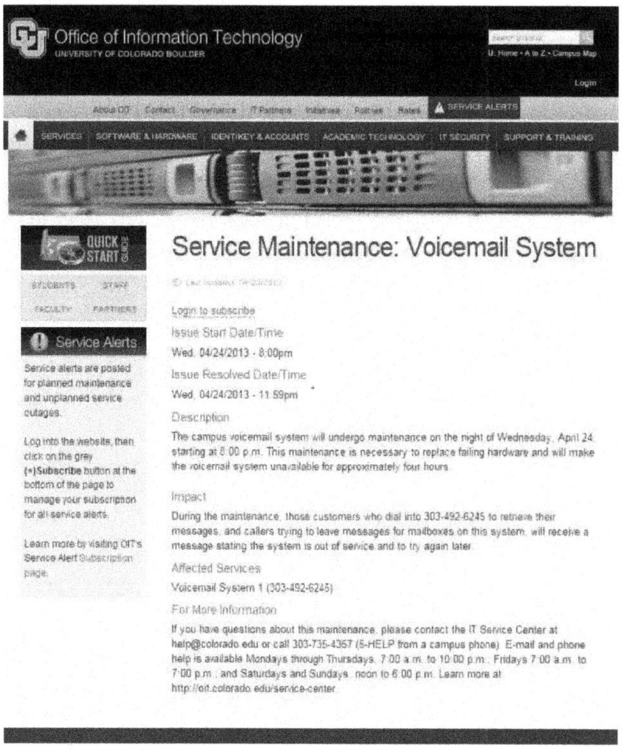

Figure 2. Service Alert Example.

Another critical communication link for service changes is an internal (to OIT) messaging service used to let OIT staff know when maintenance starts and ends. Staff receive an email, and also a text message if the maintenance goes longer than expected. This is particularly helpful if outage expectations need to be reset or a status updated in the various campus channels.

5. SUCCESSES

Although we continue to make incremental improvements to the change management process, the changes over the past three years have led to better understanding within the organization about impacts of changes, better coordination and communication of change activity, and managed expectations about service outages on the part of campus constituents.

Some of the biggest improvements are observed when large changes are planned, scheduled, and communicated to the campus. A recent example of these improvements was evidenced by a change to the firewall that protects services in the campus's main data center affected availability of the campus portals, email services, websites, online learning environment and more. The change was scheduled during the winter break when few people would be on campus or using the services from off campus. Still, we gave key campus departments a chance to provide feedback on the timing of the change in order to minimize impact. When the date had been chosen, it was first communicated to the CSRs, giving another opportunity to make a mid-course adjustment if necessary. Then messages were sent through multiple channels to the rest of campus at least a week in advance. When the day of the change rolled around—a weekday, and workday at that—the outages barely caused a ripple as most everyone knew what to expect.

These kind of well-orchestrated changes and well-established expectations of service outages have helped to not only build confidence in the services provided by OIT, but also to build confidence in OIT as a service provider on the whole. One could argue that these improvements have been a key driver to the improved perception of OIT in general.

6. FUTURE OF CHANGE

In March 2013, we implemented ServiceNow, an IT Service Management tool. ServiceNow is built on ITIL concepts. The initial roll out was focused on Incidents and Requests, as well as Problem Management. ServiceNow has an application for Change Management that we will one day configure for our organization and implement.

In April 2013, our Change Management process evolved so that we have a formal Change Advisory Board with voting members, and we're working toward approving changes in a way that goes beyond just approving the date of the change.

7. CONCLUSIONS

CU-Boulder's change management process is still a work in progress and we are continually improving the various components of our process. The integration with ServiceNow holds great promise as we expect it to automate change record reviews, reduce reliance on weekly CAB meetings, enhance reporting, and increase visibility, participation and awareness.

Some people were initially reluctant to participate in the change advisory board meetings and resistant to others having input to the timing of changes; however, most people have gotten on board with the process. The benefits to our services and the people who use them has been undeniable. The change management process has helped ensure that services are available as intended and the frequency of failed, unauthorized, and emergency changes have been minimized. Ultimately this process has allowed OIT to provide services in a manner that better meet the teaching, learning and research mission of the University of Colorado Boulder.

8. ACKNOWLEDGMENTS

Special thanks to the Office of Information Technology Project Management Office for their direction of the change management process and input to this paper. Also thanks goes to Miles France and Robert Schwander for their development of the Change Management Website and Service Alert application.

Resources

OIT Website: http://www.colorado.edu/oit/
OIT Service Alerts page: http://www.colorado.edu/oit/service-alerts
OIT Service Catalog: http://www.colorado.edu/oit/about-oit/service-catalog
ITIL Website: http://www.itil-officialsite.com/

App Development in User Services: Oxymoron or Incubator?

Lisa Barnett
Director, User Services
40 Washington Sq South, Suite B7
New York, NY 10012
+1 (212) 992-8923
lisa.barnett@nyu.edu

Darin Phelps
Director, Technology Development
40 Washington Sq South, Suite B9
New York, NY 10012
+1 (212) 998-6138
darin.phelps@nyu.edu

Brian Yulke
Associate Director, User Services
40 Washington Sq South, Suite 211
New York, NY 10012
+1 (212) 998-6283
brian.yulke@nyu.edu

ABSTRACT
User Services attracts all types. This talent develops differently, and opportunity can knock on many doors. At New York University (NYU) School of Law, we had a few Helpdesk technicians who took a web development class. When our new exam software came without robust administrative/management tools, opportunity did knock.

We started off in PHP, scarfed some data from our database guys, and cobbled together a working web app in about 6 weeks. It wasn't pretty, but it got the job done. One year later, our next iteration implemented a framework (Zend), version control (Git), and staged environments (development/testing/production). Yet another year later, we added new features, satisfying both administrative and student clients.

Today we have a small, versatile team that handles lightweight projects, and fits them into a Helpdesk schedule to accommodate an ever-growing demand for new web applications. Remarkably, we do this all without sacrificing our core mission of providing top-notch user support. While it does require better time management, it's amazing to see how flexible your Helpdesk can be with their time.

Coming from the user services group, we have a solid relationship with the end users and consequently understand their needs better than traditional programmers. Working with the core development team allowed our Helpdesk programmers to learn faster, and helped the real code-monkeys understand valuable user support fundamentals, which makes them better, too!

Finally, this created professional development opportunities within the organization. While we found equilibrium in User Services, you could also have internal moves within your larger organization. Either way, you preserve organizational knowledge and make the entire IT department stronger. While this kind of professional development opportunity may not be for everyone in your group, you can reward individuals who take initiative, have an interest in learning new technologies, and show strong time-management skills.

Categories and Subject Descriptors
•*Software and its engineering~Programming teams*

General Terms
Management, Professional Development

Keywords
Professional development, programming, career opportunities

1. INTRODUCTION
In client services, all too often our rising stars rise faster than we like and move on all too quickly. But what if you could leverage this talent and ambition? What if you could reward success with tangible professional development and give them a reason to stay longer and grow here? What if you could foster their curiosity, the desire for something more, and create a nurturing environment to stretch their skillsets beyond those expected of a productive Helpdesk member? How can we create this opportunity and not adversely affect the quality of work at the Helpdesk?

In technology, Helpdesk is a great career launching pad. Where else can you develop customer service skills, get in touch with client needs, and gain exposure to every nook and cranny that your user base has questions or problems with? Those with a mix of tech savvy, leadership, operations improvement, and good communications skills may ultimately seek out management roles in client services. Others with heavier technical prowess can still cut their teeth en route to more focused positions in a systems, networking, or programming job. The road through Helpdesk is paved with the footprints of both recent graduates and others embarking on a 2nd (or 3rd!) career. Many are eager and willing to take additional responsibilities and projects to stretch their skills and grow their resumes.

NYU School of Law is a relatively small school within New York University. Our Helpdesk supports around 2,200 students and 800 FTE. While NYU has a large central ITS organization, all of the professional schools and many of the other schools within NYU also have their own IT staffs that have a dedicated focus on the individual schools' needs.

As such, NYU School of Law has an ITS Department with 35 fulltime members, 8 of whom are dedicated Helpdesk staff (including training/documentation and management). Our Helpdesk does not target a particular part of the Law School community; rather, it supports all students (who do have a laptop requirement), faculty, administrators, and staff.

The Law School's ITS organization also has its own Technology Development Office of very busy programmers. The list of important projects that they focus on is long and there isn't any excess capacity within this technical team to work on short-term, smaller-scaled new challenges that require immediate attention. So, one challenge to the organization was how to create space for an agile team of programmers who can focus on some of these quick wins. Two frontline staff and the leadership in Helpdesk are now handling these specific programming projects, the first of which is discussed here.

2. INITIATIVE

The land of Academia is a place of learning and exploration, of discoveries both in the world around us and within us. There exists a degree of freedom often not found in the corporate world. It attracts people not with high salaries and corner offices, but with opportunities for learning and growth. We are all here with a common goal in mind: to create an environment to foster learning. This shouldn't be limited just to students and faculty, but expanded to encompass everyone, to give anyone who wants it a chance for growth.

2.1 Putting in the Effort

Academic institutions can have a wealth of knowledge and offer many avenues for learning. Many schools offer tuition benefits in the form of discounted classes and degrees. Though tuition discounts may not be available everywhere, there is often the possibility to audit classes with no more effort than a letter to the professor. Academic libraries allow access to books, journals, and databases, and most have some form of inter-library loan system connected with numerous other institutions.

The Internet is full of the collaborative efforts of so many others from all over the world: Khan Academy, Tuts+, Massive Open Online Courses (MOOCs) to name a few. These resources are sitting there just begging to be tapped. The decision to explore them is up to us. It is important that our department members know what is available to them if they seek to expand their skills on their own.

2.2 Recognizing the Work

Interest and/or hard work should not go unnoticed or unacknowledged. Taking notice of the interests and efforts of your peers and direct reports is key.

In this instance, two of the Helpdesk staff members had recently finished up some programming classes. They were eager to share what their class projects covered and their enthusiasm was obvious to the leadership of the Law School's ITS. Additionally, the Associate Director of User Services who oversees the Helpdesk had enrolled in a combined Master's program between the business school and the computer science department.

Here was an interesting subset of people with expanded skills who were ripe for the opportunity to meet a new challenge. It is a credit to the Law School's CIO that he was willing to give these tech-newbies a chance to try out their new skills in the context of a real new need the Law School faced.

3. OPPORTUNITY

Some background: Most schools typically include regular homework assignments, projects, class participation, and other factors as part of their evaluation. Law schools have a somewhat unique exam pedagogy; there is typically a single final exam on which the entire course grade is based. Additionally blind grading is instituted, where anonymous ids are used in place of student names or ids. This creates both a higher-stakes environment for final exams, and additional complications in administering them.

Opportunity arose when the decision was made to switch to a new exam software vendor. This new software brought with it new levels of reliability and usability, but lacked an administrative backend that was desperately needed, as NYU Law is one of the larger law schools in the country. We were left with the prospect of receiving nearly 7,000 exam response files each semester and no way to automatically or easily track who uploaded what, when, or where.

We needed an administrative companion to the software, but none existed. The vendor didn't offer one and there were no 3rd party solutions. A solution needed to be provided, and quickly. By the time the decision to switch was made, contracts negotiated, software tested, etc. the start of the exam period was less than two months away.

NYU Law has a committed team for developing internal applications, so why not use them? They were already engaged with other projects, and the timeline we were looking at was aggressive. There was no way they could produce what we needed in so little time.

What about an outside vendor? Someone would have to write a functional spec, negotiate price and delivery time, find money in the budget, test, and deploy. Our experience with vendors told us they would have taken too long, cost too much, and our only success would be in brokering a product that only met a semblance of what our needs were.

The outlook was bleak. There were visions of text files and Excel spreadsheets filled with lists of student course registrations and extensive formulae for manipulating exam filenames into anonymous grading IDs and course names. A task nobody would look forward to, fraught with clerical error, peril, and certain irreversible ocular damage! Helpdesk was destined to share this pain with Academic Services. But what choice did we have? Where else could we turn?

Enter our two Helpdesk technicians: they had shown interest in projects outside the scope of user support, had taken initiative on other Helpdesk projects, and conveniently taken a recent web-development course. While it seemed like a monumental task (and while there would be no hard feelings if the mission were not accepted, or completed on time), it seemed overly convenient. We considered:

- Helpdesk had been supporting exams for years, since the first semester that students started taking them on laptops. Our technicians were present in exam rooms prior to the start of each exam, and back in the office assisting Academic Services.
- ITS assisted the Academic Services with the upload of data into similar management tools for previously used products; we knew the raw material that fueled such an application.
- Since Helpdesk assisted students in uploading exams when they had technical issues, and helped them track their exam file uploads, we ended up being just as much end-users as either the students or the administration.
- Consequently we knew better than anyone what such an application would need to do.

We may not have realized it all at once, but we were perfectly poised to try writing this application. What we lacked in development experience, we made up for in a combination of domain knowledge and rookie confidence!

4. THE FIRST PROJECT

As our pioneering effort, we certainly stumbled along the way. Some valuable lessons were learned, and some wheels were likely reinvented.

After some time we realized the following:

- Resources are cheap! In a Helpdesk, there are always old machines lying around not good enough for deployment, but certainly good enough for a skunkworks project!
- VMs are even cheaper! That's right; they run on the hardware you're already using.
- Open source is also cheap! Not only that, but the documentation and online support communities are usually at least as helpful as their pricy commercial counterparts. While this may not be universally true of all open source products, those that were used (Linux, Apache, MySQL and PHP) are exemplars of the open-source community that are as popular as commercial alternatives (or even more so).

Since we weren't part of an established development team, we weren't fighting with established standards. Anything could have been used, even a new technology or programming language learned. Mercifully the choice was made easy by what was known: PHP, HTML, and MySQL.

4.1 Developing Development

A few choices had to be made and much work had to be done before even the first line of code could be written. The team had to create their own development environment capable of handling multiple contributors to the project. This manifested in the form of a Debian Linux-based server built on an old desktop PC and a process of moving code from a central file share using sFTP. Within a day or two of fumbling and searching Google, a development server was up and running and coding could begin.

We started collaboration with very low-tech protocols: word-of-mouth across the room to make sure we weren't working on the same files. Copying latest versions to a test server, and crossing our fingers we didn't break anything. This first iteration was far from perfect and would often lead to the same file being edited by two people at once.

Now we're using a distributed version control system, Github, to manage our code, and to keep different branches for development, testing, and production.

4.2 Wrangling the Data

What was being developed was, in essence, a reporting application. The problem with reporting applications is that they aren't worth much without actual data. In this case there were two main sources of data. The Student Information System contained names, IDs, courses, and registrations. An exam file receiver was needed for exam upload information such as creation and upload dates, course identification, and anonymous grading IDs.

We approached our database folks, who were appropriately skeptical but also curious. They had been given a polite nudge from management to support this new team and the project. It was important that the CIO gave the database folks a heads-up, as we wanted this project to succeed and not set up the nascent team to be viewed as a threat to anyone in the department's development team. Ultimately, they were able to help us refine our suggested database schema and supply needed data.

Getting real, live data was invaluable. Skeleton code with made-up test cases will get you only so far. With real data we finally got to see the application in action and how the 'diversity' (or less politely, the lack of quality) of real-world data can break what seemed very straightforward code (e.g., names with international characters, or course names with odd punctuation).

4.3 Testing in Production

The Helpdesk team was able to leverage their domain knowledge of the exam process while testing the application, possibly to a greater extent than traditional developers. The real gold was having both Academic Services and Records and Registration (our clients) test the application with us and provide candid feedback that was built on our already-established working relationship.

4.4 Happy Customers

Imagine our delight when the application worked well for all users during the first exam period that we used it. Academic Services and Records and Registration were very happy with the launch. Exams were administered and tracked successfully using the new exam software. Additional functionality and refinements were added to the application over time. Students now have a portal to find information about their exams, including exam schedules, room locations and anonymous exam ids. The latest feature addition includes a workflow for exam postponement request/approval/rescheduling, which continues to improve customer experience and reduce administrative overhead.

5. RESULTS

The three Helpdesk employees involved were able to successfully implement a new web application providing value to an array of customers. They were able to do so without compromising the service mission of Helpdesk by remaining efficient in their tasks and organizing their time well enough to tend to both programming tasks and Helpdesk support.

In addition to gruntling customers, the success of the project both strengthened the relationship between User Services and Academic Services, and fostered a new relationship between User Services and the ITS development team. The latter has shown additional benefits through more collaboration between the two groups, and better overall communication and understanding of projects the department is involved in.

We realized an overall net gain from the successful completion of ExamReporter. Even though we spent considerable time developing it, 5 separate departments continue to benefit from its functionality each and every exam period. Perhaps even more importantly, we have been able to help provide professional development opportunities within the organization for those involved. They have been given experience in programming a detailed web application, and in the setup and maintenance of the infrastructure involved.

Because of the success of ExamReporter, the team has been given other projects that fit within the scope of their availability and helped continue their growth as programmers.

The two frontline Helpdesk personnel involved in this programming project have been promoted to Information Technology Specialists. They are still responsible for some Helpdesk work, but they now also work on a variety of programming projects. Their time-management skills have improved, as they continue to contribute to Helpdesk and work on projects.

The Helpdesk manager was promoted from Associate Director of User Services to Lead Solutions Architect and now successfully leads a hybrid team at the Helpdesk that works on a handful of programming projects in addition to providing front-line client support.

Going forward, we will try to identify candidates with such inclinations who might be able to benefit from similar professional development opportunities. We want to foster a broader User Services culture moving forward; one where a Helpdesk developer is not viewed as an oxymoron, and can be looked to as an incubator of ideas and talent.

6. CONCLUSIONS

By taking advantage of interested Helpdesk staff for a needed project, we were able to successfully meet client needs, promote career development and improve the overall quality of service from the department.

Helpdesk staff should stay active in their education, looking for opportunities to learn, and also for opportunities to use their newfound knowledge.

Management should be supportive of any projects that may help foster growth and learning, even if off the beaten path.

When opportunities arise, make sure to be supportive. Also take advantage of inexpensive resources; they may range from recyclable hardware to open source software to supportive colleagues in other areas of the department.

Your Helpdesk environment need not suffer a drop in service. Indeed, you may see increased productivity as employees are further engaged by a new opportunity at work, and you may find you can provide more and better service from your organization.

7. ACKNOWLEDGMENTS

Special thanks to our CIO, Tolga Ergunay, for having faith in us, and taking a keen interest in our career development.

Slaying the Desktop Management Dragon with Configuration Manager 2012

Benjamin Arnold
University of Northern Iowa
1227 W 27th Street
Cedar Falls, IA 50614
1 (319) 273-2419
ben.arnold@uni.edu

ABSTRACT

Today's desktop computing environment is complex. Software eccentricities, security threats, demanding students and faculty members—why make your life harder than necessary as a desktop administrator? A strong and flexible workstation management platform is an absolute "must" in these trying times. Microsoft's System Center 2012 Configuration Manager is as robust a tool as they come.

Deploy software and operating system images with ease. Another Java exploit causing problems? Don't shudder—own that update process! Certain large software companies got you down with the threat of a software license audit? Sleep soundly, knowing the asset intelligence built into Configuration Manager has your back. This session will seek to explore the ways Config Manager can make your life easier as a desktop administrator. Even experienced desktop admins should come away with some new tricks!

Categories and Subject Descriptors

C.2.4 [**Computer Systems Organization**]: Distributed Systems – *client/server, distributed applications, distributed databases, network operating systems.*

C.5.3 [**Computer System Implementation**]: Microcomputers – *microprocessors, personal computers, portable devices, workstations.*

General Terms

Management, Reliability, Security, Human Factors, Standardization

Keywords

Desktop management, deployment, software updates, reporting, asset intelligence, self-service, security, Microsoft System Center 2012 Configuration Manager

1. INTRODUCTION

The University of Northern Iowa, known as "UNI," is a Midwest regional comprehensive university with an annual student enrollment between 12,000 and 13,000 students. The campus in Cedar Falls, Iowa, is comprised primarily of one geographical location containing approximately fifty buildings and surrounding grounds. The University manages information technology assets and support for students, faculty, and staff through a distributed model, with central "IT" providing enterprise-class services utilized by all of campus (e.g., the network and email) and each college or division maintaining their own IT units for desktop and other personalized support.

Desktop computers traditionally have been managed differently by each IT organization at UNI. With the adoption of Microsoft's System Center Configuration Manager (known colloquially as "Config Manager") in May of 2010, the campus started inching toward a standardized methodology for administering and supporting Windows desktops across the entire University.

Following the SIGUCCS 2012 combined conference in October (and, in particular, the opening plenary delivered by Sue B. Workman), the University commenced an initiative for central IT to provide a robust tool and expertise at the "unglamorous" aspects of IT, such as patching, maintenance, software updates, and OS deployment. Config Manager—particularly the 2012 release—was a platform that would allow us to achieve these goals.

2. "THE DRAGON," OR – WHY DESKTOP MANAGEMENT IN THE ENTERPRISE IS HARD

2.1 Frequently Updated Software

It is no secret that there are many software packages that see frequent exploits and, thus, require frequent update releases. Among the worst of the offenders are Java (by Oracle), Flash Player (by Adobe), and Acrobat Reader (by Adobe). Web browsers also can count themselves among those receiving frequent releases by their companies. This can prove to be a challenge for admins managing numerous desktop systems. Are users affected by the latest zero-day exploit for Java? How is Java being deployed? Is auto update turned on? Are users downloading updates themselves?

Each desktop becomes vulnerable to infection by malware (or worse) when not up-to-date with the latest software releases. Without a robust management platform, however, updating software on each and every system under your control can be overwhelming.

2.2 New Operating System Releases

Windows XP, Microsoft's flagship OS for many years, still maintains almost forty percent market share according to recent research, despite the fact that it is now more than ten years old. [1] End of life for Windows XP is coming in less than a year [2]. This scenario can be further complicated in the higher-education field, where often the best chance at migrating a large number of users to a new operating system is over the summer break. That can leave desktop administrators with a large amount of work, a short time to get it done, and the daunting prospect of trying to locate and meet with users, including professors and other faculty who may be gone over the break period.

2.3 Patching

"Patch Tuesday" is a well-known phenomenon amongst IT professionals. What Microsoft lacks in "getting it right the first time," they make up for in one of the best patch release cycles of any software manufacturer in the business. Microsoft releases six to twelve patches each month for various products. How are those going to be distributed to a desktop admin's systems? Windows Server Update Services, or WSUS for short, is a good first step, but the reporting is lacking, clunky, and slow. Out-of-band patches for zero day exploits that are known to be in the wild are not unheard of from Microsoft. There is typically more urgency in distributing these patches, both from a security department and from IT management. Being able to provide up-to-the minute reporting is something WSUS simply is not capable of doing well.

2.4 Sheer Numbers, or "What Do I Even Have Out There?"

Sometimes desktop administrators manage such a large number of machines that they don't even know what they currently have deployed. Do the computers support the next version of Windows? Do any users require RAM upgrades? What software is installed and running? This situation is even more common in higher education, where desktop administrators have not only faculty and staff to support, but also may have computer labs. In multi-site campuses, it may not be feasible to "sneaker net" it over to another location to check on one or two desktops.

2.5 Software Install Requests

It has happened to many desktop administrators at one time or another. The perfect image for a computer lab is finished, and its deployment is halfway finished before the beginning of the semester—then you get one more request from a professor who just got back from sabbatical. Or perhaps you have faculty or staff purchasing licenses for specialized software in ones and twos. (Acrobat Professional is a common example of software that may be licensed for only a limited number of users on campus). In a larger organization, these types of requests can come in fast and furious during key times of the year. Without the proper platform for handling these requests quickly and efficiently, the beleaguered desktop administrator will be overwhelmed!

3. CONFIGURATION MANAGER MAKES THE PERFECT LANCE WITH WHICH TO SLAY THE DRAGON

Microsoft System Center 2012 Configuration Manager is one of several complete desktop platform management tools available on the market today. It is part of a larger suite of software called System Center and is currently in the 2012 release. What follows will be a point-by-point comparison of problems in managing a large deployment of desktops and workstations, along with solutions provided by Config Manager.

3.1 Software Deployment

Config Manager offers a strong software deployment feature set. While many administrators have used Group Policy to accomplish this, Config Manager far surpasses the functionality found in Group Policy.

It is important to note that Config Manager is just a deployment, or delivery, vehicle for your software. It provides no assistance with packaging software appropriately or otherwise preparing it for delivery. This means that the desktop administrator, or the packaging administrator (should you be lucky enough to have one), is still responsible to ensure a software install will work as expected.

3.1.1 Agility in Software Deployments

One detriment to using Active Directory Group Policy to push out MSI installers on a computer's reboot is that doing so generally requires a desktop administrator to design her Active Directory Organizational Unit (OU) structure around the specific software packages they want to deploy and where they will be deployed. (Granted, there are ways to get around this; however, they can be complex and can slow down a computer's Group Policy processing upon reboot or logon).

With Config Manager, a computer object can be in multiple "collections," which means it can be a member of a collection for each piece of software you would like to push to it. You can create a collection that has only a single computer as a member if you wished. This gives the administrator greater flexibility in designing their software deployment strategy and also allows for a less complicated Active Directory structure.

3.1.2 Keep Software Up-To-Date Easily

At UNI, we have created a set of recommended collections that each departmental Config Manager administrator is encouraged to use. These include collections for each of four frequently updated pieces of software: Oracle Java JRE, Adobe Flash Player, Adobe Reader, and Mozilla Firefox. These collections are query-based, meaning their membership is dynamically determined by a query against the Config Manager database.

The queries that determine each collection's membership have a version number in the query language that states what the admin considers "current" at that time. Anything that does not meet that version number becomes a member of the collection by the query. This means the admin constantly has a collection of all computers that have an out- of- date version of a piece of software.

At that point, it is a simple matter to deploy the current version of the software in question to the collection. As the members install the current version, their version numbers get updated and they automatically fall out of the collection membership.

3.2 Operating System Deployment

The idea of building a desktop image for deployment to multiple machines has been around for a long time. Symantec Ghost was a prime example of an early leader in such technology. There is a constant conversation throughout the industry on thick images versus thin images, or put another way, images with all the software pre-installed versus images that contain just the baseline operating system and applicable patches and updates. In the latter scenario, the pertinent software packages are installed after the image has been applied to the machine. Thin images generally tend to allow for more flexibility and the need for simplified images to be maintained by an IT department. Config Manager makes it easy to maintain one thin image and simply deploy the desired software after the operating system has been laid down.

3.2.1 One Image, Many Task Sequences

Config Manager has the notion of the "task sequence," which is essentially a list of items or actions that need to happen and that the Config Manager system knows how to execute. A typical task sequence will reboot the computer into WinPE, clean the primary partition on the hard drive by formatting it, lay down an image that was previously specified, reboot the computer, join the domain, and install any necessary hardware drivers.

The above functionality can be extended by having a task sequence install software packages, install Windows updates, run scripts, backup and restore a user's state (primarily, their profile folder), install other devices, or any one of a number of other things the administrator might need. In this fashion, the administrator can maintain two images. One for x86 system architecture and one for x64 system architecture. After that, all applications can be installed from the task sequence, and the administrator shoud be able to tweak most settings through Group Policy.

3.2.2 Driver Repository

Config Manager has a driver repository that allows a task sequence to search for appropriate device drivers for the computer being re-imaged. This driver repository is maintained by a Config Manager administrator and drivers are uploaded and made available to those using the system.

Campuses using Dell or HP computers are particularly fortunate, as each of these vendors maintains a website with drivers easily accessible in large compressed archives through which one can download all drivers for a particular model and import them into the Config Manager system. By keeping the drivers separate from the image itself, and instead installing them after the imaging process is complete, an administrator needs to maintain fewer actual images and can get away from the need to have one image for each computer model.

3.2.3 User-State Migration

Microsoft offers a free utility called the User State Migration Tool, or USMT for short. It used to be a part of the Windows Automated Installation Kit (WAIK) and now, with the advent of Windows 8, is part of the Assessment and Deployment Kit (ADK). The USMT can be integrated into a task sequence in Config Manager. This allows an administrator to access a user's profile and other files (searchable across the local hard drive by using wild cards and file extensions), copy them to another location like a file server, wipe everything clean, lay down the new image (perhaps even with a new OS), and then restore the user's profile and files to the computer. By taking advantage of the task sequence combined with the USMT, an administrator could make a powerful and easy-to-use migration solution to bring those users still on Windows XP to a newer version of Windows.

3.3 Software Updates

Software updates, or Windows patching, is an unending process. Windows Server Update Services, or WSUS, is quite often the method of choice for ensuring Windows desktops across any organization are receiving the updates they need to stay secure and stable. Often, the nature of WSUS is such that it can be a "set it and forget it" solution. This is both good and bad. Admins who rely on WSUS for their patching are typically well-covered until

an emergency out-of-band patch arrives from Microsoft. Then management wants reports or the status of the update's deployment. That is where WSUS falls down. Config Manager offers more power and flexibility in this context.

3.3.1 Agility in Targeting Updates

Again, like with software or operating system deployments, an administrator would target Windows updates to collections. This means an administrator can selectively push updates out based on collection membership. It is easy to give different collections different timelines or rules about updates. Different collections could receive updates for different products too, based upon the members in the collection.

3.3.2 Reporting on Update Deployments

The same robust functionality that allows reporting on software deployments allows an administrator to run reports on his software updates. Such reports can provide necessary information on the status of such updates and the expected timeframe until installation is comple across the whole organization.

3.3.3 Patching Images Offline

One of the big selling points for using Software Updates through Config Manager (as opposed to relying solely on WSUS) is Config Manager's ability to patch a WIM image file offline.

If an administrator is using Config Manager to push her operating system images and has them configured and imported into the Config Manager system, then she can set a maintenance task to periodically take the WIM image offline, scan it against the current Microsoft Update Catalog, and inject any missing updates right into the WIM image.

This ensures that each month after patch Tuesday, an administrator is deploying a fully patched and secure operating system. It also eliminates the time required to download and install patches after an image is successfully pushed to a computer. Instead, the maintenance takes place at night and your WIM image is always up-to-date.

3.4 Reporting and Asset Intelligence

Out of the box, Config Manager provides approximately three hundred canned reports. These address everything from hardware inside a computer, to status on software updates, to assessing what version of driver a particular device inside a particular computer is using. These are powerful tools, and since the reporting system is based on SQL Server Reporting Services (SSRS), an administrator can write his own reports for any information that is stored within the Config Manager database.

3.4.1 Asset Intelligence Capabilities

Asset Intelligence is a feature in Config Manager that allows an admin to keep track of installed software on her deployed computers. By comparing what is installed to the list of what has been purchased, and providing the ability to run reports against those two data sets, Asset Intelligence allows an organization to keep tabs on its software license usage.

Asset Intelligence offers further functionality by collecting information from the Windows Security Event Log. This allows a computer lab administrator, for example, to keep track of who is logging on to her computers and what they are doing when they are there.

3.5 "Fancy" Software Deployment

Out of the box, Config Manager provides a few ways to deploy software to users and to computers across an organization. By coming up with some more creative solutions, Config Manager Admins can get even more advanced.

3.5.1 Using Active Directory Security Groups to Deploy Software

Consider incoming requests for licensed software installs. Traditionally, at UNI, this would mean we would verify the user was licensed, then we would dispatch a student technician to install the software on the user's computer at the first chance the technician became available. While this model works, it's often desirable to streamline the process further.

With the use of Config Manager at UNI, we now can create an Active Directory security group with computer objects as its members. In Config Manager, we have a collection set up for each licensed software product, and that collection's membership is based on a query that looks at the aforementioned Active Directory (AD) security group. When a computer object is a member of the security group for Acrobat Professional, for example, the computer becomes a member of the corresponding collection in Config Manager. [3]

There is a standing software deployment for Acrobat Professional that is targeted at the collection in Config Manager for Acrobat Professional. This deployment is set to install once and only once on each computer.

So when the next user notifies us that they have purchased a license for Acrobat Professional, we simply add their computer object in AD as a member of the appropriate security group. This will make the user a member of the collection in Config Manager; since the user will be a new member, the user will get Acrobat Professional deployed to them automatically.

3.5.2 User-Centric Installations

Config Manager 2012 also provides the ability to correlate a specific computer object with a specific user account. This is called setting the "user/device affinity." Once a primary device is set for a user, the admin can do several different things by targeting software installs at the user instead of at the computer object. For instance, their software could follow the user to other machines if need be, meaning it could be installed on any computer that the user logs into.

This might not seem like such a powerful feature until an admin considers Config Manager's integration with Microsoft's Application Virtualization platform (App-V). If you're using App-V alongside Configuration Manager, you could ensure that any time a user logs on to a device that is not their primary device (as explicitly defined by the user/device affinity settings), then instead of the full native MSI installer package, the user gets an App-V package delivered to them. In this way, an administrator can grant access to applications for specific users no matter the device the user is utilizing.

4. EXTENDING CONFIGURATION MANAGER'S USEFULNESS

Out of the box, Microsoft's Configuration Manager is perhaps one of the most powerful and useful tools a desktop administrator could ask for. There are plenty of other Microsoft products and even third party add-ons that can extend Config Manager's functionality. What follows is a brief list of those that University of Northern Iowa will be investigating and perhaps implementing over the coming months.

4.1 Cross-Platform Manageability

Configuration Manager 2012 supports a native Mac OS X and Linux client, now that Service Pack 1 was released early this year. This means administrators will be able to push software or take inventory and run reports against Mac and Linux clients in their organization. The built-in functionality is terrific and a great start; however, Parallels—the same company to make the popular desktop virtualization software for Mac OS X—now makes a Config Manager Plugin for Mac OS X.

This plugin installs in the Mac client's operating system and allows the Mac to be managed largely on feature parity with that of a Windows client. Soon, the company hopes to have full Mac OS X system imaging and deployment released as a feature set.

This will be beneficial to us at UNI, as we find more and more faculty and staff are requesting Macs for their computers. The ability to manage Macs in the same pane of glass as our deployed Windows computers, either through the built-in functionality or by leveraging a third party product, will be a great advantage.

4.2 Integrating With Other Members of the System Center 2012 Suite

4.2.1 System Center 2012 Service Manager

Service Manager is Microsoft's Information Technology Service Management (ITSM) product. It includes change and incident management, among other things. One piece that Service Manager offers is a web portal. When integrated with Configuration Manager's Application Catalog abilities, users can login to the web portal, see what software is available, and either install the software from there (triggering a Config Manager software deployment) or request access from the appropriate people. In essence, this creates the enterprise application store.

4.2.2 System Center 2012 Orchestrator

Microsoft's System Center 2012 Orchestrator is an enterprise workflow creation and management suite. Using Orchestrator, an administrator can streamline and automate the creation of software packages, Active Directory objects, or most other things in the Windows environment, based upon triggers or inputs. Combing Orchestrator with Service Manager and Config Manager makes for a powerful automation set across the desktop (or server/datacenter) landscape in any organization.

5. ACKNOWLEDGMENTS

My thanks to Santos Martinez, Microsoft Premier Field Engineer for Config Manager, who has provided a great deal of knowledge to me on Config Manager, and especially for his tireless help when my own Config Manager site went haywire in spring 2013.

6. REFERENCES

[1] Whittaker, Zack. 2013. Windows 8 Edges to 3.84 Percent Share; Still Fails to Spark. http://www.zdnet.com/windows-8-edges-to-3-84-percent-share-still-fails-to-spark-7000014746/

[2] Windows Lifecycle Fact Sheet. http://windows.microsoft.com/en-us/windows/products/lifecycle

[3] Leveraging Active Directory to Manage Software Pushes in SCCM. http://www.uni.edu/its/support/article/1131

Customer Service: Then and Now

Ashley Weese
195 Durham Center
Ames, IA 50011
1.515.294.7313
aweese@iastate.edu

Dana Peiffer
ITTC36
Cedar Falls, IA 50614
1.319.273.7137
dana.peiffer@uni.edu

ABSTRACT

Technology changes on a more frequent basis than ever before, but what is often overlooked is how customer service demands are changing along with it. In Iowa, we've seen that, as the customers needs change, so does the expectation of support. In the not so distant past, we worked with customers who wanted us to "do it for them," however, the newer generations coming to campus have much different expectations. We see two new, but very distinct types of customer technology levels, those who know just enough to be dangerous and those who just want step-by-step instructions so they can do it themselves.

Offering a different variety of support is also evolving. Customer service troubleshooting used to only involve face-to-face contact or over the phone. Now, we can offer email, chat, crowd sourcing, and even self-service via a knowledgebase. Being able to keep up with the technology is one thing, but adjusting and renewing the customer service skills, is a whole new ballgame.

One of the greatest HelpDesk challenges today is to be able to recognize the type of customer you are dealing with and adjust your Customer Service style very quickly in order to best assist that customer.

Categories and Subject Descriptors

K.6.1 [**Management of Computing and Information Systems**]: Project and People Management – *Staffing*.

Keywords

Management, Training, Support, Technology, Customer Service, Student Employees.

1. INTRODUCTION

Iowa State University, located in Ames, Iowa is a comprehensive research university with over 31,000 students and 6,000 faculty and staff members [1]. Information Technology Services (ITS) is infused into all aspects of everyday life at ISU. ITS maintains both the wired and wireless network across campus, manages and supports a University-wide web portal, Exchange 2010 for faculty and staff, CyMail, a partnership between Iowa State and Google

Apps for Education for students, as well as other classroom learning technologies, including Blackboard Learn. The department is responsible for leading and ensuring that Iowa State's information technologies support the university's mission to excel at teaching and learning, research and creative endeavors, outreach, and university leadership. [2]

The Solution Center houses the two support realms within ITS. It includes an employee side, known as Employee Technical Services, where it employs twelve full time staff members who answer questions from supported users that pay for support and acts as the single point of contact for account management troubles. Then, there is Student Technical Services, which is the single point of contact for students as well as faculty and staff who do not pay for support. STS, often times referred to as the Solution Center in general, is open an extended number of hours and staffed seven days a week with up to 60 part time student employees. We have several different positions within STS which includes a technical path and a customer service only path. The technical support path includes students answering phones, emails, working with customers in person on appointments and removing viruses from computers. The customer service only path, known as "concierge" consists of students working as the face of the Solution Center. These students are the first contact when a customer walks in the door. They assist with general questions about accounts, advise customers on where to get specific support, and help answer basic questions. No matter which track the student is hired for, each must go through a series of customer service trainings before they begin.

The University of Northern Iowa has just over 13,000 students, with a Faculty and Staff of 2,800 and is one of the three Regent Universities located in Iowa. Student Employees make up a large part of our support model for both our computer lab environment and also in the Computer Consulting Center (CCC). The Computer Labs employ approximately 60 students and the Computer Consulting Center employs 9-11 student employees.

2. CUSTOMER SERVICE - THEN

Customer Service is delivered to customers based on a need. This can range from assistance needed because of a problem, advice on a specific need or interest, or simply providing empathy in the rare case that a suitable resolution is not readily available, if available at all. "Before technology" relates to the timeliness of how this Customer Service is delivered.

2.1 EXPECTATIONS

The expectation of the customer was and still is today a resolution to the problem or question he/she has presented to the Customer Service agent. A quality resolution was more important than the speed at which it was provided. The expectation of the Customer Service agent is that he/she will be able to provide to the customer a quality resolution. Again, the quality of the resolution had a higher priority than the speed at which it was delivered.

2.2 TYPES OF SUPPORT

Telephone support was one of 3 basic ways to communicate with a customer. However, before IT the phones were analog (maybe rotary dial), may not have had caller ID, may not have had more than 1 incoming line, and in some cases did not provide the option to leave a message. Walk-in traffic was also heavily used, provided the customer was in close proximity to the Customer Service agent and that travel was at a minimum. Anyone know what this is (hold up an envelope with stamp)? Believe it or not Customer Service was also provided via snail mail. This type of Customer Service worked because our expectations of a timely resolution were flexible because we hadn't yet been exposed to the "I can have it right now" technology. Bottom line; patience on the customers' side was a virtue and the norm because that's the way it was.

3. CUSTOMER SERVICE - NOW

In today's society, many people have moved away from feeling empathetic towards others. In the customer service realm, this is no different. Because of restructuring and budget cuts many HelpDesks are seeing their first and second level support groups being merged. So now, you could have a technician with very in-depth technical knowledge that has not had many interactions with customers in the past, supporting customers. If that same technician is unable to have a conversation about a customer's problem and talk on the same level, they have failed. Just like in baseball, the technician must now be a "utility" player and wear multiple hats in order to successfully provide a positive experience and hit a homerun.

3.1 EXPECTATIONS

When a customer interacts with an employee, the customer doesn't normally think about or care about what's going on in their personal lives, if your last customer interaction went poorly, or if you are having problems with a coworker. The customer expects quality support in a timely fashion. "Customers are demanding. And they have every right to be. Today's customers have more options and less time than ever before." [3] Many times, offering different types of support and contact methods are seen as wonderful alternatives or options. In the end, the customer expects respect, acknowledgement of their time, and a knowledgeable technician.

3.2 TYPES OF SUPPORT

In this day in age, information technology can offer a wide variety of support methods. It's not just phones or email, it's live chat, social media networks, crowdsourcing, remote assistance, and self-service portals among many others. When a customer chooses to use the telephone as a support method, the customer is expecting to obtain quality service and answers within minutes.

They want the human interaction and conversation. Many times its easiest to troubleshoot an issue over the telephone as the technician can ask follow up questions or walk the customer through different resolutions. When a customer chooses to use email as a support method, often times they are too busy or don't want to speak with someone over the telephone. The emails are also very often vague so the employee must spend time compiling a list of troubleshooting questions to send them before any real resolution is given.

When a customer chooses to use a social media outlet as a way to obtain support, it is normally a question that can be answered very easily or a question/complaint that a customer feels the cyberspace world should know about. More than likely, the customer had a poor interaction with the level of support they received in the past and wanted to make others aware of it. Often times, when this happens, a reply to the message and asking them to send their contact information in a private message is recommended or advising that they'll be contacted directly by a staff member.

Using crowdsourcing or a self-service knowledgebase are other, very viable means of support as well. Yahoo Answers is a great example of a successful Crowdsourcing tool. Members of the Yahoo community can ask questions under different categories and other members respond with advice or answers. The "best" answer is then selected by the original poster. Then the page, question, responses, and answers are saved and indexed so others can use a search tool to find if someone had already answered the question. Many forums are based on the Crowdsourcing idea as well. A self-service knowledgebase is also a very helpful tool for customers. Employees create and maintain a database of answers in article form for users to view and use. Successful knowledgbases have at least one employee maintaining and reviewing articles to make sure keywords are entered, articles are correct, and that articles are easy to follow or understand.

4. HOW TO TRAIN FOR CUSTOMER SERVICE

Training employees on customer service can be very difficult in the Information Technology field. Most employees are technical thinkers and do not have "soft skills" or would rather not do customer support. Others are very customer oriented and customer service comes naturally. No matter what type of person or how long they have been in the field, it is very important to train each employee to use key phrases that build rapport, show empathy all while communicating effectively.

Many interactions with customers will have a few moments where there is "dead air" and no one is talking because either the employee or customer is looking something up. It is perfect opportunities like these that allow an employee to build rapport. Talking about the weather, the recent sports game or current events is a wonderful way to find a common ground. It will allow other, more technical interactions easier if the customer can find some way to relate.

Identifying with the customer based on their feelings is another way to "enhance the rapport you're building with customers." [4] Using phrases like "I can relate" or "I had this same thing happen to me last week" are both great examples of empathy. "Conveying empathy with customers sends a positive message that demonstrates you're listening to them and relating to what they're telling you." [4]

Effectively communicating is another, very important topic when it comes to customer service training. It could end up making a customer very happy with their experience, or it could turn into a disappointing, negative experience very quickly. Learning how to effectively communicate takes time, but remembering a few key topics can help. Be positive, attitude can be a determining factor when a customer decides they are going to listen to your advice or not. Avoid jargon, slang, and technical language. The customer wants to have a conversation, not be talked down to. Listen actively for keywords and try to rephrase their questions or concerns so you are both on the same page.

5. OBSTACLES

There are many obstacles that stand in the way of obtaining or providing excellent customer service. Some of the obstacles are easily fixed, others will not go away. Listed below are the obstacles that we believe to be important as of now:

1. Disruptive Environment

2. Language Barriers/Culture Sensitivity

3. Contacts needing assistance during non-working hours

4. Over-worked Management

5. Unplanned Outages/Lack of Staffing

6. Patience

In order to have a positive experience, the customer must not know what is going on around the technician or if something else is catching their attention, such as a disruptive environment. Coworkers could be laughing at the latest joke, discussing a current event that is very controversial, or watching last week's episode of *The Office*. When a customer calls in and hears the noise in the background or the technician has to put the customer on hold to ask others to quiet down, this can become a negative experience.

In today's environment, a time will come when there is a language barrier and the technician has troubles understanding the customer, or the customer has troubles understanding the technician. In times like these, it's best to let the other party know that you are having troubles understanding them. If this was happening over the phone, you could ask the customer to email, come into the HelpDesk, or to use the live chat feature for better service. During situations like these, there is a very fine line that you must not cross. The technician must make sure to avoid slang, jargon, assumptions and motives as different cultures have sensitivities.

Another obstacle that many customer service environments face is the lack of extended hours for customers to obtain support. At Iowa State, we have worked to extend hours over the last six years based on the needs of customers, but found that there was actually not enough need to staff the HelpDesk. We went from being open during "normal business hours," Monday through Friday, 8am to 5pm to open on the weekends (Saturday 10am to 5pm and Sunday 10am to 10pm) and open until midnight each weeknight. As we watched the metrics closely, we determined that the need stops at 9pm on weeknights and is less on weekends, so we changed our

hours yet again to Monday through Thursday 7:30am to 9pm, Friday 7:30am to 5pm, weekends from 10am to 5pm. We found a number of password resets were being performed at night for new and incoming students as well as many other, very random, questions from students. Faculty and staff did not use the extended support until a few years after we started offering it.

Additional obstacles include over-worked management. If a manager only has time to run around and put out fires, it is very unlikely that they are able to sit down and do any type of quality assurance or watch for common trends. A manager wears many hats, but at the end of the day, if they are unable to get work done, are they being effective? Many of these issues stem from budget cuts or having a lack of support system for managers to delegate tasks.

Another obstacle that seems to happen very often in the Information Technology realm is the "unplanned outage." No one can determine when an unplanned outage is going to happen, however, being staffed during these types is essential to having a positive customer experience. If you are understaffed, customers experience long wait times in the queue and are often aggravated and abandon the call. One of the ways Iowa State has gone about fixing this type of issue is to have a pre-message dedicated to the outage. Then, when a customer calls in, the first message they hear is that we are having an outage and that staff is looking into the issue. Many times, the customer hangs up after the message is heard, but it gives them a notion that there is an issue and that we are working on it.

6. WHAT THE FUTURE HOLDS (Mellenials)

Last year we were talking about how to provide quality Customer Service to these types of customers, but now our student employees are members of these types of individuals. Thus we have to not only consider their needs as customers but also their Customer Service style in how it accommodates all customers. I believe that one of the biggest challenges for this generation as a Customer Service agent will be how to deal with the customer of a past generation that lacks in or chooses not to embrace the latest technology. As mentioned earlier in this presentation "Patience is a virtue" and this new generation of Customer Service agents will be challenged to have patience when dealing with customers who have chosen to not keep up with the new technology, or rather the speed at which the new technology is delivered.

"Instant gratification" or what I refer to as the "I want/need it now" mindset will directly affect how we deliver good Customer Service as it will determine how we locate, access, and document solutions for the services available to our users. Keeping up on the latest versions of software and programs we support will be crucial and knowledge of how to use these programs will also play an important role in our ability to deliver good Customer Service. Also, given the vast availability of online resources we also have the option of quickly knowing where to access the resolution needed for our customers without necessarily containing the working knowledge of a specific product. The most important thing will be to find a resolution for customer quickly and accurately.

7. CONCLUSION

Based on the feedback we got, the number of willing applicants and the type of applicants actually hired, I would recommend this process to not only university related interviewees, but to all hiring managers looking for specific candidates that need to work together in a team environment. We ended up hiring ten of the twenty applicants and all have going through training and been more successful than any hires before. They came into the job with a sense of teamwork and had already bonded with each other to create outstanding synergy. When it comes to hire multiple students again, the Solution Center will have another hiring event. It was fun, interesting and provided us with employees who are excelling already.

8. REFERENCES

[1] Iowa State University. "ISU Fact Book 2011-2012." Last modified February 2012. http://www.ir.iastate.edu/FB12/PDF/FB2012ALL.pdf

[2] Iowa State University. "About the Office of the CIO." Accessed May 1, 2012. http://www.cio.iastate.edu/about/

[3] Performance Research Associates 2012. *Delivering Knock Your Socks Off Service*. American Management Association., New York, NY.

[4] Evenson, Renee 2012. Powerful Phrases for Effective Customer Service. American Management Association., New York, NY.

Innovate Through Crowd Sourcing

Thom Mattauch
VCU helpIT Center Manager
901 Park Ave Room B-30
Richmond, VA 23284
804-827-0532

mattauchtj@vcu.edu

ABSTRACT

In March 2012, Virginia Commonwealth University's VP for Finance and Administration created a team of innovators called team IMPACT. The task for team IMPACT was to create a viable methodology for vetting innovative ideas and to brainstorm ideas to push through this methodology. One of the ideas that came out of this project was to implement a system by which the team could gather the ideas of the entire university community. The team began the task of procuring and implementing a crowd sourcing solution. In February of 2013, team IMPACT began piloting a program called VCU Ideas, powered by IdeaScale. Through this product, team IMPACT can capture the ideas of the university as well as allow the university community to vote on the ideas. Crowd sourcing enables team IMPACT to keep their fingers on the pulse of the university.

Categories and Subject Descriptors

K.4.3 [**Computers and Society**]: Organizational Impacts *Computer-supported collaborative work*

Keywords

Support, Operating Systems, Mobile, Customer Satisfaction, Virtualization

1. INTRODUCTION

Virginia Commonwealth University (VCU) sits in the heart of Richmond, Virginia, enrolling more than 32,000 students and employing close to 18,000 faculty and staff members. Since its establishment in 1968, VCU has expanded to include two downtown campuses in Richmond, as well as six satellite locations throughout the state of Virginia, and one site in Doha, Qatar. Offering 216 degree and certification programs through 13 separate schools and one college, VCU has been able to provide students with a full range of courses, from sculpture to microbiology, engineering to foreign language, business to philosophy, and many others.

In March of 2012, the Vice President of VCU's Finance and Administration put together a team of individuals to focus on innovation throughout the university. This team is named IMPACT.

2. WHAT IS TEAM IMPACT?

IMPACT is a team composed of members from all of the departments within VCU's Finance and Administration Division. The team's mission is "To utilize creativity and collaboration to identify initiatives that result in innovative improvements in support of VCU's Quest for Distinction." The concept for team IMPACT came from the Skunk Works team, which was founded in Lockheed Martin's Advanced Development Programs [1]. The idea behind a skunk works team is to have a team that can work with autonomy and free from bureaucratic encumbrances. The team started out with a membership of 12, though currently the team operates with membership of 10 (Figure 1). The role of IMPACT was to work together to promote innovative projects within VCU's community. Though the team is sponsored by the VP for Finance and Administration, who is now the Chief Operating Officer for the university, the team was to have freedom to brainstorm, research, and bring forth projects without directives from the administration at the university.

The first hurdle that the team had to overcome was group formation. As with any group, this can be the greatest challenge and took up a good portion of the first year of its existence. However, once the group got over this hurdle, it dove head first into project brainstorming and vetting.

Figure 1 – IMPACT Team

2.1 Project evaluation

Once the team moved from formation to production mode, a process had to be in place for efficiently vetting ideas. The team chose to vet the ideas on a simple Risk vs. Benefit matrix (Figure 2). This allowed the team to rate various risks versus various benefits on a scale of 1 – 5. For Risk the scale was 1 being the highest risk and 5 being the lowest risk. For Benefit the scale was 1 being the lowest benefit and 5 being the highest benefit.

Risk factors being evaluated were:

- Time Frame
- Cost to implement
- Change to operating procedures

- Other hurdles to implementation
- Perceived Administration Support

Benefit factors being evaluated were:
- Alignment with VCU's Quest for Distinction
- Savings to the University
- Student experience
- Enhanced facilities
- Improved safety/security
- Customer Service
- Organizational transparency

The evaluation took place through a project evaluation subcommittee that consisted of three members of team IMPACT. For the first round of projects that would be moved forward in the team's process, only those projects which fell within the upper right quadrant of the matrix would be selected.

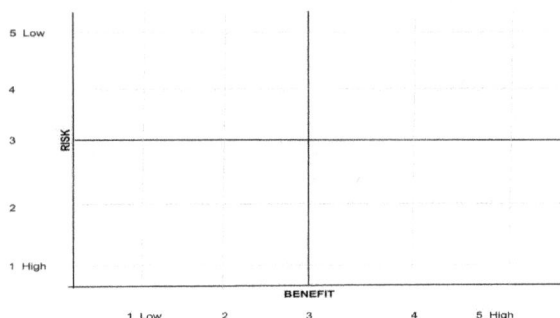

Figure 2 – Evaluation Matrix

2.2 Phase two and beyond

Once the project is vetted, it is then to be processed through a rigorous evaluation, which includes reaching out to departmental stakeholders to assist in determining the viability of the project. Once that is complete, the team assembles a project team consisting of members from team IMPACT as well as the departmental stakeholders. A full project committee then begins work on setting timelines and deliverables for the project. The final step in the process is to present the case for the project to the senior leadership of the university to obtain buy in and funding to put the project into motion.

2.3 What projects came out of the team?

After brainstorming, the team came up with a potential list of 72 projects. Of those, four projects made it through in the initial round of deliverables. Those projects were a Combined Server Center for the University, Comprehensive Space Utilization, DIY workshops for the university community and an Employee Appreciation Week. Shortly after these grew into project teams, a few more projects made it to phase two evaluations. Those were: a Centralized Training System, University Wide Utility Management, Centralized Contractual Services, and Maximizing Underutilized Resources and Expertise.

3. WHY THE NEED FOR CROWD SOURCING?

It became quickly apparent that though the team was generating many viable project ideas, that it would be impossible for a team of this size to reach its fullest potential without reaching out to the university community. With that said, the team embarked on looking at ways to capture the ideas of the entire university community. Ideas were brought up of using online forums, social

networking, email, and crowd sourcing to capture these ideas. Though all of these processes allow the team to capture ideas, it was apparent that to manage the multitude of ideas, an idea management system was needed.

3.1 Which solution was selected?

Initially the team put together an RFP committee and received proposals from three vendors. Through the RFP selection process, the team procured a system. In the initial RFP process, IdeaScale was a close second to company that was awarded the contract. This was based primarily on cost effectiveness. After issuing the award to the initial company, that company revealed many hidden costs that were not detailed in their initial RFP. As a result of this, the initial reward was revoked and the team put out a new RFP with stronger wording for what was to be delivered. Through this RFP process, IdeaScale was procured.

3.2 What does IdeaScale do?

IdeaScale is a full service idea management system. This allows the IMPACT team to reach out to the university community and enable community submissions and voting on ideas. By allowing the voting, it would quickly allow the team to put their finger on the pulse of what is most beneficial to the community. It also allows for campaigns to be created targeting specific types of ideas. While the IMPACT team will allow free flowing ideas to be generated, at times there may be a need to target certain groups, or certain ideas within the university community. Once the idea is submitted, the system enables the community to comment and vote on the idea. Once the team has evaluated an idea, it allows moderators to change the status of the idea to reflect if it has been moved into production, put on hold, or any other appropriate status change.

4. PILOT!

The IMPACT Team set up a custom install of the system for testing (Figure 3). Before rolling out a new system like this at VCU, a testing and pilot implementation has to take place. Team IMPACT opened up 200 spots for people to test the system. To entice participation, the team offered up the opportunity for testers to win an iPad Mini. To qualify, testers had to meet criteria which included actively participating in the system through idea generation, voting, and commenting. Those who actively participated were entered into a random drawing.

Within the first week of the test system being online, the community had over 50 ideas with many comments and votes. At the end of the test phase, a survey was sent out to the participants to evaluate the viability of having a system such as this on campus. The response was very positive with nearly all participants eager to see a system like this implemented. After the testing phase was complete, the team began preparation for full roll out. To phase this in and get buy in from other administrative areas, the initial campaigns for the system would be limited to ideas centered around Finance and Administration innovation. This began in April of 2013 and will continue for three months. Once that phase is complete, the campaigns will be expanded to include all areas of the VCU community.

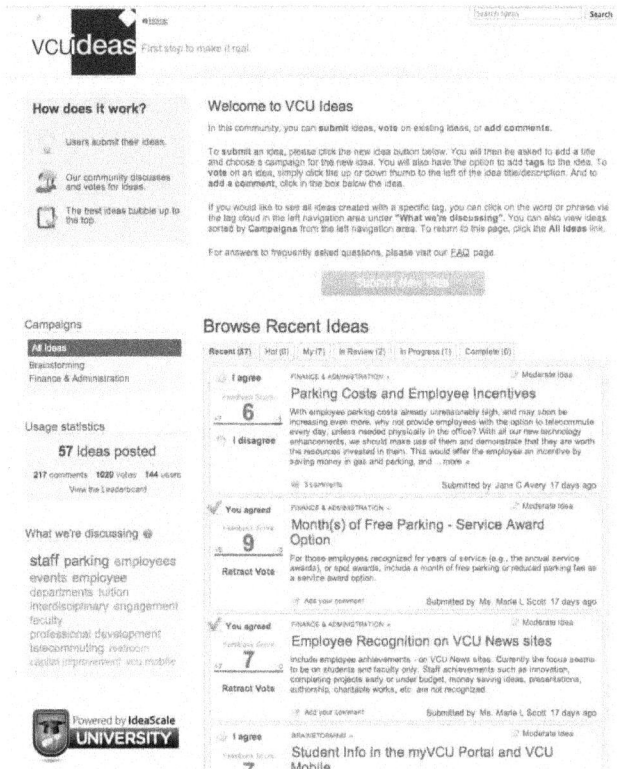

Figure 3 – VCU's IdeaScale Install

4.1 How does it work?

Simply put, users submit their ideas by clicking on a large button that says Submit New Idea. After that they are presented with a simple form popup asking for the Title, Description, Campaign, and Tags for the idea (Figure 4). By asking for their ideas in this manner, it makes for a very simple and pleasant user experience. The selection box for campaigns is useful when multiple campaigns are underway. Tags allow for ease of searching when looking for ideas which cross over to ideas already submitted.

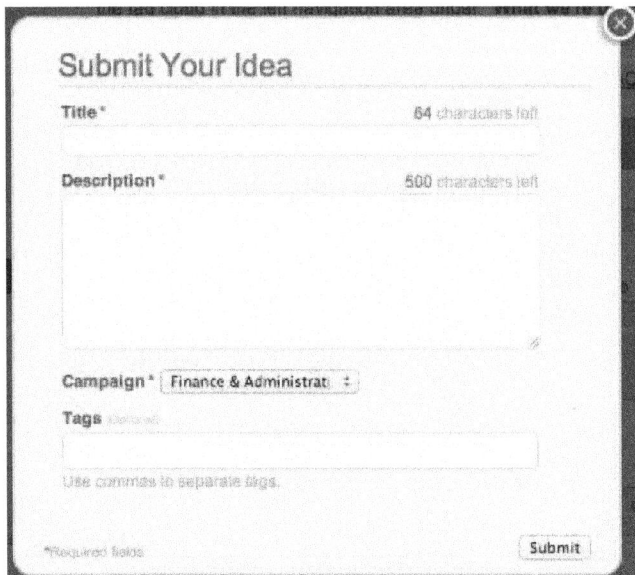

Figure 4– Submission screen

Once the user submits the idea, it goes into the database for others to view, vote up or down (Figure 5), or comment on (Figure 6).

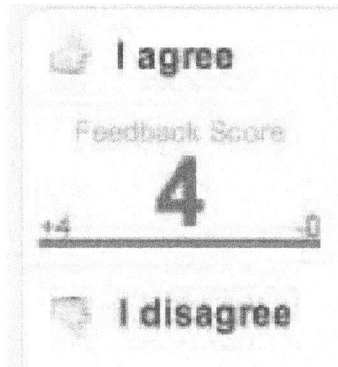

Figure 5 – Voting Options

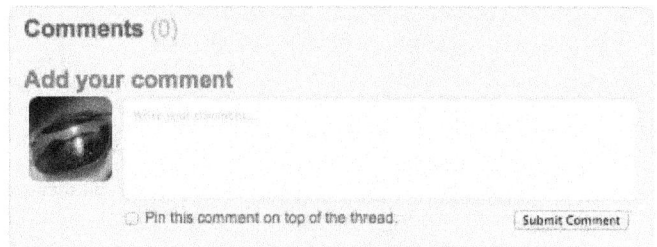

Figure 6 – Comment screen

As the community votes on items, a feedback score is calculated to give a quick view into how the community perceives the idea. There is also a dashboard view of where ideas are in the process.

End users have the ability to flag ideas to alert the moderators of potentially inflammatory or offensive topics.

4.2 Moderation

The IMPACT team has assigned three moderators for the initial roll out. The roles of the moderators are to insure that ideas submitted are on topic and well formed, to promote discussion of the the topics, and ultimately to move the ideas throughout the vetting process. Standard responses were created for the moderators to use to insure consistency in communication.

5. WHAT CHALLENGES EXIST IN ROLLING THIS OUT?

When designing the system, the IMPACT team spent many hours working out the process for how the information flows throughout the system (Figure 7

41

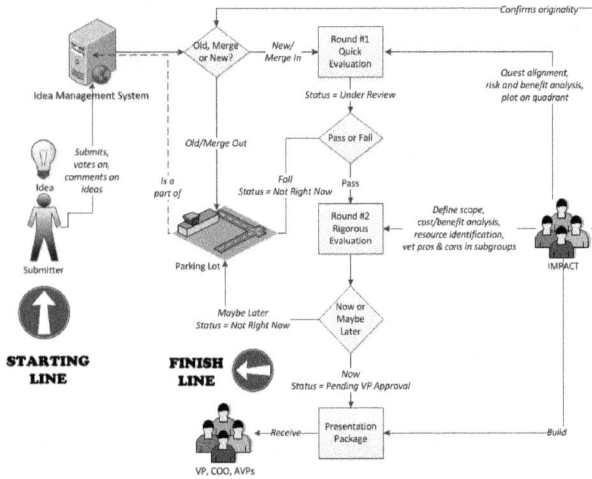

Figure 7 – Methodology Flow

Getting the flow down was the first challenge. Once this was established, a communications plan was needed. This involved how the team would communicate the existence of the system as well as how to market it. More importantly, guidelines for how to respond to ideas were needed. The team decided to let an idea sit in the system for ten days before the moderators began to move the idea through the process. This would allow ample time for the community to vote and comment on an idea. After that, it was determined that a 48-hour window would start for moderators to move the project to its next status. During this time if a project were to be moved to the next phase of development, a team would be created to begin phase two research into the idea. Projects would be deemed not viable at this point based on the vetting process defined above in section 2.1. Any project falling in the upper right quadrant of the project evaluation matrix would be designated as not viable. While the project is not viable at this point in time, the idea would be reevaluated at a later date to determine its viability. If the idea was off topic or not viable at this point, the topic would be closed and moved to the parking lot of ideas to revisit later. A note would be pinned to the top of the comments for each idea indicating the next phase for that topic.

6. THE FUTURE

Once the pilot phase of this project is complete. The IMPACT Team plans to roll this solution out to the entire university. Rolling out the solution to the university will come with a new set of challenges. First the IMPACT team will have to meet with various stakeholders to discuss communication and action plans for when ideas are processed through the system. Second, the team will have to evaluate how to best organize the system so the system will be intuitive for the end user to get their idea submitted to the proper content area. Finally, the team will have to properly scale the moderation duties of the system.

7. CONCLUSION

Virginia Commonwealth University hopes to bring about a university-wide sense of collaboration and input from faculty, staff and students from implementing this system. The university community will gain a sense of ownership over what happens at the university.

7. REFERENCE

[1] http://www.lockheedmartin.com/us/aeronautics/skunkworks.htm

Bring Your Own Computers Project in Kyushu University

Naomi Fujimura
Kyushu University
6-10-1, Hakozaki , Higashi-ku
Fukuoka Japan
+81 92 553 4434
fujimura.naomi.274@m.kyushu-u.ac.jp

ABSTRACT

At Kyushu University, we have been providing students with access to computers for education of information processing since 1979. The computers have varied from general purpose computer to personal computers (PCs). The number of PCs increased dramatically for about thirty years. The number of lectures with PCs has also been increasing rapidly for information literacy, CALL (Computer-Assisted Language Learning), and so on.

We have been always trying to arrange the PC rooms as many as possible to provide the good and comfortable ICT (Information and Communication Technology) environment for students. However, we never have the budget to equip enough PC rooms. On the other hand, the price of PCs has been going down over time. As a result, our students of 95% in first grade have their own PCs around when they enter the university.

In response to these changes, we have decided to abandon terminal rooms. We now expect all students to bring their own PCs and use them in their classes. After many meetings and committee discussions, we are going to start the new ICT environment for education in April 2013. It has taken almost two years to start up the Bring Your Own PCs (BYOPC) project.

Following were the important steps to begin the BYOPC project in Kyushu University:

-Gain agreement in the university
-How to decide the PC model, Windows or Mac, in each department
-Software (Windows, Office: EES contract with Microsoft)
-Anti-Virus software (Symantec Endpoint Protection)
-Wireless LAN (IEEE 802.11n, 80% covered of lecture rooms and so on)
-Firewall (P2P file exchange software)
-Seminar for all newcomers (Software installation, network configuration and so on)

We will report the detail and the result in the above points. It was a difficult and hard work. For example, I visited sixteen faculties and/or departments to explain the new policy and how to proceed on the project in order to get the cooperation and help. Ultimately, we had a great success on our project.

Categories and Subject Descriptors

K.3.m [**COMPUTERS AND EDUCATION**]: Miscellaneous – *Computer literacy*

General Terms

Management, Documentation, Economics, Experimentation, Human Factors

Keywords

BYOD, Education, Computer literacy, ICT environment, PC.

1. INTRODUCTION

Kyushu University is a large general national university in Japan [1]. It consists of five major campuses Hakozaki, Ito, Maidashi, Ohashi, and Tikushi in Fukuoka city. **Table 1** shows the current numbers of members in Kyushu University May 1st 2014. About 2,700 incoming students are expected to learn computer literacy. They have to use e-mail to communicate with teachers, receive important messages via the university portal site, see syllabi, register for lectures, and so on.

We have been arranging PC rooms for students to provide a good ICT (Information and Communication Technology) environment since 1979. However, lectures using PCs for not only computer literacy but also CALL (Computer-Assisted Language Learning) have been increasing for many years. Some challenging teachers expect that all students will use personal computers in their classes. It has been difficult for us to get sufficient money and to arrange enough PC rooms.

A part of small universities and colleges made their students provide their own personal computers. However, it is not easy for large universities to do so because of the number of students and the diversity of specialization. Nevertheless, the time came to challenge our policy from PC rooms prepared by the university to students bringing their own PCs

This is the report covering two years to establish the Bring Your Own PCs Project in Kyushu University. We negotiated several software contracts such as Microsoft Office and anti-virus soft-

Table 1 Current numbers of members

Status	The number of members	
Undergraduate Students	11,793	
Graduate students (MC)	3,894	
Graduate students (DC)	2,845	
Professional graduate school	393	
Subtotal of students		(18,925)
Teachers	2,099	
Administrative Staff	849	
Technical Staff	1,170	
Subtotal of staff		(4,118)
Total	23,043	

ware to decrease the cost for students. We also introduced the wireless LAN to connect student's PCs to the university LAN with IEEE 802.11n. Finally, we planned to practice the setup seminar for newcomers in early April 2013.

2. EDUCATIONAL ICT ENVIRONMENT

2.1 History

Kyushu University established the Educational Center for Information Processing in 1977. The center provided about one hundred TSS (Time Sharing System) terminals driven by the host computer in one room since 1978. It provided PCs for terminals in five PC rooms, and some open PC rooms in 1996.

We established the Information Infrastructure Initiative (III) to maintain the ICT environment for study, research, and school affair for all students and staff members in Kyushu University in 2007. The Educational Center for Information Processing was integrated into III finally. III consists of many support groups. The educational ICT environment support group is to manage and operate the educational ICT environment succeeding to the Educational Center for Information Processing.

We had been using the Windows base system, which consisted of 598 Windows PCs, printers, and servers before 2008. However, the number of PCs was not enough for 18,000 students at the time. We introduced a new system of 1,087 Macs (leased 966 and purchased 121) and servers without printers in March 2009 [2]. The reasons are as follows:

1) To provide students and teachers with the better educational ICT environment,

2) To increase the number of terminals for students and teachers

3) To decrease the undesirable cost for print service.

4) To make it possible for users to reset the login password by themselves for their convenience.

2.2 Problem

We tried to increase the number of PCs and PC rooms. However, the number of PCs was not enough to support the students and classes. The PC rooms for General Education are always occupied for lectures, and students cannot use PCs while they are free from lectures. About 400 PCs is absolutely insufficient for more than 5,000 students for General Education. We strongly wanted to increase the number of terminals as much as possible for General Education.

On the other hand, PC rooms of Center 4F and agricultural PC room in Hakozaki campus and Medical Center of Maidashi campus were not used enough. It was because the school and faculty of engineering moved from Hakozaki campus to Ito campus in 2005. In Maidashi campus, the number of PCs was not enough for lectures. We rearranged the PC room allocation to reflect the use that resulted in increased PCs for General Education and decreased PCs in the other locations.

Table 2 shows the previous and current status of PC rooms and the number of PCs in each room. It is very difficult for us to prepare PCs for students to enable them to learn at anytime, anywhere, and in their favorite pace.

3. CHANGE OF UNIVERSITY POLICY

3.1 The Decision in the University

I proposed the change of our policy as the "executive advisor to the president" to the "Management meeting" where the members are the president, board, vice president, and the executive adviser to the president. I advised that we should move away from providing the PC rooms with the university budget. I advised that it would be better for us to use our budget to improve the systems for all students and teachers.

Students can use their PCs for their learning and study at anywhere and anytime for their convenience under the new policy. I submitted the new policy to many committees in our university. Then it is accepted as the new policy of the university. However, it is not easy for the member of committees to inform the new policy to all staff members in their own faculty.

Table 2 Allocations of Terminal Rooms

Campus	Place	Current	Previous	Max User Pop
Hakozaki	Center 4F Lecture Room #1	0	77	1003
	Center 4F Open Terminal Room #1	0	20	
	Center 2F Lecture Room #2	77	75	
	Center 2F Open Terminal Room #2	25	16	
	Agricultural Terminal Room	0	26	758
	Economics Lecture Room	66	66	2280
	Central Library	*60*	*0*	
Maidashi	Medical Center Terminal Room	0	20	1242
	Medical Library	81	0	
Ito	West 4 Bld. 305	91	0	2804
	West 4 Bld. 306	*91*	*91*	
	General Education 1401	74	0	5360
	General Education 1402	*79*	*79*	
	General Education 1403	*68*	*68*	
	General Education 1501	*71*	*51*	
	General Education 1502	*61*	*71*	
	General Education 1601	79	79	
	General Education 1602	69	69	
Ohashi	Lecture Room #1	51	51	913
	Lecture Room #2	55	55	
	Lecture Room #3	14	14	
	Open Terminal Room	30	30	

Table 3 Schedule and Result of Explanation for All Division

No.	Faculty, School, Graduate school	Members	Number of Attendee (Documents prepared)	Schedule
1	Law	Over Associate Professor	52 (80)	Feb/8/(Wed) 15:00-15:20
2	Letters, Humanities	Over Lecturer	55 (65)	Feb/15/(Wed) 13:00-13:30
3	Economics	Over Lecturer	about 60 (75)	Feb/15/(Wed) 13:30-14:00
4	Education, Human-Environment Studies	Over Lecturer	about 50 (80)	Feb/15/(Wed) 15:00-15:30
5	Mathematics	Teachers selected by the Dean	9 (20)	Feb/20/(Mon) 10:00-11:10
6	Interdisciplinary Graduate School of Engineering Sciences	Over Lecturer or Associate Professor depending on the Faculty	about 70 (90)	Feb/20/(Mon) 16:30-17:00
7	Design	Teacher	about 50 (100)	Feb/2Feb/(Wed) 9:10-10:30
8	Dental Science	Professor	about 30 (35)	Feb/2Feb/(Wed) 14:00-14:30
9	Pharmaceutical Sciences	Teacher	about 20 (65)	Feb/2Mar/(Thu) 16:00-17:00
10	Sciences	Professor	about 15 (40)	Feb/29/(Wed) 10:30-12:20
11	Social and Cultural Studies	Over Lecturer	48 (75)	Mar/Feb/(Fri) 15:50-16:20
12	Health	Over Lecturer	about 30 (50)	Mar/7/(Wed) 9:00-9:30
13	Information Science and Electrical Engineering	Teacher, Technical staff members	56 (pdf)	Mar/14/(Wed) 10:00-10:20
14	Engineering	Professor	54 (pdf)	Mar/14/(Wed) 14:00-14:20
15	Agriculture, Bio resource and Bioenvironmental Sciences	Teacher, Technical staff members	about 20 (100)	Mar/2Mar/(Fri) 15:00-15:45
16	Medical Sciences	Professor	about 30 (80)	Mar/28/(Wed) 15:00-15:20

3.2 Explanation for all Faculty

To avoid any trouble, I went around the campuses to make staff members to know the new policy. **Table 3** shows the schedule, the number, and the kind of attendee. It took about two months. The total number of attendee is about 650, a fourth of teachers. It was so useful because many professors attended the meeting, and they understood the situation. The frequently asked questions and answers are as follows:

- Which kind of PCs is recommended, Windows or Mac OS X?

  It depends what you want to teach students. We wish you choose the best PC model for your educational purpose.

- How and what do III support students and us?

  III will support both Windows and Mac OS X.

- How do students and teachers connect to the network?

  III is going to introduce a new wireless LAN in classrooms as many as possible for education. That uses the protocol of IEEE 802.11n and has the high performance. We design the performance to realize the situation of about 300 students can see the video movies via the wireless LAN in a big classroom.

- How about the electric power?

  The recent PCs have a good battery to maintain the PC for more than 5 hours. It is enough for students to use it in a lecture for the beginning.

- What do you think of poor students who cannot but a PC?

  The price of PCs is now very cheap. I guess such a problem does not happen.

3.3 The PC model, Windows or Mac

I first planned to select one PC model as our "university PC model" just similar to other small universities and colleges. However, almost members of the related committee didn't agree with the one university PC model. Finally, I decided that the teachers of each faculty should decide the PC model, Windows or Mac OS X, in each department. It is difficult for all faculties, schools, and graduate schools to use one university PC model because, for example, the school of letter, engineering, and design must use the different purpose and specification for PCs. I recognized that each department should decide their own PC model after they consider their curriculum sufficiently after all.

It may be difficult for faculty members to decide the performance specification. We showed the recommended specification for PCs, whether it is Windows or Mac OS X as shown in **Table 4**

3.4 Long Range Schedule

The educational ICT environment support group of III provides the students with PC rooms of Mac as described. We have to plan the soft transition from the PC rooms prepared by the university to the student's own PCs. **Table 5** shows the long-range time schedule.

We introduced wireless LAN for education into a couple of rooms (1402 and 1403) first to confirm the performance. Then we introduce wireless LAN fully by the end of 2012 fiscal year.

Table 4 Recommended PC Specification

Item	Specification
OS	Mac OS X or Windows 8
CPU	1.6GHz Dual Core Intel Core i5
Memory	4GB
Solid State Disk	128GB(Mac) or 64GB(Windows)
USB	USB2.0x 2 or above
Voice	Headphone, Mic port
Screen Size	11.6 inch, 1366x768 pixel over
Network	802.11n
Battery	5 hours more
Weight	about 1.5Kg less
Size	17x300x192mm

Table 5 Long Range Schedule

Category		Campus	Room name	2011	2012	2013	2014	2015	2016	2017
Wireless LAN	Center BLD #1 1402, 1403 room			IEEE 802.11a/g /b 54Mbps	IEEE802.11n 300Mbps					
	Other terminal rooms			IEEE802.11a/g/b 54Mbps		IEEE802.11n 300Mbps				
Educational Information Environment	General Education	Ito Center Zone	1402, 1403	CALL (1st & 2nd grade) 150 Purchased PCs		Information Literacy (1st grade) BYOPCs	CALL (1st & 2nd grade) BYOPCs			
			1401, 1501, 502	CALL (1st & 2nd grade) 206 Leased PCs		CALL (1st & 2nd grade) Extended leased PCs	CALL (1st & 2nd grade) BYOPCs			
			1601, 1602	Information Literacy (1st & 2nd grade) 148 Leased PCs		CALL (1st & 2nd grade) Extended leased PCs	Information Literacy (1st grade) BYOPCs			
	Special course (3rd, 4th grade)	Ito West Zone	305, 306	Specialized lectures (3rd & 4th grade) Leased 500 PCs		Extended Leased 350 PCs (3rd & 4th grade)	Next Leased PCs			BYOPCs
		Hakozaki	Center terminal room, Open terminal rooms, Economic terminal room,							
		Maidashi	Medical library							
		Ohashi	Lecture room #1, #2, #3 Open terminal room : 30							
	Information Salon		Central library, Ito Library, Q-commons	Leased 232 PCs		Extended Leased 232 PCs	Next Leased PCs			Another next leased PCs

The room of 1402 and 1403 had 150 purchased PCs used for seven years. We abandoned them in the end of 2012 fiscal year. All lectures for computer literacy are expected to teach there in 2013 with students' own PCs. The lectures for CALL (Computer Assisted Language Leaning) are assigned to other PC rooms in 2013. The PC rooms for General Education disappear in 2014 by the update of leased computer systems supported by educational ICT support working group. Therefore, the lectures of computer literacy and CALL will be practiced with BYOPCs in 2014.

The PC rooms for special courses will disappear in 2017. It is because not all students have their own PCs before 2017. After 2017, some PCs are assigned to information salon, restaurant, and so on. We need more 4 years to complete our project finally.

4. ADVANCE PREPARATION
4.1 Software

We made the campus agreement (EES license) with Microsoft in 2007. In early period, we can install Office into the PCs purchased by the university budges only. However, we extended the contract to include the private PCs of students and staff members. As a result, students and staff members can install Office into their own PCs without any charge. Mac users can install Office for Mac, and also install Windows with Office for Windows in their Mac [3].

We made the contract to provide PCs with the anti-virus software of SEP (Symantec Endpoint Protection). First, we can install it into PCs purchased by the university budget only. We extended the contract to cover private PCs of students and staff members in 2011. Users can install SEP in their own PCs without any charge.

We provide all students with the latest Windows OS and Office in Windows PCs, and Office for Mac and Windows with Office in Mac without any extra charge in Kyushu University because we have the Campus Agreement contract (EES license) with Microsoft. We can also provide Symantec Endpoint Protection for private PCs of all students and staff members without any additional charge.

4.2 Network and Firewall

We planned to introduce wireless LAN of IEEE 802.11n in classrooms as many as possible. However, we could not introduce enough access points for educational wireless LAN for the first time. We have 427 classrooms in the university. The cover ratio of the first stage was about 60%. We did not have enough flexibility under the international bid because our university is a national university. We are forced to obey the strictest procedure to buy the products over 800K SDR.

We added more access points after the first introduction stage, and we are going to add access points in second and third stages this year. New wireless LAN of IEEE 802.11n started to work on April 1st 2013 successfully. It has the performance of 130Mbps when I measured before the public service in March 2013. Finally, the cover ratio becomes over 80% mainly in the classrooms.

III also introduced the firewall to cut the traffic for P2P file exchange. Many foreign students use it without any awareness that it is not permitted in Japan. Our university prohibits students to install such software even in their own PCs. However, it is safe for us to introduce a firewall to protect copyright, and to avoid the incidents and keep compliance against P2P file exchange software).

5. PC SEMINAR FOR ALL NEWCOMERS

5.1 Necessity

We planned seminars for all newcomers to install important software such as Office and Anti-virus software, set up network configuration, and so on. It must make lectures easier later. We heard that serious trouble occurred in some universities in the first several lectures because the PC environments are so various.

5.2 Announcement

First, we distributed the pamphlets that describe the necessity of PCs after the entering to our university in August 2012 open campus. We also display the same information in Web page in the university formal Web site.

The office of the student affairs sent the detailed information about the PC seminar for newcomers, such as schedule, room assignment, and what should be done to attend the PC seminar. After students finished their entrance procedure, they received the regard about PCs and power charge place.

Table 6 Checklist for Windows

Check	Item	Manual
1)	**Preparation for manuals**	
☐	Install Adobe Reader	Paper
2)	**Activation of Computer Account**	
☐	Connection to the Wireless LAN (activate)	PDF file in manual folder for Win in USB
☐	Complete of Computer Account Activation	
3)	**Installation of Software**	
☐	Check whether 32/64 bit of My PC___Bit	
☐	Connected to Wireless LAN (edunet)	
☐	Installation of Office 2013	
☐	Remove Office if exists. (If you want to use the Office software, you may skip this process.)	
☐	Completion of Authentication of Office 2013	PDF file in manual folder for Win in USB
☐	Installation of Java	
☐	Remove Anti-Virus Software if exists (If you want to use the original anti-virus software, you may skip this process.)	
☐	Installation of Symantec Endpoint Protection	
☐	Installation of Thunderbird	

5.3 Software and Documents in USB Memory

We experienced with the PC setup seminar in April 2012 to find the problem. According to the experience, we decided to adopt the write protect USB memory to provide necessary software and documents to students. If USB memory is writable, we are anxious for the possibility of computer virus. It took much time to check that USB memory is not affected by the computer virus.

USB memory contains both software and documents for Windows 8 and Mac OS X. We prepared 300 of USB memories for the seminar. It took several days to write the necessary information such as software, pdf files, and documents into USB memory.

5.4 Account

Students can use wireless LAN after they activate their account. The activation code is usually described on the student ID card. However, it was not available on time because the entrance ceremony was held on April 9th. The lecture started on April 11th. We had to finish the seminar before 9th April. We could get the information about the account activation on April 1st, and then we printed them for every student. We were anxious that students throw away the paper on which activation code is described. Someone can change the password if he/she gets the activation code. We arranged the application form that students must sign to declare they comply with the rule for computers and networks, and get it back.

5.5 Documents

We prepared documents for students. Students can find the document in the folders for Windows 8 and Mac OS X in USB memory. The total pages for both pages are so large, about 440 pages. We printed the document only necessary for the first work. The remaining documents are provided in a pdf format in the USB memory. Students are guided to copy them to their own PCs according to the type of PCs, Windows 8 or Mac OS X. It contains the documents that students are expected to work at their home because we cannot get enough time to complete the work. They are expected to install Visual Studio in Windows 8 and Xcode for Mac OS X later.

5.6 Checklist

Students set up their PCs according to the checklist as shown in **Table 6** for Windows 8 and **Table 7** for Mac OS X. They work each item in order described in checklist, and check it after they finish it. Users work the following one by one for windows 8.

1) First of all, the students install Adobe Reader because they need it to read pdf files.

2) They activate their account with the wireless LAN. We prepared the exclusive access point for that purpose.

3) They check whether their own PC is 32-bit or 64-bit machine.

4) They check the existence of Office, if so they remove it, and install Office 2013. If they want to use existing Office, they can skip it.

5) They install Java.

6) They install Symantec Endpoint Protection with Java if they want. If they want to use existing anti-virus software, they can skip this process.

7) They install Thunderbird, but do not go through the setup process at this time.

Table 7 Checklist for Mac OS X

Check	Item	Manual
1)	**Preparation for Manual**	
☐	Connection to the Wireless LAN (activate)	PDF file in manual folder for Mac in USB
☐	Complete of Computer Account Activation	
2)	**Installation of Software**	
☐	Installation of Office 2011 for Mac	PDF file in manual folder for Mac in USB
☐	Connected to Wireless LAN (edunet)	
☐	Installation of Mac に Symantec Endpoint Protection	
☐	Installation of Thunderbird ※You may install it in Windows	
3)	**Installation of Windows 8**	
☐	Installation of Windows 8	Paper
☐	Installation of Windows Support in Windows8	
☐	Install Adobe Reader	
4)	**Installation of Software in Windows 8**	
☐	Connected to Wireless LAN (edunet)	PDF file in manual folder for Windows in USB
☐	Installation of Office 2013	
☐	Completion of Authentication of Office 2013	
☐	Installation of Java	
☐	Installation of Symantec Endpoint Protection	
☐	Installation of Thunderbird ※You may install it in Windows	

For Mac users, they work their installation according to the checklist as shown in **Table 7**.

5.7 Staff Arrangement

The seminar consists of four regular days and one backup day. Three sessions are scheduled in one seminar room in a day. More than twenty staff members of III attended the PC seminar as the instructors. The twenty-one students worked as TA (Teaching Assistants) in the seminar. They are almost the students of graduate school in Ito campus. One team consists of two staff members and three TA for one classroom. One classroom contains about 40 to 50 newcomers. I think the number and combination of staff members and TA was suitable this time.

5.8 Attendee and Problems

We planned the PC seminar for newcomers on April 2nd, 3rd, 4th, 5th for regular schedule, and April 8th for backup for students who cannot attend the regular seminar. However, some students could not attend the regular and backup days. We added one extra seminar day for them on April 11th.

Table 8 shows the final status of attendance. About thirty students did not attend the seminar finally. Almost 99% of newcomers attended the seminar in total. The students, who did not attend to the seminar, belong in the school of engineering.

The ratio between Windows and Mac OS is 87:13 in total. Some department specified the Mac for their education, some specified Windows, but many departments did not specify the kind of PCs.

In such case, most students bought Windows, and very few students bought Mac. However, about a half of class bought Windows and another half bought Mac in a department of school of Design. We guess it may not be easy to teach them with such various PCs. The staff members of faculty should specify the kind of PCs corresponding to their educational policy.

Table 8 Final Status of 2013 PC setup seminar（April 2-5, 8,11）

2013/4/15 18:00

School		Total number of students	Attendance	Absence	Ratio	Win	Mac	Ratio of Win	Ratio of Mac
Letter		165	162	3	98%	153	9	94%	6%
Education		53	53	0	100%	46	7	87%	13%
Law		202	198	4	98%	188	10	95%	5%
Economics		250	249	1	100%	229	20	92%	8%
Science	(Win)	236	234	2	99%	212	22	91%	9%
	(Mac)	53	53	0	100%	2	51	4%	96%
Medicine		270	266	4	99%	234	32	88%	12%
Dentistry		54	52	2	96%	46	6	88%	12%
Pharmaceutical		82	82	0	100%	75	7	91%	9%
Engineering		852	837	12	98%	780	57	93%	7%
Design	(Win)	38	38	0	100%	35	3	92%	8%
	(Win or Mac)	91	90	1	99%	70	20	78%	22%
	(Mac)	82	82	0	100%	1	81	1%	99%
Agriculture		234	230	4	98%	211	19	92%	8%
21 Century Program		25	25	0	100%	18	7	72%	28%
Total		2687	2654	33	99%	2303	351	87%	13%

6. IMPROVEMENT AND FUTURE VISION

It took some time to login university PCs before because all students try to login at the same time. They do not need to login university PCs differently from the former ICT environment now.

Students can use only 100MB for their disk space in the former educational ICT environment. However, they can now store files as much as possible in their own PCs. They have more than 50GB disk space in their PCs. The access time is much less than hard disk because almost PCs have the SSD (Solid State Disk) as specified to recommended PCs. Teacher and students get the good computer performance during lectures.

Figure 1 Snap shot of PC rooms

At the beginning of my class, many students want to use their own PCs even if there are many university PCs as shown in **Figure** 1. It is the proof of success of our BYOPCs project.

7. CONCLUSION

We decided to change the policy for educational ICT environment from PC rooms to Bring Your Own PCs. It was not easy to get the agreement in the university. It also took much time to prepare procedure and documents for the PC setup seminar. However, it is now possible for students and teachers to use PCs at anytime, anywhere, and in their pace to learn online educational materials. Innovational Center for Educational Resource is going to provide on-line educational materials. Teachers can now use a Web learning system in every classroom. This is the beginning of revolution in educational ICT environment in Kyushu University.

8. ACKNOWLEDGMENTS

My thanks to all staff members of BYOPCs Project Task Force, Information Infrastructure Initiative, all persons related to this projects in our university, and especially newcomers who enjoyed the PC in classrooms.

9. REFERENCES

[1] Kyushu University: http://www.kyushu-u.ac.jp/english/

[2] Naomi Fujimura, Hotoshi Inoue, and Satoshi Hashikura : Experience with the Educational ICT Environment in Kyushu University, Proc. of SIGUCCS 2009 (Technical Session), pp.167-171, Oct. 2009.

[3] Naomi Fujimura, Itsuo Omagari, Masatsugu Ueda, and Keiichi Irie : Experience with Software Blanket Contract in Kyushu University, Proc. of SIGUCCS 2008 (Poster Session), pp.307-310, Oct. 2008.

Migrating from Novell to Active Directory

Jody Gardei
Ferris State University
420 Oak Street, PRK 121
Big Rapids, MI 49307
(231) 591-3025
gardeij@ferris.edu

Ashley Barrigar
Ferris State University
420 Oak Street, PRK 121
Big Rapids, MI 49307
(231) 591-4781
barriga@ferris.edu

Scott Claerhout
Ferris State University
1010 Campus Drive, FLT 412C
Big Rapids, MI 49307
(231) 591-2404
claerhos@ferris.edu

ABSTRACT

Ferris State University recognizes the importance of secure network file sharing resources to the internetworking of a university, as well as the need to reduce the number of accounts and passwords for end users to remember. Because of this and the need to reduce ongoing costs a decision was made in Fall 2010 to move from Novell to Active Directory for directory services and secure network file storage management.

Categories and Subject Descriptors

K.6.1 [**Management of Computing and Information Systems**]: Project and People Management – *staffing, strategic information systems planning, systems analysis and design, systems development, training.*

General Terms

Management, Documentation, Performance, Design, Reliability, Experimentation, Security, Human Factors, Standardization, Verification.

Keywords

Active Directory, Novell, directory, forest, structure, project planning, communications.

1. INTRODUCTION

Information technology (IT) departments at universities need to be aware of the growing costs and the growing number of services they offer to the university community. When services are duplicated, IT management and university leadership need to decide if there is value in combining services to a single platform in order to reduce costs and stay within budget. Once this decision is made, proper planning and communication is key to the success of any major change in IT services.

Ferris State University prepares students for successful careers, responsible citizenship, and lifelong learning. Through its many partnerships and its career-oriented, broad-based education, Ferris serves our rapidly changing global economy and society. Ferris is located in Big Rapids, Michigan. Annual student enrollment is about 14,500 and has a rapidly growing international student

SIGUCCS'13, November 3–8, 2013, Chicago, Illinois, USA.
Copyright © 2013 ACM 978-1-4503-2318-5/13/11...$15.00.
http://dx.doi.org/10.1145/2504776.2504792

population. Ferris employs over 2,000 people, over 46 percent are faculty [1].

Information technology services at Ferris State University are part of the Administration and Finance division. Technology resources are centrally managed by the Information Technology Services (ITS) Department. End users contact the Technology Assistance Center (TAC) for all their technology needs. The TAC service desk is staffed by one coordinator, five full time staff members, and many student employees. TAC service desk staff are trained to assist customers over the phone or by using remote assistance tools. TAC service desk staff elevate issues and requests they are not able to resolve on first contact to the other departments within ITS.

2. DEFINING THE SCOPE

The ability to successfully complete any project requires proper planning. The scope of the project must be well defined before beginning the planning phase. Migrating from Novell to Active Directory has many implications that may or may not be addressed in the scope of the project. It is important to know what will be affected by the change and if the scope of the project will address those items or if they will be dealt with later. Key IT staff made a list of the affected services and then formed sub-committees to further define the impact the migration would have on each service. Setting due dates and documentation expectations were important to the timely completion of these tasks.

During this time, IT management realized the importance of forming a steering committee and migration team. The Active Directory Steering Committee's role was to finalize the scope of the project and give direction to the migration team. Members of the steering committee included the Chief Technology Officer (CTO), the Director of Enterprise and Application Services (EAS), the Director of the TAC, the Director of Telecommunications and Student Technology Services (TTS/STS), the IT Service Manager, and the IT Project Manager. The Active Directory (AD) Migration Team was responsible for the implementation of the project plan to the entire campus community. Members of the migration team included area coordinators from server support, applications support, desktop support, and student support. This team soon realized they needed assistance with communicating these changes to the entire campus and training IT staff affected by the changes happening during the migration. An Active Directory Communications team was formed to address these needs. Members of this team included the IT Service Manager, IT trainers, and STS staff.

Table 2. Migration Teams

Steering Committee	AD Migration Team	Communications Team
CTO	Applications	IT Service Manager
EAS Director	Server	IT Trainers
TAC Director	Desktop	STS Staff
TTS/STS Director	Student	
IT Project Manager		
IT Service Manager		

3. PLANNING PHASE

Once the scope of the project was defined by the steering committee, the migration team began to plan for each of the items identified in the scope. Ferris State University's IT department's scope included: user migration, workstation migration, network file storage space for individual users and shared network file storage space for departments, printer management and distribution, primary accounts for users, implementation of a new web-based password assistance tool, and account provisioning.

3.1 Funding

Funding for the migration was granted through a three year IT plan approved by the Vice President of Administration and Finance. The migration project leader worked closely with the CTO throughout the project to secure funds for each part of the migration.

3.2 Project Management

The team utilized Innotas, a cloud-based project management software, to plan the timeline for each of the items [3]. Using project management software allowed the migration team to make changes to the timeline and see how these changes affected the completion date of the project. It also allowed IT staff to keep track of the amount of time they contributed to the project. The steering committee dictated the migration timeline to assist the migration team with their planning. In early 2013 the steering committee decided to speed up the migration and set a completion date of August 2013 for all employees of the university. There

were many projects on the horizon that would be easier to implement once the migration was complete.

3.3 Infrastructure Design

The first item to consider during the planning phase was the actual infrastructure of the new Active Directory services. During the planning phase the migration team decided it was necessary to upgrade the server environment and redesign the forest. Two forests were created, one for employees and one for students. The number of users in a forest also affects the licensing of certain applications. By creating two forests with a domain in each, they were able to reduce the cost of the Active Directory implementation and create a more secure environment.

Later on they would discover creating two Forests did impact the use of our password management tool whereas users would need to enter their domain along with their user ID when setting up challenge questions or using the online password assistance tool.

3.4 Migration Tools

Another key planning item to consider was the process for migrating university owned computers from Novell to Active Directory. At the beginning of the planning phase the majority of computers on campus were on Windows XP. IT staff wanted to avoid migrating computers one-by-one. The consultant hired to help set up the Active Directory structure recommended a tool called Quest to automate the workstation migrations on campus [4]. By the time the workstation migration started for the majority of our customers in spring 2013, the migration team realized the selection of the tool may have been in haste. By this time, the majority of end users had been upgraded to Window 7 either through attrition or computer replacement. Windows 7 required a separate tool, ForensiT, to automate the migration [2]. Both the Quest and ForensiT tool were used until the steering committee escalated the time table for the project. A decision was made to abandon the Quest tool and focus on using ForensiT with both Windows XP and Windows 7.

The switch to using ForensiT only to migrate workstations significantly reduced the amount of preparation within each department. When both tools were being used it was necessary to identify which operating system was on each workstation so the appropriate tool could be used to automate the migration. Time was also being spent making sure certain things were in place in

Figure 1: Active Directory structure

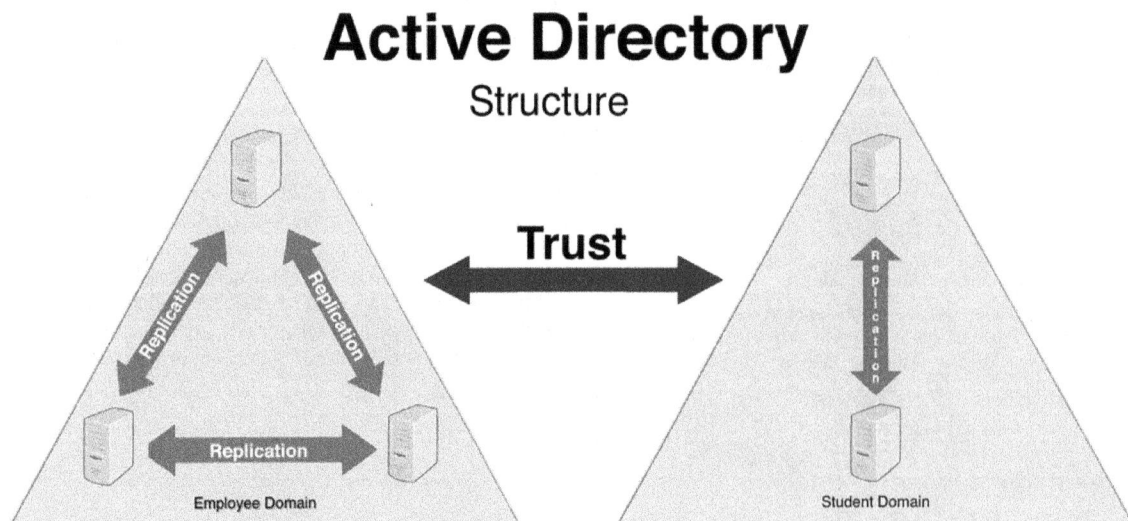

Active Directory
Structure

Trust

Replication
Replication
Replication

Employee Domain

Replication

Student Domain

order for the use of the Quest tool to be successful: Shut off simple file sharing, install client side extensions for Windows XP, set the administrator account password to a universal password, and enable the guest login account. The ForensiT tool only required a universal password on the local administrator's account

running the ForensiT tool and remove the Novell client from the computer. If the computer was not in the Domain, the ForensiT tool would compare the Novell user name used to log in to the computer with the Windows user name and query Active Directory for the same user name. If all three user names matched, the computer was added to the Domain and the Novell client was removed.

User accounts in Active Directory were manually created at the beginning of the project. Half way through the project account provisioning was enabled to automate the process. The product used was Forefront Identity Manager (FIM). FIM is able to take information provided from the Banner database and automate the creation of Active Directory accounts.

Switching to the use of one tool for workstation migrations made the job of the communications team much easier because the processes had been significantly different for each of the tools.

The ForensiT tool had a log file that was centrally monitored by the migration team. The log file reported the successful and unsuccessful workstation migrations. This notified the migration team of any failed workstation migrations not reported by the end user. The TAC service desk was responsible for adding a ticket to our work order system and assigning it to the desktop support team. The desktop support team was responsible for manually migrating workstations where the ForensiT tool would not work.

4. TESTING PHASE
A key component to ensuring IT had a working plan in place was the testing phase. The first department to migrate was the entire IT department. This helped to define the workflow that would be used in subsequent departmental migrations.

4.1 Data Gathering
The Quest and ForensiT tools for workstation migration to Active Directory were tested prior to the migration of the IT department. During the testing phase, IT staff were asked to call the TAC service desk, to report issues. The TAC used a specific classification for these tickets to make it easier to pull reports. This centralization of work order documentation provided the migration team and communication team with valuable information to assist with fine tuning the migration plan for future department migrations.

4.2 Data Review
Once the migration for the IT department was complete, the migration team reviewed the work order report and their own findings and used these to fine-tune the process. The communications team modified their customer communications to ensure they were in non-technical terms and answered any questions IT staff had during the migration.

4.3 Additional Testing
A department outside of IT was asked to participate in the testing phase and provide feedback. The migration team chose a department that had a close relationship with IT and would provide constructive feedback on their experience during the entire migration cycle from planning for the shared drive move to

and a local profile account that matched the Novell and Active Directory account of the user.

The ForensiT tool was wrapped in a conditional Visual Basic script. The script looked to see if the computer was in the domain or not. If it was already in the domain, the script would skip

the workstation migration. A follow up meeting was held with several people in their department that represented different points of view. Their feedback again helped the project teams improve their processes and communications.

5. DOCUMENTATION, COMMUNICATION, AND TRAINING
The migration from Novell to Active Directory affects the entire university; hence the need for accurate documentation, communication with the appropriate entities, and proper training options to ensure the success of the overall project.

5.1 Team Email and Calendar
The migration team set up an email and calendaring account for use by the Active Directory team chairs. All communications and meetings were initiated through this account. This allowed multiple people to have access to project related emails and to schedule meetings .

5.2 Communications Team
The Active Directory Communications Team was primarily responsible for the documentation, communication, and training for the project. Their responsibilities included developing email communications to send out at strategic times to each department and its employees during the migration of users and workstations, creating documentation for IT staff about the migration process to use as job aids and training documents, creating and maintaining a web presence for the project for IT staff, students, and employees of the university, and working closely with the AD Migration Team during the migration to ensure seamless communication and implementation of services.

The communications team worked closely with the migration team to obtain information about the migration schedule and individuals being migrated at each step of the project. The Active Directory Migration Team chairperson attended all scheduled meetings held by the communications team to pass on new information and answer questions.

At the beginning of the project, the schedule for migrating workstations and users was not set in stone, so a shared drive space was created to share working documents and host the most up to date migration schedule. The communications team relied heavily on this shared drive space to know whom they needed to communicate with and at what time. It wasn't until due dates were set that the Innotas project management software was used consistently.

5.3 End User Communications
When a department was targeting for migration, the migration team would solicit the names of two people who could work directly with the team to work on the plan. These people ideally had knowledge of how the department functions and could help design a directory structure. Each department designed their own directory structure based on guidelines provided to them on how rights are granted and how rights function in Active Directory.

Once the department's directory structure was in place, the migration team notified the communications team. Two business days prior to a departments scheduled migration, the communication team would send out an email notifying each individual affected of the date of the migration, an explanation of what to expect, and a link to find out more at the project web site. Each individual was also sent an email with his or her initial password.

After the user and workstation migration was complete, the migration team notified the communication team to send out the follow up email to the group currently being migrated. The follow up email contained information about the new drive mappings, how to change their Active Directory password, an increase in the availability of personal network drive space, and how to access their network files from the new web portal, Web Storage.

One day after the follow up email was sent, another email was sent with specific details on how to set their challenge questions and use the password assistance web site. We found this to be more effective than sending it the same day as the follow up email.

5.4 IT Staff Communication and Training
Training of service desk and desktop support staff was key to ensuring customer satisfaction. The service desk was included in all communications sent out to customers. Eventually all desktop support staff were included so everyone was aware of the status of the project. This also allowed desktop support staff to be present in the customer area on the day of the migration to assist with any issues that may arise. Staff were trained on how to manually migrate a workstation in the event of a failure.

Several training sessions were put together to address the training needs of service desk and desktop support staff before the migration began. The first session focused on the design of the Active Directory forest implemented at the university and the benefits of migrating away from Novell to Active Directory. The second session focused on user profiles and the tools available to assist in the administration of accounts.

FerrisConnect, Ferris' BlackBoard Learn system, was utilized for the permanent home of all the IT training materials related to this project. A channel was also created within the university portal, MyFSU, listing updates and quick links to information about the Active Directory project.

5.5 End User Benefits
The communications team felt it was important to stress the benefits everyone would experience once the migration was complete. For our university this meant quadrupled personal network drive space, streamlined password assistance, a more advanced web file access tool, and less complicated workstation login.

Network printers are now being distributed to end users through their Active Directory connection. End users were notified of this change and provided information on how to delete network printers not being delivered by Active Directory group policies. A printer-naming scheme relevant to the location, department, make, and model of the printer was also implemented. This new naming scheme provides the TAC with the exact location of the printer when end users call in with issues. Users can now go to any workstation, log in with their Active Directory credentials, and print to any network printer assigned to them because they are tied to their Active Directory account. Network printers no longer need to be manually installed, saving time during computer replacements.

The implementation of a new password assistance tool required extra communication to ensure end users set up their challenge questions so they are able to use the tool. The service desk was made aware of this need and they made it a part of their process to assist customers with filling out this information and using the tool for the first time whenever someone calls in for password assistance.

6. IMPLEMENTATION
The implementation phase of a project this big had enormous implications throughout the campus. Many questions were answered during the planning and testing phases.

6.1 Scheduling
We found breaking down the actual migration of users and workstations into manageable pieces worked well. We started with non-academic areas first, working one department at a time, to ensure our processes were well defined and communications tweaked to ensure a smooth transition. Being on-site during the set date of each departmental migration was also reassuring to our customers and helped to address issues before they became a public relations issue.

Initially, the data was migrated to a separate Novell server and reviewed by the department one week prior to the user and workstation migration. A new Novell server was set up at the beginning of the migration project for the move of the files to the new, department approved directory structure. End users would still log in to Novell, but the shared network drive space resembled the new directory structure. This step was necessary because the Quest tool could only migrate whole volumes. Our existing directory structure on Novell housed files from several different departments on one volume. Files from the department being migrated had to be moved to their own volume before the Quest tool could be used to migrate the files to Active Directory.

The second week of the user and workstation migration involved moving the data to the Active Directory servers, migrating individual workstations by removing the Novell client and inserting the computer into the domain, copying the user profile from the local profile to the Active Directory profile on the computer, providing end users with their login ID and password, and delivering departmental network printers.

As IT staff became more comfortable with the process and the decision was made to only use the ForensiT tool, the migration team was able to cut the time to migrate a department in half by combining the data migration with the workstation and user migration.

In February 2013, a new process was implemented. End user access to their Novell network drive space was removed at 5:00 pm on Friday evening. Data was then backed up. At 7:00 am the following Monday morning, the data was moved to the Active Directory servers through a redirected restore of the data from the back up. The workstation migration started on Monday morning when end users logged in to Novell. A login script entry was used to run the ForensiT migration tool. The entire process would take about 10 minutes to run. Then, the end user was prompted to reboot their computer and log in to Active Directory.

6.2 Student Employees
Manual migrations were used for student employee workstations because the ForensiT tool is not able to copy the local user profile

to multiple Windows workstation profiles. This allowed them to be imported into the appropriate domain and set up to share files between the many student employees that may be using the computer throughout the day. In the past, one neutral login account may have been set up on the student computer, but after the migration students logged in with their own Active Directory credentials.

6.3 Challenges

Communication is key to the successful completion of any big project. A project of this magnitude required regular updates to many different stakeholders. It was helpful to have weekly meetings set up to discuss the project and impromptu discussions to attend to issues before they could become huge problems. ITS staff had to rely on others to ensure the project didn't stop during vacations and sick days. It was a group effort to make sure the tight timeline was met.

The biggest challenge we experienced was getting end users to read the email communications being sent to them explaining the migration process. Most did not take the time to read the entire email before the migration. It was important for the department representatives working with the migration team to communicate with their staff before, during, and after the migration of their data, users, and workstations to Active Directory. We found it was very helpful to have desktop support technicians in the area the morning the migration began to answer questions and assist with any issues. The communications team also began sending out the two follow up emails on separate days. This in addition to working with the department representatives helped get end users to set up their challenge questions for the new password assistance tool. The TAC service desk was also prepared to assist callers with setting up their challenge questions when they called in for password assistance.

7. REFERENCES

[1] Ferris Fact Book 2011-2012. Retrieved electronically on May 27, 2013.
http://www.ferris.edu/HTMLS/Admision/testing/factbook/FactBook11-12.pdf

[2] ForensiT website. Retrieved electronically on June 26, 2013.
http://www.forensit.com/

[3] Innotas website. Retrieved electronically on June 26, 2013.
http://www.innotas.com/

[4] Quest website. Retrieved electronically on June 26, 2013.
http://www.quest.com/migration-manager-for-active-directory/

The Dirty Hungarian Phrasebook of Tech Support

Christopher H. King
NC State University
Box 7109 – NCSU
Raleigh, NC 27695-7109
(919) 515-5431

chking@ncsu.edu

ABSTRACT
In tech support, the customer is rarely right. Customers have a tendency to approach problem resolution by coming to their support staff with a solution rather than just discussing the visible issues and letting the professionals do the rest. Customers don't necessarily know what they need, but they can be extremely vocal about what they don't know, and it is up to the support staff member to hear one thing and understand what it means down the line. In the 2012 SIGUCCS closing keynote, Brian Janz likened this to a patient demanding a type of surgery before the doctor has even heard the symptoms. This paper and presentation will discuss the dying art of translation and discuss methods for communication, rapport, and technical association that will empower front-line staff to hear what customers are saying and translate it into useful information for problem resolution.

Categories and Subject Descriptors
H.5.2 [**User Interfaces**]: Style guides, Theory and methods, Training, help and documentation

General Terms
Design, Documentation, Human Factors, Standardization.

Keywords
Communication, Written Communication, Training, Technical Support, Incident Management, Problem Management, End-User Support

1. INTRODUCTION
In 1970, an episode of "Monty Python's Flying Circus" featured a sketch called "The Dirty Hungarian Phrasebook."[1] In it, two men attempt to communicate through the intermediary of a poorly written phrasebook, to predictably hilarious results. Unfortunately for tech support specialists, situations like that between the tobacconist and his foreign customer are all too common. Technology consumers leaf through their phrasebook of experiences and terms and try to piece together their issues, concerns and wants. The result is often incomplete, wrong or misleading. For the support professional, the next step is to try and sift through the hovercrafts full of eels and ascertain the

symptoms, possible causes and eventual solutions. At the same time, care must be taken not to offend or demean the customer through action or lack thereof.

2. KNOW THYSELF
In the sketch, the first step that the shopkeeper takes to ascertain what his customer really wants is to suggest products that he actually provides. The same applies to technology support, and in order to do that, the support staff needs to know about the products that they offer and support.

2.1 Make sure that your support staff has clear ideas about what they are supporting
Depending on their size, an organization or company can have dozens or hundreds of different services and products to offer in thousands of combinations. Add to that varying levels of support for each product based on a service-level agreement or other limiting factors and it is easy to get confused, especially as the initial voice in a support call. It is crucial that everyone in an organization know what it is that they are charged with supporting. In some cases, this is a particular product or application, and in others it is a wide range of desktops, environments, and hardware configurations. In both cases, and all of those in-between, having well-trained staff with access to the proper documentation and service levels able to identify service needs is the key to supporting those individuals looking for those services. With the tobacconist in the sketch, he knew that the customer needed matches from his actions, despite what words he was actually using. Likewise, a customer may only mention the need for offsite access to resources, which should lead the support staff to make reference to web-based tools, VPN facilities, or whatever other services are available. On the flip side, staff should not (in this example) suggest services that are NOT supported or available, like a hosted alternative or remotely accessing an internal machine.

2.2 Know the technology surrounding what you support
While support staff members may know each offering intimately, sometimes that is not enough. The customer involved may not know the product, but instead how they get to it or what it does for them apart from its usual function. For example, a customer with issues accessing a financials portal may reference the leave system, only knowing what's unavailable rather than the process they usually breeze through to get there. A good support structure understands the technology surrounding and connected to each

product, so as to better ascertain issues using only tangentially relevant keywords or references.

2.3   Service Catalogs are not just about order forms

A common tool for organizations to use is the Service Catalog. At its core, a service catalog is just a menu -- a list of offerings and descriptions of their uses, requirements, and (in some cases) costs. While this comes in handy in directing customers to what they want, it is also useful to the support staff member who may not know which version of AutoCAD is installed in a particular environment, or whether the organization supports OS X versions of Chrome. Many service catalogs began as reference materials for internal use, and although they can stay in that format, the idea of the service catalog can be expanded to extreme lengths, and there are many products out there that can link service catalogs to call tracking, change management and other ITSM solutions.

3. KNOW YOUR CUSTOMERS

With a firm grasp of the hardware and software in play, as well as the technology and policies surrounding them, the next hurdle is the wetware – the customers themselves. Customers are a very diverse lot, and come from many different backgrounds, cultures, and environments, even within the same organization. One thing that they have in common with the support professional is the technology in question, and it is important that common ground is found when discussing terminology, use cases and general descriptive terms.

3.1 When an elevator is a lift

As strange as it sounds, sometimes it is inconvenient to share a language. When another person uses similar words and grammatical structure, the mind make the next leap and assumes that those words mean what they have always meant to the listener. This can be bad, as languages have spread and mutated throughout their existence, and dialects form their own sublanguages that can cause confusing situations. Sometimes this is due to a thick accent confusing words – a friend once asked for a book on Anastasia, and was sent to the medical section on anesthesia. Other times, it's regional – ask folks from Texas and North Carolina to define "barbeque", and different answers will emerge[1]. At colleges and universities, this can go either way. A culture will develop on campus that lends itself to common words and phrases, but that culture is constantly being invaded by new students and employees who bring their own nuances to the environment. It is important that support staff members understand this and act accordingly by asking for clarification and repeating thoughts back in a different way to see if the same response is given.

3.2 One of these departments is not like the other

Colleges and universities often have dozens of departments spread out across buildings, campuses, and budgetary reporting. The needs of a vet school are similar to that of the humanities college, but in other ways they are vastly different. By the same token, the same technologies may be more prevalent or important in one area versus another area, and different technologies may be used to the same result. Knowing the frequency and importance of certain technologies based on who is using them is key to getting a support concern dealt with, as time can be saved by knowing that phone service to the dining hall is not as mission-critical as it is to campus police.

3.3 You say "S: drive", I say "Tomato"

Computing systems have common terms for things like shared resources, local drives, and network connectivity. Just as before, the same resource may be used in different ways on different parts of campus, and support staff members should be aware of the differences. While one department may use their X: drive for temporary storage, another may use it for backups. It may be that some departments use wireless networking as a convenience while others in older buildings have no other methods of connectivity. Technological terms can be a language unto themselves, and each department can have its own dialect – it's important that everyone involved is saying the same thing.

3.4 IdM to the rescue! Maybe!

Depending on the campus, there may be an internal Identity Management (IdM) system in place, telling administrators who works where and with whom in what capacity. These sorts of systems can be used by technology support folks to do all sorts of amazing things. Imagine a system where a staff member is not only linked to their supervisor and leave count, but also their service-level agreements, hardware environments and shared space allocations. When that person changes positions, or leaves the organization, the system would make it easier to reprovision or deprovision (or even automatically do these things). Even simpler than that, if support staff members could access IdM views of each person, a lot of the troubleshooting involved would be confirmation that the data in the system was up to date. That is where the "maybe" comes in – IdM, like every other database ever, is only as good as the data that it contains. An unreliable IdM is worse than none at all, so if this solution is available, then everyone involved should work hard to ensure that the data is clean, reliable, and current.

4. KNOW THE DIALOGUE

Having a common language and set of experiences between them allows the support staff member and the customer to actually converse about the problem at hand. There are still impediments to success even now, but not insurmountable ones.

---

[1] Even within North Carolina, a battle rages between Lexington style (tomato-based pork) and Eastern style (vinegar-based pork), while both join forces against the mustard-based recipes of South Carolina.

4.2 Ask the right questions (aka "it's bright green now!")

Basic troubleshooting is a very underappreciated set of skills. A customer may know what's wrong from the standpoint of lost or unavailable functionality, but that is far from describing proper symptoms that matter to the support staff member. It is important that staff members have a core set of troubleshooting questions to ask each customer, and it is just as important to be able to expand upon those answers by asking more detailed ones based on the information given. Those questions must be simple, clear and concise, while still leaving room for the customer to give good answers.

Be careful that you ask the right questions, however, because the answers that you get may not be the ones you were looking for. An old NC State University story relates how a customer called to complain that her modem connection was unresponsive. (Yes, very old.) Several minutes of questions showed that not only was that window locked up, but it sounded like the machine itself was not even powered on. The support staff member asked the customer what should have been a straightforward question: "What is the color of the light on the front of your computer?" "Green," the customer responded, indicating to the support staff member that the computer was on. A few minutes later, while checking cabling in the back of the computer, the support staff member heard the telltale "bong!" of an old-style Macintosh starting up. The conversation that followed explains it all:

Support Staff Member: What was that?

Customer: Oh, I guess the computer wasn't on after all.

Support Staff Member: But you said the light was green!

Customer: Yes, and it's BRIGHT green now.

4.3 Branding can come in handy

Previously it was discussed that different customer bases can use the same resource in different ways. On a similar note, customers in different areas can use the same terminology for different resources. Many organizations may have "home file space", files on "the web server", or a "default image", but those terms mean different things based on who they get their service from and which type of service they use. If an organization has multiple offerings of a similar type, such as storage, it helps to brand those offerings differently. If there is home file space for students in one file system, administrative users for internal use in another, and shared file space in a third, the term "file space" becomes worse than useless – it becomes extraneous and complicating. Instead, use branding – give names to these services that have little or nothing to do with the underlying infrastructure. If the students

access the drive named "Wolf Den", and the administration uses "My Drive", and the shared space is called the "Parking Lot", then it become much easier for everyone to know which resource they are using.

4.4 The difference between a concern and a complaint

A common adage in technology support is that customers are never happy. Customers may be pleasant, but they call because they do not have something that they want, whether it is software access, a password reset, or a working computer. It is for this reason that service desks exist – to provide customers with those services. Most service desks suffer from a lack of two things: staffing and authority. What this means from the standpoint of troubleshooting and support is that a service desk should be selective in the calls that they handle for a significant amount of time. If a customer calls to receive support, that is one thing, but there also are the calls where a customer calls to simply complain about a perfectly working service that is just not providing them with the results that they desire. Whether the mail system doesn't provide enough storage or the LMS gradebook isn't updating often enough or that WordPress doesn't spontaneously generate content for overworked grad students, there are times when even the most skilled support staff members will be unable to resolve the issue. That is the difference between a concern and a complaint – concerns can be fixed, but at best, complaints can be salved. A good service desk will have procedures in place for intake of complaints, knowing that extensive time should be spent elsewhere.

5. SUMMARY

In the end, the Hungarian at the tobacconist's was arrested for starting a fight due to poor communication. But, it was the phrasebook's publisher who was sent to court for willfully breaching the peace. Take a lesson – don't blame the customer for their lack of technical knowledge or the support staff member for their lack of intimate knowledge of the customer's way of life. Instead, focus on the in-between process of communication, and empower both groups to make the process smooth and efficient.

6. REFERENCES

[1] Chapman, G (Writer), Cleese, J.. (Writer), & MacNaughton, I. (Director). (1970). Spam [Television series episode]. MacNaught, I (Producer), Monty Python's Flying Circus. BBC 1.

"It's Alive! It's Alive! We've created a monster!": Implementing a New Test Scanning System at VCU

Hannah Pettit
VCU helpIT Center Supervisor
901 Park Ave. Rm. B-30
Richmond, VA 23284
804-828-4727
pettith@vcu.edu

Kendall Wylie
VCU helpIT Center Analyst
901 Park Ave. Rm. B-30
Richmond, VA 23284
804-828-0611
wylieks@vcu.edu

ABSTRACT

Every department at VCU, as well as the entire student body, utilizes test scanning services provided by our office, the VCU helpIT Center. The push for a new test scanning system was mainly so that we could work with newer test scanning technology, lower our annual maintenance costs as well as provide a system which we could personalize to fit VCU's needs. The VCU helpIT Center was tasked with implementing and transitioning the VCU faculty and students to a new test scanning system.

This paper discusses our process of transition from our Legacy Scantron test scanning system, to our new gradeIT system (which utilizes Remark OMR). Our paper highlights our "plan of attack" we developed to prepare for the transition, the implementation steps we took, our marketing campaign that we developed, the successes we celebrated, as well as the shortfalls we encountered in our attempt to provide a change in services to the VCU community.

Categories and Subject Descriptors

K.6.1 [**Management of Computing and Information Systems**]: Project and People Management – *Life cycle, Management techniques, Staffing, Strategic information systems planning, Systems analysis and design, Systems development, Training.*

Keywords

Remark OMR, Scantron, Grading, System Development, Implementation, Marketing, Communications, Project Management, Training.

1. INTRODUCTION

Virginia Commonwealth University, established in 1968, is one of the nation's top research universities located in downtown Richmond, Virginia. More than 31,000 students are actively enrolled at VCU, studying on both the academic Monroe Park Campus and the medical MCV campus, in addition to other satellite campuses around the world.

The VCU helpIT Center, which is comprised of 8 full time staff

SIGUCCS'13, November 3–8, 2013, Chicago, Illinois, USA.
Copyright © 2013 ACM 978-1-4503-2318-5/13/11…$15.00.
http://dx.doi.org/10.1145/2504776.2504795

members and 12-15 student workers (see Image 1) is the central computing support office for the VCU community. Supporting an active user base of over 120,000 people which includes students, staff, faculty, alumni and other affiliates of the university, the helpIT Center provides phone and walkup support on VCU's two campuses in downtown Richmond. In addition to tier-one technical support, the helpIT Center is also in charge of providing test scanning services for VCU faculty and students.

Image 1: Walk-up counter on Monroe Park Campus location.

2. CAUSES FOR CHANGE

For the past few decades, VCU helpIT has provided test-grading services using Scantron forms and equipment. The same scanning system had been in place since the mid-1980s, and very little aspects of it had been updated to reflect newer technology.

2.1 Issues with Scantron System

With the Scantron system, the scanning machines that were used were over 10 years old, and costly to replace or repair. Due to their age, they also suffered frequent malfunctions which would result in delaying scanning turn-around times. The software that was used for processing data and generating output files was no longer easily supported as the original creators of this script (which was built in-house many years ago) no longer worked with us. In addition to outdated hardware and software, there was an expensive annual maintenance contract, and only specific Scantron printed forms could be used.

2.2 What Did We Want in a New System?

In selecting a new system, the main desire we had was more control over the software and hardware. In the past, test scanning services came to a screeching halt when our processing or grading machine broke. Services were unavailable until a maintenance technician could come in person to take a look at the issue. In addition to more control, we also needed hardware and software that was less costly to maintain. The ability to create our own forms was also of great appeal, as we could offer many different types of testing forms to faculty to use for exams and evaluations on campus.

3.0 NEW SYSTEM SELECTION

The need to transition to a new system was there, it was just a matter of when we would have the funding to be able to do so. Eventually, funds were available for our use, so we made movement towards selecting the best system to meet our needs. A few choice members of senior staff who had worked closely with our Scantron system were tasked with finding a new system. After attending webinars, testing sample software, and comparing pricing, we finally settled on Remark Office OMR by Gravic, Inc. as the product we were going to use to create our new test scanning system. We purchased the software in 2011, and began development in Spring 2012.

3.1 Remark Office OMR by Gravic, Inc.

Remark was appealing, as it gave us the ability to create our own forms. We were able to provide many of the same test report options that we had with our previous system, which would help in easing the transition to a new system for faculty members. There was flexibility within the software to make changes to our scanning process on the fly. We had commercial support for the software if we ran into any issues or had any questions. Additionally, we could use this software with any image scanner, freeing us up from maintaining costly scanners and allowing us to purchase a variety of less expensive ones.

3.2 Bending Remark to Meet our Demands

For the entirety of the Spring 2012 semester, we worked on fine-tuning the software to meet our specific scanning needs. Working with Remark, we were able to setup our system to pull student name data from our Banner system. This way, students only had to bubble in their student ID # on their test forms, and their name would be pulled from Banner to display on the reports that instructors receive. We purchased software called Concord by Data Blocks to create our new test scanning forms. A handful of helpful faculty members were willing to assist us in testing out these new forms with their classes. By the end of the Spring 2012 semester, we had created a variety of forms that were finalized and ready to go.

4.0 SUMMER 2012 CAMPAIGN

At the start of Summer 2012, we began to outline our implementation plan, hoping to introduce the new system in the upcoming Fall 2012 semester. To do so, however, we needed to develop a marketing and communications strategy to get the word out to faculty and students about the new system.

4.1 Marketing gradeIT to VCU

To keep in line with our "IT" branding, we decided to name our new system gradeIT. This way it was easily identifiable as a system that was supported by our department. We met with our Marketing and Communications group within our department, and had them work on creating our logo for the new system (see Image 2). We worked on creating an informational website that

we could refer users to for assistance. An email account was created for gradeIT specific questions and to be used to send out test results to faculty members.

Image 2: Our new gradeIT logo.

gradeIT flyers were created that were distributed to departments, and made available from our walk-up areas (see Image 3). We manually compiled a list of all faculty members that had used test-grading services within the past year, and reached out to them via email to let them know that a new system was coming with the Fall 2012 semester. We also advertised our new system using the daily VCU Telegram service, which is a daily events email that is sent out to all faculty, staff, and students of VCU.

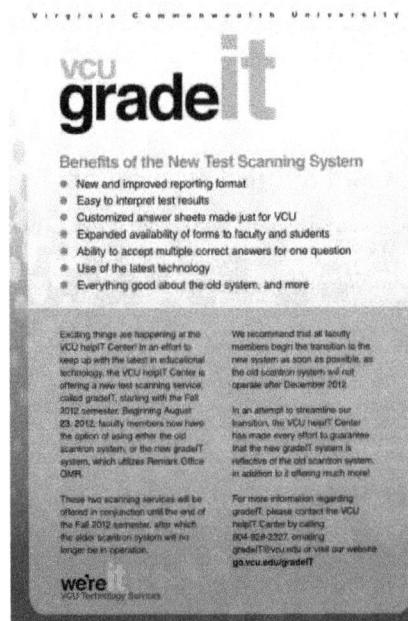

Image 3: gradeIT informational flyer for faculty members.

4.2 Making gradeIT forms available

In the past, students and faculty could traditionally purchase Scantron forms from various bookstores and businesses around campus. We wanted to keep these same outlets available, so we reached out to all bookstores and companies in the community who were distributing Scantron forms. We met with them and discussed the new gradeIT system we were implementing, and also provided them with copies of the new gradeIT forms (see Image 4) so that they reproduce them. We met with a local copy shop that traditionally works with many VCU departments, and asked them to have the forms on file to print, as many departments would want to buy them in bulk. We left the price of each form up to the establishment.

In addition to providing the forms to local businesses and bookstores, we also made the forms available to be printed on the computers located in the main library on our Monroe Park Campus. A shortcut was placed on each library computer that allows a student to quickly send a form to print using our Pay for Print system (students pay 12 cents for double sided copies). This way, if a student can't make it to a bookstore or business before a test, they can easily print a form off in the library using their VCU ID card.

To ensure that forms were being printed properly, we decided to not make the form template available to the whole VCU population on our website. Since the forms need to be printed on LaserJet printers, and can't be photocopied, we wanted to keep them out of the hands of students. As a compromise, we advertised to faculty that they could request a PDF copy of the form to be printed on departmental LaserJet printers (if they did not want to buy in bulk from the copy shop).

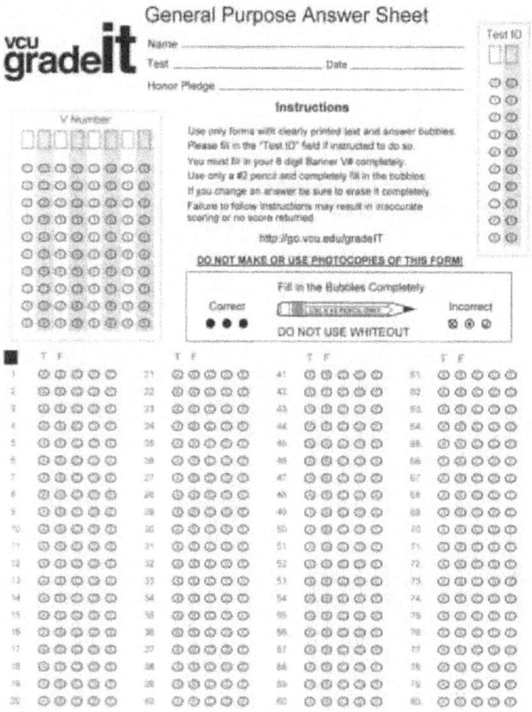

Image 4: The new gradeIT form.

5.0 IMPLEMENTATION
As the summer came to a close, and the start of the Fall semester neared, we were ready to implement the new system. We made the decision to offer both scanning systems in conjunction for the entirety of the Fall semester to ease the transition.

5.1 Fall 2012 transition semester
Since we were offering test scanning services on both systems, we were able to extend our marketing campaign into this entire semester. This guaranteed us to be able to get the word out to users who were either not around during the Summer marketing campaign, or who were not paying attention to our attempts to communicate with them. The bookstores and other outlets sold both types of forms to students (depending on what their instructors decided to use). We took this time to address any bugs in the system, and to iron out the kinks in the system (as it was being used by a larger sample than when we had done testing in the Spring).

With every Scantron test we scanned, we attached a gradeIT flyer to the scanned test set so that the instructor knew that the Scantron system was set to retire after final exams in December. Our website was constantly updated to reflect new information about the system (items were adjusted, and information was added that we had not thought to post when we first created the site). Additionally, student reporters from VCU's *The Commonwealth Times* and the School of Mass Communications interviewed us about the new gradeIT system. These interviews were streamed to the local VCU community and provided us with yet another outlet to reach users and spread information about the new gradeIT system.

5.2 Information Sessions
To aid and assist faculty members in the transition, we decided to hold informational sessions on a weekly basis during the Fall semester. These sessions were geared to discuss aspects of the new system with instructors (new forms, new reporting format, etc.) as well as clear up any questions they may have had. We advertised our training sessions on the daily VCU Telegram, as well as on our main gradeIT website. These sessions were held on a weekly basis throughout the Fall semester on both campus locations.

In addition to these public training sessions, we also met one-on-one with several departments per their request. This allowed us to meet with specific instructors who utilized the test grading system, and discuss any concerns they had about transitioning to the new system.

5.3 gradeIT Today
With the closing of the Fall 2012 semester in December, the Scantron test-grading system was retired. We kept one machine in use for the Spring 2013 semester in the event that an instructor dropped off a set of Scantron tests (note: this has only happened twice since December 2012). All staff members who performed test scanning services were trained and documentation regarding the gradeIT system was created for future training. As the Spring semester started, we held informational sessions on a weekly basis, gradually moving to twice a month as the semester advanced (demand for these classes had dropped). As we are still getting used to this new system, we continue to work out bugs in the system and are constantly adjusting it to meet our needs. We attempt to meet the demands of specific departments to fit their specific testing needs, and we continue to streamline the gradeIT system each day.

6.0 KNOWLEDGE GAINED
From this experience, both successes were celebrated and failures were met. We now have first-hand experience of the time it takes to transition our user base to a new system, and both positive and negative outcomes that arise.

6.1 Success Celebrated

Other than a few minor hiccups, we successfully implemented a new system to the entire VCU community over the past year. We've received a majority of positive feedback from both instructors and students regarding the new scanning system. The new test report options are the favorite of faculty, and students appreciate the ability to print off test forms easily in the library on their way to class. We have a larger amount of control over the new gradeIT system, allowing us to easily amend the system on the fly. Additionally, the gradeIT system is more cost efficient, as our annual maintenance of the system is thousands of dollars less than the previous system we had in place.

6.2 Shortfalls Encountered

While we knew beforehand that we needed to transition to a new test scanning system, when the time came that we had available funds, we did not have as much time as we would have liked to in order to research all possible options available on the market. We also would have liked to have had more opportunities to communicate with faculty beforehand, as some faculty expressed complaints that their input was not solicited when choosing a new test scanning system. One of the major issues we encountered was utilizing all outlets of communication to be able to notify the user base that the new system was available. We did our best to communicate using the outlets we had, but it was more of a trial and error process as we went along.

7. CONCLUSION

As we face the future, we now have the experience under our belts on how to successfully implement a new system that is used on a large scale in a university setting. Although we've had many hiccups along the way, the knowledge we have gained from implementing the gradeIT test scanning system is noteworthy.

Energy Overhead of the Graphical User Interface in Server Operating Systems

Heather Brotherton
College of Technology
Purdue University
West Lafayette, Indiana USA
hbrother@purdue.edu

J. Eric Dietz
College of Technology
Purdue University
West Lafayette, Indiana USA

John McGrory
College of Science
Dublin Institute of Technology
Dublin, Ireland

Fred Mtenzi
College of Science
Dublin Institute of Technology
Dublin, Ireland

ABSTRACT

Evidence of graphical user interface server operating system energy overhead is presented. It is posed that data centers would have substantial energy savings by eliminating graphical user interface operating systems.

Categories and Subject Descriptors

C.0 [**Systems Application Architecture**]: Operating System Energy Efficiency – *graphical user interface, system administration, data center management.*

Keywords

Data center; energy; server; operating system

1. INTRODUCTION

Energy efficiency is a hot topic in Information Technology. There are many studies in the area of hardware virtualization. However there is little in the way of scholarly studies of graphical versus non-graphical operating system energy efficiency. This may be in part because it is considered to be a moving target due to constant updates. It is also possible that it has not been considered worthy of study because of the seemingly small possibility for energy savings. This study will make a case for reducing use of the graphical user interface element of server operating systems for energy efficiency.

The rationale for the focus on the graphical user interface is to avoid focus on a particular operating system. Rather this document focuses on a broader categorization that is far more generalizable. Studying the server operating system is practical because those administering the system are trained professionals capable of working from the command line. Therefore, if there is evidence that a graphical interface at the server operating system level consumes more energy the possible negative impact of removal is lessened.

2. OPERATING SYSTEM

Operating systems reside on nearly every server, controlling systems resources. [1] Operating systems are continually designed to provide more features and these features increasingly include energy savings management. Focusing on server level operating system software allows us to take advantage of the Cascade Effect as described by Emerson. The Cascade Effect states that for every watt saved at the server level 2.84 watts are saved by the data center. [2] In addition if an operating system were chosen that required very little graphics and no sound, additional savings could be achieved. This is because it would allow the removal or reduction of components. The chart labeled figure 1 entitled watts lost per server provides a rough breakdown of the number of watts lost broken down by server component. [3] For example, if unnecessary PCI cards (these would include video and audio cards) were not installed into servers 41 watts could be saved. These components waste energy even when they are not used. [4] When these savings are multiplied into the average number of servers in a data center the savings become very significant. For example, if a PCI card such as video card were removed for a savings of 41watts from 500 servers in a data center, the cumulative watts saved would be 58220 watts per year. At an average of ten cents per kilowatt-hour this results in a savings of $51,035.65 per year.

Watts used by servers are converted to heat, which is expressed in British Thermal Units. [5] Each watt consumed by a server translates into approximately 3.4129 BTUs per hour [6]. Waste heat must then be removed from that data center to avoid damaging the servers resulting in additional energy consumed by cooling units. This is the reasoning behind the Cascade Effect. This is also the reason that the primary focus of this study will be on reducing the watts consumed at the server level.

Watts Lost per Server

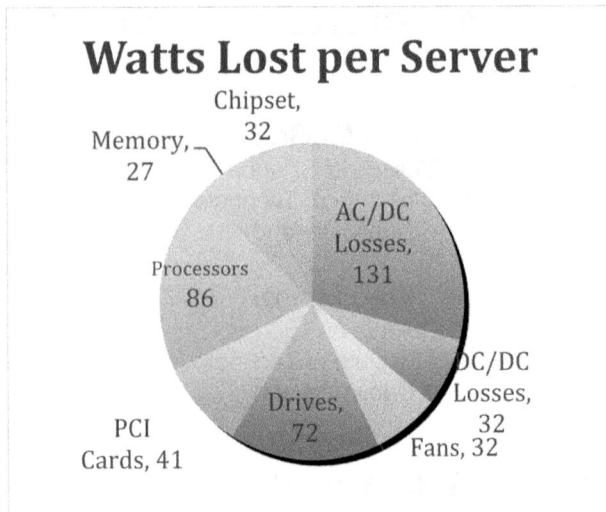

Figure 1 Watts lost per server
Source: EXP Critical Facilities Inc., Intel Corp.

3. EXPERIMENT

Quantitative data was collected to measure the efficiency of server operating systems. Experimentation and observation were employed at the server and software levels. The data collected includes observations of watts consumed by the server with different hardware and operating system software configurations. All energy readings were collected for a minimum of one hour using the Watts Up? Meter.

Linux based server operating systems ran the top command during the observations. The top tool provides data for on-going processes. A sample was taken not running top to serve as a baseline so that the load of running top can be determined. The top tool was configured via command line to take readings at intervals of one second. The results were sent to a file for possible analysis. The command used was:

top -d 1 > /home/testOSName.txt

The Windows based operating systems do not have a direct equivalent to the Linux top program. The Windows command line tool called Typeperf was configured to provide much of the same information. The command used was:

typeperf "\Memory\Available bytes" "\processor(*)\% processor time" "\Process(*)\Thread Count" > testOSName.csv

This tool was chosen in part because it would run with or without the standard GUI based Windows operating system. Another advantage to this tool is reduction in the possibility of creating the energy overhead that might come with a more sophisticated program. As this study's focus is on differences in operating systems, adding another program would unnecessarily complicate the readings. Typeperf output to file proved to be valuable during the data analysis phase as the data gathered from the Typeperf tool provided insight into the differences in what was happening at the operating system level similar to that provided by top.

4. EQUIPMENT

A custom hardware configuration was used for this experiment. The hardware was chosen for its availability, cost effectiveness, and efficiency. The hardware components used were as shown in Table 1.

The system architecture used in testing eliminated as many components as possible to reduce overhead from the hardware. Using more specialized components such as a motherboard without integrated video may have produced a more ideal testing environment, but were not readily available. Fortunately the elimination of fans, magnetic hard disk drive, and oversized components produced a surprisingly energy efficient test server.

Table 1. Shuttle XS35v2 Barebones Mini PC

Intel Atom D525 1.8GHz dual core processor
Integrated Intel Graphics Media Accelerator 3150
Gigabit LAN
SD card reader
5 USB connections
Fan-less external power supply
Intel Solid State Drive 80GB 320 Series
PNY 4GB PC3-10666 1.3GHz DDR3 SoDIMM

4.1 Server

The barebones server's baseline watt consumption mean energy consumed is 7.96 watts and the median is 8.70 watts. The barebones reading reflects the server's energy consumption prior to adding the random access memory (RAM) and the solid-state drive (SSD). The energy consumption after the addition of 4GB RAM to the server during a one hour period is 15.36 watts and the median is 15 watts. This represents an increase of 7.40 watts in the mean and 6.80 watts in the median. The server energy consumption after Solid State Drive (SSD) installation was a mean of 17.42 watts and a median consumption of 17.7 watts. This is an increase in the average of 2.06 watts and median of 2.20 watts. The data represents a baseline for the server of 17.42 to17.7 watts before the installation of the operating systems.

4.2 Monitoring Tool

The energy-monitoring tool was also chosen for availability and cost effectiveness. The meter used was a Watts up? Pro universal outlet version. This meter is capable of measuring 100 to 250v within a plus or minus 1.5 percent accuracy. The meter is also capable of logging at one-second intervals and provides a USB interface and PC software. This logging interface eliminates transcription errors and saves time. The down side of this tool is that the time stamps are not always reliable and that it has a limited memory. Even when set to overwrite, the meter will often log less than one reading per second to save space. The information provided by the manufacturer does not provide adequate information to avoid this or estimate the readings accurately.

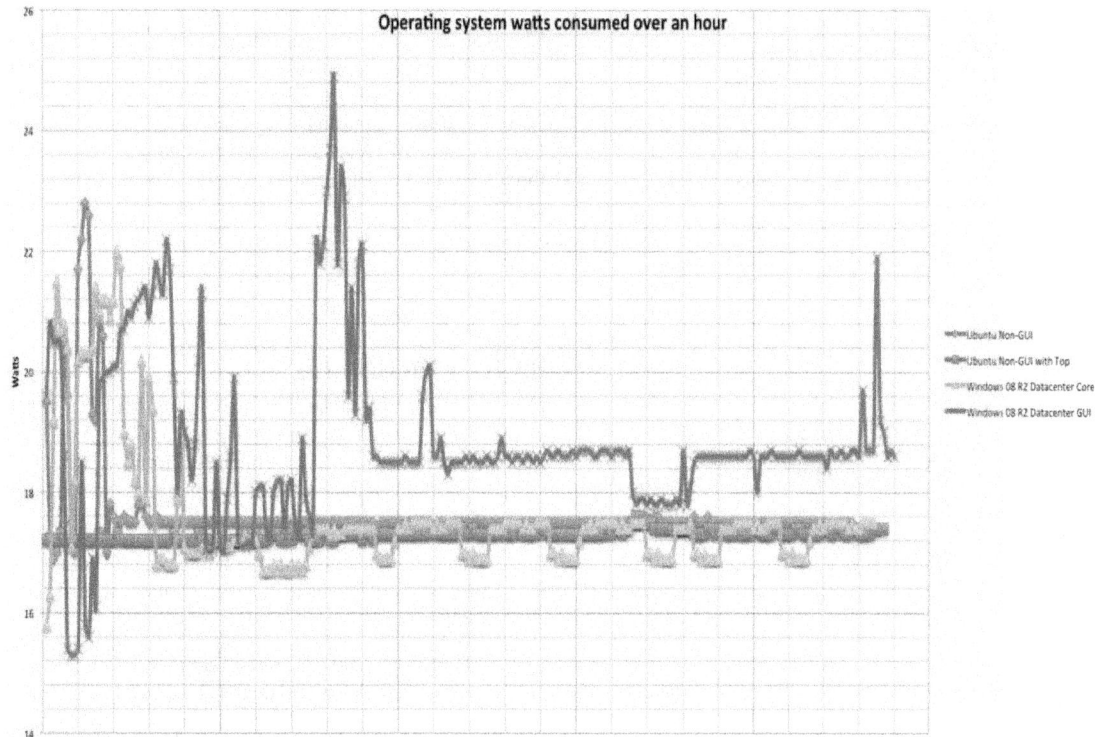

Operating system watts consumed over an hour

5. SERVER OPERATING SYSTEMS

The software used for the testing were the following x86 operating systems:

- Ubuntu 9.10 (Linux)
- Ubuntu 11.10 (Linux)
- Windows Server 2008 R2 Datacenter Core
- Windows Server 2008 R2 Datacenter GUI

No operating system configuration changes were performed; all were installed using the defaults. The systems were not connected to the Internet and no updates were performed on the operating systems.

6. FINDINGS

The data collected confirmed the expected difference between GUI based operating systems and non-GUI. One would assume that there is more energy overhead in a system that is processing and rendering graphics than one that does not. Figure 2 Comparison of watts consumed by operating system scatter chart and Table 2 both show that the operating systems that do not run a graphical user interface (GUI) use roughly 17.5 to 17.6 watts. The two graphical user interface (GUI) based operating systems tested consumed 18.1 to 18.9 watts roughly. It could be extrapolated that not using a GUI would save .6 to 1.3 watts per server.

The greatest overall variation in power usage is observed in the Windows 2008 R2 Datacenter graphical user interface operating system that varied from 15.30 watts to 24.90 watts with a difference of 9.60 watts. The data collected provides some insight into the operating system-power consumption relationship. The data collected indicates a correlation between increased energy consumption and the presence of a graphical user interface.

Table 2 OS: Windows 2008 R2 Datacenter (GUI)

Time (Minutes)	Threads (Mean Number)	Watts (Mean)
9:42	373	18.65
9:43	361	18.6
9:44	362	18.65
9:45	360	18.65
9:46	360	18.7
9:47	368	18.7
9:48	364	18.6
9:49	363	18.7
9:50	362	18.65
9:51	364	18.7
9:52	376	18.65

**Table 3 OS: Windows 2008 R2
Datacenter Core**

(Non-GUI)

Time (Minutes)	Threads (Mean Number)	Watts (Mean)
3:16	263	17.1
3:17	263	17
3:18	260	17
3:19	256	17.05
3:20	259	17.05
3:21	255	17.15
3:22	255	17.25
3:23	252	17.1
3:24	250	17.2
3:25	254	17.2
3:26	250	17.25

Table 2 and Table 3 compare the Windows 2008 R2 datacenter thread and watt consumption for a period of ten minutes The mean number of threads the GUI version of the OS is running is 365; the non-GUI mean was 256. This difference of approximately 109 threads may account for the overall difference in energy consumption. This also indicates that a reduction of the 100-thread GUI overhead can save roughly one watt at the server level.

The server hardware as configured was found to have a mean energy consumption of 17.42 watts. The Core (non-GUI) installation of Windows 2008 datacenter increases the power load by .15 watts from the baseline hardware load. The standard Windows 2008 R2 datacenter installation increases the power load from the baseline by 1.43 watts. This may not seem like much but this represents an increase of nearly ten times the load added by the non-GUI version.

7. CONCLUSION

The watt readings from the micro server tests combined with the Typeperf data provided insight into why the GUI operating system consumes more energy. The GUI version of the Windows Server 2008 R2 datacenter runs over 100 threads more than the non-GUI Core version of Windows Server 2008 R2 datacenter. This 100-thread GUI overhead represents more than one watt of additional energy consumption at the server level. Allowing for the cascade effect this would be approximately three watts per server.

8. REFERENCES

[1] A Vahdat, A Lebeck, and C Schlatter Ellis, "Every Joule is Precious: The Case for Revisiting," in EW 9 Proceedings of the 9th workshop on ACM SIGOPS European workshop: beyond the PC: new challenges for the operating system, New York, 2000, pp. 31-36.

[2] Emerson. Efficient Data Centers.com. [Online]. http://www.efficientdatacenters.com/edc/docs/EnergyLogicMetricPaper.pdf

[3] N Anderson. (2007, 27) Ars Technica. [Online]. http://arstechnica.com/uncategorized/2007/02/8932/

[4] Google. Google Data centers. [Online]. http://www.google.com/about/datacenters/efficiency/internal/#servers

[5] V Anayochukwu Ani, A Ndubueze Nzeako, and J Chigbo Obianuko, "Energy Optimization at Datacenters in Two Different Locations of Nigeria," International Journal of Energy Engineering, pp. 151-164, 2012.

[6] S Barielle. (2011, Nov.) IBM Systems Magazine. [Online]. http://www.ibmsystemsmag.com/mainframe/Business-Strategy/ROI/energy_estimating/

We Have the Technology:
Rebuilding a Department from the Ground Up

Allan Chen
Menlo College
1000 El Camino Real
Atherton, CA 94027
+1-650-543-3889
achen@menlo.edu

Omar Ali
Menlo College
1000 El Camino Real
Atherton, CA 94027
+1-650-543-3840
oali@menlo.edu

ABSTRACT

It is always important for departments - at all levels, from staff to managers to directors - to constantly evaluate how well their structure matches the needs of the institution. Sometimes changes are needed, and sometimes the transition from one model to the next can be less than smooth.

At Menlo College, because of a number of staff changes - including departmental leadership - a strategic plan to increase specialization has had a ripple effect through the entire IT organization. For instance, taking two of three Help Desk staff and diverting them to other operations and relying more on students for support has had its ups and downs. Additionally, bringing an Administrative Systems manager on board has resulted in knowledge transfer issues.

This presentation will cover the programmatic and strategic planning that went into these changes as well as how the process has gone, is going, and what we hope to do as we move forward.

Categories and Subject Descriptors

H.5.3 [**Information Systems**]: Group and Organization Interfaces – *Evaluation/methodology, Organizational design.*

General Terms

Management, Measurement, Performance, Design, Human Factors.

Keywords

Organizational structure, help desk design, gap analysis

1. INTRODUCTION

1.1 Menlo College General Information

Menlo College is a small, private undergraduate institution located in Atherton, CA, about 30 miles south of San Francisco. Roughly 700 students matriculate annually at Menlo. Curriculum is focused on business, with degrees in fields such as Accounting, Finance, and Management. A Psychology degree is also offered.

Menlo employs 30 full-time faculty and an average of 50 adjunct faculty. The full-time faculty are all PhD or otherwise hold "academically-qualified" degrees. Many of the adjuncts are "professionally-qualified" with extensive experience in industry.

Between 80-90 professional staff (not counting athletic coaches, whose numbers fluctuate quite a bit) handle operations and administration. Our largest departments are Enrollment Management (which encompasses Admissions, Financial Aid, and the Registrar), Advancement/Alumni & Development, and Student Affairs.

1.2 Menlo College Office of IT

The Office of IT (OIT) includes seven staff making up six FTE positions. As of spring 2013, these positions include:

- Chief Information Officer
- Help Desk Supervisor
- Desktop Manager
- Systems Manager
- Web Applications Developer
- ERP and Business Operations Manager (50%)
- Database Administrator (50%)

All professional positions report to the CIO in a flat organizational structure.

OIT operates a Help Desk, located in the college library, which is staffed primarily by students. An average of eight students have worked in this capacity throughout the 2012-13 academic year.

OIT sources actively and diversely. E-mail and Calendaring is completely outsourced to Google, and our LMS is handled by an outside vendor as well. We partner heavily with our preferred Value-Added Reseller (VAR) for consulting. Networking, in particular, is handled primarily outside of campus resources. This is due to staff capacity and resources.

A number of special projects and services are noteworthy:

- Significant investment in a Virtual Desktop Infrastructure (VDI)

- Recent roll-out of campus-wide LMS (1 semester)

- Relatively recent ERP implementation (~1.5 years)

- Updates to almost all servers and a number of networking components

- New trouble ticket system (6 months)

2. HISTORY AND STAFF CHANGES

OIT has undergone a number of staff and organizational changes in the last 12-18 months. Figure 1 illustrates the staff departures during spring 2012. Note that over a 3 month period 3.5 staff FTE left the department. The Database and ERP position was officially 50% but actual operated only "as needed" – he did not have set hours when he was in the office. This dramatically changed his availability.

Figure 2 illustrates the change in titles during spring 2012. It is important to note that two of the now three Help Desk Consultants were new hires, effectively creating organizational parity across all positions. Coupled with the rapid change in staff, almost no differentiation or specialization developed between the individuals.

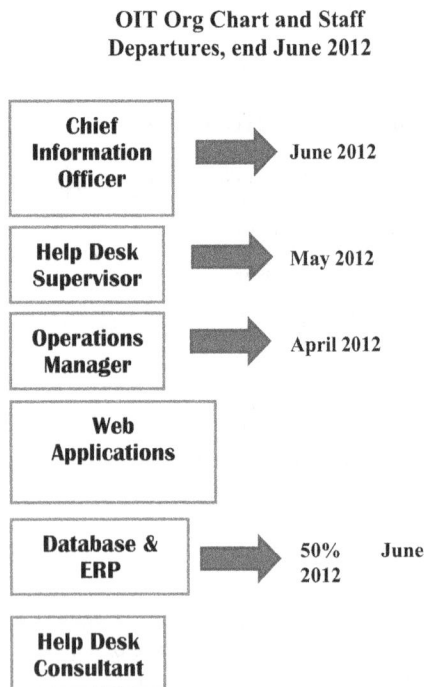

OIT Org Chart and Staff Departures, end June 2012

Figure 1

**OIT Staff Title Changes
June-August 2012**

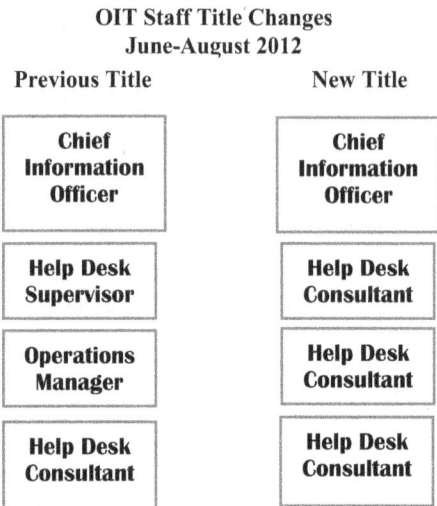

Figure 2

A number of characteristics made these transitions more difficult. Institutional knowledge, shifting responsibilities and timing of staff moves had a significant impact on OIT operations. This was exacerbated by the general trend of the previous five years – OIT had gone through a significant change in scope, operations, and infrastructure and had seen an increase in staff. In such situations, it is not uncommon to find job duties far removed from descriptions as staff fill in gaps as they emerge. These incongruities should be addressed over time, however, to maintain alignment between staff and operations.

Of course, these issues are universally applicable to other departments and schools. Very few organizations withstand personnel change without any challenges. These situations can also provide the opportunity to reshape a department or organization from the ground up.

2.1 Institutional Knowledge

The Help Desk Supervisor handled much more than just Help Desk itself. He was a position of incredible responsibility and one deeply involved in nearly all aspects of operations, from networking to desktop support to help desk structure. This came about largely through the rapid growth of the department in earlier years. The specific individual had a diverse set of skills, and was able to take on responsibilities as they emerged.

This position was replaced, essentially, by a Desktop Support Specialist. Not only were the duties radically altered, but the amount of institutional knowledge that left was substantial. To fill in the gap on responsibilities, an existing technology partner was asked to take on more duties. This, in turn, created another risk of losing entire sections of departmental knowledge – we were virtually outsourcing significant parts of our operations.

2.2 Shifting Responsibilities

Much of the reorganization was done "on the fly" – rather than an orderly transition of duties, responsibilities were moved back and forth between and among the remaining staff. This led to more problems. For example, the aggregate responsibilities of the Operations Manager were not passed along to anyone in particular. For example, the in-person support for our learning management system fell upon the web applications developer, whose other responsibilities are focused on programming and coding. Classroom support, previously handled personally by this one staff member, became the domain of the Help Desk in general, with consulting and field support from the CIO.

This also happened with the Help Desk Supervisor role. All of the responsibilities managed by that individual did not fall upon any specific new staff in a planned, logical manner. Things were dropped and duties lost along the way.

Finally, immediately prior to the departure of the previous CIO, a general Help Desk staff member was elevated to the role of Help Desk Supervisor. On the one hand, this formally filled the gap created by the predecessor's departure. On the other, this particular individual was a recent graduate with no professional experience. Regardless of any "intangibles" that might make this a sound decision, there is an inherent disruption created and responsibilities must move even more.

2.3 Timing
The majority of these staff changes occurred in very rapid succession. From April to June, 2012, three senior staff – including the CIO – left. In addition, the Database Administrator – the primary contact for the college ERP – went to part-time during that same period.

Notably, there was a 45-day gap between the previous and current CIOs. A change in leadership at such a time caused a number of issues. The fiscal year turned during this period and several financial decisions had to be made by the previous CIO in a very short amount of time before departure. Also, the three Help Desk staff operated in maintenance mode – "keeping the lights on." This caused progress on a number of projects to slow down until the incoming CIO arrived. The office was busy, but was not necessarily making progress.

3. REDESIGNING OIT
Menlo College OIT needed a significant structural overhaul after the staffing changes of the previous 6 months. The key was identifying the gaps in service and finding the right people to step forward to fill those spaces. This meant identifying latent talent and fostering a culture that allowed for taking on new responsibilities for professional growth and out of personal interest yet also maintained a high quality of customer service.

Subsequently, it became clear that there were certain key operations that had to be addressed before significant change could occur. We needed to make all changes at once, but focus on a few key items in particular.

This formal process began roughly three months after the change in leadership and arrival of the new CIO. The first 90 days were focused on critical change needs, budget issues, and forming key partnerships. For the purpose of this paper, we ignore these initial efforts as they were more about gaining momentum for the coming reorganization.

3.1 Needs/Gap Analysis
In any reorganization, there should be some kind of needs or gap analysis. Coupled with this is identifying services that cannot be delivered efficiently, are legacy and should be retired, or both. We utilized both approaches in this process.

3.1.1 Service Catalogs
OIT constructed two different service catalogs based upon the ITIL 3.0 framework.

The Business Service Catalog allowed us to identify what we were offering to the customer. Many were obvious – email, help desk, and field support. Others required more thought. We never really considered that we were the group providing telephone service, for instance. Technically there was another company behind us, yes, but when it came to the customer, OIT was the group that would be answering questions and ensuring quality of service.

We then used the Business Catalog to develop a Technical Service Catalog. These were the internal operations that we ran to support the business services. For example, we operated a trouble ticket system (technical) to allow for service requests (business). Technical services often covered multiple business services. Our virtual machine infrastructure (VMI), for instance, supported everything from telephony to network storage to the virtual part of our desktop provision service.

Importantly, the catalogs were developed without consideration of whether we had the staff to actually deliver all of the services at our desired level(s). The goal was to review what we delivered and what we had to do, technically, to provide those services. This laid the foundation for a more thorough gap analysis.

3.1.2 Pain Points
Using both metrics from our ticket system (Web Help Desk from Solar Winds) and open discussion, we identified bottlenecks. It was important that we combine both hard statistics and personal observations. The numbers certainly gave us a good view on what types of questions were coming in from our customers, but we had to dig into other information to find out if certain topics were statistically skewed through multiple requests by the same person for the same issue (an e-mail, phone call and web submission for a single issue, for instance). The personal observations helped build on these numbers to address what individual staff felt were our true weaknesses.

In combination, we could see where we were inefficient vs. actually low on dedicated resources. We found that if something came up often in the metrics but not in the minds of staff, we were probably getting the job done but not efficiently and/or with long-lasting positive results. We were applying band-aids repeatedly. If the tickets did not match up with a topic that came up often to staff, it was likely something prominent (thus the notice from staff) that was under-provisioned. Staff are going to worry about insufficient resources to manage the firewalls, whereas users only notice if the network connection is working or not.

3.1.3 Gap Analysis
Pulling these two activities together, we could complete a comprehensive gap analysis. Building the catalogs meant that we could see what we were at least trying to deliver. Identifying pain points illustrated where additional resources were needed.

A foundational issue was that our operations had grown beyond what we had the capacity to support, at least in our current arrangement. We could no longer get away with every staff having dual and sometimes opposing roles – deep project dive *and* daily support, for example. Some staff had specialized so much that they were effectively removed from front line support. Some systems had grown to the point of needing direct attention (rather than 3rd party support from our technology partner). The gaps, therefore, were not only in our operations, but also our structure.

3.2 Realignment

OIT went through a significant change in structure and responsibilities over the course of three months.

3.2.1 Consulting vs. Development

We separated consulting with constituents about needs and potential solutions from the actual development and implementation of those solutions. Specifically, the Web Applications Developer and Database Administrator roles moved towards a focus primarily on technical implementation – getting things to work. The CIO and a newly created ERP and Business Operations Manager engaged in actual consultation with departments.

Obviously we should not completely separate consulting and implementation. However, by changing the emphasis and better defining roles, each group was able to be more efficient. When all parties did come together, discussions were more focused and productive. Customers better understood how to express their needs in a way that would help developers properly design solutions, a discussion effectively moderated by those in the consulting role.

3.2.2 Infrastructure Focus

A glaring gap in our resource allocation was that we had no one formally dedicated to our infrastructure, from VMI to VDI to networking. Two staff did some work, but only in addition to their primary roles at the Help Desk. We also completely outsourced our networking needs after the previous Help Desk Supervisor left

These two staff were formally tasked with managing the infrastructure – specifically the servers and desktops, both physical and virtual. Within a month of this change, it became clear that one person was more in line with a systems administrator and therefore took over management of all of our physical and virtual servers. The other staff member took over desktops, from building virtual ones to imaging physical ones. These roles are symbiotic – the systems administrator runs the virtual servers that manage our virtual desktops, and maintains the physical servers that actually power the virtual desktops. The desktop manager relies on the systems administrator for a reliable environment and platform, and is instrumental in providing feedback to keep the overall systems optimized.

Networking would remain largely outside our domain, though support would be through a partnership with an outside group, rather than complete outsourcing. It was a conscious decision not to devote personnel resources to greater network management. While relying on networking specialists made more sense than trying to manage our system ourselves, we still needed to understand the monitoring alarms, notifications and other symptoms. We therefore undertook a process of working side-by-side with a reseller.

3.2.3 Sourcing

We also intensively reviewed to whom we outsourced services and the resellers that handled our network and general infrastructure. Contracts were examined, agreements changed and, ultimately, the two separate resellers were replaced by a single, new reseller with a broader set of services.

This reseller now handles all consulting services and does almost all of our infrastructure design and build work (again, working alongside our staff to keep knowledge internal). We still aggressively pass bids for equipment to other resellers to ensure best pricing and to avoid the potential conflict of interest of a reseller and its "preferred" partner vendors. This is a fine line but an important one in ensuring the best solutions for Menlo College.

3.2.4 Help Desk Self-Sufficiency

The most important change was making the Help Desk a self-sufficient operation staffed mainly by students, managed by the Help Desk Supervisor. The other two staff – now working on infrastructure – still spent some of their time with general support issues. But if we were to succeed in this new organizational model, we needed to free up staff time through a more independent Help Desk.

Over the next few months – leading up to early Spring 2013 – the need for this "first domino" became increasingly pointed. Therefore, the remainder of this paper focuses on the experiences and evolution of the Help Desk.

4. MENLO COLLEGE OIT HELP DESK

The Menlo College Helpdesk serves three primary groups of users--fulltime staff, faculty, and students. Menlo College has very few part-time or contract staff. To a manageable extent, the Help Desk also supports coaches in the Athletics Department, where there is very high turnover. For the purposes of this paper we are mostly discussing the physical Help Desk and its operations, which is located in the Menlo College Bowman Library. The core services we offer include:

- o Limited troubleshooting of personal hardware (no direct, hands-on support)
- o Full support of college-owned equipment
- o Support of classroom hardware
- o Event hardware set up and assistance
- o Assistance with Virtual Infrastructure issues

In addition, the Help Desk also acts as a filter for the rest of OIT. Staff such as the Web Applications Developer or the other professional Help Desk staff serve as tier 2 support in one manner or another. Via our ticket system, all IT-related inquiries are sent to the same queue. These tickets are then routed to various tier 2 staff by the Help Desk team, which includes both the Help Desk Supervisor and the student staff themselves. In most cases, the tier 2 staff are specifically not the first point of contact to customers. In fact, we found any system that made them the front-line contacts to be inefficient. Most times it was asking too much of them to provide top-tier, high-touch customer service and be productive at concentration-intensive activities such as software development or database management. We also found that they would be quickly overwhelmed by all the direct interactions – they needed the ticketing system to stay organized. This method also improves unity and fosters collaboration so that we can work as a team toward problem resolution. Many occasions arise where a ticket needs to be passed down so that a Help Desk member may complete a part of the request.

4.1 Prior to Summer 2012

From 2009-2012, Menlo College's Help Desk enjoyed very heavy professional and student staffing. Our resources included two full-time employees (Help Desk Supervisor, Operations Manager), one part-time employee (Help Desk Consultant), one full-time intern and a handful of students. The full-time staff were split between serving faculty and staff, offering a very high professional staff to customer ratio. Everyone else was set to assist wherever they could. For greater consistency, the part-time professional staff member and the entire student work force were all managed by the single Help Desk Supervisor.

4.1.1 Strength in Numbers
Service was very balanced under this model. The faculty population was small enough that one person could handle all their needs. Staff and student body made up the larger customer base so naturally they received their service from a larger group of techs. Our big investment in Help Desk staff let us handle the normal flow of tickets with little overhead. Productivity was mixed depending on the level of technician but the ratios meant that any slowdown from one person was quickly resolved with the aid of another. Student staff and the intern were always very timely in their ticket resolutions. In general, the professional staff tackled the more difficult tickets. This did mean that they took longer to resolve but also that the customers felt a sense of dedication and attention when a professional staff member was on the job.

4.1.2 Opportunities
Starting in 2010, specialization arose from new technologies and services. The increased need for not only a web presence but an interactive one with integrated features necessitated the addition of a Web Applications Developer position. This position was also responsible for the implementation of the new email and calendaring system, based on Google Apps for Education. With a new ERP system came the need for a Database Administrator for implementation and support. In 2011, the contractor hired to fill this role became a full-time staff member and part of the OIT team. The final major adoption during this time frame was that of a virtual server (VMI) and desktop (VDI) infrastructure. We tested and deployed virtual desktops to both staff and learning environments. The Help Desk Supervisor was made responsible for configuring and supporting the VDI deployment and, by extension, also managed the VMI environment.. As technology on campus modernized, we expanded the student work force in order to give the employees more time to do their respective tasks, but professional staff remained heavily involved in day-to-day support.

In many ways the relationship between OIT staff makeup and workload/scope of responsibilities were at a tipping point. There were enough staff of varying skills and interests to cover our daily operations and our new ventures at the same time. We did not yet have to remove staff from working at the Help Desk in order to roll out virtual desktops.

4.1.3 Challenges
Of course, as we added services and complexity to our operations, we did run into some problems. The first and foremost was training, which was required to spread institutional knowledge and improve support of this growing structure. In particular, student staff had no training options and there was no formal documentation available. Most skills were taught "just in time" and as needed. Higher level tickets saw a slowdown in completion because student techs would have to wait for someone to be available for training.

Another problem the team saw was in communication. The student staff were not used to making contact with clients directly. What was normally arranged ahead of time became the full responsibility of the student. A lot of the time clients were left

seeking updates to their tickets. The system was beginning to show some strain - while the full time Help Desk staff knew exactly what had been accomplished, they did not have time to provide updates.

4.2 Summer 2012
During the summer of 2012 we experienced a huge staff loss. Both Help Desk employees and our CIO left in rapid succession. This left us with a huge deficit in institutional knowledge. Before leaving, the previous CIO hired two full-time employees in an attempt to cover the loss. The part-time Help Desk member also converted to a full-time role. In reality, there was some overlap of whom was hired when to do what, but by mid-year there were essentially now three full-time staff – all with the title of Help Desk Consultant. It was unclear whether these three positions were meant collectively to take the place of the now-departed Help Desk Supervisor and/or Operations Manager.

4.2.1 Challenges
Official service roles were not assigned to the three-person Help Desk team. However, we identified our strengths and were able to delegate work fairly evenly, provided that one staff could easily address the issue at hand. Unfortunately, not every problem had an obvious solution, or an obvious support person. We fell behind trying to solve problems that we had not addressed before. Lack of documentation, the timing of staff changes and loss of institutional knowledge meant that we were not only once again learning on the fly but also from scratch and without backup. This caused us to take longer than average when addressing tickets.

The Help Desk suffered a large loss in reputation across the entire campus. Our ticket system was not yet fully deployed which affected self-service, voicemails were not answered in a consistent manner, and each time we had to "put out a fire" we were severely distracted from our day-to-day support tasks. Customer service suffered. Fortunately, the relationship between faculty and students did not change too dramatically because the most were not present until the summer ended, but this was merely a fortune of timing and one that therefore would not last.

The team also found itself relying more and more on an outside reseller that had been an integral partner for many years. Entire projects that had great impact on our operations – rebuilding our Domain Controller and troubleshooting the VDI deployment – were essentially outsourced.

4.2.2 Leadership Gap
The time in between leaders was only a few months and because the previous management had left us with tasks to accomplish, the staff in general had more than enough to do. These tasks where seen through by the interim management, which was handled primarily by the CFO. Outside of checking up on project progress and managing the budget, we rarely felt the presence of any significant leadership or management. The Help Desk staff fell into a routine of "keeping the lights on."

4.3 Fall 2012 - New Leadership
The current CIO joined us on the eve of the fall semester. The summer had been plagued by hardware failures as well as a major network disruption when the fiber optic cabling was damaged. At the time, the Help Desk team was composed of three full-time employees as well as two student techs. The fall semester saw consolidation of management, as one of the Help Desk

Consultants was promoted to Help Desk Supervisor. The student team quickly grew to six to meet needs. It was clear early on at both the staff and management levels that we were going to attempt to have a self-sufficient Help Desk. The other two full time employees needed to branch off to handle the rebuild of the VDI and the maintenance of our server infrastructure. They were to remain parts of the Help Desk team, but in many ways were more akin to advanced technicians and tier 2 support than "in the field."

4.3.1 Rough Beginning

The initial transition was very rough. The two employees that were moved out of the tier 1 Help Desk operations found themselves naturally pulled into the work flow repeatedly. This was compounded by our physical spaces - our office space includes all three of the full-time employees. Users and customers feel comfortable enough to enter and seek out help from whomever is available. This was great when our responsibilities were shared and we still do not see this as an issue because the problems are often small enough to be taken care of in a few minutes. But there is a definite decrease in sense of ticket ownership in the other two staff. They do not have the same sense of obligation towards the maintenance of their tickets. Often tickets would be listed as "in progress" for a long period of time in the system when in fact they had been completed or should have been updated with new information that might have let others complete them.

4.3.2 Refocus on Communication and Service

Helpdesk communication is still lacking overall, but is improving. One point of emphasis is that there is a need to work hard at customer service and to stay highly engaged with our customers. We have adopted the concept of "Total Ticket Ownership." This was first presented in a discussion during the 2013 SIGUCCS Management Symposium (no paper). Every time a ticket is addressed, the tech or employee involved must update the client in some personal way. The obvious method is to utilize our ticket system to send a personal message, but staff and students are encouraged to call or even visit as well. Customers have responded positively from the extra effort that we are making to work with them. We do not have a perfect track record yet and student techs are still responding with mixed reliability. Every semester has seen an improvement in their communication and we will continue to emphasize this.

4.3.3 Evolving Student Staff Roles

With the changes in professional staff responsibilities came changes for the student staff as well. We are seeing student resources increase in efficiency. The supervisor is acting as a resource monitor for the team. He is constantly watching the Help Desk queue and deploying students to assignments as they come on shift. Instructions for work are given when techs come on shift. This is similar to the old system in that there is not official training regimen for the students to go through. The difference is that the supervisor is making time to assign assignments to tickets or projects. This way the students get some amount of training every shift. one-on-one interviews have revealed that the students feel they receive enough information before each assignment to be able to execute. After a few weeks, some of the techs have identified "daily duties" that they can take care of before they begin addressing tickets. In addition to the Help Desk duties, the two ex-Help Desk employees do not hesitate to teach the techs about enterprise-level operations.

This summer will see two of the student technicians assisting with the deployment of our newly rebuilt virtual environment. They will be interacting with layers by performing regular maintenance on them and then managing deployment to the campus. In addition to maintenance, they will also get to participate in the creation of virtual labs around campus. Leading into the next semester we hope to elevate these two individuals to "level 2" technicians. They will be expected to sort through the simpler tier 2 tickets that would normally go to the employee responsible for the VDI environment. The idea is to alleviate some of his workload so that he can focus on other projects.

The overall goal is to create a student staff with tiers indicating skill and knowledge set. "Level 2" students would have proven proficiency at certain topics that would allow them to not only better support the community on those topics but also potentially train other students. "Level 3" technicians would be able to take on additional work away from the desk itself. This could potentially even lead to a kind of formal internship program.

4.3.4 Ongoing Challenges

A number of challenges still persist, some of which do not have a clear cut remedy. The staff are still pulled in multiple directions. Transitioning from "keeping the lights on" before the arrival of the current CIO to a fast-paced rebuild and reorganize effort after the change in leadership was easy. But we continue to operate in a sub-optimal manner with items falling through the cracks. We have not reached a point of equilibrium at which we can transition to a smoother and more controlled approach.

At the same time that student staff are transitioning into tiers of differing training and skill levels, we continue to face challenges in consistency. With a student staff this small, having any one student under-trained in an area affects 25-40% of the actual Help Desk hours. It is a good sign that some staff are gaining skills and becoming "level 2" technicians. But that leaves several that are still "level 1." This also highlights the challenge of trying to create tiers and levels at such a small institution – with a proportionately-sized student staff of only six, creating different levels of skill sets becomes quite a challenge. Increasing our student staff is a desire, but funding issues do not allow for many additional hours, either at the desk or on projects.

The fundamental challenge is that we are building a newly-designed, self-sufficient, student-staffed Help Desk "in production." We are experimenting in procedure and methods while trying to actively support end users. We do not have time or money to train the students outside of their regular shifts. We need students that have just signed their employment forms to somehow become seasoned technicians overnight, so that the other staff can be free to meet needs elsewhere. We realize, of course, that this cannot happen instantaneously and that we have to dedicate time to training, documentation, and management.

4.3.5 Next Steps

Work flow at the college is beginning to stabilize almost a year after the new CIO joined us. As we continue to move forward the Help Desk needs to work towards standardizing their expertise While there is nothing official in terms of training now, we are going to work towards documenting as much of our daily duties as we can so that incoming students will have resources readily available to successfully address tickets. Those techs that are able to take their roles to the second level of service will also be expected to document their growth so that those under them can learn by example.

5. CONCLUSION

Menlo College OIT still has a long way to go in its reorganization. We have identified a number of gaps and have undertaken significant projects in redesigning and rebuilding our virtual infrastructure and creating a self-sufficient Help Desk. We have reassigned duties to staff, changed job descriptions, and picked up new skills in a formal but still just-in-time manner. Our conversations with our partners are more structured and with clearer goals underlying those discussions. Project management has become a part of our processes.

Yet, as we move forward, a number of questions persist. Importantly, it is not just an issue of whether we can run a Help Desk operation almost entirely on a small pool of student staff, or if we can run an enterprise infrastructure. The fundamental question is whether we can reorganize the department and rebuild the Help Desk model without sacrificing reliability, accountability, and customer service. This is a tightrope that we continue to inch along, with the occasional slip. But we do have the methods (gap analysis, open team discussions, outreach, etc) to help get us there.

Leverage Your Mac to Support Multiple OS Environments

Thom Mattauch
VCU helpIT Center Manager
901 Park Ave Room B-30
Richmond, VA 23284
804-827-0532

mattauchtj@vcu.edu

Kendall Wylie
VCU helpIT Center Technician
901 Park Ave Room B-30
Richmond, VA 23284
804-828-0611

wylieks@vcu.edu

ABSTRACT

Would you like to use a single machine to support multiple platforms? Would you like a single point of support for Windows, Mac, Chrome OS, Android and more? This paper demonstrates how the VCU helpIT Center is leveraging Virtual Box to provide a single point of support through the iMac. In this paper we discuss how VCU sets up and uses Virtual Box to load various environments and discusses a use case of the system to provide support to an end user.

Categories and Subject Descriptors

K.6.2 [**Management of Computing and Information Systems**]: Computing equipment management.

General Terms

Management, Documentation, Performance, Reliability, Experimentation, Standardization

Keywords

Support, Virtualization, Operating Systems, Mobile, Customer Satisfaction

1. INTRODUCTION

Virginia Commonwealth University (known to the locals as VCU) sits in the heart of Richmond, Virginia, enrolling more than 31,000 students and employing over 18,000 faculty and staff members [1]. Since its establishment in 1968, VCU has expanded to include two downtown campuses in Richmond, as well as 6 satellite locations throughout the state of Virginia and Doha, Qatar. Offering 216 degree and certification programs through 13 separate schools and one college, VCU has been able to provide students with a full range of courses, from sculpture to microbiology, engineering to foreign language, business to philosophy, and many others.

The helpIT Center (see Image 1) is the central computing support office for the VCU community. Supporting an estimated user base of over 120,000 people, the helpIT Center provides "over the phone" tech support and two walk-up support locations on

our main downtown campuses. It is currently staffed by eight full-time employees, and an additional 12-15 part-time students and hourly workers.

Image 1. Walk-up counter at the main office on the VCU Monroe Park Campus.

Bring Your Own Device (BYOD) is the current trend at VCU. For Faculty and Staff, VCU has eliminated the purchase of institutional phones and has opted for offering a stipend for those using their personal cell phones for business use instead. Also, for those who did not have a smart phone, they offered up to $200 for the purchase of one for any Faculty and Staff member who wished to get one for business use. As a result, an influx in new smart phone mobile users began to come into the helpIT Center. Along with this, the increase in the use of Tablets caused an increase in the number of alternative OS devices to begin showing up (Windows Mobile, iOS, Android) on campus and off.

2. WHY THE NEED FOR VIRTUALIZATION?

Supporting multiple environments used to consist of the purchase and ownership of multiple devices. However due to shrinking budgets, the purchase of the various devices to support the wide array of Operating Systems was cost prohibitive and logistically challenging. Supporting a user base as large as one at VCU means nearly every version of operating system and nearly every variation of mobile device will be used by the users at VCU. In addition, consumer technology is a rapidly evolving industry; to keep up with it in a physical means would involve a nearly constant supply of devices to support the ever-changing landscape of the consumer market. To support the mission at the VCU helpIT Center means that no user will be turned away from our desk. To enable the staff to support these users, a centralized tool needed to be developed for the technicians. This is where the idea of virtualizing all environments came from.

2.1 What platforms are supported?

To provide comprehensive support at the VCU helpIT Center, we evaluated the needs of the end user. Out of that evaluation we determined that we would need to support the Windows environment from XP through Windows 8, Mac OS 10.4 through 10.8, iOS, various versions of the Android OS, Chrome OS, and Linux. The use of the Mac for the virtual host system was simple. Licensing dictates that the Mac OS can only run on Apple hardware (for the purpose of virtualization). Furthermore, the technicians at the helpIT Center all have either an iMac or a MacBook Pro at their disposal. By virtualizing on the Mac, all OS's supported at the VCU helpIT Center area available on one machine.

2.2 What solutions exist for virtualization?

There are several solutions available for virtualizing on the Mac Platform. Virtual Box is an open source solution that works for most of the OS's that need to be virtualized but does have limitations [2]. VMware Fusion and Parallels are both commercially available and supported platforms, which offer the ability to virtualize all platforms which the VCU helpIT Center requires.

3. WHAT IS THE VCU HELPIT CENTER DOING TO SUPPORT ALL PLATFORMS?

The VCU helpIT Center is currently piloting virtualization with two employees with a roll out planned for summer 2013 to all technicians. The current setup involves 27" iMacs loaded with Mac OS 10.8, 8GB of RAM, and Virtual Box (see Image 2). For our Windows platforms we have a Lenovo desktop with dual monitors. We chose Virtual Box as our virtual machine host because of its open source nature, low cost, and broad community support.

Image 2. Desk Setup with windows and Mac Platforms side by side.

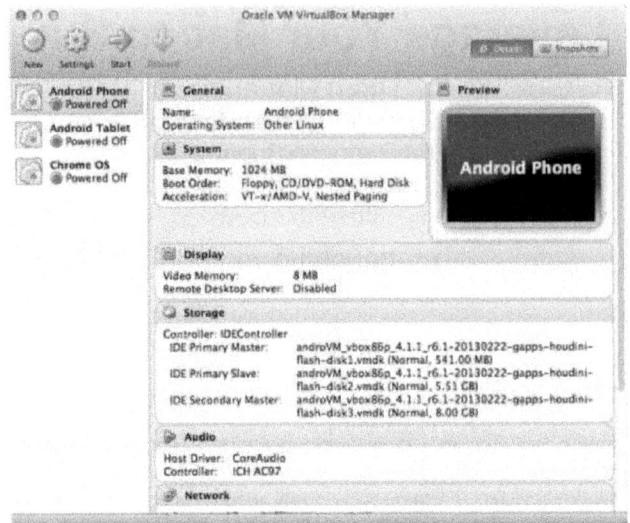

Image 3. Landing page of Virtual box on a Mac.

3.1 What Operating Systems does the VCU helpIT Center support through VM?

Currently the VCU helpIT Center is running Android Phone (Image 3), Android Tablet (Image 4), Chrome OS (Image 5), and Linux in a virtual environment. Windows 7 and 8 were excluded from this project at this time because each technician currently has a Windows box at each workstation. This may change in the future to assist with the growing number of new and old Windows versions we are expected to support.

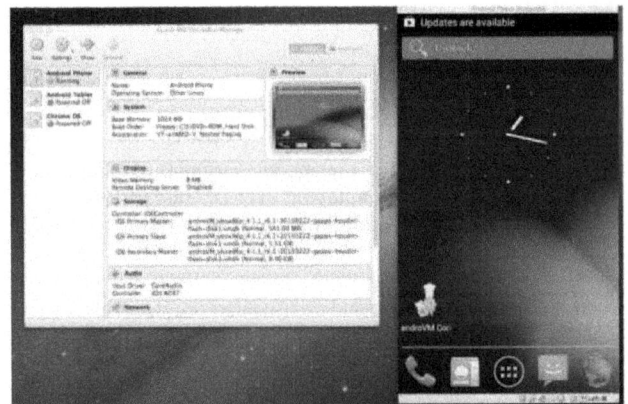

Image 4. Android Phone VM running.

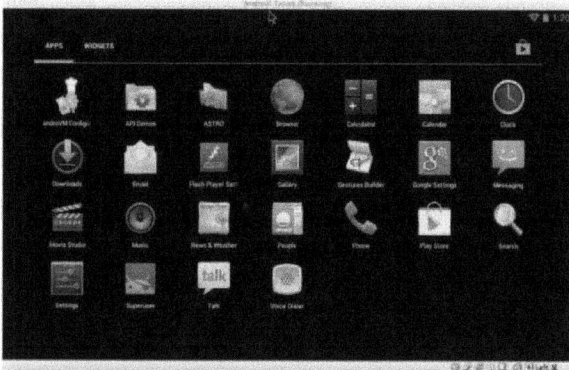

Image 5. Apps screen in Android Tablet running.

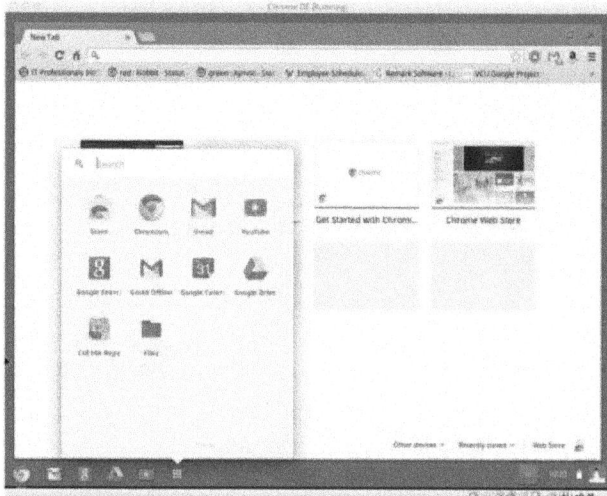

Image 6. Chrome OS instance VM running.

3.2 Limitations

The only limitations presented in this environment are with the Android OS. Because of the open source nature of Android, various device manufacturers load a custom build of Android on their devices. Because this is a Virtual Machine, the VCU helpIT Center is leveraging generic installs of the Android OS. Additionally, because this is a generic install, full functionality of some aspects of the Android OS are unavailable. Furthermore, the install of the Google Play store is challenging. The Chrome OS version that we use is not an official release and therefore as the developer states: "does not represent the full Chrome OS experience."

3.3 Why not iOS?

iOS is one of the most popular platforms we support on campus however, licensing is one of the biggest hurdles to get over when it comes to iOS. iOS is not licensed to be run in a virtual environment. An iOS emulator is included in the XCode development suite available on the Mac App Store for free. However it is designed for the development and testing of iOS apps. The critical areas of the OS are not available in the emulator. For example, the mail app and calendar are not present. However, for the purposes of support at the VCU helpIT Center, the need did not exist for an out of the box solution for providing

support for iOS environments because, simply put, everyone of the technicians at the VCU helpIT Center already had an iOS device. We do have one communal iOS device available to all members the support team, but it is rarely used due to the previously stated reasons. iOS also has the added benefit of consistency in menu structure between the iPod Touch/iPhone OS, and the iPad OS. For example, the sequence to update the stored password for an email account is the same between an iPhone and iPad.

3.4 Not all OS's covered?

While there are other players in the Mobile OS market, the VCU helpIT center based its decision on which OS's to support on the needs of the user base. Windows Mobile has not registered on VCU's support radar. Blackberry has been a big player at VCU, though its user base is slowly dwindling. However, Blackberry does not offer an option for Virtualization at this point and we have noticed a huge drop in requests for support. In these cases we fully rely on existing written documentation and web searches to support users with these OS's.

4. USE CASES

With the practical application of these virtual machines we can better assist customers setting up university email, calendar, contacts, mobile sites, and the VCU Mobile application. We unfortunately cannot emulate the setup of the wireless networks because the virtual machines are using virtual bridged network adapters; therefore no "wi-fi" chip exists. Sometimes users will also call in for help navigating around their mobile device. It's beneficial to have the virtual machines because documentation does not necessarily exist for that type of request.

4.1 Example Use Case

A user may call in and need assistance setting up their VCU email account on their Android mobile device (Image 6). We launch the virtual machine we have and create a live visual reference while assisting the user. We can make verbal references for the user like "Tap the grey sign on button" or "The icon that looks like a stamp." Additionally, we can go through the process ourselves and setup an email account along with the user. This is very helpful when the instructions we have on file do not match up with what the user is seeing.

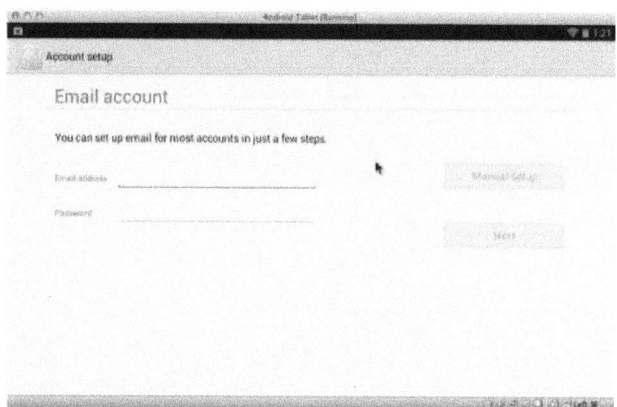

Image 7. Initial email setup screen in Android Tablet.

5. CONCLUSION

Going forward virtual machines seem to be a viable solution to supporting more and more platforms. We have been able to utilize virtual box in walking users through email setup and trouble shooting on their Android Phones. The virtualized Chrome machines have allowed us to become more familiar with its functionality and prepare us for eventual support calls. It is a proven tool in the arsenal we can use. It's common knowledge that you can virtualize traditional desktop operating systems, but virtualizing mobile and newer alternative OS software is relatively new. Since we now have this experience under our belt we can easily add future operating systems as they become available and deploy this tool to the rest of our staff.

6. RFERENCES

1   DOI= http://www.vcu.edu/about/stats.php.

2   https://www.virtualbox.org/

80

Climbing the Microsoft Mountain: Deploying Microsoft Solutions for Directory Services, Email, and Calendar

Beth Rugg
Ithaca College
953 Danby Rd
Ithaca, NY 14850
607-274-7349
erugg@ithaca.edu

ABSTRACT

In 2010, Ithaca College began making significant changes to the desktop environment. Over the course of three years and four different projects, we moved email, calendar, and directory services to Microsoft. This paper will discuss migrating our users from Novell to Active Directory, moving from a locally hosted email solution to Microsoft Live@edu, moving from Oracle Calendar to Microsoft Live@edu, and finally migrating email and calendar to Microsoft Office 365. Each project was unique in scope, involved a separate timeline and implementation schedule, and presented its own unique challenges. Some of the highlights of these projects include physically touching 4000 Macintosh and Windows computers as part of the Novell to Active Directory migration, determining what email clients to support for the Live email migration, and teaching 1500 users a new way to schedule and manage meetings during final exam week! Once all that was done, we still faced one final migration from Microsoft Live@edu to Microsoft Office 365. This paper will provide a high level overview of these projects, key policy and implementation decisions and lessons learned from a client services perspective.

Categories and Subject Descriptors

H.4.1 [**Information Systems Applications**]: Office Automation – *time management.*

H.4.3 [**Information Systems Applications**]: Communication Applications – *electronic mail.*

K.6.1 [**Management of Computing and Information Systems**]: Project and People Management – *strategic information systems planning, training.*

General Terms

Management, Documentation, Human Factors, Standardization.

Keywords

email, calendar, Novell, Active Directory, Microsoft, systems, project management, enterprise, change, transitions, users, Windows, Macintosh, support.

SIGUCCS'13, November 3–8, 2013, Chicago, IL, USA.
Copyright © 2013 ACM 978-1-4503-2318-5/13/11...$15.00.
http://dx.doi.org/10.1145/2504776.2504797

1. OVERVIEW

Ithaca College is a private residential college in Upstate New York with 6000 undergrads and 1500 faculty and staff. There are five schools within the college, Humanities and Sciences, Business, Music, Communication, and Health Science and Human Performance. The college's computer inventory is 2/3 Windows and 1/3 Macintosh workstations. Information Technology Services (ITS) is a centralized IT organization supporting both the academic and administrative needs of the campus community. The ITS teams involved in these projects were Desktop Services (9 people), User Support Services (8 people), Network Services (5 people) and System Administration (4 people).

2. NOVELL TO ACTIVE DIRECTORY

In 2008, as part of a network redesign, the ITS leadership made the decision was to move from Novell to Active Directory. Novell had lost market share to Microsoft and Active Directory had become the directory standard for computing environments. At this time, the network infrastructure was being completely redesigned from a flat structure to one based on security and limited access. This paper will focus on the Novell to Active Directory change but, because of other changes, traditional Novell to Active Directory migration strategies, tools and processes would not work; every workstation, all 4500 of them, had to be physically touched to accomplish our goals.

Our Novell environment consisted of three file servers, one for faculty, one for students, and one for staff with 2 terabytes of data supporting 105 departments each with a unique file structure and access rights. It also included one print server with more than 350 printers that involved over 8000 user accounts for faculty, staff, and students. Windows workstations were using XP and required logins. The Mac environment included four operating systems, 10.4, 10.5, 10.6, and 10.7, was not managed and did not require directory login. Users had administrative privileges on their computers.

The new Active Directory environment would consist of 1 file server for faculty and staff users (not students) and two print servers, one for labs and one for administrative use. Both Windows and Mac computers would be joined to the domain and require authentication to use the machines.

The scope of this effort was to place the computer on the new network, join the computer to the Active Directory domain, migrate the user profile, create the new Active Directory account, and help users add the new Windows printers. The project was divided into two phases, workstation migration and file migration. The planning for this project began in 2009; workstation implementation started summer 2011 and continued through

February 2012. File migration began in July of 2012 and was completed by October 2012.

Everything was new to the team. The team was composed of ~twenty people representing networking services, desktop services, system administration and user support services. Over the course of the project we determined how to manage user credentials, developed numerous processes and procedures for migrating profiles, learned about and implemented use of the Bradford Network Access control device, developed processes for managing Mac and Windows computers, developed staffing strategies and goals, developed metrics, schedules, and tracking mechanisms for the migration, developed extensive training, documentation, and communication channels for users and technical staff. We developed an implementation schedule, hired extra desktop technicians to visit every workstation, and came in ahead of schedule and under budget with over 99% of the assets migrated by close of the project.

2.1 Key Decisions

There was not a pre-defined process or methodology to help us figure out what to do. From what we could tell, no one had done what we were trying to do. Vendors could offer limited assistance with parts of the project. There were many key decisions that affected the outcome.

A network engineer consultant was brought on board to work side by side with the project team. This consultant had expertise in network redesign and network access control.

The decision to have the project lead come from User Services forced the team to wrestle with security and usability issues throughout the project. Helpdesk specialists led the testing, quality assurance, and process development aspects of the project. Everything we did was viewed from a user experience lens. That didn't mean usability "won out" over security but it did mean usability factored into the decisions that were made.

The project was divided into standard phases: research and development, testing, quality assurance, piloting and implementation. Each phase was important because of the work accomplished and the team dynamics. The research phase was important because the team defined vocabulary, functional requirements and options, contacted vendors, and researched what other institutions had done. The recommendation to redesign the network and move from Novell to Active Directory was made by consultants and approved by college leadership. Technical leads had had a limited voice in the decision. During this phase each team member began taking responsibility for implementing the change. Initially, the team was very large, over twenty people, over time the team divided into working groups to tackle specific tasks.

With the new emphasis on security, the organization wrestled with whether or not users would continue to have administrative rights in the new environment. Because of human resource restrictions, we decide to maintain status quo and the users kept these rights on their local workstation.

Because we are a mixed operating system environment, we wrestled with managing the Mac computers. We knew Windows computers would be managed through group policy and researched whether or not to create the same managed experience for Mac users by setting up the Apple dual directory. In the end, we decided to not implement these Mac management tools.

The team wanted to design an experience that had minimal impact on the user. That decision forced us to figure out how to migrate user profiles. We ended up using the ForesnIT tools for Windows users and developed a script for Mac users. However, because we were also setting up a new printer environment, we did not find a way to migrate printers and had to have users add printers after the migration. We left detailed documentation for them and the majority of users were able to successfully do this.

We spent a lot of time figuring out how to integrate Active Directory user credentials into the existing environment. We do not have single-sign on. During the migration process, users would have four or five primary institutional accounts: one for the human resources and the financial system, one for email, one for student information system, one for Novell, and one for Active Directory. We made sure the Active Directory and the email account (Sun One Directory Services) had the same policies applied to them: length, complexity, and password expiration. We modified the existing home grown password reset tool to pass credentials to both SODS and Active Directory. To the users, it appeared that there was only one account. We did rebrand the tool from "email password utility" to "Netpass utility" to reflect this change.

Windows 7 was released during the course of the project. Because all of our processes and scripts were developed and tested against Windows XP, ITS decided to delay the release of Windows 7 until after the project completion. Other releases and projects were also delayed including the release of Office 2010/2011 and the email and calendar migration.

We decided to phase in the implementation and developed a schedule that took regular academic and technology refresh cycles into account. We decided to start the process with labs and eclassrooms because we fully manage the computers in those spaces. In our technology refresh program, administrative computers get replaced in the fall and academic computers get replaced in the spring. We decided to implement the faculty and staff computer migration by doing the opposite, academic computers first and then administrative computers. It was simply too complex to develop a schedule that took both major efforts into account. This approach worked well for us.

We identify project liaisons for every department. We used them as communication liaisons with their department and as trainers. They became our primary contact with any given department. We also communicated directly with every user. Each user would receive a direct email 2 weeks, 1 week, and the day prior to the scheduled migration date.

We piloted everything before we started an implementation. The pilot usually involved migrating one computer, testing and using it, and then migrating the rest of the computers. Before we started with the department migration, we reached out to all of the departments and asked for volunteers. This effort helped to identify issues and make the department coordinators more comfortable with the changes. We modified our asset tracking system to track the computer migrations. This enabled us to maintain accurate records and inventories. We hired seven temporary desktop service technicians for the department implementation. Because they were temp staff we decided to work over the December shutdown. But, once we started we were committed to the implementation; we wouldn't be able to delay or stop and re-adjust our processes. We also had to develop schedules that kept seven people busy 40 hours a week for 12 weeks. The actual workstation migration took on average 45 minutes per computer. Macs tended to be more difficult to join to the domain at took longer than Windows workstations.

Once we decided to migrate workstations and files in two phases, we had to figure out what to migrate first, files or computers. Because the new network was more secure than the old network, we decided to move the computers first into the more secure environment, leave the Novell client on the workstations, and allow the new network to have access to the old network so that users could still access their Novell files.

The migration and configuration of eclassroom computers presented a unique challenge. We knew it was going to take a significant amount of time to migrate everyone and that once we started the implementation, some faculty would be using their Active Directory credentials on their personal workstations while others would be using the Novell credentials. We needed a consistent environment that worked the same regardless of how their office workstation was configured; we also needed fast login time so that class time was not negatively impacted. We decided to have the eclassroom computers login to a local account. If the faculty member needed to access Novell files, he/she would use the Novell client; if access was needed to the Windows file system, active directory credentials could be used. As it turns out if Novell and Active credentials were the same then Windows computers would "pass through" the credentials to Novell; the user didn't have to actually use the Novell client.

We decided to migrate files over the summer because fewer users would be impacted. From a scheduling perspective, we planned to migrate the majority of user' files prior to fall start-up. We looked into moving all the files over one weekend but because of the complexity of access rights, this strategy was abandoned. We devised a schedule that started with user home directories and then moved into department files starting with simplest security group access settings first. We migrated home directories for 1500 users over one weekend and then migrated three or four departments three nights a week, 5-6 pm usually, for about six weeks. We would migrate on one day and leave the next free so that we could handle problems. We left the most complex departments to the end. We also decided not to require users to "clean up" data however we did work with specific departments regarding specific data questions. The file migration process was to do a large copy and then run a differential copy at cutover. At cutover, user access to Novell was disabled. We also decided to move from three file servers to one for ease of use and better collaboration. Prior to the file migration, we also migrated email to Microsoft Live@edu. Because SkyDrive cloud file storage was a service, we did not allocate file server space to students and promoted the SkyDrive offering instead.

2.2 Timeline

This project was extremely complex and implemented in many phases. There was a research phase (September 2009 – March 2011), a testing phase (March 2011-July 2011), and an implementation phase (July 2011 – February 2012). The implementation phase for the workstation migration involved these steps: beta testers, lab and eclassroom pilot, lab and eclassroom implementation, Information Technology Services pilot, department pilot, academic department implementation, administrative departments implementation, and exceptions and special needs.

The File Migration steps included department pilot (not ITS since our access rights were very complex), simple to complex security group departments, and finally exceptions including Admissions, Res Life, Financial Services, and FTP access. In general academic departments had simpler access rights than administrative departments.

2.3 Challenges

We encountered many human and technical challenges along the way. Team dynamics were challenging. We had to figure out how to work together in a coordinated way. Accountability in a project can be a challenge since there is not a direct reporting structure between the project manager and the technical leads. Communication itself can be perceived to be a threat. Some ITS departments are more transparent than others, some individuals are more team-oriented than others. Agreement on timelines, schedules, and deadlines was difficult. Workload was always an issue. Despite these challenges, over time, individuals worked through these issues and were able to achieve the goals of the project. Language was a barrier. We had to spend time as a team defining vocabulary and refining language so that we were all talking about the same thing. It was difficult to come to consensus as to what had to be accomplished.

We had to implement many changes all at once and could not find a blue print for developing the processes we needed. So, we had to develop everything from scratch. Finding the balance between usability and security was, and continues to be, a challenge. None of the support staff knew Active Directory and had to learn about it in the midst of this project.

Taken in its entirety, this project was overwhelming but the team learned to tackle each question and problem individually and kept digging until all of the questions were answered. Then, we developed the processes, tested them, refined them, and implemented them. Internal and external communication was challenging especially during implementation. We held daily morning and afternoon touch base meetings with desktop services, support, networking, and system administration to keep everyone on the same page. We developed robust Helpdesk tracking mechanisms. We held weekly planning meetings to coordinate future migrations. All of this communication and coordination was difficult, tedious, time consuming, and yet critical to ensuring our success.

The Mac migration and subsequent support tended to be more difficult than the Windows migration. We created a "make admin" script for the Mac environment that worked for the most part during the initial migration but has presented subsequent problems. Wireless printing "broke" during the migration because of differences between Novell and Windows print environment. Novell mapped drives created login problems for users during the migration. Mapped network drives would send credential requests prior to authentication creating lock out situations. The Helpdesk understood the symptoms and came up with work-arounds.

2.4 Outcome

Over 4000 workstations and 315 printers were migrated between July 1, 2011 and May 31, 2013. The eclassroom, lab, and individual department migrations went well. We were able to successfully implement the plan and stay on schedule. The maximum number of computers that were migrated in a single day with seven technicians and two network engineers was 70; the maximum number of printers migrated in a day was 17. Each migration took no more than 45 minutes per workstation. One student computer had over 400 individual profiles that were migrated. We offered 44 workshops and over 100 people attended the hands on training.

Over 400 planning meetings were held, over 600 planning tasks were completed, over 600 Helpdesk tickets related to testing were generated and solved, over 930 user notices sent out, and over 1100 Helpdesk tickets were generated during migration implementation (33% of migrations generating a ticket.) We only had to re-image one computer and we couldn't get one computer to join the domain. Migrating users of Dropbox, an unsupported piece of software, was problematic because the profile didn't copy properly.Thirty eight hundred additional man hours were used during the implementation and 275 workstations were considered exceptions that required individual consultation and took us from March to May to get them migrated. We came in ahead of schedule and under budget. A major success story for the department and the project team!

2.5 Lessons Learned

If working with a consultant, try and get the right consultant. Personality issues with the first consultant reduced the team's effectiveness. I attribute much of our success to the second consultant who understood security and usability, could explain highly technical issues in a way the majority of people could understand, was willing to work as part of a team, was readily available and developed creative solutions when needed.

Internal and external communication, training, and documentation are very important in a project of this size. Agendas, meeting notes, regular touch-base meetings, space for a testing environment, thoughtful planning, developing clear goals, and milestones cannot be overlooked. Team dynamics can't be ignored. If you have a large project team, divide it into smaller working groups to increase effectiveness. Keep team sizes small and focused if possible. The length of the project will be affected by individual work load. If we had back-filled positions and allowed team members to work on this project full time, we may have been able to accomplish our goals in a shorter time frame.

We still have not implemented tools for managing Macs. The Macs are working fine so there seems to be little interest in doing the work to provide a more managed environment. Project managers should know that whatever doesn't get done during the project probably won't get done, its human nature. Other key lessons: identify the right people for the project team, plan the project, the devil is in the details, take it one day at a time, you can never over communicate, document everything, and set up a project governance structure and process for those issues that the team can't agree on.

3. EMAIL TO MICROSOFT LIVE@EDU

In 2011, it was obvious we needed a new email system. The current email system, provided by Mirapoint, was 4 years old and had significant capacity and performance issues. Costs increases for the Mirapoint solution were projected to be in excess of 50% the next fiscal year. The College's enterprise calendar system, Oracle Calendar, was nearing end-of-life. ITS management and staff looked into options: Google versus Microsoft versus a third party vendor; outsourcing student mail but keeping faculty and staff mail local, setting up a local Exchange environment etc. ITS wanted a solution that would integrate with our new Active Directory infrastructure. Research revealed that more than half of 4-year colleges had outsourced student email services, and around

40% had either done the same for faculty and staff email or were considering it. After researching alternatives, the decision was made to outsource all email to Microsoft's Live@Edu.

This recommendation was made to the campus community and administration. Information sessions were held across campus in January of 2012. Some students would have preferred Google, but faculty and staff didn't seem to care. The email performance issues were so bad that the community was eager to accept anything better. The recommendation was approved by college administration.

3.1 Key Decisions

Early on, the project team had to decide whether to do the work internally or consult with a vendor. Because of the performance problems, compressed project schedule, and limited mail migration knowledge, we decided to contract with a vendor to actually create the mailboxes and migrate the email. We chose Business 2 Business Consulting (B2B); B2B could guide us through the decision-making and the steps of this transition. B2B had experience migrating from a locally hosted Exchange environment to Live@edu, but no experience going from a 3rd party email system to Live@edu (no vendor did).

We had to decide whether it would be a phased in migration or a precipice migration. We decided that a precipice migration would work best for our community because it allowed us to control adoption. The Mirapoint contract had to be renewed in the middle of June so we were highly motivated to get everyone onto the new system prior to that deadline. We needed to decide if we would migrate email and calendar at the same time. There were too many variables; we did email first and calendar later. We hoped that the calendar migration would take place within a few months of the email migration, before the fall semester, but in the end, there was a six-month gap between the migrations. This gap allowed us to ramp up support for Outlook, get users to adopt Office 2010/2011, and provide users with some breathing room between all the changes we were inflicting on them.

When we made the decision to outsource, Microsoft had two offerings for the education community: Microsoft Live@edu or Office 365. Live@edu had SkyDrive; Office 365 did not but came with Sharepoint and Lync (the A2 license offering). Live@edu was 1.5 years from end of life but it was a more mature service offering. We decided to migrate to Live@edu knowing that we would be forced into another upgrade in the near future. We had low risk tolerance and wanted to migrate to the mature solution with more proven migration processes.

We decided not to do any username clean-up. But we had to decide what to do with users who already had a Hotmail account that used the @ithaca.edu domain name. Those users were "evicted" from the Microsoft environment prior to the move. The @ithaca.edu name was proprietary and would only be associated with college-managed accounts. Users were notified of this change and had to go into the Hotmail system and change their username prior to the migration.

We needed to decide whether to do separate domains for students, faculty, and staff. For ease of use we decided to go with one domain. We also were having student email for life discussions with Alumni Affairs and Microsoft Live@edu could meet this need. We are implementing student email for life beginning June 2013. From a support perspective, we had to determine what email clients would be supported with Microsoft Live@edu. This decision was difficult because we knew that we would also be upgrading calendar in the near future and we were in the midst of the Microsoft Office 2010/2011 rollout. The supported email clients prior to the migration were Thunderbird for Windows users and Apple Mail for Macs. Many Mac users also used Thunderbird. The majority of users had Office 2007/2008. Outlook email client for the Macs is only available in Office 2011. So, if we went to supporting Outlook right away, Mac users would also be forced to upgrade their versions of Office. The project team (~ fifteen people) was comprised of a project manager and representatives from IT leadership, system administration, desktop support, networking and user support services. The team weighed usability, ease of support, functionality, and user change impacts against each other and decided on a phased in approach of moving users from Thunderbird to Outlook 2010/2011.

We decided that in June 2012, at the point of migration, we would continue to support Thunderbird for Windows environment and Apple Mail for the Mac environment. Users would have to make configuration changes but they would not have to learn a new application. We would tie Outlook support to the calendar migration, at that point all calendar users would have to use Outlook email client. Webmail users would be largely unaffected but would see significant user interface changes. We also needed to get everyone to one version of Office, either 2010 for Windows or 2011 for Macs. In January, when we released Office 2010/2011 to the user community we had announced that Office 2007/2008 would not be supported after December 2012 but user adoption had been slow.

In October 2012, we released Outlook 2010/2011 documentation to the user community and announced support for Outlook and email, but not calendar. We encouraged users to move from Thunderbird to Outlook at that time, in front of the calendar migration. In order to do that, users had to upgrade to Office 2010/2011. There were pros and cons to this approach. Support services staff and the user communities were both in constant transition between June and December. But, users were given plenty of time to adopt into these changes on their own prior to the forced migration. This process allowed ITS staff to manage the change variables.

3.2 Timeline
Once these decisions were made, we set the schedule. Because we didn't want to renew the Mirapoint license in mid-June 2012, we decided to migrate all users over the weekend of June 11th. This date was after the spring semester but before summer freshman orientation. Pilot testing would begin in May 2012.

3.3 Challenges
Finding the right vendor, the short timeline, learning the new environment, and defining support were a few of the challenges we faced with this project. The system administration team had to set up the account provisioning infrastructure. We decided to use ILM (identity lifecycle management) and PCNS (password change notification service) instead of the federated option, ADFS. We could get ILM and PCNS up and running faster than ADFS and ADFS would require five to six additional servers. But, by not going with ADFS we would be forced into another migration prior to 2014.

Defining Mac support was challenging. Because Apple Mail was the supported email client and it is part of the operating system,

the team did not want to "stop supporting" that client. However, by supporting multiple clients, the support burden would increase for the Helpdesk. We ended up being "fuzzy" about our Mac support.

We had to decide what to tell users to do with their local mail. We could migrate all mail on the servers but did not have access to local mail. We thought the mail could remain local but the Outlook email client does not read Thunderbird local mail. This factored into our decision to delay support for Outlook. This gave users six months to move their local mail to the Live servers. Thunderbird contacts are also stored locally so a process was documented telling users how to migrate their local contacts.

Not all of the college's email was migrating to Live@edu, only faculty, staff, and student accounts. List serve email would still be managed locally. Our local spam filter and list serve server would still be managed locally. This had minimal impact on the end users, but system administration had to do some reconfiguration. Bulk emailing was an issue. Users can only send 1500 individual messages in a 24 hour period from Live@edu. We had to create a bulk mailer option for the user community. The test system was set up about four weeks in advance. Testing and documentation had to be done in a very compressed time frame. SkyDrive and Messenger are two additional services that are provided with the Live@edu suite. The focus of the project was email and yet we couldn't ignore these services since they are part of the user interface. User Support team members spent some time understanding the service offerings and documenting the account set up process. We had to make sure our users received timely email communications about the change and that we pointed them to other resources in advance. If they relied on looking at email and they couldn't access their email after the migration call volume would dramatically increase.

Live@edu has a message size limit of 25 MB. We ran a report that showed over 1000 messages were greater than that. We notified individual users about this problem in advance and asked them to either save the messages locally or delete the files. We wanted to integrate Live@edu with our portal environment and had to use a non-Microsoft supported way to do that. We didn't want to move unnecessary mail so we asked users to voluntarily clean-up their mailboxes. About three weeks prior to migration we started doing email synchronization with Live@edu servers. After the initial sync, the process would do a differential sync. However, because we didn't want to lose any mail at cutover once the MX record was changed to Microsoft Live@edu, the last sync did not delete any messages so any messages that the users had deleted the week prior to cut over were still in the new system causing frustration for a few of our good citizens.

Users had to make configuration changes to their email clients. These changes were well documented, however some of the mobile devices did not auto discover the server name so users had to hard code the server settings in their mobile devices and we had to scramble at the last minute to update our documentation.

We were very concerned that our users would start using the calendar feature in Outlook and OWA prior to the calendar migration. This problem had the potential to cause mass confusion for meeting schedulers. We had no technical way to prevent this and asked the community to wait to use this feature. They did.

Live@edu has system names that are reserved for folders: Contacts, Tasks, and Calendar. If there is a user-generated folder at the top level with these names, the folder and their contents will

NOT be migrated. We sent the list of reserved names out to account holders and asked them to fix it prior to migration.

The initial directory mapping showed too much user information including the college ID number. Since we didn't realize what directory information was visible, we fed it all to Microsoft. Once it was there, we couldn't undo it. But, the scripts were redone so that only the email and name fields were shown. Users had to reset forwarding addresses.

Usernames have a 20 character limit in Microsoft so 6 account names had to be shortened. These were mainly departmental account names.

3.4 Outcomes

The actual mail migration went extremely well. It happened over a weekend starting on Friday evening. The production system was available for testing on Sunday morning. A miscommunication occurred and the production system was made available to the user community through the portal during the final testing but since we had told people the system would be down until Monday morning, this mistake didn't cause any system issues. According to the error logs, less than 100 users had issues related to their mail. Most of these issues were related to individual emails.

We migrated server email and contacts, we linked to the Global directory and we migrated user forwarding information. Users had to recreate contact groups and migrate local contacts and local mail.

The Helpdesk experienced high call volume on the first three days after the migration as was expected. The majority of issues were user oriented. No mail was lost. We did have problems with Word documents on Live@edu servers and accessing them with Thunderbird but it turned out to be a setting in Thunderbird that needed to be tweaked.

3.5 Lessons Learned

Overall, the email migration went very well. No mail was lost; the majority of users had access to their email Monday morning. Since we didn't force users to change their email clients, there wasn't much of a learning curve for our users. Many people reported liking the new webmail interface and its increased functionality.

The team worked well together to achieve the project goals with limited time. It is obvious that the more time the support team can have in a testing environment, the better. Because some of the scripts were tweaked right before migration, we had to do a second round of testing. Project team staff were devoted to this effort for the six weeks prior to implementation. Detailed planning, working with a vendor to guide us, in-depth testing, detailed change documentation, and training are all requirements for a successful project.

4. ORACLE CALENDAR TO MICROSOFT LIVE@EDU

Oracle Calendar was the institutional calendaring system we used for many years. The Oracle Calendar product was at end of life with support ending in 2013. Oracle Calendar did not work on the 10.7 and 10.8 Mac operating systems. Since Microsoft Live@edu provided a calendar solution along with email, ITS decided to migrate user data from Oracle Calendar to Outlook Calendar over the December 2012 shut-down, six months after the email migration. The original plan was to migrate calendar much closer to the email migration date. We were concerned that having the possibility of two calendar systems for the community would become confusing. However, the user community was beginning to suffer "change fatigue" and the calendar migration would have occurred in August around semester start up. So the decision was made to delay the migration for one semester.

For Oracle Calendar users, this change was big! The interface was completely new, functionality, delegate rights, and handling meeting responses were all different. Out of all of the Microsoft changes (Novell to Active Directory, email, and now calendar), this one had the most user impact.

ITS developed five pieces of documentation and four hands on workshops to help users with this change. Unfortunately, the timing was such that the users had to learn about the new application at semester's end. But, since the impact was primarily on administrative users, this was manageable. We warned the users that it would take time and effort to get used to the new system and to not ignore our messages. We also direct emailed all calendar users multiple times so that they were very aware of the change, the downtime, and the training opportunities.

4.1 Key Decisions

Mac and Windows users would have to use the Outlook 2010/2011 client to access their calendars. We would not support the Mac calendar app. That meant we had to start supporting Outlook for email first and then calendar. Three months prior to migration, ITS officially started supporting the Outlook 2010/2011 email client. All users were notified of this change and Oracle Calendar users were strongly encouraged to voluntarily adopt its usage prior to the calendar migration. Non Oracle Calendar users could continue to use Thunderbird until June 2013. Many faculty are not calendar users and were not going to be affected by the calendar migration so we didn't want to force them to change email clients mid-stream. Users had to first upgrade their Office suite and then learn how to use Outlook email. Of course, the majority of users waited until the last minute to upgrade.

We had to decide whether we would migrate user data for them or have users do it themselves. We were advised users that converting Oracle Calendar files into .pst files and migrating them to Live@edu was not ideal and very time consuming. We didn't want users to have to recreate data as that was too time consuming and not acceptable. We decided to get a vendor to help migrate user data. We chose CalMover as the vendor. We had to decide how much old data to migrate. Because we were not sure about how long the migration would take, we decided to migrate one month of historical data. If we had time after the migration we could go back and migrate more. We decided it was important to differentiate migrated data from new calendar entries and accomplished that by placing an asterisk (*) in front of the migrated meetings.

Since there was not a one-to-one correlation between designate rights (Oracle Calendar) and delegated rights (Outlook) we decided not to migrate any access rights but to train users to do it themselves. We also decided to do individual consultations with the President's Council support staff to assist them and teach them how to set up proper delegate rights. Since access rights were not being migrated and we were relying on users to do that for themselves we didn't want any upper administration calendars to be unintentionally visible to the public. We had to decide if and how long Oracle Calendar would be available to the campus community after migration. It was important that no new meetings get created in Oracle Calendar. We wanted users to have read access only but that was not technically possible. In the end we decided it was a training issue and continued to allow users to view their Oracle Calendar data until March 2013.

4.2 Timeline
We had the vendor identified in October 2012 leaving us three months to do testing and develop documentation and training. The schedule was set to migrate calendar data over December shut down. The actual data migration took about three days for 1600 accounts.

4.3 Challenges
The support staff had to learn the Outlook client. Understanding delegate rights and translating how those rights would and should be used by the community members was difficult. We relied on the test system being set up for learning and experimentation. The test system was available to us six weeks prior to migration creating a very short window of time from access and testing to delivering training (about one month).

We also weren't familiar with current designate right practices and couldn't easily make recommendations to the campus community. Individual consultations with President's Council helped. We quickly decided that we would recommend "editor" rights over "delegate" rights because we thought that was closer to the Oracle Calendar experience. Setting up delegate rights continued to be the most difficult aspect of this migration.

Because we are a multi-platform environment, we needed to learn OWA, Outlook for Windows, and Outlook for Mac. There are significant differences between the two clients; Mac users tend to have less functionality. We needed to know and document the differences.

We had over 300 room resources in Oracle Calendar. Not all of those resources were actual rooms, some were more like department planners. We needed to clean up this list before recreating the room resources in the Microsoft Live environment. We identified the resource owners, emailed them directly to find out what resources were actively being used and ended up reducing the number of resources by 50%.

The experience for room resource owners was very different because of mailboxes being associated with the room resource. We had to decide what the default resource settings would be (publicly available or limited access) and communicate that to the resource owners so they could change the settings if needed. It took some time to understand the default setting options. We decided to make all resources private and let the owners make them public.

There was some confusion about room resources in general. The room resources in Oracle Calendar are primarily private conference rooms, and not classrooms or publicly reservable spaces. This difference was important to the Registrar's Office and Conference and Event Services staff who are responsible for centralized scheduling. The confusion was easily cleared up.

Because of the short timeline and the time of the year, we could not use our student training staff to help deliver training. This put a lot of stress on our professional trainer. She was developing curriculum and delivering it the next day. We also had to figure out how to set up the training environment and ended up creating 20 user accounts and 20 room accounts on the pilot system.

Because our trainer was devoted to developing workshop curriculum, Helpdesk staff and the User Support Director developed the documentation (quick guides).

Our goal was to get all users off of Oracle Calendar at the time of the migration. However, the migration was happening at a critical time in the Admission life cycle. Admissions staff relies on calendar to schedule prospective student visits. After several consultations, we realized that they were really using it like a daily planner instead of an actual calendar and recommended that they create their own calendars, not ones managed by the institution, to accomplish their goals. We had to delay their migration from Oracle Calendar to Outlook until March 2013. New calendars were NOT created in Live@edu and data was not migrated for these calendars. Admission staff continued to use Oracle Calendar until February 2012 when they set up new calendars in Live@edu.

4.4 Outcomes
Overall, the calendar migration went very smoothly. No data was lost. Delegate rights were a challenge but that was not unexpected. Only 16 accounts had to be manually touched to correct migration issues.

4.5 Lessons Learned
Ideally support staff needs a minimum of six weeks in a testing environment to learn a new system. We should always plan for some kind of data cleanup with these types of enterprise migrations. We now know the minimum time required to develop comprehensive training and documentation; we had about two weeks to develop four workshops and five quick guides. The effort was extremely stressful for all involved. More time should have been devoted to this effort. Support staff were dedicated to these efforts for the four weeks prior to the migration. .

The hard part of a migration like this is being the translator; understanding the current environment and translating that to the new environment. Microsoft provides application specific training but we were the only ones who could be the translators for our community moving from Oracle Calendar to Microsoft.

This was the first truly enterprise calendar system that we have had putting students, faculty, and staff all in the same environment. However, some faculty don't like being associated with an enterprise calendar system. They see it as an invasion of privacy to have someone else be able to schedule their time. The institution has not made a declarative statement otherwise so time is still being wasted calling individuals instead of just scheduling them. This is obviously not a technical issue.

5. MICROSOFT LIVE@EDU TO OFFICE 365
By August 2013, we need to upgrade from Microsoft Live@edu to Office 365 (O365). Office 365 comes in two flavors O365 Wave 14 which has an Exchange 2010 backend and O365Wave 15 with an Exchange 2013 backend. According to Microsoft the migration to O365 Wave 14 is riskier than the Wave 15 migration. Once you agree on a basic date with Microsoft, it seems impossible to change the date. Once you migrate to Wave 14 the migration to Wave 15 is managed by Microsoft Engineering and the timing is non-negotiable and it should happen anywhere between two weeks and six months after the Wave 14 upgrade.

SkyDrive and Messenger are eliminated from the O365 services. Live SkyDrive accounts become personal user accounts having the same username and password until the user changes it. The URLs to access email and calendar are different from the URL to access SkyDrive. This becomes a user training issue and Microsoft provides template user messages that one can personalize.

O365 Wave 14 provides the option of bringing on Sharepoint and Lync and new services. In Wave 15, Sharepoint is renamed SkyDrive Pro (confusing I know but I am not making this up).

For this migration we were initially told we needed to change our account provisioning process and our password synchronization tool; we needed to go to a federated environment and set up ADFS. In January 2013, Microsoft said there was funding available to help with this configuration change; by February 2013, that offer was no longer available. To hire a vendor was going to cost more than $20,000. Microsoft then said that we could upgrade to O365 using our current configuration using ILM and PCNS so we started down that path. Later it turns out that we can only use that configuration for 30 days after the upgrade. At that point we would need to either put in a new PCNS tool currently in development or switch to ADFS. Unfortunately for us, the new PCNS tool was scheduled to be released right before our 30 days runs out. So, we were back at looking into ADFS.

This is the point we are at as I write this paper. We will detail the rest of the story in my final presentation, or in a subsequent paper. I will document what we have done and learned so far.

5.1 Key Decisions
The main decisions for this upgrade for us relate to the account provisioning and password synchronization architecture and whether or not to bring on Sharepoint and Lync.

Since we never hosted a local instance of Exchange, we have no prior experience regarding Sharepoint; nor do we understand the implications of bringing Sharepoint online at this time. Initial testing and experimentation seem to reveal complex procedures for setting up access rights. Sharepoint also seems redundant at this this point in our organizational life cycle. We have many collaborative options that we are currently supporting including a home grown solution, myHome community, and Sakai project sites. Many users are already using DropBox and SkyDrive so why bring on another cloud storage solution?

It is slightly less clear the role Lync might play. We already have an AdobeConnect license and many users connect to Skype on a regular basis. So, in the end, we have decided not to bring on these service offerings at the point of migration but will investigate them further at a later date.

5.2 Timeline
The upgrade is scheduled to happen June 6th, approximately one year after the migration from Mirapoint to Live@edu.

5.3 Challenges
The biggest challenge has been working with Microsoft. What we are told seems to change at every meeting. We are used to having more say into environment changes that affect our user community. Microsoft Engineering doesn't seem to care; the goal is to move all of the Microsoft clients to one environment.

Time is of the essence. We are still unclear as to what our account provisioning and password change infrastructure will be and we are five weeks from migration and nine weeks from when we need to make the infrastructure change. We have expressed concerns to Microsoft and have been directed to our account

manager. We would like to have the 30 day restriction removed but we don't believe that will happen. All of this has left us scrambling for answers and options.

6. CONCLUSION
Since 2011 we have taken our user community through some major. As a result of these changes we no longer rely on third party products like Notfylink to sync calendar entries with mobile devices. Our disaster recovery posture is in better shape since email and calendar are hosted in the cloud. Email performance issues have almost disappeared. We have an enterprise calendar system available to all faculty, staff, and students instead of a limited subset. We are working in a much more integrated environment; the user interfaces for Outlook Web Apps and Outlook clients are very similar and for the most part have similar functionality. Now that we are on Active Directory, we are starting to shift directory services to Active Directory instead of SunOne Directory Services. Over time, we hope to be able to standardize on the one directory. We have also saved on licensing costs. We are no longer paying annual licenses for email and calendar or Novell.

As expected, the Mac environment lags behind the Windows environment from a management perspective. That is our fault and one we will correct over time. However, the functional differences in Outlook are not something we control. Some Mac users have even installed Fusion so they can run the Windows OS on the Mac and use the Windows version of Outlook (not an ITS supported practice).

The support demands of mobile devices has significantly decreased. Password synchronization just works; users are not getting locked out of their accounts every 4 months. The service is a much more reliable and integrated experience.

We have accomplished a significant amount of change in a relatively short time period. Project planning and prioritization was key to our success. By defining the scope of the project, understanding key project components and milestones and developing realistic plans; we achieved all of our goals and original target dates. We never had to adjust a go live date.

The professionalism of the staff can't be minimized. Everyone involved in these efforts already had a full time job; each individual rose to the challenges each of these change efforts threw at us. There certainly is and was the potential for burn out and yet that doesn't seem to have happened. Leadership heard us when we asked to delay the calendar migration. That helped both the user community and our support staff. We have learned the importance of a testing environment and making sure there is enough time to have detailed testing take place. Having the front line support teams involved in testing is key since they know user behaviors and needs the best.

We know our technology environment! Over the last three years we have talked with every user in our community multiple times. The Novell to Active Directory project forced us to understand how every computer was being used on campus. The oldest machine we found was from 1998! We talked with every faculty member running a workstation server and determined how we could meet their needs in a more secure environment. We have talked with every administrative assistant about how they support their bosses using either email or calendar. We have done a lot of data clean up. The shared file structure is much improved allowing for easier collaboration and navigation.

All of these changes happening in a short amount of time is hopefully unique to this part of our organizational life. The project teams had success with every migration. However, just because we can doesn't mean we should. Individual team members went above and beyond many times over these last three years. There is the chance that leadership could begin to expect this level of effort all of the time. This would be a mistake and potentially lead to higher rates of turnover among the professional staff.

Having an open and transparent relationship with the user community is critical. We always gave them advance notice as to the changes that were coming. Communication is handled by the user support team so there was always a unified plan with documentation and training being a critical piece of that plan. Although there are many resources available online, our community requires us to deliver the change training for them. Our goal is to not have the technology prevent anyone from doing his or her job. And, for the most part, we have largely accomplished that.

Having resources for consultants and finding the right consultants for the project also helped us be successful. Working with consultants helps support staff to learn new systems and not make critical mistakes in the process. We are grateful we had this type of support.

Because we are using the free email and calendar system, Microsoft has more leverage into our environment. We seem to have very little power to leverage the timing of these changes and are relying on Microsoft for several critical components to make the system work.

After all of these changes, the user community still trusts us. We must have done something right. Strategically, we are in a much better technical and support environment now then we were in 2011.

7. ACKNOWLEDGMENTS

Many thanks to the professional staff involved in these efforts: Karen Sunderland, Adam Lee, Tony Tabone, Sharon Beltaine, Bill Kaupe, Terry Ruger, Drew Hammond, Dale Reigle, Steve Adams, Mike Taves, Paula Wedemeyer, Dave Weil, John White, Ed Fuller, Benjamin Costello, Mike Testa, Bill Weeks, Brian Edwards and many others!

Concerto – Digital Signage on the Cheap

Todd Swatling
Vassar College
124 Raymond Ave
Poughkeepsie, NY
1-845-437-7759
toswatling@vassar.edu
todd.swatling@gmail.com

ABSTRACT

Concerto Digital Signage is free and open source software (FOSS) developed by students at Rensselaer Polytechnic Institute (RPI) and tailored to the needs of educational institutions. Being a web application, it has minimal requirements for both server and client, allowing it to run on commodity hardware. Concerto facilitates distributed, yet targeted, announcements in a way that encourages interdepartmental communication. I will discuss the Concerto implementation at Vassar College, which uses old and low powered hardware for cost savings, ties into VC's emergency alerting system, and harnesses screensavers to increase coverage to wherever computers are already deployed.

Categories and Subject Descriptors

H.5.1 [Multimedia Information Systems, Animations]

General Terms

Performance, Design, Economics, Experimentation

Keywords

Digital Signage; Open Source; Concerto; Raspberry Pi

1. Introduction

Rensselaer Polytechnic Institute (RPI) launched Concerto digital signage in 2008. Concerto was created by the Web Technologies Group, a student organization and part of the Student Senate. This origin is especially relevant because much of the design of Concerto reveals that it was designed for the way educational institutions operate. Specifically, the fact that Concerto is a low-cost solution that was designed to grow organically in a decentralized manner makes it a perfect match for the needs of colleges and universities.

There are a lot of definitions for digital signage. It can mean everything from a simple scrolling LED sign to the panels in airports showing arrival and departure times all the way up to the animated menus at some newer fast-food chains. Our particular project displays non-animated slides and RSS text.

Vassar Computing and Information Services (CIS) gave up looking at commercial digital signage software and implementation because it was too expensive. The content management side alone cost approximately $10,000. Although we are still only in the pilot stages of the project, Concerto has made this project a possibility due to its free and open source nature. Right now, we have three screens installed plus a handful of other on-and-off clients like screensavers.

2. Organization in Concerto

We are currently using manually created local accounts, though Concerto can make use of CAS (Central Authentication System) for authentication. Groups in Concerto are always locally managed in the web interface, regardless of whether CAS has been integrated. Groups are used to give control over a feed or screen. A group can own many screens and feeds, but each screen or feed can only be owned by one group.

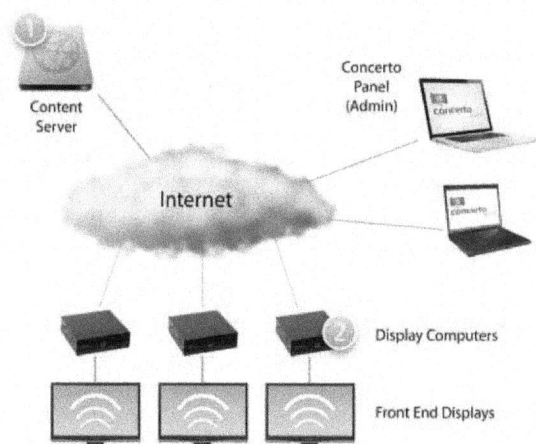

Figure 1. Network Diagram of a Concerto deployment showing the server (1), clients and screens (2), and computers running Concerto Panel, RPI's branded Concerto screensaver. [1]

Groups also own screens. Members of the group subscribe their screen to one or more feeds and choose how often each is displayed. This is one of the things that I really like about Concerto. It allows CIS to show our feeds most often on the screens in our building, but also include content from the rest of the campus. This allows campus-wide advertising of events without compromising the owning group's information dissemination. It also allows other content to fill in the gaps if and when the local group's content is sparse.

The items displayed on Concerto-controlled screens are generally text and images, but Concerto does allow support for audio and video. The decision to enable audio or video depends on your use and the location of the sign. If outside classrooms, for example, looping audio would be distracting. It's also important to keep the content from getting stale; the idea, after all, is to get students, faculty and staff to turn to these screens for information, not to ignore them. Also worthy of note, most of the people we imagine using our Concerto install will probably barely be comfortable creating images, let alone the idea of creating audio-visual content. We recommend that people uncomfortable with image editing software to use something like PowerPoint to create slides and then export them as JPEG files for upload to Concerto.

Anyone with a Concerto (or CAS) account can submit content to a feed. Once it is submitted, a member of the owning group must approve it. If you are an owner, anything you submit to one of your feeds is automatically approved. Feeds can have many different types of content. There are two types of special feeds. Dynamic feeds pull their information from an external source, typically via RSS. There's a whole complicated language for parsing dynamic feeds, which the developers promise will be simplified in Concerto 2, but is still in alpha testing at present.

A designated emergency feed can be created for the system. Once something is posted to the emergency feed, it overrides all content of that type on every screen. The emergency feed can be a dynamic feed, but it does not have to be. Vassar uses Rave Alert from Rave Mobile Safety for sending out SMS alerts in the event of an emergency. Rave Alert can also offer alerts via RSS. Unfortunately, I have not had time to integrate Concerto with our emergency alert system at this time, so my knowledge of this function is limited to what I've read.

```
#!/bin/bash
## loadtest.sh
url="http://concerto.vassar.edu"

for i in {1..300}
do
        open $url
        sleep .2
done
```

Figure 2. Bash script for testing web server load.

3. Performance

Concerto is simply a PHP application with a MySQL database backend, which allows it to run on a simple Apache install. Vassar is using a Linux server running in a VMware environment with 1 CPU and 2 gigabytes of RAM. The server is currently running three signs with no noticeable load. In order to test the server's capacity, I wrote a quick bash script (see Figure 2). The URL variable in quotes will need to be modified for use at other institutions.

Using this script on my MacBook Pro, I generated 300 tabs in Chrome. The Concerto server did not go above a 0.26 load. Pages took much longer than usual to do the initial load. But, when I spot-checked a few of the tabs they all were performing at normal speed. The change in load time is most likely a bandwidth issue, due to 300 connections occurring within a few seconds. Most of the work, like image resizing and slide transitions, is done in client-side JavaScript resulting in normal performance once the page is loaded.

The fact that Concerto is a LAMP (Linux, Apache, MySQL, & PHP) application allows it to scale well. (Linux is definitely not a requirement, just a common Concerto was written with built-in memcached support, memcached being an object caching system that caches database results and images. This can significantly speed up system performance. I turned off memcached in the early stages while we were playing around with templates because it was doing its job too well and continued serving up the old image. I am sure we will turn it back on when the load increases, but for now it is just an added complexity. Like all PHP/MySQL applications, if the server is unable to meet the load, MySQL can be split off onto another server.

Another benefit of Concerto being a LAMP application is that the only software needed on the client side is a web browser with a decent JavaScript engine. I have had very good experiences with Chromium, the open source version of Google's Chrome browser. It is very difficult to find a device that is unable to meet the modest hardware requirements for this browser. At Vassar, our clients are all running Debian Linux, which also has very minimal hardware requirements. This allows us to make new use of old, but perfectly functional, equipment. One of our signs is powered by a circa 2007 Mac Mini; another is running on a Zotac nettop from a few years ago.

4. Client Hardware

The initial cost of deploying existing hardware is zero, but older hardware generally uses more electricity. This is a consideration for Vassar because our digital signage pilot is partly due to a request from our Sustainability Committee. The nettop listed above uses about 25 watts per hour. At 12 cents per kWh, the average cost for electricity in the country, that would cost $131 over 5 years in constant operation. For long-term savings we wanted to find the lowest cost, lowest wattage computer that is out now. This turned out to be the Raspberry Pi.

The Raspberry Pi was released in early 2012 as a tool for teaching computer science in K-12 schools, but has since gained a massive following with hardware hackers, artists, and makers. The device retails at $35 for just the board, and is about the size of a deck of cards. It uses a SD card for storage and a standard micro USB phone charger for power. Chargers like this use about 3.5 watts per hour, resulting in a 5-year electricity cost of about $18. Plan to spend about $60 for a Raspberry Pi plus the accessories mentioned above. This makes the total 5-year cost of a Raspberry Pi sign $53 cheaper than using "free" old hardware.

By happenstance, the first Raspberry Pi's were shipping at the same time I was searching for hardware to run the Concerto screens. Luckily, I found a forum thread on rasbberrypi.org about using them for Concerto. With favorable results from that thread, and such a low price, I was able to acquire a Pi to use for testing.

Figure 3. Raspberry Pi Concerto client mounted behind monitor. ©Todd Swatling

There are other similar low cost, low power computers on the market, such as the Beagle Board and a myriad of devices with Rockchip processors. These devices are designed to be plugged into an HDMI port on the back of a television and play HD video. They have more powerful hardware, more fit and finish, and the higher price tag that comes with it. Since our screens will only have images, not video or sound, this is unnecessary for our needs, but may be useful for others.

Since Raspberry Pi's are a hot commodity, (depending on the level of tech savvy among the student body) I was concerned

about theft. All of the reasonably priced Raspberry Pi cases are designed to make it easy to insert and remove the SD card. Rather than buy a case, we are using uncommon square bit screws and nylon spacers to physically secure our Raspberry Pi behind the display. (see Figures 3 and 4) Note that the holes we are using for mounting are for aiding in the manufacturing process, not for mounting; it is possible to damage your Pi by over-tightening. My hope is that if one is stolen, it will be damaged in the process and be a disincentive to steal more of them.

Another tip for Raspberry Pi Concerto deployment is to use the smallest SD card that will fit the operating system. Operating system images are copied to the SD card using a block-based copying program such as Unix's dd command. A dd image can be put on a disk with more space, but an image cannot be shrunk. Smaller cards result in smaller images, which take less time to

Figure 4. Another view of the Raspberry Pi showing the mounting hardware. ©Todd Swatling

write and allow you to use whatever sized SD card is on hand.

Since all of the storage is on the SD card, supporting them is very simple. If a Raspberry Pi-based sign is misbehaving, simply replace the SD card with a freshly-imaged one. If that does not fix the problem, the Raspberry Pi itself needs to be replaced. Since they're both so inexpensive, it is quite affordable to have a stockpile of spares.

An inexpensive client for a commercial system can cost upwards of $600. The Concerto project's website [1] offers a configuration for a small form factor computer with a cost of

$250. Using a Raspberry Pi as a client makes the client's hardware almost negligible compared to the cost of the display. Be sure to use a commercial display that is designed to be in continuous operation without image burn-in.

Figure 5. iPad mounted securely behind the glass of a locked door. ©Todd Swatling

We have also been able to breathe new life into some first-generation iPads, formerly in our loaner pool, that were otherwise virtually unused (since Apple significantly upgraded the hardware of later versions, there was no longer any interest in borrowing original iPads). We mounted an iPad behind the glass door of our training room, keeping it safe but still visible to passers by. (see Figure 4) iPads are capable of displaying a website full screen if the page has <meta name="apple-mobile-web-app-capable" content="yes"> in the page header. Once that change has been added, browse to the page, tap the Share button, and tap Add to Home Screen. That will create a link to the full screen version of the page.

RPI developed a Windows screensaver, which can attach to your Concerto instance and display content from select feeds. I have had mixed results with making it work as described. The official screensaver is not a true sign; it displays select content one at a time on a black background rather than multiple feeds on the institution's template. In any case, it does not support MacOS, which is our primary workstation platform. To remedy this, I found a project on Google Code called WebSaver, [2] which loads a webpage when the screensaver is initiated. WebSaver only supports MacOS, though I am working on getting a similar setup on Windows.

Concerto screensavers will allow us to put a sign anywhere that already has a computer. This will be especially useful in places such as the library, which already has a large number of computers in high traffic areas. I can also see this as useful for getting the word out to lesser-traveled parts of campus, like office buildings, which would probably not merit a dedicated sign.

Normally, a screen's resolution is set when it is initially deployed. My first solution was to create a screen for each of several monitor resolutions and have a script to direct clients to the proper screen for its resolution. This would have cluttered the list of screens and it would have been a lot of work to maintain and up-to-date list of common resolutions. Luckily, I was able to modify the code to detect the resolution with JavaScript and resize it on the fly. Unfortunately, this breaks down when using multiple monitors with different resolutions. My current method uses a cookie in order to communicate the display size to the various PHP and JavaScript files that need it. Presently, the monitor that loads the page first sets the resolution for all of the system's displays, but that is still something I need to work on.

5. REFERENCES

[1] Concerto Team. 2011. Deploy. Retrieved June 21, 2013 from http://www.concerto-signage.org/deploy.

[2] Gavin Brock. 2010. Websaver. Retrieved June 21, 2013 from https://code.google.com/p/websaver/.

Meeting the Technology Needs of the Differently-abled Student

Carol Currie Sobczak
University of Southern Maine
96 Falmouth Street
Portland, ME 04104
207-780-4339
sobczak@usm.maine.edu

ABSTRACT
IT provides installation of and training with various software and hardware applications to students with a wide range of disabilities.

Categories and Subject Descriptors
C.0 Computer Systems Organization, GENERAL, Hardware/software interfaces

C.3 Computer Systems Organization, SPECIAL-PURPOSE AND APPLICATION-BASED SYSTEMS
Microprocessor/microcomputer applications

C.5.3 COMPUTER SYSTEM IMPLEMENTATION
Microcomputers

D.2.9 Software, SOFTWARE ENGINEERING, Management

K.3.1 Computing Milieux, COMPUTERS AND EDUCATION

General Terms
Documentation, Human Factors, Management

Keywords
Assistive Technology, Adaptive Technology, Imaging, Disabilities, Deployment, Education, Training

1. INTRODUCTION
The University of Southern Maine is part of the state university system. It is spread across three main campuses in three cities (Portland, Gorham, and Lewiston-Auburn). The Division of Information Technology is responsible for classroom and lab support, helpdesk administration, telecommunications, media services, software support for faculty and staff, videoconferencing support, student computing support, network infrastructure and management, technical services (hardware), database and application development/support, and the campus computing store.

All public institutions must comply with federal mandates. There are three key pieces of legislation pertinent to this discussion: 1986 Re-authorization of the Rehabilitation Act of 1973, the Telecommunications Accessibility Enhancement Ace of 1988, and the Americans with Disabilities Act of 1990. According to the Americans with Disabilities Act of 1990, Section 508 establishes requirements for electronic and information technology developed, maintained, procured, or used by the Federal government. Section 508 requires Federal electronic and information technology to be accessible to people with disabilities, including employees and members of the public.

An accessible information technology system is one that can be operated in a variety of ways and does not rely on a single sense or ability of the user. For example, a system that provides output only in visual format may not be accessible to people with visual impairments and a system that provides output only in audio format may not be accessible to people who are deaf or hard of hearing. Some individuals with disabilities may need accessibility-related software or peripheral devices in order to use systems that comply with Section 508.[1]

What pro-active steps should a University take to address anticipated needs? While determining factors should address immediate need (as measured by an analysis of disability types and incidences across the existing student population, for example), and be in accordance with legislated guidelines addressing reasonable accommodation, qualifying students with disability, etc. the foundation element should be adherence to the intent of the now well-established guidelines.

Pro-active steps taken by a University to provide accommodations using assistive technology should address the following considerations:

- Initial accommodations should concentrate on areas of high-incidence need by addressing the most prevalent disability types: learning disability, low vision, low hearing, and mild physical disabilities.

- Initial accommodations can focus on increasing the accessibility of the most commonly-used university resources: libraries, computing services, and academic support services.

- Initial accommodations should concentrate on improving the accessibility of activities commonly required of most students: reading, writing, communicating, and other aspects of information access.

---

[1] http://www.ada.gov/cguide.htm#anchor62335

- Planning for accommodations should include the provision of hardware/software support, maintenance, and training.

- The university should anticipate that needs for individualized assistive technology will arise, and accommodation planning should include procedures for identifying and procuring this technology on a student by student basis.

- Planned adjustments or upgrades to the university's computing services should anticipate an increased need for assistive technology.

There are a number of software standards that have become quite commonplace over the past 10 years or so that allow assistive technology products (like screen readers, text-to-speech, etc.) to work with software. Some current or past APIs (automated programming interface) include: Microsoft UI Automation and IAccessible2 on Microsoft Windows, AT-SPI on UNIX and Linux, Mac OS X Accessibility, and Java Accessibility and the Java Access Bridge for Java software.

Accessibility features in mainstream software can also make input easier at the user level, for example: Keyboard shortcuts, MouseKeys, Macro recorders, Sticky keys ClickLock, ToggleKeys, Customization of pointer appearance, such as size, color and shape, Predictive text, and Spell checkers and grammar checkers.

Other approaches that may be particularly relevant to users with a learning disability include:

- Cause and effect software

- Switch accessible software

- Hand-eye co-ordination skills software

- Diagnostic assessment software

- Mind mapping software

- Study skills software

- Symbol-based software

- Text-to-speech

- Touch typing software

Enabling access to Web content for all users is the concern of the Web accessibility movement. Websites can be designed to be more accessible by their conformance to certain design principles.

Screen readers are of limited use when reading text from websites designed without consideration to accessibility; this can be due to the differences between spoken and written language and the complexity of text, but it is mainly due to poor page design practices. The tendency to indicate semantic meaning using methods that are purely presentational (e.g. larger or smaller font sizes, using different font colors, or images or multimedia to provide information) restricts meaningful access to some users. Therefore designing sites in accordance with Web accessibility principles helps enable meaningful access for all users.

For example, web designers can ensure that navigation and content is as plain and simple as appropriate and long texts should provide summaries.[2]

2. BACKGROUND

In the summer of 1995, the University of Southern Maine engaged consultants to complete a site visit and audit, and report of the availability of assistive technology at the University pursuant to the mandates of federal and state law.

It was agreed that the assistive technology audit would concentrate on an array of University services and analyze each area with respect to assistive technology presently available. In those areas where the curriculum, research or reference materials, or learning supports or equipment available to the students were inaccessible to students with disabilities, the consultants were requested to recommend strategies and/or equipment acquisitions that would eliminate those deficiencies.

The centralized control of the USM data network makes the system fast, powerful and efficient. Troubleshooting can often be accomplished centrally, and upgrading software and system functionality can also be done efficiently. Conversely, the same uniformity that provides maintenance efficiency creates difficulties for diverse learning needs. Systems that are based on uniformity eliminate adaptability from end-user control, resulting in a computing environment that requires the user to adapt to the system rather than vice versa.

The report included several recommendations for basic assistive technologies in two basic categories: equipment and resources, and training, support and maintenance.

Equipment and resources included:

- Screen magnification

- OCR optical character recognition for digitized and text (requires flatbed scanner)

- Text-to-speech

- Word prediction software

- Availability of adaptive input devices (generally USB access)

Training, support and maintenance included:

- A clearly defined protocol for identifying, acquiring, implementing, training on and maintaining assistive technology for staff in the Office of Support for Students with Disabilities

  This organizational framework should not be viewed as incidental to the need for the acquisition of specific hardware and software, but the reverse: specific hardware and software needs to be a component of a clearly defined service effort.

- Assistive technology support staff from the university should receive hands on training with the assistive technology that will be available to the university students.

  The training should be designed to increase the expertise of other trainers, not just end users. This training model is predicated on the assumption that the university intends to develop a core of assistive technology expertise in-house.

---

[2] http://www.w3.org/WAI/intro/accessibility.php

In 1997, USM received funding from the University of Maine System to establish a collection of adaptive technology hardware and software, as well as a support person to maintain those collections. A Software Support Specialist (Adaptive Technology Specialist) was hired and the initial equipment collection was started. Initial purchases included CCTV, MS-DOS-based computer equipment, Braille printer and supplies, AlphaSmartPro for electronic note taking, handheld tape recorders, as well as preliminary software like early versions of DragonDictate and JAWS.

With the elimination of the Adaptive Technology Support Specialist in 2008, IT was faced with the continued collaboration with OSSD (Office for Support to Students with Disabilities) to provide adaptive technology training to students.

USM has AT stations in various locations across a three campus array. These stations have historically been Windows-based computers, running the full array of student-based academic software, with adaptive applications installed after the base image has been applied. Each station has typically included a large display (monitor), adjustable height table, seating with adjustable arms, a scanner with sheet feeder, and a headset.

In 2012, we found that many student users preferred Macintosh computers and were able to utilize applications that are included as a part of the operating system, i.e., VoiceOver. A Mac "prototype" developed in 2012 and put in service in 2013. GhostReader, and enhanced audio reader was added, as well as more "double-clickable" settings will make it easier for students with vision impairments to turn on voice navigation aids.

Computers are refreshed on a three year cycle. The annual software application renewal costs (typically for 10 licenses per application) approximately $7000.

Over the years, we have simplified documentation for training procedures with several applications. Some of our team have gained enhanced knowledge of software available by installing and using them on their office computers.

Training individuals with a variety of applications was becoming imposing and difficult to maintain. We focused on documenting our procedures. We made these documents available to the OSSD staff, as well as our student lab staff. They could then make themselves familiar with the products and begin the process with a student at an earlier contact. (Some of those documents will be featured in a display to accompany this project.)

Students' personal devices including laptops, iPads and tablets have flooded our campuses. Support for these could have become a nightmare. We chose to focus on a small collection of applications that were available to download and install for free or relatively inexpensively. To date, this has not presented a problem. Students have adapted quickly to new technologies that meet their individual needs.

3. CURRENT STUDENTS
During spring semester 2013, the Office for Support to Students with Disabilities (OSSD) had 238 students requesting accommodations. Of those, 62 or 26% have alternative text format as an accommodation, meaning they receive PDF copies of texts for use with a screen reader. We do not have data on what screen readers people use. There are 2 students who use Kurzweil exclusively and own their own copies. Students with Macintosh computers typically use VoiceOver. We introduce students to Natural Reader and several students choose to use Abode's built

in reader. We have three students who are approved for and use JAWS regularly. We have one student at this time who is approved for and uses Dragon regularly. Anecdotally, there are other students on campus who use Dragon who are not eligible or choose not to register with our office. All totaled, about 1/3 of our students have some kind of technology as part of their academic accommodations.

4. CURRENT APPLICATIONS
Hardware/software includes: Braille printer, scanners, Dragon NS, JAWS, Kurzweil, pdf to MP3 conversion....

2012:

JAWS 13 http://www.freedomscientific.com/products/fs/jaws-product-page.asp

Kurzweil3000 v 12 http://www.kurzweiledu.com/kurzweil-3000-v13-windows.html

Dragon 11 http://www.nuance.com/dragon/index.htm

Inspiration http://www.inspiration.com/

2013:

Natural Reader http://www.naturalreaders.com/

MAGic http://www.freedomscientific.com/products/low-vision/MAGic-screen-magnification-software.asp

VoiceOver (Mac) http://www.apple.com/accessibility/voiceover/

GhostReader
http://www.convenienceware.com/product/ghostreader

5. DEFINITIONS

Assistive Technology is an umbrella term that includes assistive, adaptive, and rehabilitative devices for people with disabilities and also includes the process used in selecting, locating, and using them. AT promotes greater independence by enabling people to perform tasks that they were formerly unable to accomplish, or had great difficulty accomplishing, by providing enhancements to, or changing methods of interacting with, the technology needed to accomplish such tasks.

The term **Adaptive Technology** is often used as the synonym for Assistive Technology, however, they are different terms. Assistive Technology refers to "any item, piece of equipment, or product system, whether acquired commercially, modified, or customized, that is used to increase, maintain, or improve functional capabilities of individuals with disabilities,"[3] while Adaptive Technology covers items that are specifically designed for persons with disabilities and would seldom be used by non-disabled persons. In other words, "Assistive Technology is any object or system that increases or maintains the capabilities of people with disabilities," while Adaptive Technology is "any object or system that is specifically designed for the purpose of increasing or maintaining the capabilities of people with disabilities."[4] Consequently, Adaptive Technology is a subset of

---

[3] "Assessing for Adaptive Technology Needs". Retrieved 2013-04-05.

[4] "Tennessee Science Standards". Retrieved 2013-04-05.

Assistive Technology. Adaptive Technology often refers specifically to electronic and Information Technology access.[5]

Accessibility software: In human–computer interaction, computer accessibility (also known as accessible computing) refers to the accessibility of a computer system to all people, regardless of disability or severity of impairment, examples include Web accessibility guidelines.

Assistive Technology for Visual Impairment: For general computer use access technology such as screen readers, screen magnifiers and refreshable Braille displays has been widely taken up along with standalone reading aids that integrate a scanner, optical character recognition (OCR) software, and speech software in a single machine.

Computer accessibility (also known as *Accessible computing*), in human-computer interaction, refers to the accessibility of a computer system to all people, regardless of disability or severity of impairment. It is largely a software concern; when software, hardware, or a combination of hardware and software, is used to enable use of a computer by a person with a disability or impairment[6]

6. CATEGORIES OF DISABILITY

There are four general categories of disabilities:

Visual

Visual impairment including blindness means an impairment in vision that, even with correction, adversely affects an individual's educational performance. The term includes both partial sight and blindness.[7]

Auditory (hearing impairment)

An auditory processing disorder interferes with an individual's ability to analyze or make sense of information taken in through the ears. This is different from problems involving hearing per se, such as deafness or being hard of hearing. Difficulties with auditory processing do not affect what is heard by the ear, but do affect how this information is interpreted, or processed by the brain.[8]

While sound user interfaces have a secondary role in common desktop computing, usually limited to system sounds as feedback, software producers take into account people who can't hear, either for personal disability, noisy environments, silence requirements or lack of sound hardware. Such system sounds like beeps can be substituted or supplemented with visual notifications and captioned text (akin to closed captions).

Motor

A physical disability is any impairment which limits the physical function of one or more limbs or fine or gross motor ability.

Orthopedic Impairment that adversely affects a child's educational performance includes impairments caused by a congenital anomaly, impairments caused by disease (e.g., poliomyelitis, bone tuberculosis, arthritis), and impairments from other causes (e.g., cerebral palsy, paralysis, carpal tunnel syndrome, repetitive strain injury, amputations, and fractures or burns that cause contractures).[9]

Some people may not be able to use a conventional input device, such as the mouse or the keyboard. Keyboard shortcuts and mouse gestures are ways to achieve this. Speech recognition technology is also a compelling and suitable alternative to conventional keyboard and mouse input as it simply requires a commonly available audio headset.

Cognitive, including learning disabilities, dyslexia, ADHD, Autism

Students with cognitive disabilities often are unable to read or to gain meaning from standard print materials. They may struggle with reading due to difficulties with functional abilities such as problem-solving, memory, attention, and comprehension.[10]

7. FUTURE PLANS

For the foreseeable future, the partnership with OSSD continues. There are no plans (or budget!) to support the reinstatement of an Adaptive Technology Specialist in IT. Hardware (computer stations) is replaced on a three-year cycle. Staff continue to build training outlines for the currently installed applications. Collaboratively, we investigate new and/or proven applications. We plan to expand some of the dedicated stations to include a Macintosh computer with limited applications. And, of course, the quest to reduce the annual licensing costs continues.

We have recently started investigating EduApps. *AccessApps* is an initiative supported by the Joint Information Systems Committee[11] (JISC) Regional Support Centres (RSC) and JISC TechDis. It consists of over 50 open source and freeware Microsoft Windows applications, running from a USB stick. AccessApps provides a range of solutions to support writing, reading and planning as well as sensory, cognitive and physical difficulties.

From their website (eduapps.org):[12]

EduApps consists of eight useful software collections that are free for you to download and use.

The EduApps Family covers a range of user requirements to support teaching and learning, so just choose the one that's right for you.

- AccessApps, provides a range of solutions to support writing, reading and planning, as well as sensory, cognitive and physical difficulties.

---

[5] http://en.wikipedia.org/wiki/Assistive_technology

[6] http://en.wikipedia.org/wiki/Computer_accessibility

[7] http://nichcy.org/disability/specific/visualimpairment

[8] http://www.ldonline.org/article/6390/

[9] http://nichcy.org/disability/categories#ortho

[10] http://aim.cast.org/learn/disabilityspecific/cognitive

[11] JISC (formerly the Joint Information Systems Committee) is a United Kingdom non-departmental public body whose role is to support post-16 and higher education, and research, by providing leadership in the use of ICT (Information and Communications Technology) in learning, teaching, research and administration. It is funded by all the UK post-16 and higher education funding councils.

[12] http://www.eduapps.org

- TeachApps, is a collection of software specifically designed for teachers or lecturers.

- LearnApps, as its name implies, is specifically designed for learners. All learners or students can benefit from LearnApps.

- MyStudyBar, is our most popular program, providing a suite of apps to support literacy.

- MyVisBar, a high contrast floating toolbar, designed to support learners with visual difficulties.

- MyAccess, a portal to all your favourite and accessible applications providing inclusive e-learning options for all.

- Create&Convert, is our new kid on the block, designed to help publish accessible information for all. Version 1.5 now available to download!

- Accessible Formatting WordBar, create accessible Word documents with ease using our innovative WordBar.

  All EduApps collections can run from a USB thumb-drive plugged into a Windows computer. Therefore, they offer a portable, personal solution – with you wherever you go.

8. RESOURCES

University of Athens Speech & Accessibility Lab Offers Online Software Directory

http://assistivetechnology.about.com/od/ATCAT11/a/Downolad-161-Free-Assistive-Technology-Applications.htm

General Sources of Disability Rights Information

ADA Information Line

www.ada.gov

Regional Disability and Business

Technical Assistance Centers

www.adata.org

National Dissemination Center for Children with Disabilities

http://nichcy.org/disability

9. ACKNOWLEDGMENTS

The author gratefully acknowledges the efforts of the Student Computing Support team at the University of Southern Maine, especially Jennifer Hanscom and Cheryl Thompson. Further population information was provided by Joanne Benica, Director of Support for Student with Disabilities, and Heather Dilios, Administrative Support for Students with Disabilities.

Enhancing Information Security of a University using Computer Ethics Video Clips, Managed Security Service and an Information Security Management System

Takashi Yamanoue
yamanoue@cc.kagoshima-u.ac.jp

Tamotsu Furuya
furuya@cc.kagoshima-u.ac.jp

Koichi Shimozono
simozono@cc.kagoshima-u.ac.jp

Masato Masuya
masatom@cc.kagoshima-u.ac.jp

Kentaro Oda
odaken@cc.kagoshima-u.ac.jp

Kunihiko Mori
mori@cc.kagoshima-u.ac.jp

Kagoshima University
Korimoto, Kagoshima
890-0065, Japan
+81-99-285-7187

ABSTRACT

An experience of enhancing information security for the ICT service department of a Japanese national university corporation is described. Information security is realized by the integration of people, processes, and technology. In order to enhance the people's side of information security, we have been using digital video clips, which are produced by a group of faculty members of Japanese universities. In order to enhance the technology side of information security, we have been using a managed security service and other means. We could reach 24 hours a day and 365 days a year monitoring at the doorway of the university using the service. However, we had no standard means to enhance the process side of information security until recently. This deficiency became an obstacle to making agreements between other universities on inter-university activities. This need also may be an obstacle to gaining reliance from users. In order to cope with this problem, we have decided to implement an information security management system (ISMS). It takes a lot of time and work to implement the ISMS. However, many parts of the ISMS were processes that we were already doing without any clear rules. The ISMS helps not only enhance information security but also improve daily work and management of the staff.

Categories and Subject Descriptors

C.2.0 [**Security and protection**]: Installation Management – *Benchmarks.*

General Terms

Management, Security.

SIGUCCS'13, November 03–08 2013, Chicago, IL, USA
Copyright 2013 ACM 978-1-4503-2318-5/13/11...$15.00.
http://dx.doi.org/10.1145/2504776.2504816

Keywords

Network security, Computer Ethics, Security Monitor, ISMS

1. INTRODUCTION

Most universities and colleges provide networked computers, and students have been using e-mail and other services on their campuses for many years. The information security of campuses is one of the most important matters for all universities and colleges today. Information security is realized by the integration of people, process and technology[1]. We have been using computer ethics video clips for the people aspect, and a managed security service and other measures for technology aspects; both are meant to enhance the information security of our campus. We have acquired a certificate of ISMS (Information Security Management System) in April 2013 for the process side measures. This paper provides an outline of the computer ethics video clips and the managed security service, and then describes the process of acquiring the ISMS certificate.

2. COMPUTER ETHICS VIDEO CLIPS

The Association of National Universities' Education Center for Information Processing (AECIP) in Japan produced the "digital video clips of computer ethics" ("Part I") with the National Institute of Multimedia Education (NIME) in 2002. The "Part I" acquired a good reputation. After that, the other three parts of video clips, Part II[2], Part III[4], and Part IV were produced to catch up to latest computer ethics and security issues by the NIME, the Open University Japan, and the Academic eXchange for Information Environment and Strategy (AXIES).

Many of the clips consist of one episode and its explanation. Episodes are dramas concerning students. Almost all of them are followed by an explanation from technical and legal points of view. Some problems in the drama have no 'correct' answer and are designed to prompt discussion in a class session.

For example, these video clips can be used as follows in a class.
1. Show an episode to students.
2. Discuss the episode in the class.

3. Show its explanation to students.
4. Discuss the explanation in the class
5. Assign homework to write a paper on the basis of the clip and discussions.

In our university, in order to prevent losing and leaking personal information and important information, the clip of "Protection of personal information (clip no. 4 of part III)" was used for training courses for faculty and staff in 2011. The courses took place before faculty meetings for every school of the university in order to show the clip to all faculty and staff. As part of computer literacy classes of the university in 2012, it was encouraged that all freshman students were shown clips of "Login and logout (clip no. 1 of part I)", "What if you forget the password? (clip no. 1 of part III)", "Problem with using an easy password (clip no. 2 of part III)", "Protection of personal information (clip no. 4 of part III)", and "Friends of friends are friends in the internet? (clip no. 15 of part III)" All students of our university can see the clips of part IV by logging into a Moodle server for liberal arts education in 2013.

3. MANAGED SECURITY SERVICE

A campus network is similar to a city. There are good packets and bad packets in the network just like there are good people and bad people in the city. There are also packets which came from outside of the campus. A manager of the campus network is similar to a police officer in the city, and has to keep the network safe. In order to keep the city safe, the police officer has to patrol the city. Without the patrol, crimes will not be discovered. The patrol of the city by the police officer corresponds to the monitoring of network security by the network manager. Monitoring network security is one of the most important jobs for the network managers today. Without monitoring of network security, it is hard to keep the network safe. It is common for the security policy of a university to have a clause that states that monitoring network security is a mandate, the same as the law of the city. However it is very hard to monitor every part of a university's network with the limited number of staff and a limited amount of time and expense. In order to cope with these problems, we bought a commercial managed security service (network security monitoring service) for the doorway of our campus network. With the commercial monitoring service, we could achieve 24 hours a day and 365 days a year monitoring at the doorway. We are using a firewall with logging function for monitoring inside of our campus network. If an incident was found by this combined monitoring, we could deal with it as quickly as possible. By these efforts, there were no serious incidents like unauthorized manipulation of important web pages by crackers or the leak of serious personal information by using P2P file sharing software as in recent years[3].

4. ISMS

Process is also an important element to preserve security. We had no standard means to enhance the process side of information security until recently. The lack became an obstacle to making agreements with other universities on inter-university activities. The lack also may be an obstacle to gaining reliance from users. In order to cope with this problem, we decided to implement an Information Security Management System (ISMS or ISO 27001). After the following process, we have been certified with ISMS (JIS Q 27001, Japanese version of ISO 27001) April 23, 2013.

ISO 27001 is a well-known information security standard and has become globally famous for its systematic approaches and methodologies. It helps organizations to achieve their desired level of information security by using a so-called ISMS Plan-Do-Check-Act (PDCA) methodology that establishes policies, controls and security organization within the organization. ISMS ensures the processes of the preventive, detective and corrective controls to the ultimate level.

4.1 Our Process to Implement the ISMS

The 2011 Tohoku earthquake and tsunami reminded us that it is important to prepare for unpredictable accidents.

Our department, Computing and Communications Center of Kagoshima University (CCC), began the inter university data backup experiment between us and Media and Information Technology Center of Yamaguchi University (MITC), Japan, in September 30, 2011. MITC had already been certified with ISMS and the director and other members of MITC asked us to get a certificate of ISMS. We started to explore how to get the certificate after that. The process of implementing the ISMS after that was the following.

- Dec. 2011. Have started surveying ISMS consultants.
- Apr. 2012. Have decided to implement ISMS in CCC at the staff meeting.
- May 8-9, 2012. A part of our staff participated in ISMS training course at Yamaguchi University.
- May 28, 2012. Have started the process to choose the ISMS consultant.
- June 20, 2012. Have meeting to survey other university's case and choosing of the consultant.
- July 2012. The consultant was decided by a bid.
- August 2012. Have started meetings with the consultant. Table 1 shows the dates and the agendas of this and following meetings. Start to make inventory of information assets to protect.
- September 2012. Start to write the manual using a sample which is provided by the consultant. We have made the risk assessment with the consultant.
- October 2012. Conduct employee training and BCP test.
- November 2012. Conduct internal audit with the help of the consultant. We have surveyed another ISMS certified university. We have found that they extracted norms from the manual. A norm defines a concrete procedure and it is easy to improve. We have adopted this method in our process.
- December 2012 to January 2013. Have responded to the nonconformity report of the internal audit. In this step, we have made many norms and records. This work was the most fruitful work to improve the manual, norms and other documents. Table 2 shows the list of the documents and records.
- February 2013. Have the first external audit by the certificate institute. The audit was mostly interviews on documents.
- March 2013. Have the second external audit. The audit included site tour and interviews.
- April 23, 2013. Certified.

4.2 Effect of the ISMS

We have seen the following effects since receiving ISM certification

- We could offer a good to MITC's questions. Cooperation, which requires standard security process, between us and other universities or companies, became easier than before.

Table 1. Meeting with the consultant

No.	Date and Agenda	No.	Date and Agenda
1	Aug 8, 2012 ● The first meeting with the consultant ● Sample manual ● Survey of current documents.	9	Oct. 11, 2012 ● Site tour ● Report of the risk assessment report and risk ● Confirming the internal audit.
2	Aug 17, 2012 ● Sample manual explanation	10	Nov. 13, 2012 ● Confirming the BCP and BCP training ● Confirming the internal audit
3	Aug 24, 2012 ● Risk assessment ● Creating an inventory of information assets to protect ● Risk and vulnerability ● Review of the policy statement and the scope	11	Nov. 15, 2012 ● Internal audit ●
4	Sep. 7, 2012 ● Review of the inventory of information assets to protect ● ISMS manual ● Review of the policy statement and the scope	12	Nov. 16, 2012 ● Follow up the internal audit ● Explanation of the management review ● Advice of preparation for the external audit
5	Sep. 11, 2012 ● Confirming the first and the second section, and a part of the fourth section of the manual.	13	Nov. 22, 2012 ● Confirming the BCP and BCP training ● Discussing and deciding the mesurement elements of effectiveness
6	Sep. 21, 2012 ● Confirming the scope ● Review of the inventory of information assets to protect ● Sample of the risk assesment ● Applicable legislation	14	Dec. 4, 2012 ● Following up the internal audit
7	Oct. 3, 2012 ● Training of the security ● Explanation of the BCP ● Explanation of documents and records ● Confirming the third and fourth section of the manual	15	Jan. 8, 2013. ● Preparation for the external audit
8	Oct. 10, 2012 ● Training of internal auditor	16	Feb. 8, 2013 ● Confirming the progress of the Nonconformity report ● Confirming the plan for risk response ● Confirming the mesurement elements of effectiveness ● Preparation for the external audit

- Making documents and records help us to have common knowledge on our information assets and work. For example, a written norm helps to resolve a conflict among members of our staff

- The security control on the "clear desk and clear screen" made our office rooms tidy. The "clear desk" control aims to prevent the staff from losing important information in the messy room. The "clear screen" control aims to prevent the staff from stealing IDs, passwords, or other information when the staff leaves the PC without logging out.

5. CONCLUSIONS

It takes a lot of time and work to implement the ISMS. However, many parts of the ISMS were processes that we already have been following without any clear written rules. The ISMS helps not only enhance information security but also improves daily work and management of the staff. Combining the ISMS, video clips and managed security service gives us confidence to maintain information security.

6. ACKNOWLEDGMENTS

We thank Mr. Honda, who worked very hard on office work for implementing the ISMS. We also thank SUN Partners, who is the consultant company.

Table 2. Documents and Records

Documents ID	Documents/Records name	Documents ID	Documents/Records name
ISMS-1-01	Information Security Policy	ISMS-5-R18	Security card issue ledger
ISMS-1-02	Information Security Management System Manual	ISMS-5-R19	Key rent ledger
ISMS-1-02-01	Scope	ISMS-5-R20	Physical access record and Non-disclosure agreement
ISMS-1-02-02	Inventory of information assets to protect	ISMS-5-R21	Privileged identity management ledger
ISMS-1-02-03	Report of the Risk Assessment	ISMS-5-R22	Software management ledger
ISMS-1-02-04	Statement of Applicability	ISMS-5-R23	Access control list
ISMS-1-02-05	Risk treatment plan	ISMS-5-R24	Privileged Identity Account Form
ISMS-3-01	BCP	ISMS-5-R25	USB keys management ledger
ISMS-4-01	Applicable legislation	ISMS-5-R26	School virtual machine hosting ledger
ISMS-4-02	Documents management ledger	ISMS-5-R27	Important information assets storing and classification record
ISMS-5-R01	ISMS yearly schedule	ISMS-5-R28	Clear desk and Clear Screen check record
ISMS-5-R02	Security Education record	ISMS-5-R29	Mobile PC management ledger
ISMS-5-R03	Effectiveness Measurement Sheet	ISMS-5-R30	Web servers and mail servers hosting ledger
ISMS-5-R04	Internal Audit Report		
ISMS-5-R05	Internal Audit matrix		
ISMS-5-R06	Internal Audit Checklist	ISMS-6-N01	Norm of user registration
ISMS-5-R07	Internal Audit Report	ISMS-6-N02	Norm of user's password management
ISMS-5-R08	Non-Conformity Report	ISMS-6-N03	Norm of user's password using rule
ISMS-5-R09	Preventive Action Report	ISMS-6-N04	Norm of passing of user's list
ISMS-5-R10	Management review record	ISMS-6-N05	Norm of passing of host list
ISMS-5-R11	BCP risk assessment	ISMS-6-N06	Norm of outside working
ISMS-5-R12	BCP test results record	ISMS-6-N07	Norm of schools' server hosting service
ISMS-5-R13	Improvement suggestion	ISMS-6-N08	Norm of short term using
ISMS-5-R14	Trouble log	ISMS-6-N09	Norm of server management
ISMS-5-R15	Hardware list	ISMS-6-N10	Norm of network management
ISMS-5-R16	Server housing management ledger	ISMS-6-N11	Norm of working log
ISMS-5-R17	Access level list	ISMS-6-N12	Norm of outsourcing

7. REFERENCES

[1] Amanda Andress: Surviving Security: How to Integrate People, Process, and Technology, CRC press, 2003.

[2] Takashi Yamanoue, Michio Nakanishi, Atsushi Nakamura, Izumi Fuse, Ikuya Murata, Shozo Fukada, Takahiro Tagawa, Tatsumi Takeo, Shigeto Okabe, Tsuneo Yamada : Digital Video Clips Covering Computer Ethics in Higher Education, Proceedings of the 33nd annual ACM SIGUCCS conference on User services, pp.456-461, Monterey, California, US. 6-9 Nov. 2005.

[3] Masato Masuya, Takashi Yamanoue, Shinichiro Kubota : An Experience of Monitoring University Network Security Using a Commercial Service and DIY Monitoring, Proceedings of the 34nd annual ACM SIGUCCS conference on User services, pp.225-230, Edmonton, Alberta, Canada. 5-8 Nov. 2006.

[4] Izumi Fuse, Takashi Yamanoue, Shigeto Okabe, Atsushi Nakamura, Michio Nakanishi, Shozo Fukada, Takahiro Tagawa, Tatsumi Takeo, Ikuya Murata, Tetsutaro Uehara, Tsuneo Yamada: Improving Computer Ethics Video Clips for Higher Education, Proceedings of the 36th annual ACM SIGUCCS conference on User services, pp.235-242, Portland, Oregon, US. 6-9 Oct. 2008.

ECCS2012 Makes PCs and Printers in Computer Labs Accessible from Off-Campus Environment

Kazutaka Maruyama
Information Technology Center
The University of Tokyo
2-11-16, Yayoi, Bunkyo
Tokyo, 113-8658, Japan
kazutaka@acm.org

Takayuki Sekiya
Information Technology Center
The University of Tokyo
3-8-1, Komaba, Meguro
Tokyo, 153-8902, Japan
sekiya@ecc.u-tokyo.ac.jp

ABSTRACT

Information Technology Center, The University of Tokyo provides Educational Campuswide Computing System (ECCS) to approximately 60,000 users at our university. ECCS includes computer labs for class and self-study and a mail service for sta and students. ECCS2012, launched in March 2012, focuses on integrations of hardware and various channels to access the system. For example, a single kind of terminals in the labs, an integrated le server for the terminals and the mail service, and a printing service portal which connects printers in the labs to o -campus PCs and terminals in the labs to o -campus printers in commercial stores. In this paper, we describe the detail and usage statistics of ECCS2012.

Categories and Subject Descriptors

K.6.2 [**Management of Computing and Information Systems**]: Installation Management; K.6.4 [**Management of Computing and Information Systems**]: System Management; H.4 [**Information Systems Applications**]: Miscellaneous

Keywords

Educational computer system, Remote access, Remote desktop, Printing service, E-money

1. INTRODUCTION

Information Technology Center, The University of Tokyo, provides the *Educational Campuswide Computing System* (ECCS) for students and teaching and faculty sta of the university. Students and teaching sta use ECCS for their classes, and faculty sta use it to read and write e-mails and as a SSL-VPN gateway in order to access web pages only accessible from on-campus PCs. ECCS provides computer lab and e-mail services to approximately 60,000 users.

ECCS2012, which was launched in March 2012, resolved some problems of a prior ECCS, ECCS2008. The problems of ECCS2008 were as follows:

- there were two types of PC terminals for Mac OS X and Windows,

- there were three separate le servers, two for home directories of PC terminals and one for a mail service,

- a mail service consisted of two di erent systems,

- only a prepaid card was available for payment on a printing service,

- users o -campus could only use the mail service.

In this paper, we describe how ECCS2012 resolved these problems, especially the improvement of services accessible by o -campus users. The rest of this paper is organized as follows. Section 2 describes an overview of ECCS2012 and some subsystems of PC terminals, le servers, a mail service, and a printing service. Section 3 includes the services for o -campus users, remote access to PC terminals, a printing portal, and payment on a printing service by e-money. Section 4 summarizes our achievements and provides future work.

2. OVERVIEW OF ECCS2012

ECCS2012 includes following subsystems:

- PC terminals for classes and private study of students, and related management systems[4],

- a mail service for the PC terminal users and mail hosting service users,

- le servers for the PC terminals and the mail service,

- a printing service[3],

- authentication servers and a user management system,

- network facilities and rewall equipment.

In this section, we describe some subsystems which improved considerably, but do not provide any o -campus services.

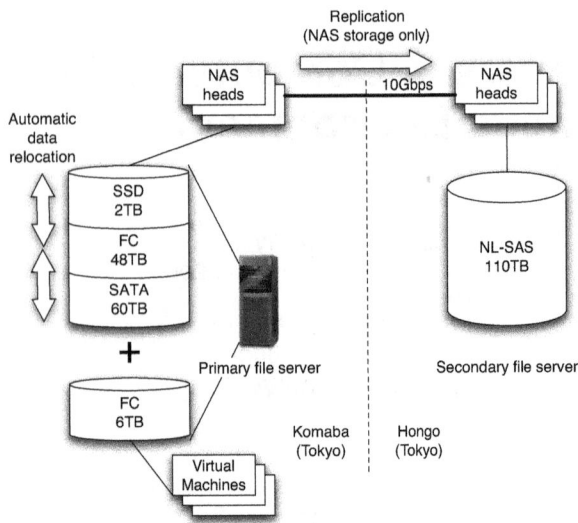

Figure 1: File servers of ECCS2012.

2.1 PC Terminals

PC terminals of ECCS2012 differ from those of ECCS2008, because they are a single type hardware, Apple iMac, which can run both Mac OS X and Windows by Boot Camp. There are 1,300+ PCs located in classrooms and libraries of 18 buildings on three separate campuses, (1) Hongo, Tokyo, (2) Komaba, Tokyo, and (3) Kashiwa, Chiba. Since the six full-time technical staff that maintain them are located only on campuses (1) and (2), remote management systems are required. The following three management systems enable us to update installed operating systems and applications, boot and shutdown terminals and maintain consistency.

- Making an image of a master PC and distributing the image to all other PCs in classrooms and libraries. Canon IT Solutions Inc. provides these features to us as a part of *Total Manager for Mac*. Total Manager for Mac also enables us to boot and shutdown all the PCs remotely.

- Installing and uninstalling separate OS updates and applications into all the PCs by using *Kaseya* of Kaseya Int'l Ltd.

- Keeping the content of PCs stable. *Deep Freeze* of Faronics Corporation is installed on both Mac OS X and Windows partitions.

2.2 File Servers

ECCS2012 requires network attached storage for both the PCs and the mail service. The PCs store users' own files in home directories via NFS from Mac OS X and CIFS from Windows. The mail service, which consists of eight separate Linux servers with a load balancer, also stores mail spools and personal settings of users via NFS. Since ECCS2008 included three discrete file servers, two for the PCs and one for the mail service, the total cost of ownership (TCO) was rather high and any available free space could not be used by the other file servers. ECCS2012 uses a single high-end file server with high performance, availability, and reliability as a primary file server, instead of three mid-range file servers.

Figure 1 shows the structure of the ECCS2012 file servers. EMC Symmetrix VMAX and Celerra VG8, as a primary file server, located at Komaba Campus in Tokyo, provides files to the PCs and the mail servers via NFS and CIFS. The primary server also provides virtual disks for virtual machines via Fiber Channel. EMC VNX 5700, as a secondary file server, located at Hongo Campus in Tokyo at a distance of 9.5 kilometers from Komaba, receives replication data from the primary one. The primary server includes three different types of drives. NAS heads of the server manage 110TB storage, which is put into a single storage pool and whose blocks are relocated automatically according to the statistics of accessing to them by EMC FAST VP. The features of the file servers are as follows.

- Since the PCs and the mail service use the same storage pool, we can assign available free space to either service.

- A combination of different types of drives keeps I/O performance high and saves on installation and electric energy consumption costs.

- A replication from the primary server to the secondary one allows us to eliminate a backup server used in ECCS2008 and gain the additional benefit of disaster recovery (DR). Elimination of the backup server also reduces the management cost of backup schedules to zero.

2.3 Mail Services

ECCS2012 provides mail service to both users of the PCs and of a mail hosting service. The hosting service hosts numerous mail domains used in the university, which are typically sub domains of the university. In ECCS2008 we provided two different types of mail servers to reduce the burden of users' migration, but the TCO was extremely high. In ECCS2012, we focused on reducing our TCO instead of the burden of users and consolidated two mail servers into a single type, DEEPSoft MailSuite. It runs on Linux, not an appliance, and includes not only daemon services for e-mails, but also web mail, anti-virus, and anti-spam.

2.4 Printing Service

The ECCS printing service has provided *on-demand printing* and *printing with a charge* since 2004. On-demand printing in this paper (1) spools a printing job from a user first, and then (2) prints out the spooled job only when the user who sent the job designates "really print" on a *job handling PC* by the side of a printer. On-demand printing and printing with a charge reduce waste and encourage eager students to promote their private study[2].

ECCS2012 provides multi-function printers (MFP) for the following additional requirement of users.

- Digitizing paper materials using an automatic document feeder and an OCR unit.

- Directly printing Word, Excel, and PowerPoint files on users' own USB sticks using job handling PCs, eliminating the need to first log into the PC terminals. A preview of the files appears before printing so that users can check the compatibility of MS Office on the job handling PC.

All other features of the printing service are described in section 3.2.

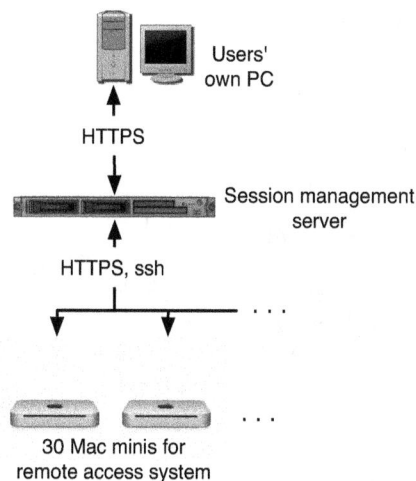

Figure 2: Remote access system of ECCS2012.

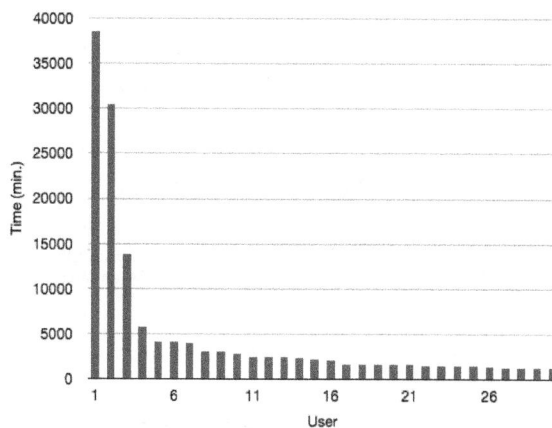

Figure 3: Top 30 of total login time.

3. ACCESS FROM OFF-CAMPUS

Most services of ECCS2008 could not be remotely accessed by o -campus users. Now, ECCS2012 makes the graphical desktop of the PC terminals and the printing service remotely accessible to promote greater use of our system.

3.1 Remote Access to PC Terminals

Since applications highly specialized for classes are installed on the PC terminals of ECCS, students are required to come to classrooms or libraries with the terminals when they want to use these applications. ECCS2008 provided only ssh remote access based on a command line method. Graphical applications were available on-campus only. The *remote access system* of ECCS2012 focuses on providing access to these graphical applications to both students at home and part-time lecturers in their own o ces without any special clients.

The remote access system consists of 30 Mac minis and a session management server at a server room (Figure 2). Mac OS X provides a VNC server feature and is already accessible remotely. Guacamole[1] enables Mac OS X to be accessible by standard web browsers with HTML5. Therefore, the remote access system requires no additional clients. The session management server acts as a mediator between users' own PCs and the Mac minis. When a user accesses a login page on the server with his/her browser and succeeds in logging into a session, the server picks an available Mac mini from its pool and assigns it to the user. Once the assignment is made, the user's browser displays the Mac mini screen with the standard login window of Mac OS X. He/She enters his/her user name and password again to log into Mac OS X. If the authentication succeeds, his/her desktop, the same as what appears on the PC terminals, appears in his/her browser. When a session unexpectedly disconnects, the server clears the session information and forces the Mac mini to reboot through a ssh connection at which point it is put back into the pool.

1,584 unique users have logged into the remote access system. Figure 3 shows the top 30 of total login time. There are a few heavy users and many light users. About 15% of source IPs are on-campus and 85% are o -campus. The 30

Mac minis are too many because the maximum number of simultaneous login users is only eight.

3.2 Printing Portal and Payment by E-money

The printing service is connected to o -campus resources to allow users to do the following:

1. Printing their jobs to o -campus printers, provided by Net Print Service described below, in the same way as to on-campus printers,

2. Sending print jobs from their own PCs at home or research laboratory to on-campus printers,

3. Paying for printing charges with e-money.

The rst and the second above correspond with (1) and (2) in Figure 4 respectively. A printing portal located in Fuji Xerox DC (o -campus) is connected with our printing job spooler via VPN and mediates between on- and o -campus resources. The PC terminals and the users' own PCs with a special printer driver can send a print job to the printing portal. The driver can be set to direct the portal to either send the job to the on-campus spooler and/or the o -campus MFPs. The driver is provided by Fuji Xerox Co., Ltd., which operates *Net Print Service* (NPS) and the MFPs at 7-Eleven Japan stores. NPS is an independent commercial service. If a user uses NPS, he/she does a free registration of NPS, uploads his/her le to NPS via web browsers, and can print it at any 7-Eleven Japan store. ECCS users who wish to print at 7-Eleven stores, need to register NPS and set up the printer driver prior to sending a printing job.

The only printing payment method in ECCS2008 was 1,000 yen prepaid cards. The ECCS2012 printing service accepts e-money, Suica, as well as prepaid cards. Suica, a prepaid and rechargeable e-money card, was developed by East Japan Railway Company, a.k.a. JR East. Since Suica and Suica compatible IC card, are widely used at railway stations and commercial stores in Japan, most students already have these cards. If a user wants to print out only a few pages, all he/she has to do is to put his/her Suica on a reader connected with on-campus MFPs. There is no need to purchase a prepaid card.

The number of printing jobs sent to the printing portal is 1,285 from March 2012 to March 2013. About 9% of them

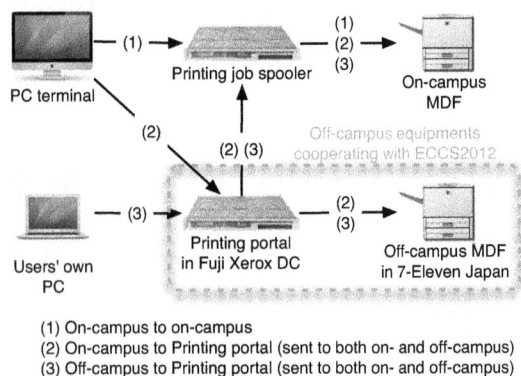

(1) On-campus to on-campus
(2) On-campus to Printing portal (sent to both on- and off-campus)
(3) Off-campus to Printing portal (sent to both on- and off-campus)

Figure 4: Printing job flows of ECCS2012.

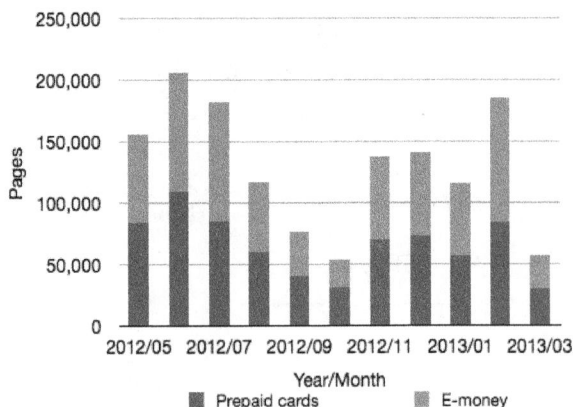

Figure 5: Details of payment methods.

are jobs sent to NPS. The percentage is low because the NPS service charges 20 yen per an A4 monochrome page, double the cost of printing on-campus. NPS may be too expensive for students who do have a less expensive alternative. About 68% of source IPs of connections to the portal are on-campus. This includes users' own PCs connected to the university's Wi-Fi service and PCs located in research laboratories. 32% are located o -campus. These users install the driver on their own PCs and can then send printing jobs to on-campus MFPs.

Figure 5 shows details of payment methods from May 2012 to March 2013. The total printed using prepaid cards is 726,543 pages and the total for e-money is 704,846 pages. The number of pages paid for by e-money appears to be increasing, but the prepaid cards total is still higher. One reason may be that a 1,000 yen prepaid card includes a print allowance equivalent to 1,050 yen.

4. SUMMARY

In this paper, we provide an overview of ECCS2012, especially the ability to connect to o -campus resources, such as the remote access system, the printing portal, and e-money. These services increase usefulness for users. The complexity of the system, however, increases and makes solving problems harder. We will continue to measure the usage of services and provide feedback on the next ECCS.

5. ACKNOWLEDGMENTS

Thanks to NEC Corporation, Canon IT Solutions Inc., and Fuji Xerox Co., Ltd. for supporting us in implementing and operating the remote access system and the printing service of the ECCS2012.

6. REFERENCES

[1] *Guacamole - HTML5 Clientless Remote Desktop.* http://guac-dev.org/.

[2] K. Ando and T. Sekiya. New Approach for Printing System Management in University Environment. In *The Special Interest Group Technical Reports of IPSJ*, volume 2005, pages 13–16, 2005. (In Japanese).

[3] K. Maruyama and T. Sekiya. Printing Service for Educational Computer System in Cooperation with O -campus Services. In *The Special Interest Group Technical Reports of IPSJ*, volume 2012-IOT-16, 2012. (In Japanese).

[4] K. Maruyama, T. Sekiya, T. Imogawa, and Y. Wada. Agent Based Management of Dual Boot PC Terminals in Classrooms. In *Proceedings of Internet and Operation Technology Symposium 2012*, pages 39–46, 2012. (In Japanese).

High-Speed Network Infrastructure between KIT's Campuses for Computer System Redundancy

Hideo Masuda
Kyoto Institute of Technology
Matsugasaki, Sakyo
Kyoto, JAPAN 606-8585
+81 75 724 7956
h-masuda@kit.ac.jp

Kazuyoshi Murata
Kyoto Institute of Technology
Matsugasaki, Sakyo
Kyoto, JAPAN 606-8585

kmurata@kit.ac.jp

Yu Shibuya
Kyoto Institute of Technology
Matsugasaki, Sakyo
Kyoto, JAPAN 606-8585

shibuya@kit.ac.jp

Yasuaki Kuroe
Kyoto Institute of Technology
Matsugasaki, Sakyo
Kyoto, JAPAN 606-8585
kuroe@kit.ac.jp

ABSTRACT

In our university, we have updated our network infrastructure from Cisco-based 1-gigabit Ethernet system to Brocade-based 10-Gigabit Ethernet system in December 2012. We use a Brocade VDX Switch for aggregation Switch. It enables not only IP networking but also provides Fibre Channel and/or Fibre Channel over IP/Ethernet. Moreover, it provides connectivity between the Matsugasaki and Saga campuses (about a 10km distance) with 10GBASE-ZR Ethernet via our regional data center. It enables a campus-wide IP Storage Area Network (SAN), allowing computer systems to be operated with distributed environments, so our computer system will have redundant features against disasters. In this paper, we will discuss the merits and drawbacks of our system.

Categories and Subject Descriptors

C.2.3 [**Computer-Communication Networks**]: Network Operations – *network management*

General Terms: Design, Management, Experimentation.

Keywords: Network Infrastructure, 10Giga-Ethernet, VCS Fabric, Disaster Recovery.

1. INTRODUCTION

Recently, TCP/IP network systems have been widely used in most universities and companies as information system infrastructures. At our university, we developed a FDDI (Fiber-Distributed Data Interface) based network system (KITnet1) in 1994. In 1996, an ATM-based network system (KITnet2) was in service. Since

2001, a Gigabit Ethernet-based network system (KITnet3) was in service. In 2009, we replaced KITnet2 with a 10-gigabit Ethernet based network system (KITnet4) described in SIGUCCS 2009 [1], and operated and managed both KITnet3 and KITnet4 as the University's backbone networks. Our replacement policy has been based on a "tick-tack" model since KITnet4. We do not replace the network infrastructure at once, but instead replace half of our edge switches and secondary backbone routers. This way, users can use the network as long as possible in spite of the system replacement project. When we reach the end-of-life period for the devices of KITnet3, we plan to replace the old part of KITnet (KITnet3). For this purpose, we received government funding for the network system replacement in 2011.

In this paper, we introduce the new network infrastructure called "KITnet5".

2. REQUIREMENTS

Network infrastructure must have sustainability, reliability and ease of management. To satisfy these requirements, we decided to do the following five things described in [1], that is, [R1] use newer network technology, [R2] use open and standard technology, [R3] use hardware redundancy system, [R4] use heterogeneous system and [R5] use the same type of hardware throughout the system.

Moreover, we suffered the great earthquake and tsunami disaster in 2011, so disaster recovery is one of the most important matters for new network infrastructure. Our campus consists of two parts: the main Matsugasaki campus and the Saga campus. The two campuses are about 10km apart. According to [2], damage to the Saga campus is assumed to be less than that to the Matsugasaki campus. Therefore, the Saga campus is the best candidate for the backup site. We decided to do [R6], providing a high-speed network between Matsugasaki and Saga.

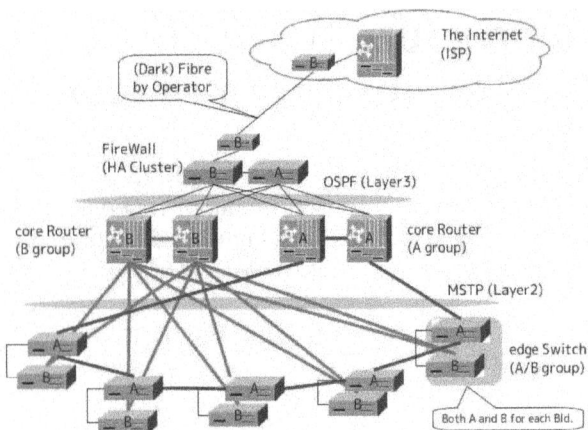

Figure 1. Basic Design of KITnet for Tick-Tack model.

3. IMPLEMENTATION

KITnet5 is a very orthodox 3-layered star topology. It consists of a core layer 3 switch (Brocade CER2024), aggregation layer 2 switch (Brocade VDX6720), and an edge layer 2 switch (Brocade ICX6450) (see Figure 2). On the other hand, KITnet4 is a ring topology and consists of four distributed stacking switches built on Virtual Chassis technology including core to edge.

KITnet5's features are as follows:

- 10Giga-Ethernet (10GBASE-LR) including inter-campus
- Star topology
- STP free (VCS and Protect-Link)

- Network and fabric feature in one device
- Limited lifetime warranty (all edge switches)

Figure 2 shows our network infrastructure configuration for KITnet4 and KITnet5. KITnet4 (Figure 2 right side) uses Juniper EX4200-48T switches for the core and edge switches. The link between switches is 10 Giga Ethernet (10GBASE-LR) with VC stacking. KITnet4 uses MSTP (Multiple Spanning Tree Protocol) and VRRP (Virtual Redundancy Router Protocol).

4. CONCLUSIONS

In this paper, our new network infrastructure is shown. KITnet5 is a star topology, inter-campus connection which is STP-free with 22 edge buildings.

We plan to continue the management of this network system and acquire further operational know-how.

5. REFERENCES

[1] Hideo, M., Kazuyoshi, M., Yu, S. 2009. Low TCO and High-Speed Network Infrastructure with Virtual Technology. In *Proceedings of the 37th annual ACM SIGUCCS fall Conference*, 321-324. DOI= http://dx.doi.org/10.1145/1629501.1629563.

[2] Kyoto disaster prevention map (In Japanese): http://www.city.kyoto.lg.jp/gyozai/page/0000086399.html.

[3] Brocade Networks: Brocade VCS Fabric Technology. http://www.brocade.com/solutions-technology/technology/vcs-technology/index.page.

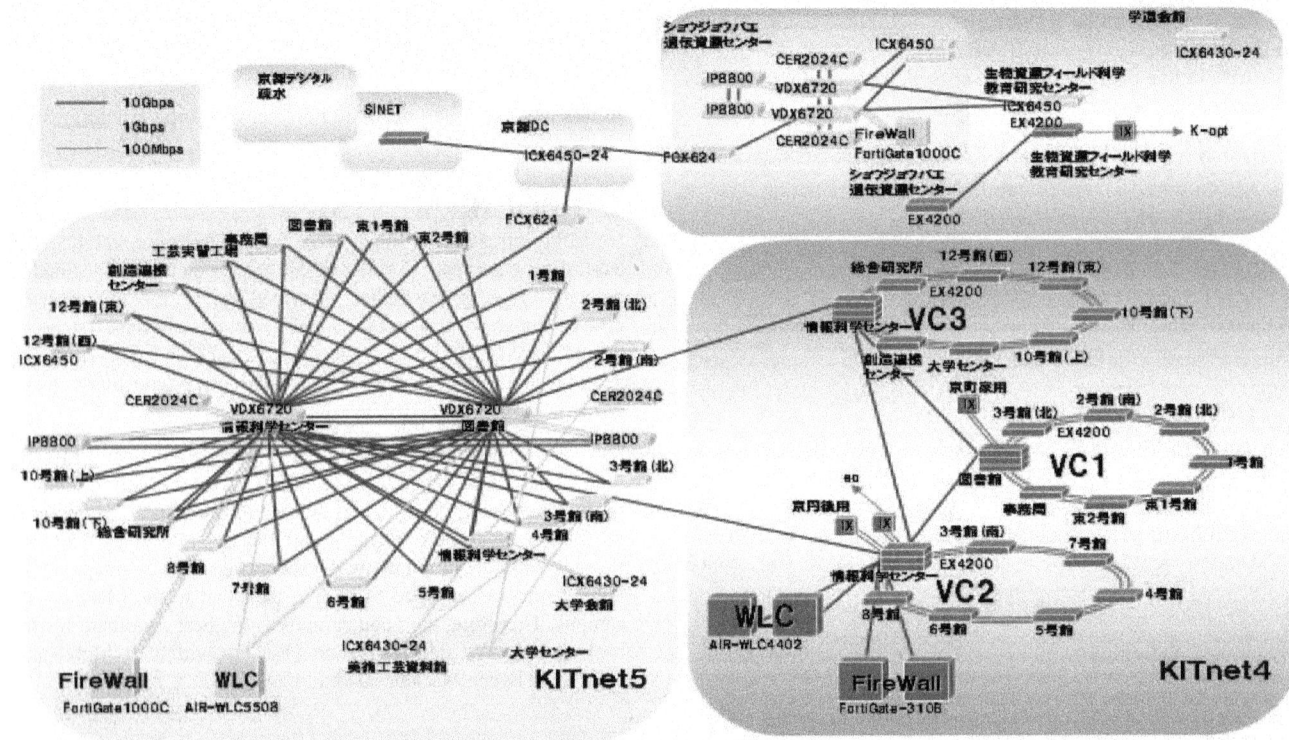

Figure 2. Network Configuration of KITnet

Creating a Mobile Computer Lab for Staff Training

Chris Washington
UC Berkeley
Educational Technology Services
Berkeley, CA 94720
(510) 643-9490
chrisw@cafe.berkeley.edu

Jon Crumpler
UC Berkeley
Educational Technology Services
Berkeley, CA 94720
(510) 643-9490
crumpler@cafe.berkeley.edu

ABSTRACT

UC Berkeley's Operational Excellence initiative is a multi-year, multi-project approach to make operations more efficient so that the University may direct more resources away from administrative expenses and towards teaching and research in supporting the UC mission statement.[1] One such project to help with the overall goal of OE is the creation of a 10 seat mobile computing lab in response to the growing need of staff training for OE projects across the UC Berkeley campus. The mobile lab was originally created and managed in March 2012 by a single FTE-technician who had to dedicate a significant amount of time managing the logistics of a new mobile computer facility. The project was then transitioned to the Educational Technology Services-Computer Facilities and its staff of 70+ student employees in November 2012. The pairing allowed for a flexible, affordable solution, which focused on the staff training needs of the campus. This allowed for the Computer Facilities staff to offer lecture-style training sessions in a traditional computer lab environment, with the new option of a mobile lab setup for smaller staff training sessions held in a departmental meeting room or office space.

Categories and Subject Descriptors

K.6.1 **[Project and People Management]**: Training

General Terms

Documentation, Management, Human Factors

Keywords

Staffing, training, student employees, hardware management, maintenance,

1. INTRODUCTION

The mobile lab was envisioned by a project manager and a project coordinator at CalPlanning, a division of the Berkeley budget office that was asked to provide support for a campus-wide rollout of a new departmental budget. Sara Teacle and Catherine Lloyd devised a plan to hold traditional training lab sessions, but also wanted to provide the many campus departments with individual support through a series of breakout sessions. These breakout sessions would be held in departmental conference rooms and

would offer a substantial 3 hour block of time for the department budget team to work on its assignments with the training staff on-hand to answer questions. The computer facility staff set up ten laptops with a computer facility image, which was configured to deliver a fast boot and a no-frills user experience.

1.1 A Campus in Transition

The mobile lab operated with minimal issues for the spring 2012 semester. Over the summer sessions, a campus-wide efficiency initiative began transitioning the mobile lab to the computer facilities staff. Once in the hands of this staff, the challenges of operating a campus-wide mobile lab came to light.

1.2 Analyzing Initial Challenges

In its initial state, the mobile lab was set up and monitored on-site by a full-time employee. The flexibility of the tech's hours allowed for the mobile lab to be set up on short notice, but having the tech remain present for the duration of a potentially 3 hour training session was not an effective use of University resources. The challenge posed to the computer facilities staff was to find a way to offer the mobile lab to a host of departments, deliver a consistent experience in a variety of rooms across campus, create a scenario that allowed for short notice setup, and also allow for flexibility in the full-time employee's schedule. The solution was students.

2. SERVICE BREAKDOWN

The following is a breakdown of the workflow established to screen new clients, new locations, and the policies used to create a student-managed project.

2.1 Reservation Policy

New clients are directed to the computer facility instructional scheduler. This instructional scheduler then assesses whether the client's needs would be better met by a mobile lab or traditional computer facility. Ten days' notice is required for preapproved rooms or clients with no software requests. Three weeks' notice is required for appointments that require a software install or room check (wireless, available outlets, projection space, etc.).

2.2 Software Requests

Software installs or changes to the stock image require three weeks' notice. A rush order option is available when the technical staff schedule permits. In order to avoid a bloated image, the client is told that all installs will be deleted after the appointment unless specific arrangements are made. Clients must provide software keys with every request, as the machines are regularly reverted back to the standard image.

2.3 New Conference Rooms

New locations are tested for reliable wireless connections, potential power or projection issues, and space for the student consultant to remain on-site. The coordinator of mobile lab appointments must arrange for early access for this initial test.

2.4 Appointment Setup

Student staff are booked for 30 minutes before and after an appointment. Coordinators are asked to admit student staff 15 minutes before a given appointment, to allow for setup time. Students are asked to introduce themselves to the meeting facilitator and will give warning that they will be approached in the last 10 minutes of an appointment. This interaction gives the facilitator the chance to extend the meeting past the original appointment while allowing the student staff to arrange for a replacement from one of the 6-12 currently shifted employees.

3. OUTREACH

Having successfully delivered 2 months of service for 75 booked hours with the current model using a restricted client base, the next step is identifying upcoming training initiatives that would benefit from a traditional computer lab training that would be supplemented with breakout sessions. UC Berkeley is currently going through a multi-step efficiency initiative, and the result is a steady list of campus-wide programs that are perfect candidates for the mobile lab's offering.

Another potential avenue for clients to find the mobile lab is through the campus event services. Several requests have come through this channel, but clear communication of the service is essential as one time clients with software requests can quickly generate more work than we are equipped to handle at this early phase.

4. STUDENT STAFF

The 80 students working for the computer facilities were pooled to manage the setup, staff scheduling, and training for the mobile lab. The project was assigned to Cynthia Tang, a student employee. Cynthia was added to the scheduling calendar for the mobile lab and was asked to monitor this calendar for updates. She then assembled a small team of students from our existing staff and through the use of training documentation and checklists she was able to train students to manage the setup and assessment of a location within one hour.

4.1 Training Documentation

Cynthia Tang created three training documents to quickly on-board student staff. The speed with which a student employee could be trained was key, as many last-minute appointments were made with less than a day's notice. In these instances, Cynthia would pull staff scheduled in the general computer facilities and train them during or shortly before setup.

The three training documents were entitled "Laptop/Projector/Printer Setup," "Client Service Options," and "Room Assessments." "Laptop/Projector/Printer Setup" was a step-by-step walkthrough of hardware setup with captioned pictures. "Client Service Options" outlined policies for the mobile lab and procedures for how and when to approach the clients. "Room Assessments" is a checklist that the student employees review to verify that the room is ready for an appointment (outlet count, surface suitable for projection, etc.).

5. TECHNICAL SPECIFICATIONS

The laptops are loaded with a basic image that prioritizes boot speed and client requests. Local profiles are used to access the laptops and upon logout the profile reverts to its original state, deleting any newly added local content. Reservation specific software requests are placed in labeled folder on the desktop. Once a week the laptops are connected to a port replicator for remote updates.

5.1 On-site Set-up

Once at the location, the student staff log in to the laptops using a local profile. The laptops and surge protector power strips are arranged according to the client's specifications, each laptop is connected to a mouse for ease of use, and the coordinator is reminded of the available projector and printer options. The computer is configured to load Internet Explorer and this brings up the campus wireless login screen. Clients are asked to use their own credentials to access the campus wireless network.

6. INITIAL AND ON-GOING COSTS

The initial labor costs for the first semester the lab was in use was $999.15, which included mobile lab scheduling, communication, technical administration, software configuration, staff supervisor planning, location vetting, and logistics with student support staff. Ongoing costs were estimated at $275.00 per week, including all tasks previously mentioned.

Ten Dell Latitude E6220 laptop computers were purchased for $1350.00 per computer. Equipment costs, including the initial purchase of the ten Dell laptops, were $16,531.15, which also included a portable projector, portable printer, Netgear Ethernet switch, Ethernet cables, and an AV cart used for transportation.

For future costs and expansion of the mobile lab service, an additional ten Dell Latitude E6230 laptop computers and sleeves will cost $11,720.00. Additional future equipment costs are projected to be $8517.90 for laptop power cords, Dell port replicators, a Netgear Ethernet switch, a storage cabinet with power, Ethernet connections, and fans for ventilation.

Table 1. Estimated Total Costs

Total Labor Cost – Start Up	$999
Total Labor Cost – Ongoing (One year equals 50 Weeks)	$13,750
Total Equipment – Current	$14,761
Total Equipment – Future	$20,238
Total	**$49,748**

6.1 Cost Recovery

In terms of cost recovery, we would consider proposing a two-tier recharge rate. For campus departments needing a laptop lab with custom software install and other requests, we would consider charging $500-999 for startup costs and a weekly rate of $275. For departments needing the mobile lab for a short term with no additional requests, (they would use the base software image), the recharge rate would be an initial startup fee of $275 and a weekly rate of $275.

7. CONCLUSION

The usefulness of the mobile labs service was certainly proven in the pilot test case and the coming semesters will hopefully illuminate further uses for the mobile labs. The service is posed to add a truly dynamic element to our instructional offerings. Internally we were very pleased with the results of trusting aspects of this project to students. Allowing the students to design and write their own training materials and management model cut down on the amount of hours needed on our end, and in the end gave the students a real sense of ownership over their stake in this pilot.

8. REFERENCES

[1] *UC Berkeley Operational Excellence What is Operational Excellence* http://oe.berkeley.edu/vision/whatisoe.shtml, 2009 Web September 2009

Make the SIGUCCS Experience Last
Become a Local Chapter

Lisa Brown
University of Rochester
Rush Rhees Library
Rochester, NY 14627
1 585-275-9162

lisa.brown@rochester.edu

Mat Felthousen
Cleveland Institute of Art
11141 East Boulevard
Cleveland, OH 44106
1 216-421-7384

mfelthousen@cia.edu

ABSTRACT

In 1997, as a result of conversations that started during a SIGUCCS conference, several NY state schools formed a regional conference called NYCHES (New York Computing in Higher Education Symposium). SIGUCCS attendees from these schools wanted to continue the 'SIGUCCS dialogs' throughout the year, so NYCHES has met a few times a year since 1997, with participation increasing to include dozens of schools across central and western NY state.

Schools would volunteer to host the day-long meeting, and provide food for the attendees. There was no membership fee to be involved in NYCHES, so costs to attendees were minimized to travel expenses. Cost containment, particularly in the face of constricting travel budgets for many schools, made a regional conference an attractive option for schools that could not afford to send many people to national conferences. Even so, based on their experiences in NYCHES many members became active SIGUCCS attendees, and conversations started during SIGUCCS would continue on in NYCHES meetings through the year.

On March 19 2012, NYCHES became the first local chapter for SIGUCCS. SIG Chapters, and their membership, receive considerable benefits from the Association of Computing Machinery (ACM) including website hosting, membership tools, mailing list hosting, recruitment tools, ACM email addresses, subscriptions to ACM publications, and access to the ACM Distinguished Speakers Program. Chapter members are not required to pay for membership, unless they wish to serve on the Board of the Chapter, so despite the substantial benefits, costs to their respective institutions are still minimized.

This paper will discuss how NYCHES was successful as a regional conference, and how this format could be duplicated in other parts of the country. It will also discuss how the members of a regional conference would benefit from a formal association with both ACM and SIGUCCS.

Categories and Subject Descriptors

K.3.1 **[Computers and Education]**: Computer Uses in Education; K.6.1 **[Management of Computing and Information Systems]**: Project and People Management; K.7.2 **[The Computing Profession]**: Organizations

General Terms

Management, Standardization

Keywords

Regional conference, Helpdesk

1. INTRODUCTION

On March 19 2012 the first local chapter of SIGUCCS, called 'NYCHES Chapter of ACM SIGUCCS', was established, with a Board comprised of Lisa Brown from the University of Rochester (Chair), Laurie Fox from SUNY Geneseo (Vice Chair), and Mike Allington from St. John Fisher College (Secretary/Treasurer).

The origin of this chapter can be traced back more than 15 years to a SIGUCCS conference, when several attendees discussed how to continue the SIGUCCS experience and networking opportunities throughout the year. From that conversation, a regional group called NYCHES - New York Computing in Higher Education Symposium - was formed. NYCHES representatives have typically been from four-year higher education institutions in western and central New York.

NYCHES has met three to four times a year since 1997, with a school hosting a day-long meeting based on topics proposed in advance by attendees. There are no fees for membership. Schools would volunteer to host the meeting, including providing food, so that the responsibility and costs involved in the meeting would be minimized and equitably distributed. The meetings usually concluded with a tour of the host's facilities so that each school has an opportunity to showcase their accomplishments. NYCHES participants have included dozens of institutions and more than a hundred participants, many of whom became active in SIGUCCS as a result of NYCHES.

In addition to SIGUCCS, NYCHES participants have also attended conferences such as EDUCAUSE, NERCOMP (a regional extension of EDUCAUSE), ResNet, LabMan, Infocomm, and HDI. NYCHES meetings benefitted from this wide range of experiences as the information would be shared back to the group. A frequent comment at NYCHES meetings over the years was that in terms of opportunities to network with peers, SIGUCCS is a unique resource.

It was a logical progression therefore for NYCHES to become a Local Chapter for SIGUCCS. The sole requirements for establishing a chapter are to have three Board members who are members of both ACM and SIGUCCS, and to have ten members who would be willing to carry out the mission of the chapter. Nearly 40 NYCHES members voted unanimously to establish a SIGUCCS Chapter.

Chapter members are not required to pay for membership, unless they wish to serve on the Board of the Chapter. Board members must be members of both SIGUCCS and ACM (Association of Computing Machinery). Despite the substantial benefits of being associated with both ACM and SIGUCCS, costs to chapter members and their respective institutions are still minimized. SIG Chapters, and their members, receive considerable benefits from the ACM including website hosting, membership tools, listserv hosting, membership recruitment tools, '@acm.org' email addresses, subscriptions to ACM publications, and access to the ACM Distinguished Speakers Program.

2. WHAT / WHO IS NYCHES?
NYCHES was formally established in 1997 based on efforts of IT professionals from Syracuse University and Cornell University. These two individuals made contact with IT professionals from four other schools to pull together the first ever meeting. That small group decided that a forum was needed to provide an ongoing idea exchange. More information about the early NYCHES years can be found in the 1999 SIGUCCS conference proceedings.[1]

Much has changed since 1999. People have changed jobs and left the group, but word about the group has spread. We now have participation from over twenty schools in the central and western NY region and over eighty active members subscribed to our listserv.

We meet annually at least twice a year at participating host schools and model our meetings around the SIGUCCS experience. Sometimes a host school will present about a new technology that they are in the process of implementing and discussion/questions will follow. Other times, the topic will be an open forum for discussion of a specific topic so participants can get an understanding of how that service is being provided at other schools. In addition, we always leave time for a round robin of quick questions that have recently come up at the schools.

3. WHAT / WHO IS ACM?
The Association of Computing Machinery (ACM) is the largest educational and scientific computing society in the world, with more than 96,000 members. ACM publishes more than 40 publications, organizes more than 150 conferences annually, and has 34 Special Interest Groups, including SIGUCCS. ACM is also home of the premier Digital Library[2] for the computing industry, which includes 50+ years of content.

Individuals can become members of ACM for $99/$198 yearly, with lifetime memberships being available. Membership benefits include:

- Email digests, 50+ journals
- Learning Center, aimed at lifelong learning
    - 4500+ online courses
    - Online books (Safari ® and Books24x7®)
- ACM Career & Job Center
- Email forwarding/filtering (you get an @acm.org mailing address)
- Discounts, such as on insurance, shopping, subscriptions, car rental, credit cards
- Access to ACM Digital Library, at the higher price level

4. WHAT / WHO IS SIGUCCS
SIGUCCS is the Special Interest Group on University and College Computing Services. With a membership of several hundred people, SIGUCCS' content includes the annual conference, webinars, listservs, Facebook, and LinkedIn sites.

For more information on SIGUCCS, please visit http://www.siguccs.org/

5. SIGUCCS MEMBERSHIP
For $25 per year SIGUCCS members receive the following benefits:

- Access to ACM Digital Library for SIGUCCS content
- Access to a members-only listserv and webinars
- Discounted registration fees for conference ($110 for the combined conference this year)

For more information on SIGUCCS membership, please visit http://www.siguccs.org/involve/join.html.

6. BENEFITS OF BEING A LOCAL CHAPTER OF ACM SIGUCCS
Local chapters of ACM Special Interest Groups are entitled to a number of administrative tools, including the management of membership rosters and an ACM-hosted website. Additionally, events offered by the chapter can be posted on the ACM Activities calendar[3] to broaden the exposure of the organization.

If your local chapter has less than ten members, ACM will help recruit members from your area. They can also provide ACM promotional materials[4] for chapter events and offer access to a list of distinguished speakers[5] for your events with over 250 lectures from nearly 100 different speakers.

For more information on Special Interest Group Chapters, please visit http://www.acm.org/chapters/sig.

---

[1] http://dl.acm.org/citation.cfm?id=337125&dl=ACM&coll=DL&CFID=102793126&CFTOKEN=11014398

[2] http://dl.acm.org/dl.cfm

[3] http://campus.acm.org/public/chapters_conf_cal/index.cfm

[4] http://campus.acm.org/public/profqj/promotional_materials.cfm

[5] http://www.dsp.acm.org/

7. INDIVIDUAL BENEFITS OF CHAPTER MEMBERSHIP

Aside from the benefits a chapter enjoys from being associated with ACM, individuals who are members of a chapter receive:

- A complimentary three-month electronic subscription to ACM's publication *Communications of the ACM*

- Eligible for an "acm.org" email forwarding address with Google Postini filtering

- E-Newsletters: *TechNews* 3 times weekly, *CareerNews* bi-monthly, *MemberNet* monthly

8. FORMING A LOCAL CHAPTER

Becoming a local chapter is easy. A group needs ten members and a Board comprised of a Chair, Vice Chair, and a Secretary / Treasurer. The three Board members must hold membership in both ACM and SIGUCCS. Every year the chapter must submit an annual report consisting of information about meetings, as well as a financial report (if necessary).

For NYCHES, we already had over 10 members participating on a regular basis at our meetings. We also had eight people willing to participate as board members, so we scheduled a vote. We do not collect dues or have any financial standing, so an annual report will simply be a recounting of our meetings and planning for the future.

9. OUR DECISION

In November of 2011, we decided to bring information on being a local chapter to the group and make a decision. Various factors were weighed when we made our decision.

9.1 PROS

Since NYCHES grew out of the SIGUCCS conference and meetings are modeled after SIGUCCS, a relationship with both ACM and SIGUCCS would be a good thing. It would provide a level of professional association to the group, and it would bring broader exposure to the group.

Chapters are offered a number of services through ACM, including a listserv and website. While NYCHES had always been fortunate to have a stable listserv presence through one of the participating schools, we had not been so lucky with a website presence. The opportunity to have both of these hosted in one location that allowed shared maintenance was a bonus.

Being affiliated with both ACM and SIGUCCS offers professional development opportunities beyond what was possible with remaining a separate regional conference, in terms of networking with a broader audience. This networking would also benefit SIGUCCS with recruitment of attendees for the annual conference.

Finally, we considered the many ACM and SIGUCCS membership benefits, including access to the Digital Library.

9.2 CONS

One of the drawbacks of becoming a local chapter was a fear of losing our branding. We had been NYCHES for so long that we had hoped to keep this name recognition. This ended up not being an issue as we learned after our vote that we were able to keep NYCHES in our chapter name.

A second potential drawback is the expenses for the three board members. Each is required to have individual membership in both the ACM and SIGUCCS organizations. For most people willing to participate on the board, this was not an issue.

Third, expansion of membership may make it more difficult to identify host locations for meetings, or force us to choose central locations for the main meetings.

Despite these concerns, NYCHES voted unanimously in favor of becoming a Local Chapter.

10. FUTURE PLANS

At our first official chapter meeting in April 2012, we talked about how to make the best use of our new organization. Volunteers from various schools stepped up to take charge of different identified gaps, specifically membership management, hosting challenges, and our website. We also talked about continuing to meet twice annually (spring and fall) for general topics, but added that we should identify more specific topics to engage smaller groups between meetings.

General, large group meetings would consist of NYCHES business, as well as broad topic discussions. Smaller meetings would focus on a specific topic, possibly things that drew a lot of discussion or interest during a general meeting, such as desktop virtualization, as was the case from our inaugural meeting as a chapter. Future small meetings may also address areas like learning management systems, audio/visual support, and staff/team management issues.

We have also received interest from a number of schools about hosting future events, while identifying problems that have come up in organizing past meetings. Previous hosts are planning to put together a checklist for future hosts so that we can help overcome these issues.

The group also discussed accepting vendor support for meetings and decided that they did not want to lose touch with the spirit of NYCHES. NYCHES meetings had typically been a venue where individuals could discuss both pros and cons of products and vendor relationships. They did however indicate that they wanted individuals from the group to share opportunities with the rest of the chapter for meeting with vendors of specific technologies, so that multiple schools could attend.

Membership was discussed, and we determined that anyone from the NY region willing to travel to our host location should be allowed to attend. We will continue to recruit members from area schools and encourage them to join us. We will also encourage hosting in all locales, with the expectation that the host school provides information on low-cost accommodations for those traveling long distances.

Since that initial meeting, the chapter has continued to flourish. We've held our fall and spring meetings and had great attendance at each. We've developed a new web site, hosted by ACM. We've developed an informational spreadsheet where each school provides information about the technology that they support so members can easily find colleagues working in similar environments. We continue to make use of the listserve to remain in contact with each other, ask questions, and share ideas. And we share information about technology events on our campuses. We've also done a new officer election and passed the reins on to a new chair, vice chair, and secretary/treasurer.

11. CONCLUSION

As travel and conference budgets shrink due to economic pressures, regional conferences are very cost-effective ways to achieve some of the benefits of attending the SIGUCCS conference. The time commitment is minimal, just a day in most cases, and the travel costs are typically limited to mileage reimbursements. In exchange, chapter members develop the same types of long-lasting connections with peers at other institutions that they do at SIGUCCS, and the conversations can continue throughout the year.

ACM and SIGUCCS both benefit from increased awareness and potential increases in membership, as institutions who could not otherwise afford to send personnel to the annual SIGUCCS conference will still learn from the experiences shared by other chapter members. For more information on NYCHES ACM SIGUCCS, please visit http://nyches.acm.org/

Mixing and Matching Usage Data:
Techniques for Mining Varied Activity Data Sources

Owen G. McGrath
Educational Technology Services
University of California, Berkeley
omcgrath@berkeley.edu

ABSTRACT

Digital systems underlie a wide range of teaching and learning activities in higher education today. The scope and reach of digital systems now increasingly extend to activities as they occur even inside lecture halls, classrooms, and informal study areas. Learning management systems, interactive student response systems, lecture capture systems, and digitally controlled smart classrooms are examples of technology trends that bring along with them an unprecedented amount of instrumentation quietly collecting lots of data about teacher and learner activities in and across these various spaces. In snapshots, these usage streams offer data that can be helpful for understanding and supporting a particular service. If combined across time and location, the varied data sources potentially open windows onto even more interesting activity patterns and relations. These mosaics, however, can be somewhat difficult to analyze due to the dimensionality of the combined data. Matrix techniques can ease the difficulties of exploring and discovering user activity patterns in such situations. This paper surveys commonly implemented matrix techniques that can be used to enable data mining of user activity information when temporal and spatial data sets are mixed and matched from varied sources.

Categories and Subject Descriptors

K.6.1 [**Management of Computing and Information Systems**]: Project and People Management – *systems analysis and design.*

Keywords

Usage data mining, usage analytics, matrix techniques

1. INTRODUCTION

Encompassing a wide range of goals and approaches, data mining of user activity in e-learning systems has become a research field

in its own right in the past decade [1]. Typical approaches to data mining of e-learner activities focus on how to find patterns in learner on-line behavior. Often what gets analyzed are the so called click stream trails left behind by students visiting, browsing, and interacting with e-learning content and tools. Various patterns are arranged into groupings (e.g., based on the activities, roles, and timing involved) that can shed light on issues such as how to evaluate student progress or improve system usability.

Data mining of e-learners and their distributed activities throughout the day and night can present technical and analytical challenges, especially in terms of the dimensionality of the combined usage data sources. With web-based teaching and learning systems, two aspects of data tend to hinder analysis: many variables and broad time scales. When combined, the multitude of variables and the extension of usage patterns across time can overwhelm basic analysis algorithms. One favored solution to the dimensionality and time scale problems is to put the data into large matrices [2]. Once in a large matrix, the combined data some common matrix manipulation techniques can be applied that render the data more accessible for basic data mining. This paper offers an example of how such matrix manipulation techniques can be applied in supporting usage analyses data mining for a large web-based Sakai CLE e-learning deployment. The matrix techniques demonstrated can be carried out in a freely available package for Matlab [3][4], but can also be carried out in freely-available software such as Weka, Gnu Octave, or the R software for statistics [5].

2. BACKGROUND

2.1 E-Learner Data Mining Approaches

Usage analysis of e-learner behavior depends on data logged as users navigate through various online learning systems. The variety of data mining investigations is broad and ever increasing, but one of the most common approaches is clustering analysis. The goal of clustering analysis is to see what inherent groupings if any exist in the data, i.e., what items in the data are alike. In the context of e-learning system usage, a clustering analysis might reveal that the site's users fall into groupings based on their evaluated performance on assessments or the pathways they took through the on-line content [6][7].

Before clustering usage analysis can begin, the source data must be combined in a phase that involves resolving not just variations between data formats but more fundamental differences in underlying information models. At this mixing and matching stage, logged data from across the system is strung together based on common dimensions such user event location and time span. In a Sakai system, for instance, nearly all core tools log activity in about sequence, timing, and location of user-generated activity. The various sources can be brought together on dimensions of user, location, and time.

2.2 Multi-Dimensional Usage Data

In considering Sakai usage, the data involved lends itself well to a matrix representation. In a matrix approach to user activity data combination, the various data sources are first merged into a large flat file of rows and columns, with rows representing individual user sessions. To create the a mosaic, the source data can be merged into a spreadsheet with columns representing, for instance, each possible event and flag variables for attributes such as location or user type (e.g., undergraduate, graduate).

In the specific context the Sakai on-line learning environment, the data mining project might seek to understand how the system's many thousands of users are accessing and using the various sites and tools of the collaboration and learning environment in different locations over time. Across a semester, what do user sessions look like in terms of duration and actions? What many different activities do students and instructors carry out during different sessions? Which activities go together? In data mining, to examine differences and similarities across many thousands of on-line sessions is to reveal useful characteristic aspects of users' interaction with the system that might otherwise remain invisible. These analyses can identify common groupings and trends in data sets across large spans and dimensions.

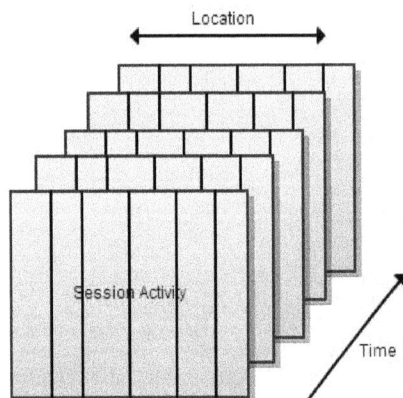

Figure 1. Multi-Dimensional Matrix of Sakai user actions.

Although the data could be made easier to process at this point by collapsing some or all of the dimensionality, such a reduction brings with it the disadvantage of information loss. Flattening observations across the time dimension, for example, is usually done by binning the observations into certain fixed time labels (e.g., morning, afternoon, evening). From then on in the analysis, time patterns that might exist across or beyond those categories are lost. An alternative technique uses one big multi-dimensional

matrix for holding observations. Keeping all the data in one large matrix opens up the possibility of looking at relations across a large number of variables simultaneously without loss of detail along any of the dimensions. Investigating e-learner behavior can then turn towards looking at how user session patterns might be changing across various locations (e.g., classrooms, computer labs, libraries) and arbitrary periods of time. Extending the usefulness of a simple two dimensional matrix, it is easy to imagine having many matrices layered together across time. If a single large matrix is like on frame of a movie, many matrices might be layered together in a sequence like the frames of a movie.

2.3 Mining Time & Location Usage Data

The key matrix techniques for making multi-dimensional data accessible for further mining analysis are the so called decompositions that can be performed. Matrix decompositions might be thought of as techniques for unfolding a matrix. Different unfoldings can be used to get different perspectives onto the ways the data relate across dimensions of the matrix. Depending on the ordering and size, different decomposition can be applied to in order to open up a high dimensional matrix for use in a data mining clustering investigation. Clustering of the subcomponents can then be performed, in turn, to reveal a lot about the essential data relationships that were otherwise difficult to discern in the original form [8]. The output of the decomposition analysis allows the original matrix in a sense to be teased apart, with its essential data displayed in parts aligned in different ways.

Using the matrix decomposition technique to explore multivariate usage data from the Sakai CLE system can lead to the discovery of interesting relationships. When looking, for example, at user session activity data across dimensions of time and location, the output of the matrix decomposition allows for a clustering analysis revealing a spectrum of different session types. Examining the spectrum, it is possible to see groupings of usage activity that characterize the neighborhoods usage activity. In the case of evaluating participants session activity patterns, clustering reveals different usage activity neighborhoods around short sessions of on-campus locations during various periods the day where the activity is primarily access to course documents. In contrast, particularly in the afternoon and evening, off-campus usage cluster show activity more oriented towards document editing and assignment submissions. This approach to analyzing user session data provides a quick gauge for measuring thousands of users' session activity patterns across hundreds of locations during long periods of time. The basic partitioning can reveal whether particular activity types in the system are more prevalent in particular time and location orderings and what sort of content and tools characterize the different activities.

For making sense of user session activity across locations within a particular time window, the matrix analysis approach breaks the core multi-way matrix down into a subset of two dimensional matrices that provide insights into system usage. Using decomposition functions separates the sessions orderings across several smaller matrices. As a starting point towards allowing clustering of the system usage and other next steps towards exploring activities, these unfolding techniques can be done in different ways across dimensions of the larger starter matrix. The decomposition approach to unfolding user session data from one large matrix provides a way of opening up for inspection the many characteristics and patterns held within the giant snapshot of user sessions. For analyzing e-learner user sessions along time dimensions with matrices, practical solutions can be found in the freely-available Tensor Toolbox for Matlab [4] or the PTAk package for R [10]. Both provide techniques for constructing and analyzing multi-dimensional matrices. The uncovering of relations using a matrix decomposition can become the starting point for more extensive data mining to user activity clusters. Clusters of student interactions with the learning management system might reveal aspects of the environment that need re-design in order to meet individual needs in the online user experience more effectively [11] [12] [13].

3. CONCLUSION

Gathering and analyzing usage activity can be a very time consuming task. With the matrix techniques, however, the analysis process is made much easier, allowing for pattern discovery in the enormous amount of data involved. This paper has been intended mainly as brief overview of how efforts to address the particular usage reporting needs of one Sakai CLE production service. Through mining user activity across many dimensions, trends and patterns can become discernible, and their contexts better understood. This process, as noted, benefits from follow-up empirical investigation in the evaluation phase [14]. The deployment phase can lead towards a repeatable process that leverages the potential and promise of data mining for assisting those in higher education who are responsible for implementing and maintaining internet-based services.

As a complement to data mining, educational matrix techniques provide a toolkit for uncovering usage structure and access patterns within the enormous volume and variety of multivariate user data generated in such systems. For Internet-based services in higher education to keep up with the increasingly high standards that institutions place on them, the analytical tools and processes we employ will need ever greater power and flexibility. In most cases, practical aims are motivated by the ongoing need for understanding, supporting, and managing users and usage. Given the problems posed by high-volume usage data, these matrix techniques offer crucial aid in exploring data sources commonly encountered in today's production e-learning systems. Data sources and methods are varied here. This is understandable given the range of contexts and systems involved, but the processes have much in common.

4. REFERENCES

[1] Welser, H. T, Smith, M. A. Gleave, E., & Fisher., D. (2008). "Distilling digital traces: Computational social science approaches to studying the internet." In N. Fielding, R. L. Lee and G. Grant (Eds.), Handbook of online research methods. (pp 116-140). London: Sage Publications.

[2] Cadez, I., Heckerman, D., Meek, C., Smyth, P., and White, S. 2000. Matrix of navigation patterns on a Web site using model-based clustering. In Proceedings of the Sixth ACM SIGKDD international Conference on Knowledge Discovery and Data Mining (Boston, Massachusetts, United States, August 20 - 23, 2000). KDD '00. ACM, New York, NY, 280-284.

[3] Kolda, T. G., & Bader, B. W. (2009). Tensor decompositions and applications. SIAM review, 51(3), 455-500.

[4] Bader, B. W., & Kolda, T. G. (2007). Efficient MATLAB computations with sparse and factored tensors. SIAM Journal on Scientific Computing, 30(1), 205-231.

[5] Romero, C., et al. Mining and Visualizing Visited Trails in Web-Based Educational Systems. In Educational Data Mining 2008: 1st International Conference on Educational Data Mining. 2008.Montreal, Quebec, Canada.

[6] Mazza, R. and Dimitrova, V. 2005. Generation of Graphical Representations of Student Tracking Data in Course Management Systems. In Proceedings of the Ninth international Conference on information Visualisation (July 06 - 08, 2005). IV. IEEE Computer Society, Washington, DC, 253-258.

[7] Skillicorn, D. B. (2007). Understanding complex datasets: data mining with matrix decompositions. Chapman & Hall/CRC.

[8] Sun, Y., Janeja, V. P., Mcguire, M. P., & Gangopadhyay, A. (2012, April). Tnet: Tensor-based neighborhood discovery in traffic networks. In Data Engineering Workshops (ICDEW), 2012 IEEE 28th International Conference on (pp. 331-336). IEEE.

[9] http://cran.r-project.org/web/packages/ptak

[10] Buket Dogan, A. Yilmaz Camurcu. (2010) Visual clustering of multidimensional educational data from an intelligent tutoring system, Journal of Computer Applications in Engineering Education, Wiley Publishing Company, Volume 18, Number 2, February 2009, pp. 375 - 382.

[11] Romero, C. and Ventura, S. 2007. Educational data mining: A survey from 1995 to 2005. Expert Syst. Appl. 33, 1 (Jul. 2007), 135-146.

[12] Stenmark, D. 2008. Identifying clusters of user behavior in intranet search engine log files. J. Am. Soc. Inf. Sci. Technol. 59, 14 (Dec. 2008), 2232-2243.

[13] Zdravko Markov , Daniel T. Larose, Data Mining the Web: Uncovering Patterns in Web Content, Structure, and Usage, Wiley-Interscience, 2007.

[14] McGrath, O. (2010). Data Mining User Activity in Free and Open Source Software (FOSS)/Open Learning Management Systems. International Journal of Open Source Software and Processes (IJOSSP), 2(1), 65-75.

Creating Your Master Mind: Personal and Professional Development through MasterMind Groups

Benjamin Arnold
University of Northern Iowa
1227 W 27th Street
Cedar Falls, IA 50614
1 (319) 273-2419
Ben.arnold@uni.edu

Lucas Friedrichsen
Oregon State University
121 Valley Library
Corvallis, OR 97331
1 (541) 737-8244
Lucas.friedrichsen@oregonstate.edu

Mo Nishiyama
Oregon Health & Science University
3505 SW Veterans Hospital Road
Portland, OR 97239
1 (503) 494-1406
nishiyam@ohsu.edu

ABSTRACT
Do you find it easier or more enjoyable to pursue your personal or professional goals in concert with other like-minded people? If so, a "MasterMind group" might be just the resource you have been searching for. A MasterMind group, as described by the business author Napoleon Hill, is "The coordination of knowledge and effort of two or more people, who work toward a definite purpose, in the spirit of harmony." By gathering regularly with a like-minded set of people, one can find camaraderie, advice, differing points of view, and perhaps most importantly, accountability. Within a peer mentorship environment, members are willing to hold each other responsible for their growth and progress. The MasterMind group stands in contrast to a mentor/mentee relationship because in the former, each participant stands to gain from the relationship equally.

Categories and Subject Descriptors
K.4.3 [Organizational Impacts]: Computer-supported collaborative work, Employment, Reengineering

General Terms
Management, Performance, Experimentation, Human Factors, Theory

Keywords
MasterMind Group, professional development, personal development, collaboration, group learning.

1. INTRODUCTION
The age-old saying that there is strength in numbers can apply to many facets in life, including one's professional development. It is far too common for people to internalize their own professional or personal development as a way of hiding their shortcomings from others or perhaps because they are in direct competition for advancement with others. It stands to be mentioned that going it alone for advancement or development isn't necessarily the wrong way to go about the process, just that perhaps you are missing out on a whole other facet of growing and learning: the challenges

SIGUCCS'13, November 3–8, 2013, Chicago, Illinois, USA.
Copyright © 2013 ACM 978-1-4503-2318-5/13/11...$15.00.
http://dx.doi.org/10.1145/2504776.2504791

and ideas that come from face-to-face interaction with others. You can benefit from prospering in an environment where others can provide perspectives and reality checks.

In Napoleon Hill's *Think and Grow Rich*, he devotes an entire chapter to the concept of the MasterMind group. One of the three sources of knowledge, he writes, is accumulated experience. [1] Where better to get access to such than through the collective experience and wisdom of a group of like-minded people, who work together for the advancement of all members of the group? Hill asserts that Andrew Carnegie attributes his entire accumulated fortune to the power he gained through his personal MasterMind group. Carnegie's MasterMind group consisted of approximately fifty peers, for the purpose of manufacturing and marketing steel. [2]

If the principle worked for Andrew Carnegie, who is widely recognized as one of the most successful businessmen of the twentieth century, it can work for others. This paper will outline the experiences of one such MasterMind group from formation to running successful meetings to making sure everyone participates and is benefiting from the group equally.

2. CHARACTERISTICS OF A MASTERMIND GROUP
Napoleon Hill, in *Think and Grow Rich*, defines the MasterMind group as "Coordination of knowledge and effort, in a spirit of harmony, between two or more people, for the attainment of a definite purpose." [3] This simple definition reveals several key characteristics of a MasterMind group.

2.1 The Spirit of Harmony
Collaborating in a harmonious manner is important. People tend to internalize or hide professional development for many reasons. These include the fact that they are competing with the others around them for salary, that next promotion, or maybe just for recognition from management. In an environment of competitors, one will rarely be truly open and share experiences, knowledge, and wisdom. One is always holding something back If you are in competition with any in your group you will not feel truly free to open up for fear of your weaknesses getting spread around the office or having them used against you.

That's why involvement in professional groups outside of your own organization can be beneficial. You get around the issue of competitors or generally awkward situations. You are able to improve your network, and you are introduced to others with whom you may be able to share knowledge.

2.2 Working Toward a Definite Purpose

A MasterMind group is typically focused on one purpose or theme—physical fitness, career advancement, becoming more productive, becoming better mothers or fathers, or something similar. In the case of this MasterMind group, professional development and personal improvement are the primary purposes. Tangential benefits to each member's working organization are also realized from time to time through shared resources, such as process improvement documents, publications that pertain to members' interests, and acquired knowledge of members.

2.3 Mutual Benefit for All Group Members

The difference between a MasterMind group and a mentor/mentee relationship is that all members of a MasterMind group stand to benefit from their participation equally. In the traditional mentor and mentee relationship the mentee tends to be the primary person to benefit from their relationship. "Mastermind groups create a win-win situation for all participants. New friendships develop and everyone grows because of the support and encouragement of the Mastermind group." [3]

2.4 Benefits of a MasterMind Group

Both tangible and intangible benefits can be realized from the MasterMind group. One benefit is a stronger professional network. Professionals often say "it's not what you know, it's whom you know" and the MasterMind process can you help build that network wider and deeper. Imagine the richness and depth that one gets from a conference. For example, SIGUCCS Conferences are great opportunities to meet like-minded professionals who are motivated to succeed and share knowledge in a challenging academic IT support profession.

Another benefit is developing new friendships. We are social creatures and connections happen naturally, particularly when interests and outcomes are shared. The relationships we build when meeting at conferences, which tend to be professional and social, will be enriched by interacting throughout the year. Our MasterMind group was formed after members met at SIGUCCS 2012 conference in San Diego, and discovered common interest in promoting professional development year-round. Group founder Ben Arnold initiated the first meeting few months after the conference, and we continued to meet on a regular basis. The group spent a lot of time together at the SIGUCCS 2012 conference, which improved the conference experience that much more!

With the open, nurturing and non-competitive nature of a MasterMind group, new ideas are easily and readily shared. Documents, input and feedback, and work are also generally shared. For example, one member of the group led his first interview and hiring process in early 2013. He requested input for any step in the process and received sample interview questions, a hiring process checklist and a set of staff expectations. That member reported less stress during the interview and on-boarding process because of the help and support he received. Plus he did not have to reinvent the wheel which saved time and money for his university!

Life can be full of stress and sometimes disappointment, but the MasterMind group provides a fresh breath of encouragement. Members continually encourage each other through tough times and recognize accomplishments. The positive energy this generates can help sustain members between the meetings, through rough patches at work or even motivate them to seek new challenges by changing their work environment.

The group can provide external accountability and motivation, through the mechanism of gentle peer pressure, particularly if a member has a tough task or deadline to meet. Generally, the member dos not want to disappoint the team, so effort is made to accomplish an item. Though our group hasn't, a MasterMind group could go so far as to assign action items and formally check up on their completion at the beginning of each meeting.

Imagine a group outside of work, family and close friends that constantly pushes you to do your best, looks out for your best interest and is genuinely interested in the topics and input you provide—not to mention, a group that will listen to your ideas and respond in kind with honest feedback and different perspectives before you present to your colleagues. All of these elements can be found in a MasterMind group.

3. FORMING YOUR OWN MASTERMIND

3.1 Reach Out to Your Network

Strengthen your network and leverage your existing connections to find people interested in joining a MasterMind group. Examples of networks to consider include:

- SIGUCCS
- EDUCAUSE
- LinkedIn
- Former college colleagues
- Former student employees
- Local professional groups (Young Professionals, technology user groups, etc.).

Expand your network with professionals in similar situations or positions within your local area. Consider reaching out to people at other universities in your area who work in the same job field. Often people in the same job area, regardless of company or organization, encounter similar circumstances and can help each other out.

3.2 Similar Drive and Commitment

Similar to a professional organization, a MasterMind group benefits from a shared drive and a set of goals. Elements of our MasterMind group include continual learning, encouragement, helping each other and looking out for the best interest of the group. Our focus on continual learning helps keep the group on track. Topics change with each meeting, which helps keep each other on our toes and thinking about new things. Encouragement is provided during the meetings, particularly when a member is having a rough time at work or with something outside of work (the MasterMind group provides a safe harbor for offering condolences, providing advice, and venting). Between meetings, group members often seek out the MasterMind group to vet ideas, gather feedback on upcoming presentation methods and ideas, or to gather insight before addressing tough topics. Having a group to lean on outside of work that provides helpful and objective advice has been useful and timely. The group will deviate from the standard meeting time to accommodate changes in schedules or life's hiccups. The group feels it is important to include everyone as often as possible. We have discovered that accommodating the schedules of our members also provides the maximum benefit to the individuals and the group.

3.3 Diverse Skill Sets or Experiences

Diversity is the spice of life and MasterMind is no different. Incorporating professionals from all levels of the organization brings a new and sometimes surprising perspective to the discussion and interaction. Our MasterMind includes a Chief Information Officer (CIO), a director, an IT manager, lab manager and support and documentation staff member. The CIO offers high level strategic input, while managers and staff provide the daily operational level of input. This diversity provides a rich and comprehensive discussion. If the group were comprised of people at a single organizational level (e.g., managers), the discussion would generally focus around topics that are specific to the job class: diversity of perspectives would be limited. Our MasterMind group also treats all participants as equals regardless of their job titles or rank.

Additional diversity can be achieved by looking outside of your current job type. Imagine a MasterMind group comprised of a programmer, helpdesk staff, database administrator, system administrator and a director or CIO. The richness of ideas and input from that group has unlimited potential. A helpdesk staff member with limited coding experience might bring up a topic that could be simplified by automation through programming, which is a skill that a programmer or DBA uses on a more daily basis. The interaction might yield a method to save the helpdesk staff member time by writing a script to perform a certain set of routine and mundane tasks. In an ideal situation that would free the helpdesk staff member to eliminate that work, add a quick check and balance and perform more value-added work. But why limit it to IT professionals? As long as a member is invested in growth and and committed to the group, there is no reason to exclude people from other business units such as human resources, finance, facilities, etc.

4. TIPS AND TRICKS FOR RUNNING YOUR GROUP

4.1 Expectations and Culture of the Groups and Meetings

As with any organizational group, the culture will often reflect the values of its members. When the MasterMind group consists of individuals who value fostering a supportive environment in which mutual support of its members and betterment of the entire group are expected, less time needs to be spent on setting ground rules and addressing housekeeping issues. MasterMind members who value progress and accountability will meet their goals and accomplish their action items with greater frequency than those who do not hold themselves to higher standards. In situations where members stray from the group's culture, other members may need to intervene to preserve the spirit of the group. An effective MasterMind group will be self-policing and self-correcting as long as expectations are communicated in advance.

4.2 Organization

To be effective, a MasterMind group needs to have a manageable membership size. Although the diversity of ideas can enrich larger groups, the logistics of coordinating meetings and organizing groups will outweigh any benefits gained from having perspectives of large membership. An ideal size for MasterMind group is no greater than seven members. All members are viewed as equals, regardless of titles they possess in their professions: members regularly rotate roles for facilitating meetings, setting agendas, and note-taking.

4.3 Topics

Discussion topics tend to be quite dynamic and generally based on the meeting facilitator's decision. More often than not, the meeting topic is influenced by something that is happening at work or will take place in the near future. Another method to consider for topic creation is to work with the group during the first few sessions to brainstorm ideas for the next few weeks and

set out an agenda. This will allow additional preparation time for participants on topics where they feel that they can't effectively contribute.

Some examples of meeting topics for our group include:

1) Confrontation and Conflict at Work: Difficult Discussions.
2) Personal and Employee Development: Goals for Next 1, 5, 10 Years
3) Experts: How to Work With and Learn From Them?
4) What Transformative Technology or Solution Would You Implement?
5) Time Management and Avoiding Burnout
6) Keeping Current on Knowledge
7) Your First 90 Days in a New Position

4.4 Agendas

Productive meetings generally start with an agenda provided to attendees ahead of time to allow time for preparation. For the MasterMind meeting, the agenda is shared at least 24 hours prior to the meeting. The facilitator and organizer of the meeting selects the topic, determines the questions and talking points and provides links to resources as required. A sample agenda from a past meeting is listed below.

7:00 p.m.- (PST) - Call Starts

7:05 p.m - Covering Old Business. Any important quick updates on items from last meeting?

7:25 p.m. - New Discussion Topic: New manager or boss (new boss brought into your department)

1) How do you build the relationship to foster mutual respect and trust? What has been effective in the past?

2) How to properly on-board them? What methods do you use to bring them into the department effectively?

3) What if the previous vision of the department is different than the new manager's or boss's vision? How do you deal with that?

4) You have been in the department for years and know how things operate; you have a vision for the department and respect of colleagues and staff. What are the best ways to approach the new manager or boss about new ideas, improvements, etc.?

5) Any other questions or feedback the group has on this topic.

8:20 p.m. - Discuss New Goals and Challenges for the Next Two Weeks

8:30 p.m. - Call Ends

Our group experienced "meeting creep" from time to time, a situation where the group is meshing well and one part of the agenda lasts for much longer than anticipated (something that never happens in the working world...!). For situations like that, our group found it helpful for the facilitator to check in with the group, either to keep the meeting agenda moving forward or to stay focused on that topic and defer the agenda to a later time. Meeting creep can also happen if the agenda is too extensive. If you want each group member to contribute, keep in mind that each person will take 1-3 minutes to respond. Subsequent follow-up meetings may be scheduled if an agenda is too big to fit to be accommodated in a single meeting. Our group encountered that situation with the agenda listed above and had to shorten some of the later questions.

4.5 Recognition

Sustaining energy through tough topics or situations is improved by providing time for reflection and recognition. Our MasterMind group has found an effective method of sharing "wins" from each individual during every session. These are "wins" or items of self-recognition since the last meeting and serve as a reminder of how much is accomplished. Often that discussion sparks ideas or prompts other members on things they can do within their own organizations. To help move the "wins" category along, each member shares his or her goals to achieve by the next session.

4.6 Meeting Duration and Interval

Coordinating a group of people to meet on a regular schedule can be a challenge. Committing to meeting regularly takes away time from members' other commitments (e.g., family, work). Therefore it is essential to respect each member's time. The meeting duration should be sufficient to cover both ongoing business and discussions. The interval for meeting should be long enough to allow for participants to work on challenges between meetings. Our group has found that meeting every two weeks for ninety minutes each session provides time for each person to participate effectively and reflect on lessons learned during meetings. Meeting every two weeks also provides the group with momentum that would not be as strong if the meetings only occurred once every month or longer.

4.7 Notes and Minutes

Keeping timely and accurate notes is essential for maintaining the effectiveness of the MasterMind group. Notes taken from MasterMind meetings can be used to track the progress of the group, monitor peer accountability, and track best practices and suggestions that are offered by other members. A good practice for taking meeting notes is to have someone other than the meeting facilitator take notes. Rotating responsibilities on a regular interval is suggested.. Another good practice is to prepare for upcoming MasterMind meetings by formulating loose notes based on the agenda items before the scheduled meeting.

Our MasterMind group has experienced success using cloud-based collaborative systems. Google Drive and Google Docs are used for maintaining ongoing meeting notes, for sharing references which relate to meeting topics, and even for one-off collaborations which occur between meetings. By leveraging the powers of these tools, our MasterMind group has overcome the limitations of being geographically separated from each other.

4.8 Interaction Methods and Tools

There are several collaborative software solutions, both free and commercial, that can be used to facilitate MasterMind group meetings. The free version of Skype video chat software allows up to three participants in a group chat (more participants can be added with a premium Skype subscription.) Zoom.us is another free solution which can be used for this purpose.

Our MasterMind group has relied almost exclusively on Google HangOut video chats. The advantage of this platform is integration with other Google service apps that are used in the course of meetings: Gmail for sending calendar invites, Google Drive and Google Docs for managing meeting notes, and Google Chat for messaging.

The value of collaborative video solutions can be extended for SIGUCCS members' benefit beyond MasterMind meetings. These solutions have potential for hosting online Birds-of-a-Feather sessions, informal hangouts, and for presentation collaborations.

5. LESSONS LEARNED

The early MasterMind group meetings were less structured and more casual. Over time, we added structure to meetings to ensure that we dedicated time to discussion topics in the meetings. We began assigning the rotation of meeting facilitators, defined roles for each meeting (e.g., facilitator, note-taker), and stressed amongst ourselves the importance of keeping meetings on schedule.

Our group has found that a facilitator needs to focus on the conversation and should not also take notes or minutes for the meeting. That has become a standing rule for each meeting and provides members with valuable experience leading meetings and writing notes for a wider audience.

Although technology is a powerful enabler which allows remote collaborations to occur, there are several important items which must be taken into consideration when holding MasterMind meetings online. Access to a reliable high-speed Internet connection is an essential prerequisite for an effective meeting experience. Any multimedia hardware and software, including video cameras, microphones, and even new computers, need to be tested for functionality before pressing them into service. Our MasterMind meetings begin with five minutes of "grace period" where members are expected to rectify any technical issues which may arise with their computing equipment.

Finally, even though technology plays a major role in the creation, execution, and success of the MasterMind group, the most important element of the group involves building and maintaining relationships with other members. Our MasterMind group started with professional relationships which were built and solidified at past SIGUCCS conferences. After discovering mutual interests in career and professional development, and a desire to promote ongoing dialogue and exchange of ideas throughout the year, the MasterMind group was formed.

As a high-performing and resource-intensive group, starting a MasterMind group will require time commitment, trust, being open to suggestions, and a desire to learn and better oneself. Having solid relationships with other members is essential for MasterMind groups to succeed. It is advisable to nurture relationships with other members before diving into the full-blown MasterMind process. Another method is to find people with similar interests and use the first set of MasterMind meetings to create the relationships.

6. ACKNOWLEDGMENTS

Many thanks to Allan Chen, Jacob Morris, Mo Nishiyama, Ben Arnold and Lucas Friedrichsen for the success of the MasterMind group. The dedication to each other's productive improvement and success has been a breath of fresh air at all times, both personally and professionally. These are strong relationships that will continue to improve and stand the test of time. Mad props to Ben Arnold for finding the topic of a MasterMind group and approaching the group to start it up!

7. REFERENCES

[1] Greenstreet, Karyn. 1997. How to Create and Run a Mastermind Group. In *Passion for Business*. http://www.passionforbusiness.com/articles/mastermind-group.htm

[2] Hill, Napoleon. 1937. *Think and Grow Rich*. The Ralston Society. Meriden, CT.

[3] Hill, Napoleon.

Facebook: How We Lost Control and Found Empowerment

Cate Lyon
Whitman College
345 Boyer Ave
Walla Walla, WA 99362
(509) 527-4976
lyoncd@whitman.edu

Robert Fricke
Whitman College
345 Boyer Ave
Walla Walla, WA 99362
(509) 527-4976
frickerg@whitman.edu

ABSTRACT

Whitman College Technology Services (WCTS) constantly strives to find new and interesting ways to engage and connect with our student body as well as to empower our student staff. Additionally, social media engagement has been challenging; of the two separate Facebook pages associated with WCTS, the most recent update was several months ago. A marriage of problem and solution was discovered: we let go of control and let our student staff manage our Facebook presence. This solution not only allows us to better engage the student body but also gives our student staff more responsibility and "real world" experience.

Categories and Subject Descriptors

K.6.1 [**Management of Computing and Information Systems**]: Project and People Management – *management techniques*

Keywords

Facebook, Whitman College, Student Staff, Student Employment, Social Media, Management.

1. INTRODUCTION

Whitman College is a liberal arts college located in Walla Walla, Washington and was founded in 1882. Whitman's student body consists of approximately 1600 students from 45 states and 30 nations[1].

Whitman College Technology Services (WCTS) consists of 25 staff members and typically 35 student staff. WCTS is divided into different work groups consisting of Support Services, Network Infrastructure, Enterprise Technology, and Instructional and Learning Technology. The student staff is employed at the Helpdesk, Library Technology Desk, Instructional Media Services (IMS), and the Multimedia Development Lab (MDL).

WCTS currently has ownership of 2 Facebook pages and 7 Twitter accounts. As of February 1, 2013, the WCTS Facebook page had last been updated in November 2012. This page had 97 Likes and 7 administrators. Over half of the Likes are of current or former WCTS staff and student staff. The Whitman College Multimedia Development Lab Facebook page had last been updated in May 2010. 1 of the 7 Twitter accounts is currently in use while the rest have never tweeted. The currently used Twitter

---

[1] http://www.whitman.edu/about-whitman/fast-facts

account (@WCTS), is used to update the community about network and service outages. The use of these accounts is sporadic and ineffective as the messages being sent out were going to those that currently work for the organization and not to the Whitman community as a whole. WCTS has never made social media a priority.

The role of the student staff at WCTS has been underutilized; they generally fill their downtime on the job with homework, socializing with friends, or just browsing the internet. The role of the student employees has changed little in the past several years. A supply runner, for instance, goes from computer lab to computer lab stocking paper and toner in the printers as well doing general tidying up of the room. When they have that completed, they have nothing else to do. We saw this as an opportunity for them to get more involved and take on more responsibility within the department. However, we weren't decided on what form that responsibility should take.

While attending the 2012 SIGUCCS conference in Memphis, TN, we attended several sessions that addressed social media use on college campuses as well as sessions about managing student workers. While attending one of the sessions, an idea was sparked. Why not let go of control of our Facebook and allow our students to design and develop WCTS' social media presence on campus. This would allow us new ways to engage our student staff and give them experiences that can be included in their resumes. Additionally, this allows us to address their stated interest in expanding their responsibilities and becoming more involved in WCTS.

2. WHAT WE THOUGHT WE WERE GOING TO DO

It was very important for us to be guides in this process; we did not want to dictate the project. However, there were certain goals and objectives that needed to be decided upon prior to starting the project.

- Define goals
- Determine our audience
- Define our strategy
- Determine rules and guidelines

While we had many objectives, our most important one was to engage the students. Our aim was not just the WCTS student staff participants, but to engage the greater Whitman community. The initial rules and guidelines we came up with were very broad – things such as nothing personal, acceptable language, frequency of posts, etc.

Because we weren't certain exactly what social media vehicle to use, we decided to survey our current student staff. The survey was designed with questions such as – "What social media do you use?" and "Do you "like" the WCTS page currently", etc. Our survey results reflected those of the survey the Whitman College Pioneer newspaper found, "According to a *Pioneer* survey of 120 students, Facebook is the primary form of social media used by students. 95 percent of survey respondents have a Facebook account. Of the Facebook users, 60 percent of survey respondents check their account multiple times per day."[2]

Once we received our survey results, we decided to test the water with one of the WCTS Help Desk student managers, Greg Dwulet. Greg confirmed the use of FB as the social media of choice. This was due to the fact that a large number of students already have a FB account. He also agreed with our choice of creating a "new" FB presence, one that would be independent of the current WCTS FB page as many of our survey responses found that the current WCTS page is "dry".

3. OUR PROJECT STARTS TO CHANGE

It was now time to meet with our immediate supervisor. We needed her buy-in to move forward with the project. She agreed that WCTS showed a need for someone to direct our social media communications and encouraged us to go forward with this project in order to expand our professional growth.

In addition, she gave us 3 questions to answer.

1. Clarify what you're trying to accomplish and why:
2. How do you measure what you're trying to accomplish?
3. What is the beginning and what is the end of your project?

These questions forced us to solidify what we're trying to do and how we're going to accomplish it.

An initial timeline was developed as a result of this meeting as well. Within 3 months, we wanted to have an advertising campaign launched including the choosing of a mascot, a page name, advertisements and a campus-wide campaign developed. Within 6 months, the page should be launched and sustained almost exclusively by the WCTS student staff. By the end of the school year, the page should have 100 fans (likes). A summer project should be developed that will advertise to the incoming freshman class. Within 1 year, we want to have at least 250 fans (likes).

Our next steps were to start student involvement in the project. We decided to meet with the student managers after break in order to discuss volunteers, a mission statement and a minimum time commitment. An additional goal was to involve the students on an added project that would be to create a campaign for the Higher Education Information Security Council's Information Security Awareness Video and Poster Contest. We decided that the timeline to complete this goal for the current submittal year would be unrealistic and adjusted our goal to have a project for the 2014 contest.

3.1 Our Project Changes More

Prior to our initial meeting with student staff, we met with the Assistant Vice President of Communications, Ruth Wardwell, to discuss Whitman College's social media guidelines. To our surprise, we discovered that there are none documented. The college does have a style guideline to which we will adhere as this page is an official representation of Whitman College. The

---

[2]   http://whitmanpioneer.com/news/2012/10/04/social-media-communications/

meeting with Ruth also provided us the opportunity to get another perspective on this project. She gave us some recommendations on how to better involve the students in the project. She suggested that the students should create their own guidelines for the project as well as that the Facebook page be name Whitman College_____ so that it could be easily found while doing a search on Facebook. Ruth also offered the services of the official Whitman photographer for any photographic needs that may present themselves for the Facebook page.

3.2 First Meeting with Student Managers

The first meeting with student managers occurred two months after our meetings with our management and the communications department. The meeting was requested with the student managers with little to no prior context. A few of them had heard rumblings of a "Facebook project" but none were sure what exactly that meant. When we all finally met, the topics of this initial meeting were to:

1. Determine rules, regulations, and guidelines
2. Discuss project measurements and set expectations and goals from both the WCTS and Student Staff viewpoints
3. Create a campaign for the CyberSecurity Awareness Month
4. Determine the name of the Facebook page and if a mascot will be used
5. How to recruit volunteers and how the hand off will occur from one year to the next
6. Determine what the student managers want to achieve with this project

Great conversations were started at this meeting. The student managers were enthusiastic and very interested in the project. We began by discussing what we as WCTS could do with social media. This led to what content could be used for posts and the mentioning of the fact that the MDL was also currently working on another project that would parallel this project. The MDL is working on creating blog posts about questions that are commonly asked in their area. These could be questions about Photoshop, Final Cut Pro, general layouts, etc. Other potential topics that were brought up included "non-techy" items like general campus events. We felt that the page should be well rounded and could draw and keep the attention of a variety of users, not just the "tech savvy." Finally, we discussed the issue of whether or not the current Facebook page should be kept or deleted entirely and started from scratch. Opinions varied in the room. A pro that was presented was that the page already exists and has current followers whereas it could be more difficult to attract followers to a page in its infancy. A con for keeping the current page was that the current posts and material were dry, infrequent, and may detract a potential follower from liking the Facebook page. The meeting was left with the student managers giving their buy-in into the project and the group of them some tasks to complete before the next project meeting.

3.3 The Students Take Over

The next meeting was called about a month later by the student managers. They came prepared with a PowerPoint presentation which addressed the tasks that were assigned to them from the previous meeting. The following is a list of the tasks they were given with their responses below them.

1. Creating Guidelines for the Facebook page:

a. Posting will occur bi-weekly

b. Posting will be managed by the student managers, and each manager will be assigned on a weekly rotation

c. Managers may delegate responsibilities as needed to other student staff

d. All managers should review the page frequently and assess content.

e. Manager will choose subjects that fall within an umbrella of topics that have been predetermined

f. Managers will be responsible for addressing a diversity of topics.

g. Managers are collectively responsible for keeping a buffer of 4 weeks worth of content.

h. There will be a "borrowing" policy for the buffer posts. If you take one, you must put one back within 2 weeks.

2. Creating a Timeline as to when key items will be completed and when the Facebook page will be launched

a. Submit CyberSecurity video by March 8, 2013

b. End of spring 2013 confirm 6 topics of interest and have created 3 potential posts from each topic.

c. Page should be running by August 2013, ten posts will be posted prior to freshmen arrival to kick off the page.

d. Begin consistent, bi-weekly posting starting fall 2013.

3. Creating sample posts and topics for the "new" page

a. Topics

   i. Campus facilities

   ii. In the News

   iii. Gizmo Geek Out

   iv. How-to Guides

   v. General Computer Tips

   vi. Q&A

   vii. Pertinent Updates

   viii. Leisure

b. Posts

   i. Computer Availability Map

   ii. Manual Device Registration

   iii. GoPrint setup

   iv. Detecting Phishing

   v. WCTS Department Summaries and overview of services available

vi. Basic Guide to Computer Maintenance

vii. Outage Notifications

viii. Etc....

4. Creating a Mission Statement as to guide them and future members of the Facebook team

a. To increase student access to and knowledge of the technology services that are available to them on Whitman's campus by engaging them in social media.

5. Coming up with a plan for doing a campaign for the Cybersecurity Awareness Month

a. A rough draft video was presented

6. Creating a Marketing Plan

a. Competition at the beginning of Fall 2013 semester to design the cover photo for our page. Rewards incentive.

b. Put "like us on Facebook" on everything. Signs at the helpdesk, library desk, IMS, MDL.

c. Encouraging consultants to like and share our page.

d. Getting in touch with the Pio (school newspaper) about advertising.

7. Deciding on the state of the current Facebook page: out with the old and bring in the new or revamp what is there.

a. We need a chance to grab people's attention

b. This project is student generated content

c. Students are more likely to "like" a new page than look at an old page they've already liked.

d. Easier than trying to clean out the old page.

8. Deciding on any resources that they may need for the project. This includes money, marketing materials, etc.

a. Need access to posting sites such as

   i. Vimeo

   ii. Imgr

b. Access to the equipment in the MDL and IMS

Their presentation was very thorough but left us with two questions that we felt still needed to be answered.

1. Will the rest of the WCTS student staff participate? When?

2. What is the exact timeline for page launch?

3.4 Selling the Project to Stakeholders

A meeting was held with our immediate supervisor, the Whitman College ISO, and the CTO for final consent. As the driving force on the project, student managers David Wilson and Greg Dwulet, presented on behalf of the WCTS student staff. They came prepared with their PowerPoint and to answer any questions that the stakeholders may have had. Our goal was to quell any fears about handing over something that is so visible and representative of WCTS to our student staff. This was the meeting where we asked the stakeholders to let go of control. To achieve this we discussed our motivations for the project and WCTS' history with social media. At the end of the meeting, the following concerns were brought up.

1. The destruction and recreation of the current WCTS page was very troubling to some attendees. The argument was that people would be forced to re-like a page that they have already liked. The concern was that we would lose followers.

2. If a post needs to be removed immediately (copyright, inappropriateness, etc.), would there be someone available to remove them?

3. Inconsistent security-related advice. Could the ISO still post to keep the message consistent and avoid any potential of any "unsafe recommendations getting out there?"

These were very strong objections that needed to be resolved. However, we as the project managers were not going to make these decisions for the students. We stated that "this is a page that is being 'led' by the students. We are there to guide, not to jump in and try to persuade them one way or another. We have strong feelings that this is the perfect opportunity for them to deal with opposition to the way they want to do the project – let's see what they say." We stated that the arguments that were presented in the meeting will be addressed with the students at our next group meeting.

One of the really positive outcomes was the suggestion by management that we bring a student to help us present at SIGUCCS and bring their perspective.

3.5 The Bump in the Road

As a culture, we keep our doors open and encourage anyone to stop by our desks and just talk. At the beginning of April, during one of these moments, it became clear that there was some underlying stress in conjunction with the project. The semester was beginning to wind down and finals, orals and theses were on the horizon. At this point we realized that we had not asked ourselves, "Are we prepared to allow this to fail?"

Our resounding answer to this was "No." Falling back to status quo was not an option. Fortunately, we had a meeting already scheduled and we decided to ask.

1. How is your stress level? Do you need anything from us?

2. Are the timeline and scope still achievable?

3. Has a decision about keeping or discarding the page been made?

In addition to this, we asked them to read the WCTS Mission Statement as well as an article about launching successful Facebook competitions.[2]

All of the student stakeholders were able to attend this meeting for the first time. Without being prompted, they as a team presented to us a new timeline and scope of the project. Due to 4.5 weeks being left in the semester, decisions were made to keep the old page versus a new one and to delete the old content, and bring in more of the WCTS student staff to help. They also adjusted the timeline for advertising the campaign. Rather than beginning at the end of the school year, they made the decision to wait until the end of August as content will be available on the page. The one drawback to this timeline is that the incoming freshman will be inundated with information so we must figure out a way to make the Facebook campaign standout. One idea was to collaborate with the Student Advisors and get this project highlighted during their training and tours of campus.

"Why are you doing this?" was asked to the group. The first response from many was "because you asked us to." This led into more discussions about how to get information about WCTS dispersed to students on campus. This information is stuff that we take for granted. We are not even cognizant of the fact that many students don't know it. For instance, many seniors still have no idea how to setup the printers on campus, they don't know where the helpdesk is, and what other resources are offered. Our favorite response to the question was from Jake. "At first I thought this was stupid, then I thought it was hopeless. Now it is a challenge." His reasoning was due to the various ways that people use or don't use Facebook.

Finally, we reminded them that this page is a representation of WCTS as a whole and we gave them a copy of the WCTS mission statement. We asked them to keep this close while planning, developing content, and posting.

4. A REMINDER OF WHY

Five months post SIGUCCS 2012, we found the original notes that we had passed back and forth during one of the sessions we attended. The notes were as follows:

RF – "Problem w/ our FB & Twitter accounts is that WCTS staff are the majority of followers. Does us no good."

CL – "That's why we need:

1. New Accounts

2. Students to have ownership – there should be an 'advisor' but no policing of posts – just approval

3. Discussion based

4. Develop strategy. Again, not dictated from the top down. Let them develop it.

We will continue to monitor progress as the project develops. At this point, we have handed over nearly all control of the WCTS Facebook page to our student staff. They plan to continue development throughout Summer 2013 and have designated August for the page launch.

Office 365: Tips to Avoid Turbulence While Moving Faculty and Staff to the Cloud

Beth Goelzer Lyons
Cornell University
B06 CCC
Ithaca, NY 14853
607 255-3928
bgl1@cornell.edu

Tom Parker
Cornell University
739 Rhodes Hall
Ithaca, NY 14853
607 255-7521
tom.parker@cornell.edu

ABSTRACT

Moving more than 23,500 locally hosted Exchange email and calendar accounts to Microsoft's cloud-based Office 365, with almost no disruption to the work of Cornell University's faculty and staff, was a carefully choreographed, well-practiced yet dynamic dance. Ten key factors:

1. Close coordination, partnership, and collaboration with Microsoft to plan and implement the migration and to escalate and resolve issues

2. Early campus awareness

3. CIO periodic updates to the University leadership and campus community on plans and progress

4. Early and continuous involvement of IT leaders and IT staff both within the central IT organization and throughout the campus

5. Early awareness and management of business-affecting changes

6. Local expertise with Exchange

7. Extensive Cornell-provided web pages on preparing for Office 365

8. Targeted email guiding individuals to complete specific to-do's at three weeks before their move date, two weeks, one week, the day of, and the day after

9. End-user support at the unit level and through the central IT Service Desk

10. Daily web conference call with the project team for IT leaders to discuss status and issues

Categories and Subject Descriptors

Electronic mail; *Training, help, and documentation*; Microsoft Exchange; Microsoft Outlook; Microsoft Office 365

SIGUCCS'13, November 3–8, 2013, Chicago, Illinois, USA.
Copyright is held by the owner/author(s). Publication rights licensed to ACM.
ACM 978-1-4503-2318-5/13/11...$15.00.
http://dx.doi.org/10.1145/2504776.2504813

Keywords

Microsoft Office 365, Microsoft Exchange, Outlook, Email Migration.

1. INTRODUCTION

Moving more than 23,500 locally hosted Exchange email and calendar accounts to Microsoft's cloud-based Office 365, with almost no disruption to the work of Cornell University's faculty and staff, was a carefully choreographed, well-practiced yet dynamic dance.

In the fall of 2011, a small team of Cornell IT professionals evaluated the suitability of cloud-based email services for the University's faculty and staff. The students had been using Google Apps for Education since 2008, but at that time, the available cloud-based services did not yet meet the requirements for faculty and staff. By 2011, those deficiencies had been addressed, and the significant service efficiencies and improvements offered by the competing cloud-based email and calendar vendors became extremely attractive.

Microsoft's Office 365 service was ultimately selected as the best fit. Cornell's faculty and staff were already using Microsoft Exchange, so transitioning to Office 365[1] would mean minimal disruption, little change in the functionality the campus depended on, and familiar email and calendar clients and practices. Ten key factors made this a reality.

2. TEN KEY FACTORS
2.1 Close coordination, partnership, and collaboration with Microsoft

While somewhat new to large-scale migrations in the higher education space, the Microsoft team arrived with considerable experience doing high-volume moves for corporations. The overarching goals of the project, as well as project fundamentals defining the scope, recommended methodologies, roles and responsibilities, and conditions of satisfaction, were outlined in a lengthy and detailed Statement of Work document that was

---

[1] The use of the term "Office 365" in this paper refers only to Cornell's migration to Office 365's Exchange service. Office 365 also includes integrated communication features (instant messaging, voice, video), collaboration and shared work spaces (SharePoint), and other productivity tools. At Cornell, these Office 365 services were deferred for future deployment phases.

carefully reviewed and refined to the satisfaction of both Microsoft and the Cornell team.

For most projects, Cornell relies on a fairly mature set of project management methodologies developed for higher-education environments. In this case, an early project decision was to make use of Microsoft's experience and recommendations, wherever possible, in building our detailed project plan. A Microsoft-maintained SharePoint project site facilitated the sharing of Microsoft's standard process documents for Office 365 migrations and was used to track progress, to-do's, and open issues.

At the request of the Cornell Project Management Team, Microsoft provided a dedicated project manager to serve as the point person for the Microsoft effort. Close cooperation at the project-manager level proved valuable in both directions. It allowed the Cornell team to make full use of Microsoft's considerable experience while helping the Microsoft team navigate some of the complexities that are unique to our higher education environment. In addition, regular, ongoing communications among various levels at Cornell and Microsoft, both technical and on the customer account side, built a strong, effective foundation.

2.2 Early campus awareness

In March/April 2012, Office 365 was identified as the option that would offer the fastest transition with the least amount of change for Cornell faculty and staff. Chief Information Officer and Vice President Ted Dodds engaged University leaders to gather community feedback and concerns.

Their input considered, Dodds announced the decision to the campus in early June. Separate emails were sent to Cornell's deans and vice presidents, to IT leaders, to IT staff, and to general faculty and staff. This strategy established Dodds as the visible, enthusiastic project champion for all levels of the university. Throughout the project, we followed this model of communicating directly with these constituencies to great success, with some communications coming from Dodds and some from the project team.

It was crucial that the June communications set the right tone about what to expect, so that we could begin building confidence that switching the email and calendar system in such a short amount of time was a good decision and one that would be successful. Three years before, Cornell faculty and staff navigated a tremendous change to email and calendar, when the University switched from a Cyrus IMAP/POP system plus Oracle Calendar to an all-in-one Microsoft Exchange system. A key attraction to Office 365 was that the transition this time would be relatively minor, for the most part. With the memory of the previous move still so fresh in people's minds, we built the reassurance of sameness and "minor changes" into all of our faculty/staff communications.

The June faculty/staff message was just a few sentences:

"In fall 2012, the Cornell email and calendar system for faculty and staff will be switched from the locally provided Exchange service to a Microsoft cloud-based service called Office 365. This service provides the same email and calendar system faculty and staff use today, and everyone will be able to continue using the same Outlook, Outlook Web App, Thunderbird, Apple Mail/iCal, and other ways of accessing email and calendar. It is not

necessary for faculty and staff to take any action at this point. Specific details will be provided in later communications."

A link to the project website and our standard contact information for the IT Service Desk concluded the message.

The messages to the deans and vice presidents, IT leaders, and IT staff added details on estimated timing for the move and the rationale. Throughout the project, we provided more extensive information to these constituencies to position them to provide guidance and answer questions from their management and from faculty and staff. For IT leaders and IT staff, these details also helped them prepare to support the move.

The June messages marked both the start of campus awareness and the project itself. The tradeoff with such early communications was vagueness. We had a good sense of the scope of the change, but could offer only our best guess as to precisely when migrations to Office 365 would start. To compensate, we used time ranges, such as mid-September to November/December, along with phrasing to indicate that dates would be validated later on as part of internal pilot migrations. This proved to be a wise strategy, since the dates did in fact shift by about 10 weeks.

The next update to faculty and staff came in early August. Signed by Chief Information Officer and Vice President Dodds, it briefly answered why the email system was changing, the timing (now October 2012 to February 2013), the fact that faculty/staff could expect to take some steps to prepare (with the specifics to come later), and reassurance that support would be available both centrally and within their unit.

2.3 CIO periodic updates to the University leadership on plans and progress

Every 8 to 12 weeks during the Office 365 project, Chief Information Officer and Vice President Dodds provided high-level progress reports to the University's senior administrators. Prior to the start of migration, these succinct email messages recapped the nature of the project, outlined the timeline and the expected impact to the campus, and reiterated the close partnership between the project team and the IT leaders in each academic and administrative unit. During the migration, the focus shifted to a report on the percent moved, the fraction reporting issues after migration, and our process for working with Microsoft to resolve issues. These email updates, as well as Dodds' in-person meetings, created top-down awareness of and social support for Office 365.

2.4 Early and continuous involvement of IT leaders and IT staff both within the central IT organization and throughout the campus

In Cornell's decentralized IT model, the central IT organization provides University-wide IT services and an IT Service Desk to support all members of the Cornell community. Most academic and administrative units also have a small IT organization that provides unit-specific IT services and support for their faculty and staff. In the past few years, a formal structure has been established through which the central IT organization and the IT leaders in each major unit collaborate, coordinate, and set direction.

In keeping with this model, both the Office 365 project team and its steering committee included a few IT leaders from the academic and administrative units. The regular IT leaders' meetings had a standing agenda item for Office 365. Each IT leader also partnered with the project team to set the migration dates and account groupings for their unit. We sent regular status updates by email to all IT leaders and all IT staff, on average once a week when migrations were underway. These updates were also posted to our IT@Cornell News site (itnews.cornell.edu), which is targeted at IT staff but open to anyone.

Working so closely with the IT leaders gave us critical insight into the widely varying challenges and degrees of readiness in each unit, both technical and social. They provided a necessary check on our assumptions about optimal migration timing for any given unit. They also helped us tune our communications both to IT staff and to general faculty/staff, and served as a continuous feedback loop for the project as a whole.

2.5 Early awareness and management of business-affecting changes

No transition, even from on-premise Exchange to cloud-based Exchange, can be done without requiring some amount of preparation and adjustment from the campus. And it is virtually impossible to communicate too soon about practices that people will have to change. Faculty and staff, not to mention University leadership, have deeply entrenched work practices, and they expect email and calendar, rightly so, to facilitate their work, not get in the way.

So it was strategically important to communicate about the two most significant impacts of Office 365 right from the beginning. One was a 50 percent decrease in the size of messages people could send. The other was discontinuing support for BlackBerry devices.

The message size limit affected faculty and staff in two ways: they would no longer be able to rely on email for sending files larger than 25 MB, and any existing messages in their mail account that exceeded 25 MB would not be moved to Office 365. About 7,000 accounts fell into the latter category.

To keep this population from growing, and to give campus as much time as possible to adjust to the new limit, we lowered the limit from 50 MB to Office 365's 25 MB in July 2012. We alerted faculty and staff to the change and increased their awareness about the University-supported alternatives for sending large files. Our communications included an email to all faculty and staff, an article in the employee e-newspaper Pawprint, and new web content explaining these options.

For the 7,000 accounts that already had oversized messages, we began a "large message remediation" campaign that ran from August to October 2012. Account holders were encouraged to review each message and decide whether to save the attachments, delete the attachments but save the message, delete the message (including the attachments), or save the message to local storage. Each account owner received a series of personalized email messages listing the date, size, folder path, and subject line of their oversized messages, along with a link to how-to instructions. The email briefly explained why and when the account holder needed to take action, and what would happen if they did nothing. In early December, as a safety net, we created PSTs of any oversized messages remaining in the accounts. These PSTs are on a local file store accessible only by the account holder.

Because IT support for most of the academic and administrative units at Cornell starts at the department level, we also leveraged the IT leaders to help with this campaign. We sent each IT leader a list of the affected accounts within their unit and periodically provided updated lists. This model increased the overall success by enabling the IT leaders to provide hands-on support, check on the progress of their faculty and staff, confirm the legitimacy of the information we were sharing as the central IT organization, and alert us to business needs that the new limit might affect and other concerns or issues.

Discontinuing support for BlackBerry phones followed a similar course. About 200 BlackBerry users, along with the IT leaders of their academic or administrative units, were notified in September 2012 that Cornell's BlackBerry Enterprise Server Express (BES) would be discontinued in March 2013. This decision was made because BES is incompatible with Office 365, and the terms of the cloud-based alternative from Research in Motion were not appropriate for Cornell.

Most of the users had personally owned phones and were eligible for a phone upgrade by March 2013. Subsequent reminders urged action before the start of migrations to Office 365 if possible. By the beginning of February, 80 users remained. In collaboration with their IT leaders, we adjusted migration dates as needed to allow these stragglers to reach their phone upgrade date or make the decision to keep using their BlackBerry in a more limited way.

Although we knew that RIM was rumored to be planning a launch of ActiveSync-compatible BlackBerry devices in the first half of 2013, we could not justify continuing to allocate resources to support BlackBerry devices until then. In 2012, only about 3% of the smartphones connecting to Cornell's Exchange system (via BES) were BlackBerry phones, mirroring the nationwide usage trends. As it played out, the ActiveSync phones were not available in the U.S. market in time for our migration window.

2.6 Local expertise with Exchange

The same technical team who deployed the University's central Exchange service three years earlier served as Microsoft's local partner in orchestrating the migration to Office 365. This team also manages all other aspects of Cornell's email infrastructure. Their deep understanding benefited Cornell throughout the project and they took the lead in minimizing the disruption that faculty and staff would see.

The lessons learned in managing the faculty/staff move to the central Exchange service (and later the upgrade from Exchange Server 2007 to 2010), and the scripts, routines, and tools developed to support those efforts, gave us a strong starting point. We were able to reuse scripts and the methodology for batching groups to minimize disruption largely due to experience of that project. The technical team had a rich knowledge of the technical characteristics of the email accounts and the technical challenges we would likely face in the migration. We also had a still relevant and mostly accurate (in hindsight) take on the social dimensions of planning who would migrate when.

In addition, this in-house expertise enabled the project team to fully evaluate and plan for the interaction of Office 365 with some legacy features that have become an expected part of email at Cornell. These include special-purpose accounts that multiple individuals can access (for example, to handle department business, or room/equipment reservations); complex calendar delegation relationships; and the option to have Cornell email routed to an external account while preserving the original envelope information. The technical team's depth also proved invaluable in partnering with Microsoft to troubleshoot issues with individual accounts and with overall service performance once the migration was underway.

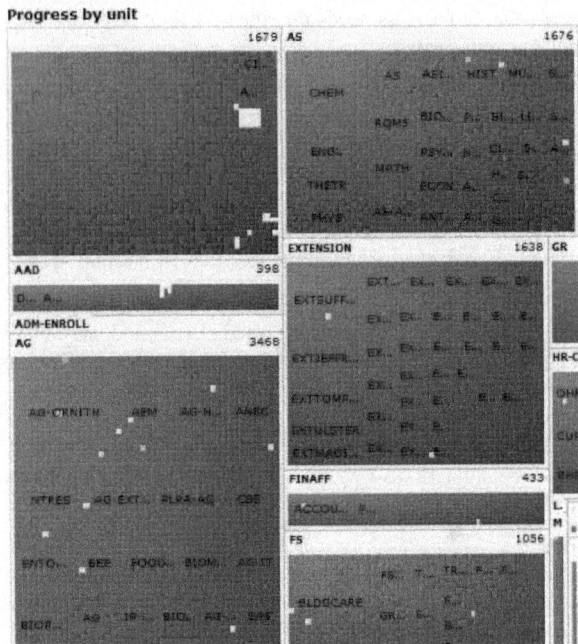

Figure 1. This custom application of MagnaView visually represented migration progress by academic and administrative unit. Each pixel is an email account. Green (*dark gray*) is Office 365, blue (*light gray*) is on-premise Exchange, and the other colors (*whitish*) indicate account issues or anomalies. A member of Cornell's technical team developed this visualization.

2.7 Extensive Cornell-provided web pages on preparing for Office 365

Cornell's central IT organization invests in providing extensive self-service documentation for most of the services used by faculty, staff, and students. This model is evaluated with every cloud-based service, to determine whether to provide local documentation or point to the vendor's. For Office 365, we decided to continue with local documentation.

Much of the information we developed for the local Exchange service was still relevant for Office 365. Also, Microsoft, understandably, needs to offer generic documentation covering all supported clients and pointing users to their institution for certain bits of information. For faculty and staff, a mix of Microsoft documentation and local documentation would not only have been confusing, but would also have introduced an expectation that the IT Service Desk supports more clients than it does.

The investment in local documentation meant the project team could offer a consistent, streamlined, Cornell-oriented guide to the Office 365 migration, with the flexibility to rapidly adjust the content to fit communication campaigns and to respond to new needs as the migration unfolded. The Office 365 site offered this information:

- General awareness of the project
- Frequently asked questions
- Differences to expect with Office 365
- Steps for each client to take before and after migration
- Known issues and troubleshooting tips
- Steps to manage oversized messages
- Options for very large mailings

At the conclusion of the project, the existing faculty/staff email site and the accompanying client sites were updated with the relevant Office 365 information, and the Office 365 site used to guide campus through the transition was taken down. A project summary site, with examples of the communication materials used, is available at www.it.cornell.edu/office365-project/

2.8 Targeted email guiding individuals to complete specific to-do's

Migrating to Office 365 required configuration changes for all of the email clients that we support. After investigations into possible ways to automate the changes came up empty, an email campaign with five standard messages was developed to steer individuals through the process. Each email was personalized with the migration date and account name, set the expectation that some steps would need to be done before and after the migration, and guided people who needed help to contact their local unit's IT staff or the IT Service Desk. Then each message presented a short checklist of tasks to do that week.

- *Three weeks before migration:* Summary of what's different with Office 365, and steps to do before the migration.

- *Two weeks before:* Reminder to do any steps that are needed before migration, and to learn the differences with Office 365.

- *One week before:* Reminder to do any steps that are needed before migration; suggestion to print or bookmark the steps you'll need to do after migration (could not be done in advance); and a recap of the differences with Office 365.

- *Day before:* Final reminder to do any steps that are needed before migration and to print or bookmark the steps you'll need to do after migration; instruction to verify your account move by going to Outlook Web App and looking for the confirmation message; and temporary limitations that might be seen until all accounts have been moved.

- *Day after:* Confirmation of move; steps to do after migration; and temporary limitations.

Sending four staged messages prior to the migration was an effective way to ensure that faculty and staff were aware that their account was being moved and that action from them was required. The day-after confirmation message preemptively answered the "did my account move?" question, so that IT staff and the IT Service Desk could focus on the unexpected issues instead. Overall, this investment in preparation and awareness resulted in the migration being seen as minimally intrusive and almost a non-event for most faculty and staff.

2.9 End-user support at the unit level and through the central IT Service Desk

In Cornell's decentralized IT model, many faculty and staff typically seek support from their academic or administrative unit's IT staff as their first step. University-owned computers vary from completely managed and locked down to entirely user-maintained, depending on the unit or department. This kind of diversity is problematic to adequately support on lean IT budgets, so the central IT organization had already ended support for older versions of Outlook and Entourage in May 2012.

For Office 365, that meant the project team would provide step-by-step migration guides and troubleshooting for the newest versions of Outlook (2010 for Windows and 2011 for Mac) and Outlook Web App, with less extensive support for Apple Mail/iCal, and the University's chosen IMAP/POP alternative, Thunderbird. This posed an immediate challenge for IT leaders in some units, where a sizable portion of Outlook users were still on older versions.

In August 2012, we reiterated the necessity of standardizing on Outlook 2010 and 2011 as the University's supported Microsoft desktop clients, and we did not provide Office 365-related documentation or support for the older versions. For cases where upgrading was not possible, we began positioning Outlook Web App as the best solution. These limitations added a support burden for the units that faced barriers to upgrading. But for the University as a whole, they allowed us to provide better support, faster, to the greatest number of individuals.

The support model for Office 365 was essentially the same one used by the central IT Service Desk normally: providing known answers to known questions for faculty and staff (level 1 support), troubleshooting for both faculty and staff and IT staff (level 2), and escalating and tracking cases they couldn't resolve to the technical team for Office 365 (level 3). The IT Service Desk leveraged the remote desktop tool Bomgar to guide faculty and staff through configuration changes and to verify correct setups as part of troubleshooting. Two differences: a separate Office 365 queue was maintained for the duration of the project, and three full-time staff from a Microsoft-selected contract agency were brought in to augment the IT Service Desk staffing, primarily for level 1 support.

Table 1. IT Service Desk Summary for Office 365 Cases Reported Between 9/1/2012 and 3/31/2013

Total by Assigned Group	Reported	Distribution by Assigned Group	Percent Resolved
Level 1	1,973	72.2%	99.6%
Level 2	574	21.0%	97.9%
Level 3	185	6.8%	69.7%
Total Cases Reported	2,732		

Rapid sharing of information between the IT Service Desk, the project team, and IT staff was instrumental in providing effective support across the campus. Troubleshooting tips and known issues were posted to a public site and announced directly to IT staff, so they could differentiate between problems they should attempt to resolve and problems that required intervention from Microsoft or the technical team.

Initially we shared this kind of information once we could present a full picture, following the philosophy of our standard documentation. Early feedback from IT staff shifted our approach to iteration: describing a trend as soon as we saw it and gradually providing specifics as they became known. IT staff could then reference our list of known issues and troubleshooting tips for every new situation they encountered, and, where our information was still at the early vague stage, contribute additional details from the cases they were seeing in the field.

2.10 Daily conference call with the project team for IT leaders

For all but the first few migrations, the project team invited IT leaders and IT staff to join a Monday-Friday, half-hour WebEx conference call as their units were being migrated. Cornell has a site license for WebEx, so the only cost for these calls was resource time. IT staff from any unit, whether migrated or waiting to migrate, were welcome to join any call.

Led by a member of the technical team, these calls summarized the results of the latest moves, reviewed IT Service Desk activity to date, provided updates on known issues, and answered questions unique to the most recent migrations. This began as an experiment to provide a dedicated channel for sharing information between the project team and the IT staff in the days following a migration. It quickly became a powerful part of our strategy as another way to assess the success of a migration.

3. ACKNOWLEDGMENTS

Cornell's transition to Office 365 was orchestrated through the thoughtful planning, diligence, and dedication of small core groups from Microsoft and Cornell. From Microsoft, we acknowledge Mike Gussin, Tony Lanzafame, Dave Pearlman, Ryan Rager, John Serrato, the Migration Factory, and BrightPlanIT, among others. From Cornell, we acknowledge Moe Arif, Andrea Beesing, Bryan Benning, Chuck Boeheim, Pete Bosanko, Lee Brink, Joanne Button, Bob Carozzoni, Rick Cochran, Laurie Collinsworth, Kassy Crawford, Aimee Decker, Ted Dodds, Dan Elswit, Philip Halcomb, Dan Hawryschuk, Bill Holmes, Jim Howell, Shari Kearl, Todd Kreuger, Mike Leiter, Pat McClary, Wyman Miles, Todd Olson, Ken Ridley, John Ruffing, Keshav Santi, Steve Schuster, Ron Seccia, Diane Sempler, Jenny Signor, Andy Slusar, Jeff Truelsen, Bill Turner, Dave Vernon, and Dan Villanti, among others.

Implementation and Operation of the Kyushu University Authentication System

Eisuke Ito
Kyushu University
6-10-1 Hakozaki, Higashi-ku
Fukuoka 812-8581, Japan
+81 92 642 4037
ito.eisuke.523
@m.kyushu-u.ac.jp

Yoshiaki Kasahara
Kyushu University
6-10-1 Hakozaki, Higashi-ku
Fukuoka 812-8581, Japan
+81 92 642 2297
kasahara.yoshiaki.820
@m.kyushu-u.ac.jp

Naomi Fujimura
Kyushu University
4-9-1 Shiobaru, Minami-ku
Fukuoka, Japan
+81 92 553 4434
fujimura.naomi.274
@m.kyushu-u.ac.jp

ABSTRACT

Nowadays, a university needs to build and maintain a central ID database and authentication system for better ICT (information and communication technology) services. In 2008, the headquarters of Kyushu University had defined medium-range policy of ICT infrastructure preparation, and the policy had indicated construction of a central authentication system. According to the policy, the authors elaborated an installation plan of the Kyu(Q)shu University authentication system (QUAS, for short). Since 2009, Information Infrastructure Initiative of Kyushu University, to which the authors belong, has been issuing ID cards to all employees, and also operating LDAP servers. This paper introduces the action plan and outline of QUAS. This paper also describes two recent topics of QUAS. One is high load of LDAP servers because of rapid increase of mobile devices, and the other one is development of a multifactor authentication Shibboleth Identity Provider (IdP).

Categories and Subject Descriptors

K.6.5 [**Management of Computing and Information Systems**]: Security and Protection – *authentication.*

General Terms

Measurement, Performance, Design, Reliability, Security, Human Factors.

Keywords

ID management, Central user authentication, LDAP, Shibboleth, Multifactor authentication.

SIGUCCS'13, November 3–8, 2013, Chicago, Illinois, USA.
Copyright © 2013 ACM 978-1-4503-2318-5/13/11...$15.00.
HTTP://DX.DOI.ORG/10.1145/2504776.2504788

1. INTRODUCTION

Nowadays, a university needs to build and maintain a central ID database and authentication system for better ICT services. A University has many ICT services, such as E-mail, e-learning system, wireless LAN, and the results DB. ICT services are also indispensable to university activity. If there wasn't the central ID database and authentication system in a university, individual ID and password pair must be published for each service, and users must remember ID-password pairs for services. Password management is not only complicated for users, but also complicated for the service administrator.

In 2008, the headquarters of Kyushu University had defined medium-range policy of ICT infrastructure preparation, and the policy had indicated construction of a central authentication system. According to the policy, we elaborated an installation plan of the Kyu(Q)shu University authentication system (QUAS, for short). Since 2009, Information Infrastructure Initiative of Kyushu University, to which the authors belong, has been issuing ID cards to all employees, and also operating LDAP servers [1][2].

The Academic Access Management Federation in Japan (nickname: "GakuNin") started in 2009 [3]. It is a federation of universities (users of academic e-resources) and organizations like publishers (providers of such e-resources) to mutually trust rules/policy and utilize federated access among them. GakuNin adopted Shibboleth [4] as the common distributed web authentication system as same as InCommon in U.S. [5], and UK Federation [6]. Kyushu University installed a Shibboleth IdP server in 2011, and participated in GakuNin. Students and staff members can use federated services such as E-Journal.

This paper introduces the action plan and outline of QUAS. This paper also describes two recent topics of QUAS. One is high load of LDAP servers because of rapid increase of mobile devices, and the other one is development of a multifactor authentication Shibboleth IdP.

The composition of this paper is as follows. Section 2 explains the outline of QUAS. We describe the IDM (ID management DB system), and provisioning flow from IDM to various systems, such as LDAP, Active Directory (AD), and E-mail server. Section 3 explains our SSO environment. Section 4 shows the high load problem of LDAP occurred in 2012, and also shows a solution to the problem. In Section 5, we describe development of a multifactor authentication Shibboleth IdP. Finally, we conclude this paper in section 6.

2. OUTLINE OF QUAS

2.1 Mission and Action Plan of QUAS

We defined the mission of QUAS as QUAS should realize convenient, reliable, and safe (secure) information services in our university. We also defined following seven action plans.

(1) Construct an authentication server which can be referred by intramural ICT services.

(2) Issue user IDs to all persons who work/study in Kyushu University.

(3) Construct an ID management DB system that keeps current status of members.

(4) Realize SSO (Single Sign On).

(5) Participate in the Japanese academic federation GakuNin.

(6) Integrate legacy services.

(7) Introduce a multifactor authentication system for security.

2.2 The Outline of QUAS

Figure 1 shows the outline structure of QUAS system as of March 2012, and Figure 2 shows that of April 2013.

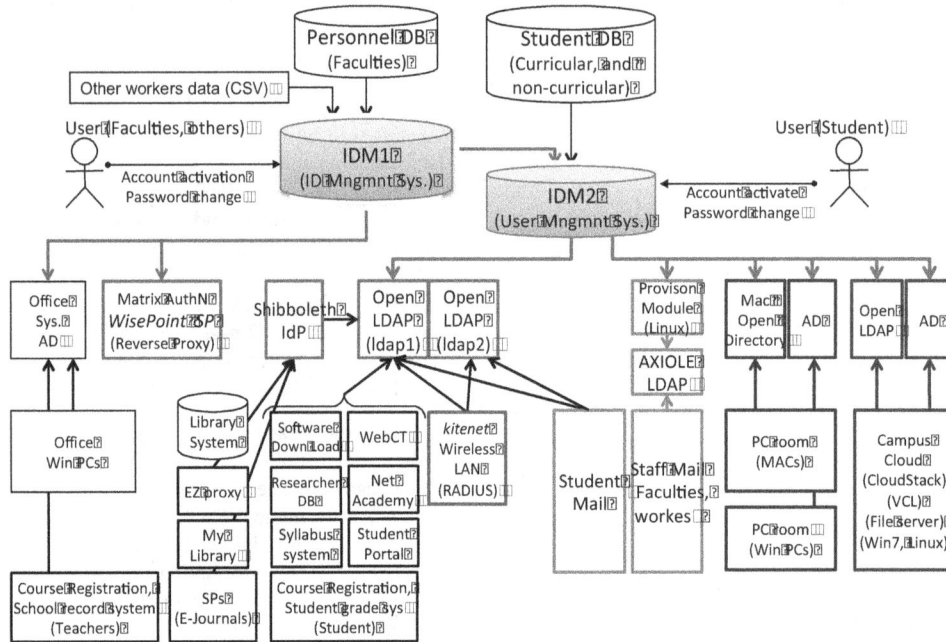

Figure 1 Outline of QUAS (Mar. 2012)

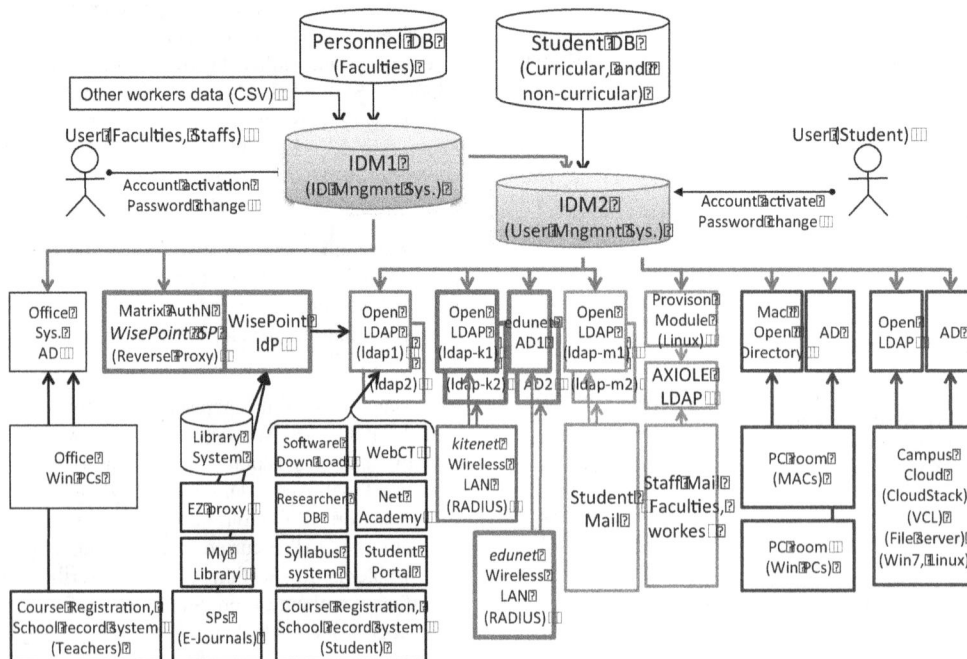

Figure 2 Outline of QUAS (Apr. 2013)

To realize the action plan (1) of section 2.1, we installed two LDAP servers with OpenLDAP [7], and provided them to intramural ICT servers. In 2012, overload of LDAP servers occurred because of rapid increase of mobile devices, and chronically massive access from Gmail. This paper mentions the overload problem in section 4. After that, we installed additional LDAP and AD (Active Directory) servers.

2.3 Two Identity Management DB Systems

There are two user data sources, the personnel DB and the student DB. The personnel DB has all records of faculty members who are employed in Kyushu University. The student DB has all curricular and non-curricular student records. Non-employee worker records are typed by hand into a formatted CSV (comma separated value) file.

As shown in Figure 1 and 2, QUAS has two user IDMs (ID management DB systems) because of historical reasons. One is staff's IDM (IDM1, for convenient), and the other one is student IDM (IDM2). IDM1 is a Fujitsu product, and IDM1 was installed in 2009 at the starting time of QUAS. IDM1 keeps records of faculty members and non-employee workers, but it doesn't have student records. IDM2 is a NEC product, and it manages student accounts. IDM2 was installed as a part of education system in 2008. IDM2 has all persons' records. IDM1 only provisions faculty member data and other worker data. IDM2 can provision all member data.

2.4 User ID System

To realize the action plan (2) and (3) of section 2.1, we checked persons who work/study in Kyushu University. The main members of our university are students and faculty members. Faculty members are employed by Kyushu University. A student is an undergraduate student, a graduate curricular student or non-curricular student. Non-curricular student is a foreign student, or a research student. In addition to students and faculty members, there are various non-employee workers with various roles such as research fellows, visiting researchers, temporary staff, and so on. Most of them are employed in external organizations such as other universities, research institutes, or worker delivery companies. Table 1 shows approximate numbers of members in Kyushu University as of March 2012. The total numbers of each class are equal to the number of account in the IDM (ID management) system.

Table 1 The number of IDs in Kyushu University (Mar 2012)

Role	Total No. of IDs (approx..)
Curricular students	19,000
Non-curricular students	500
Faculty members	9,000
Non-employee workers	800
Total	29,300

Next, we describe the user ID system. The student ID card has been issued to each student and each non-curricular student by the university office. Student ID has been used as the user ID of ICT services since 1995. There wasn't user ID for faculty members

and non-employee workers before QUAS was introduced. We designed user ID system of faculty members as follows. The user ID of faculty members is a unique 10-digit random number, like '1893740523'. For other workers, we issue a unique string like 'a982746519' to a worker, where the first letter is 'a', and following is a unique nine-digit random number. We started user ID assignment and user ID card issuing to faculty members and other workers since 2009, at the starting year of central authentication LDAP service.

3. SHIBBOLETH and REVERSE PROXY

To satisfy action plan (4) and (5) of section 2.1, we constructed Shibboleth IdP. Shibboleth is a recent technology for distributed Web SSO using SAML (security assertion markup language) based data exchange. It is difficult to "Shibbolize" legacy services, and the open-source version of Shibboleth IdP didn't support multifactor authentication in 2009. To integrate legacy web services and realize multifactor authentication as action plan (6) and (7), we installed a reverse proxy based SSO system called WisePoint produced by FalconSC [8].

3.1 Policy for Single Sign On

The more services refer the QUAS, the higher the risk of impersonation, because there are more attacking surfaces and the QUAS provides only one pair of ID and password for a user.

To reduce security risks, we defined a policy for SSO. Table 2 shows the policy. We classified ICT services into two types. One is security oriented service such as the student grade DB and researcher DB. They manage important data, and they require a high security level. The other one is usability oriented service such as e-mail and wireless LAN. They are commodity services and they don't require high security level.

ID and password authentication is enough for usability-oriented services. However, for security oriented services it isn't secure enough. A multi-factor authentication system is necessary for security-oriented services. We introduced a matrix code authentication system as a multi-factor authentication system.

Table 2 SSO Policy

	Intramural	Extramural
Usability oriented services	Mail, Wireless LAN, Student Portal, MyLibrary, … ID/PW authN Shibboleth SSO	E-Journal,
Security orient services	Student Grade DB, Researcher DB Matrix Code AuthN, Reverse Proxy	

3.2 Matrix Code Authentication

We have been using a FalconSC product "WisePoint" which is an implementation of matrix code authentication. WisePoint is also a reverse proxy SSO product, so it can integrate legacy services. A unique matrix code is issued for every faculty member (not for students). The code is printed on the reverse side of a staff card.

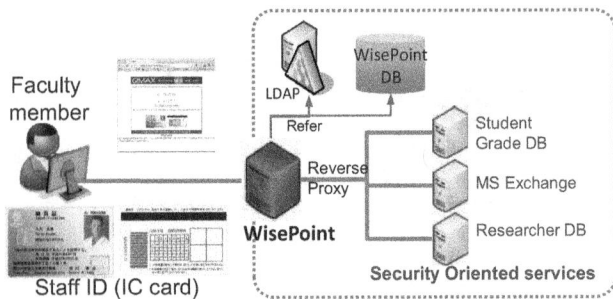

Figure 3 WisePoint Matrix Code AuthN (until Oct. 2012)

3.3 Shibboleth and GakuNin

We introduced an experimental Shibboleth IdP in 2009 on a CentOS machine using open source IdP software provided by Internet2. We refined the IdP system through the IdP test operation. Second IdP system consisted of two servers for tandem operation and we opened the IdP to intramural usability oriented web services from October 2010. The first SP (Service Provider) was the MyLibrary web service of Kyushu University Library.

The academic authentication federation GakuNin started in Japan in 2009 [3]. GakuNin adopted Shibboleth as the distributed web authentication system as same as InCommon in U.S. [5], and UK Federation [6]. After having a discussion with CIO, Kyushu University participated in the GakuNin federation in 2011. Since participation of GakuNin, students and staff members can use federated services such as E-Journal.

4. HIGH LOAD of LDAP

The load of the LDAP authentication servers was increasing from 2012. Because of high load of the authentication server, the user authentication failure incident was occurred on January 25, 2012, and some students couldn't login to the e-learning system (Blackboard learning system). An initial investigation suggested that the student mail server and the radius server for wireless LAN were sending massive authentication requests [2].

4.1 Student Mail and Wireless LAN

Student mail server provides e-mail service to all the students [9][10]. Figure 4 shows the system architecture. In order to prevent unsolicited junk e-mail submission, SMTP-AUTH is attested at the time of e-mail submission. For e-mail retrieval, POP3 and IMAP4 are provided to users. Therefore, user authentication is performed at the time of mail submission and retrieval, and all authentication requests come to the LDAP server.

The load in the 802.1X authentication by wireless LAN also went up. The wireless LAN service named "kitenet" is provided on all the campuses, and kitenet requires 802.1X PEAP authentication at the time of connection. Figure 5 shows rough composition of authentication system. The user authentication request at the time of kitenet connection is forwarded to a LDAP authentication server via the RADIUS server.

The smart phone and the tablet computer increased rapidly from the second half of 2011. Wireless LAN access was needed for these devices, so the load of the authentication server became high.

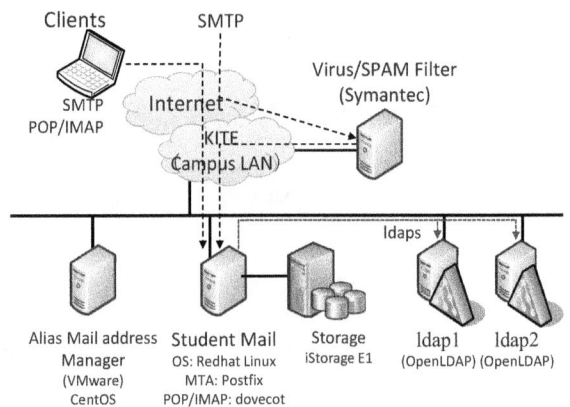

Figure 4 Student Mail System and LDAP (until Oct. 2012)

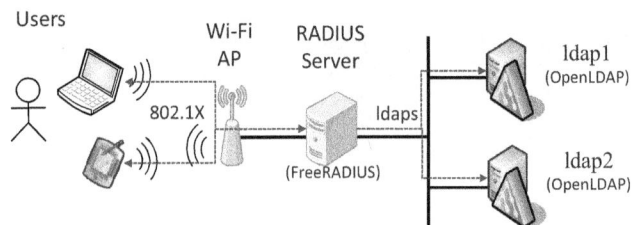

Figure 5 Wireless LAN _kitenet_ and LDAP (until Oct. 2012)

4.2 Statistics of LDAP accesses

We analyzed logs of the LDAP authentication server. The period was from December 1, 2011 to December 31, 2012. Table 3 shows actions of LDAP, which we extracted from the log for load analysis.

Table 3 Counted LDAP actions

Action	Description
CONNECT	The number of LDAP accesses.
Failed	Total number of failed actions.
BIND	The number of ldap_bind action.
SEARCH	The number of ldap_search action.

We didn't count UNBIND action, because UNBIND is the resource release and connection cutting operation, and it corresponds to ACCEPT. We omitted other actions because there were only few numbers, and they did not influence load analysis. Failed is the number of authentication error (RESULT is err=49), and most of them are BIND failure according to user's login failure.

Figure 6, 7, 8 shows the statistics of two LDAP servers (ldap1 and ldap2). Figure 7 shows statistics data of requests from kitenet RADIUS, and Figure 8 shows requests from student mail server.

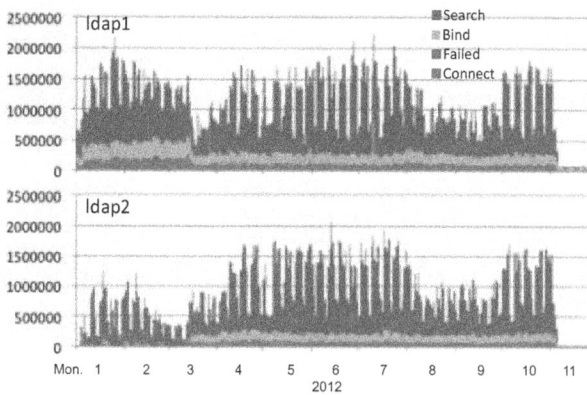

Figure 6 Stat. of ldap1 and ldap2 (Jan. 2012 – Nov. 2012)

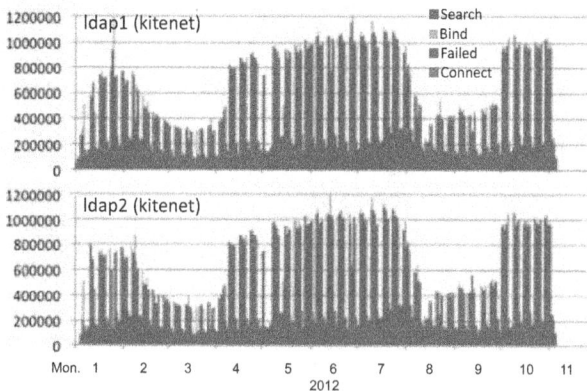

Figure 7 Stat. of ldap1 and ldap2 (Jan. 2012 – Nov. 2012) (from kitenet RADIUS server)

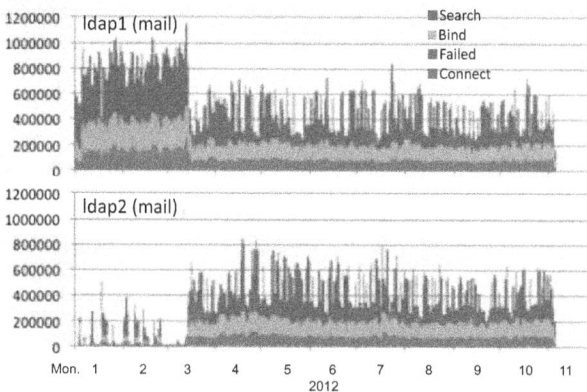

Figure 8 Stat. of ldap1 and ldap2 (Jan. 2012 – Nov. 2012) (from Student Mail server)

4.3 Analysis

We divide in three periods for analysis, (a) Jan.–Feb., (b) Mar.–Oct., and (c) after Nov. 2012. During period (a), request overflow was observed because it was before we tuned server configuration and installed counter measures. In period (b), we did the load balancing of LDAP servers by DNS round robin, and we also tuned configuration of syslog daemon for OpenLDAP. In period

(c), a drastic measure was deployed that new LDAP/AD authentication servers were introduced.

4.3.1 Requests from kitenet RADIUS

Figure 7 shows that the number of LDAP accesses from wireless LAN "kitenet" RADIUS server. It shows fine correlation with university activity. There was a large amount of requests in a weekday, but few on Saturday and Sunday. During winter and summer vacation, requests were reduced. LDAP requests were increasing gradually from July to April, 2012. It might illustrate increase of smart phones and tablets on campus.

In Figure 7, the number of requests from kitenet RADIUS are fine balanced to two LDAP servers. FreeRADIUS [11] can specify multiple referring LDAP servers with "redundant-load-balance" directive. In this setup, FreeRADIUS accesses multiple servers by round robin, and it automatically selects available LDAP servers in case of trouble.

Most LDAP requests from kitenet RADIUS are SEARCH. The password hash value required for 802.1X PEAP MS-CHAPv2 authentication is provided in the sambaNTPassword attribute. RADIUS server can find the hashed value by SEARCH and validate user-supplied password by itself.

4.3.2 Requests from Student Mail Server

Figure 8 shows that most requests were SEARCH, and SEARCH followed human activity. However, about 20,000 CONNECTs and 20,000 BINDs were observed every day. The reason was accesses from Gmail. Gmail has a function to retrieve other servers' messages through POP3. A few thousands students configured his/her private Gmail account to retrieve messages from the student mail server and Gmail periodically accessed the POP server. Therefore, the number of POP accesses to the mail server was almost stable, and it represented the number of authentication request to the LDAP authentication server.

4.4 Additional LDAP Servers

We tried to tolerate high load of authentication request with two OpenLDAP servers using the load sharing by DNS round robin, during March, 2012 to October. But when one of them stopped due to malfunction or maintenance, authentication requests concentrated to another server and it overflowed.

For radical solution, we installed new additional LDAP servers in November, 2012. Figure 2 shows the present QUAS structure. We added two OpenLDAP servers for kitenet RADIUS, two OpenLDAP servers for student mail server, and two Active Directory servers for edunet RADIUS. Edunet is a new 802.11n broadband wireless LAN service for ICT based education. After that, the load of existing OpenLDAP servers are rapidly decreased.

5. MULTI-FACTOR AUTHENTICATION SHIBBOLETH IDP

A possible damage of impersonation became higher because of increasing GakuNin federated service. If an ID and password are stolen, an impersonated user can use federated services illegally.

To reduce an impersonation risk, we considered developing much stronger authentication mechanism into Shibboleth IdP, such as one time password, multi-factor authentication, or PKI digital certificate authentication. Kyushu University already introduced WisePoint, a matrix code based multifactor authentication server. In late 2011, we proposed joint development of multifactor authentication Shibboleth IdP to the FalconSC which was the vender of WisePoint. After some negotiation between FalconSC and Kyushu University, joint development was begun from February 2012. Figure 9 shows developed WisePoint IdP and WisePoint SP (a reverse proxy).

Beta level development of WisePoint IdP was completed in August 2012. We experimented the beta level WisePoint IdP with actual Kyushu University services in October 2012. We found a case sensitivity problem of user ID as a result of experiment.

Although the OpenLDAP of QUAS doesn't distinguish upper case and lower cases of user ID, the default setting of WisePoint distinguish them. Case sensitivity problem did not appear in previous services because WisePoint was used by faculty members, and user ID of faculty member was a 10-digit random number, like '1893740523'. WisePoint Shibboleth IdP are used not only faculty members but also students. The student's user ID includes alphabetic characters, like '1AB013001X', and user ID is registered with the capital letter at LDAP and AD. Some students input their user ID in lower letters like '1ab013001x', then case sensitive setting became a problem.

We proposed to add a directive to change user ID case sensitivity to FalconSC, and they developed our proposed directive. And we tested the improved WisePoint IdP. Finally, we replaced OSS version IdP to WisePoint IdP in November 2012. As a side effect, we could reduce maintenance cost of IdP, because the server machine of old Shibboleth IdP was removed.

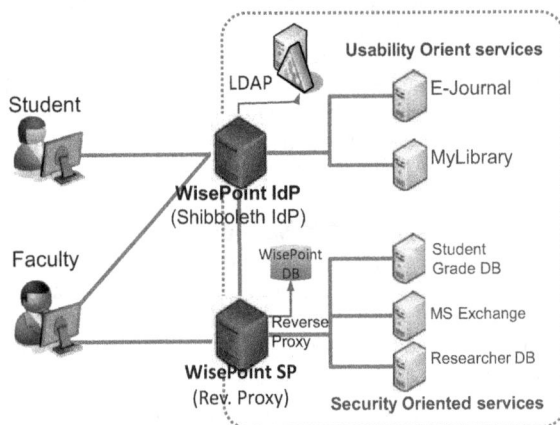

Figure 9 Multifactor AuthN Shibboleth IdP by WisePoint

6. CONCLUSION

In this paper, we described the outline of QUAS. In 2009, we had defined missions and action plans for QUAS implementation, implemented the QUAS, and have been operating it until now. We introduced system composition of QUAS, user ID system, SSO policy, and SSO systems.

We also described two recent topics of QUAS. One was high load of LDAP servers. We analyzed LDAP log files to research the reason of high load, and found that student mail and wireless LAN service sent massive LDAP requests. We added four LDAP servers for radical solution. The other topic was development of a multifactor authentication Shibboleth IdP. We had a joint development between the vender and Kyushu University, and installed developed system to real service.

In the near future, we'll integrate two ID management DB systems into one system. ID management and authentication service is a most fundamental service. It must be persistent, and also we need to continue improving it.

7. ACKNOWLEDGMENTS

Our thanks to all students and staff members who are using the QUAS in Information Infrastructure Initiative in Kyushu University.

8. REFERENCES

[1] Ito. E., Kasahara, Y., Nogita, M., and Suzuki, T. 2007. Institutional authentication platform for trustful inter/intra-institutional ubiquitous services, In Proceedings of the 2nd International Conference of Ubiquitous Information Technology (2nd ICUT), pp.103-108.

[2] Ito, E., Kasahara. Y., and Fujimura, N. 2012. A study of LDAP load balancing for University ICT services. *IPSJ SIG Technical Report*, Vol. 2012-CSEC-57/2012-IOT-17, No. 11, pp.51-56.

[3] GakuNin, https://www.gakunin.jp/docs/fed

[4] Shibboleth Consortium, Shibboleth, http://shibboleth.net/ .

[5] InCommon, http://www.incommon.org/

[6] UK Federation, http://www.ukfederation.org.uk/

[7] OpenLDAP, http://www.openldap.org/

[8] FalconSC, WisePoint, http://wisepoint.jp/

[9] Fujimura. N., Masuoka, K., and Masaki, Y. 2010. Experiences with Individual Receipt Confirmation System and the University Primary Mail Service. In Proceedings of SIGUCCS 2010 (Norfolk, VA, October 24 – 27 2010), pp.65-70.

[10] Fujimura, N., Togawa, T., Kasahara, Y., and Ito, E. 2012. Introduction and experience with the Primary Mail Service based on their names for students. In *Proceedings of the SIGUCCS 2012* (Memphis, TN, October 17 - 19, 2012). ACM, New York, NY, pp.11-14.

[11] FreeRADIUS, http://freeradius.org/

Personality Inventories and Cognitive Frames: Understanding the Balance in Managing and Leading IT Organizations

Kenneth Janz
Winona State University
Somsen Hall 111i
Winona, MN 55987
1-507-457-2299
kjanz@winona.edu

Robin Honken
Winona State University
Somsen Hall 207
Winona, MN 55987
1-507-457-2215
rhonken@winona.edu

ABSTRACT

With the complex dynamics of higher education and the ever-changing nature of information technology, leaders/managers find it difficult to effectively lead the effort to integrate technology into the academic and administrative culture of higher education institutions. Leadership and organizational literature is rich with ideas, theories, and models about viewing organizations. Because we work in complex organizations, these models provide tools that enable a leader/manager to understand environments and people. This presentation will combine the personality inventories of DiSC with the cognitive frames discussed by Bolman and Deal [10] and Birnbaum [7]. This will create a platform for conversation for both current CIOs and staff aspiring to leadership positions.

Categories and Subject Descriptors

K.6.1 [**Project and People Management**]: Management

Keywords

Leadership, Chief Information Officer, Higher Education, Organizational Performance, Cognitive Frames, Personality Inventories

1. INTRODUCTION

The complex innovative use of information technology that is found on college campuses today requires a level of leadership found in a CEO executive team or cabinet level position. By 2002, a majority of doctoral granting institutions had appointed a CIO that provided executive level leadership for the organization [18].

Given the increasingly visible role of CIOs, combined with the enormous resource investment dedicated to information technology, the CIO has become a target of criticism. Leadership in higher education often fails to recognize their dual managerial and technical roles. Potter states that CIOs must manage their supervisors' expectations if they want to survive [36]. This takes a "keen sense of what the boss anticipates from information technology projects as well as a diplomatic understanding of what

the boss really does—and does not—know about information technology" (p.75) [36]. Zastrocky and Schlier assert that CIO misunderstanding of this dual role is one reason that the longevity in the CIO position is still limited when compared to other senior executive management positions. Within higher education the CIO position exists in a complex, loosely coupled organization [46]. Stakeholders bring multiple perceptions and expectations to the leadership and management role of the CIO. Because of this complex political environment, CIOs are finding it difficult to effectively lead efforts to integrate technology into the disparate cultures of the academy.

2. CIO LEADERSHIP

2.1 Role of the Chief Information Officer

The CIO is responsible for the overall leadership in the area of information technology Synnott and Gruber first used the title, "Chief Information Officer" or CIO. They defined the CIO as "the senior executive responsible for establishing corporate information policy, standards, and management control over all corporate information resources" (p. 66) [42]. In the 1970s, private and public sector organizations began to create positions generally called Chief Information Officer (CIO) in order to provide high level coordination over increasingly complex information technology resources and needs [42].

Rockart, Ball and Bullen carried out one of the first studies that looked at the emerging role of the CIO. In their study, successful CIOs and researchers were asked to describe the responsibilities of the CIO position. The study found that the role of the CIO was becoming shaped by external forces beyond the control of the organization itself [38]. The three role characteristics described by many in the study were: (1) the CIO are responsible for information infrastructure, (2) the CIO have a staff orientation and utilized communication, education, standards, and other indirect controls to perform integrator and gatekeeper roles for new technologies and finally, (3) the CIO have become a integral member of the executive management team [38].

Benjamin, Dickinson, and Rockart interviewed 20 CIOs to test the role characteristics defined by Rockart, Ball and Bullen [2]. These researchers concluded that the role of the CIO had evolved faster than anticipated and was becoming a high level executive, "primarily concerned with issues of long-range planning, consultation, and support of the broad range of constituencies throughout the organization" (p. 178) [2]. As described above, the literature showed a continually upward ascension of the CIO position into higher levels of executive management throughout the eighties and nineties. As the CIO position moved into these higher levels of executive management, the role he or she performed within the organization become more and more complex.

By the 1980s, turnover in the CIO position was common in business and industry. Hayley and Bolek reported from data collected in a Touche Ross and Company survey that nearly one-third of the 568 CIO participants replaced individuals who were dismissed or demoted [19]. Frenzel, using data from a Coopers and Lybrand's Highbarger survey, concluded that the CIO was a victim of power politics and unrealistic expectations in corporate environments [17]. This same survey data also showed that very few CIOs remained in their companies for more than four years.

By the 1990s, it became evident that the need for a skilled leader/manager to head information technology was increasingly important and had grown out of need to have a skilled technical specialist heading information technology for the organization. In her study of the literature and previous research, Stephens concluded that seven elements were common responsibilities of the CIO by the mid-nineties: (1) policy procedures and standards for information resources, (2) strategic planning for information resources, (3) budgetary oversight for information technology, (4) coordination of information technology units, (5) education of top management in the role of information technology in the organization, (6) consulting services to top management, and (7) understanding the internal political environment of the business [41].

By the early 21st century, the CIO role had developed into a position that had become a full member of the CEO management team. McClure described the role of a CIO in the early 21st century as an individual who worked with senior administration in the organization to implement effective information management in order to achieve the organizations goals [26]. This would assist the organization in establishing a sound investment process to select, control, and evaluate information technology spending for costs, risk, and benefits. In addition, the CIO was to promote improvements to the work process and increase the value of the organization's information technology resources. The literature on CIOs changes from research on roles and responsibilities to factors that contributed to successful and failed CIOs. This is demonstrated in research by McClure and the reporting of Kwak and Datz [26], [23], [13].

Kwak, in covering the research results of Enns, Huff, Golden, and Higgins, reported that CIOs with strong technical backgrounds were equally as effective as less technically specialized CIOs with greater general management experience at mobilizing the support of other top executives [23]. Datz reported from data collected from a 2002 survey of Global Conference Board's CEOs that six habits contributed to highly effective CIOs: (1) commit to the care and feeding of top management, (2) govern wisely, (3) assign direct reports to be business unit ambassadors, (4) join hands with business leaders at every opportunity, (5) advertise your technology strategy, and (6) make information technology user-friendly for everyone [13]. McClure found three critical factors associated with successful CIOs. The factors included (1) aligning the information management leadership with organizational goals, (2) promoting organizational credibility, and (3) executing information management responsibilities effectively. [26].

2.2 The Chief Information Officer in Higher Education

By 1990, the position of CIO began to appear in the higher education literature reflective of information technology's growing importance to the college campus [32]. The roles and responsibilities of the CIO in higher education began to evolve and expand even more rapidly since that time [1], [24], [32], [35].

Lattimer conducted a survey of 204 CIOs in higher education to update the Penrod et al. EDUCAUSE CIO study of 139 CIOs [24]. Lattimer found most CIOs report to a Provost or Executive/Other Vice President, and the majority had responsibility for administrative computing, academic computing, voice and data communications, and planning, but not for television, institutional research, printing, copy services, media services, mail services, or the library. Most CIOs approved information technology purchases throughout the organization and established standards for information technology purchases. Over half the CIOs surveyed were involved in leadership, planning, and communication with the greater campus community.

Penrod et al. placed CIOs into three categories in higher education. The categories they identified are as follows:

1. policy officer reporting to the president/chancellor or vice president for academic affairs who also serves as an executive officer of the university and holds line responsibility for substantial information resources;
2. policy officer reporting to the provost or vice president without major technology units reporting to them but who is still expected to provide leadership and vision; and
3. a senior administrator who is unlikely to interact with executive officers except when there are difficulties or at budget time and typically the institutional strategy toward information technology is undefined [32].

Zastrocky and Schlier identified seven issues that effective CIOs in higher education are regularly confronted with in his/her institution. These seven issues are: (1) politics and public relations, (2) finance, (3) marketing, (4) knowing the concerns of the CEO, (5) understanding the needs of others on the executive team, (6) understanding the drivers of higher education, and most importantly (7) the ability to read, look, ask and listen [46].

Many institutions of higher education are using information technology as one of the primary means by which they can improve their competitive advantage [27]. As higher education looks to information technology as a means to improve competitive advantage, there is increased interest from stakeholders in the organizational position with overall responsibility for integrating information technology on campuses of higher education. The centrality of the information technology on the college campus, and its leader, the CIO, is evident by its impact on the wider institutional mission, increased salary of the CIO, increased resource allocations for information technology, and growing literature base focused on this functional area and position. It is important to remember that the CIO position exists in a complex, loosely coupled organization. Stakeholders bring multiple perceptions and expectations to the leadership and management role of the CIO.

3. FRAMES AND MODELS

The leadership and organizational literature is rich with ideas, theories, and model about viewing organizations. Bolman and Deal, Weick and Bougon, Morgan, Quinn, Slater, Bergquist, and Birnbaum are a few examples of authors who argue that organizations can be better understood using multiple lenses, images or frames [6], [7], [8], [10], [30], [37], [40], [45]. This is due to that fact that the nature of organizations is complex, surprising, deceptive and ambiguous. These lenses, models, or frames provide a tool for a leader to examine and make sense of organizations. Four frames or images of organizations: structural (bureaucratic), human resource (collegial), political (political), and symbolic (anarchical) have been developed by Bolman and Deal and Birnbaum [10], [7]. Bolman and Deal, in developing the four frames, "consolidated major schools of organization thought" (p. 12) [10]. Birnbaum extends this theory base into higher education. All of these authors argue that the ability to use a multiframe perspective is important for effective leadership [7]. Each of the four frames are described in the following sections.

3.1 Structural (Bureaucratic)

"The structural frame emphasizes goals, specialized roles, and formal relationships" [10] (p. 13). It draws from the disciplines of sociology and management science. In the structural frame, the metaphor for the organization is that of a factory or machine. Organizations designed and operated as if machines are called bureaucracies [30]. Frederick Taylor and Max Weber's work forms the bases of what we think of as the structural frame today. Taylor used time and motion studies to break down and reconstruct tasks in a more efficient manner [43]. Weber sought to develop a model of organizations based on rationality [44]. He describes bureaucratic models of organizations. Mintzberg provides a modern perspective to the structural frame [29].

Bolman and Deal provide six assumptions of organizations that make up the structural frame:

- accomplish and recognize goals and objectives;
- rationality triumphs over individual choice and outside demands;
- design structures to match circumstances;
- enhance effectiveness through specialization;
- coordination and control are essential to benefit organizational goals; and
- troubles occur from structural deficiencies [10] (p. 40).

A structural frame approach to organizations operates efficiently under the same conditions where machines or factories operate efficiently [30], (p. 27).

The structural frame focuses on the coordination of work. This coordination takes place both vertically and laterally. Examples of vertical coordination are through authority, rules and policies, and planning and control systems [10]. Conversely, one can describe lateral coordination with meetings, task forces, coordinating roles, matrix structures, and networks. It is important in the structural frame to know and understand the characteristics of power and authority [7]. Structural leaders assume an active role in decision-making and execute well-researched solutions to organizational problems [4], [5].

3.2 Human Resource (Collegial)

The human resource frame focuses on the individuals who make up the organization. Family is the metaphor for the human resource or collegial frame. The central concepts of the human resource (collegial) frame are that individuals have needs, skills, and relationships and the leader must empower employees to successfully lead the organization [10]. Morgan uses the metaphor of an organization as an organism in describing features of the human resource frame [30]. The work of Maslow's hierarchy of motivation [25], McGregor's Theory X and Y [28], and Argyris' people's need for self-actualization, create the theoretical basis for this frame.

Bolman and Deal provide four assumptions of organizations that depict the human resource frame:

- organizations serve human needs;
- people and organizations need each other;
- when the fit between individual and system is broke, one or both suffer; and
- a good fit benefits both the individual and the organization [10] (p. 102 - 103).

Organizational success and effectiveness are linked to people-conscious strategies that seek to meet the needs of the individuals as well as the organization [4], [5], [7]. [10]. The faculty members within a collegial college or university see the president (or other senior administration) as a first among equals [6]. Effective human resource leaders rely on participation, collaboration, and empowerment of the individual to advance organizational goals and strategies [7], [10]. Positive campus results are linked to collegial leadership [4], [5].

3.3 Political (Political)

The political frame was created and developed by political scientists. The metaphor for the political frame or system is the jungle. The central concepts of the political frame are power, conflict, competition, and organizational politics. The leader must be an advocate for employees to successfully lead the organization [10].

Bolman and Deal provide five propositions of organizations that represent the political frame:

- organizations are coalitions of various individuals and interest groups;
- enduring differences exist between coalition members in values, beliefs, information, interest, and perceptions of reality;
- the allocation of scare resources become the most important decisions;
- scarce resources and enduring differences give conflict a central role in organizational dynamics and make power the important resource; and
- goals and decisions emerge from bargaining, negotiation, and jockeying for position [10] (p. 163).

Leadership within the political system depends upon the leader's presence and timing [7]. Political leaders are seen as negotiators or mediators working with shifting power blocs [5].

Understanding Higher Education Organizations
Using Cognitive Frames as a Guide

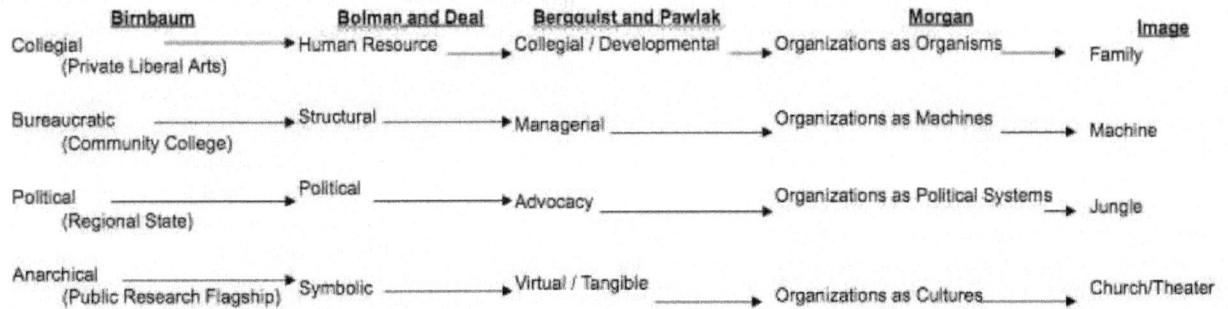

Birnbaum	Bolman and Deal	Bergquist and Pawlak	Morgan	Image
Collegial (Private Liberal Arts)	Human Resource	Collegial / Developmental	Organizations as Organisms	Family
Bureaucratic (Community College)	Structural	Managerial	Organizations as Machines	Machine
Political (Regional State)	Political	Advocacy	Organizations as Political Systems	Jungle
Anarchical (Public Research Flagship)	Symbolic	Virtual / Tangible	Organizations as Cultures	Church/Theater

Figure 1. Alignment of various authors' descriptions of organizations

3.4 Symbolic (Anarchical)

The symbolic frame draws on social and cultural anthropology and assumes that the meaning underlying events is more important than the event itself. People within symbolic or anarchical institutions must deal with issues of attention and meaning [7]. The metaphor for the symbolic or anarchical frame represents organizations as tribes, theaters or temples. The leader must inspire employees to successfully lead the organization by using culture, meaning, ritual, ceremony, stories and heroes [10].

Bolman and Deal provide six assumptions of organizations in the symbolic frame:

- it is not what happens but what it meant that is important;
- activity and meaning are loosely coupled;
- life is ambiguous;
- high ambiguity undercuts most issues;
- people create symbols to resolve confusion; and
- events are important for what is expressed, not what is produced. [10] (p. 216 - 217)

Goals are realized through the communication of organizational vision, as well as through the use of symbols and stories [4], [5].

3.5 Integrating Multiple Frames and Models

It is important to remember that frames are viewpoints from which organizational leaders process events and determine actions. Leaders who view their organizations through only one of the four frames are likely to have an unbalanced view of the institution [7]. Morgan proposes using multiple frames or metaphors to view and understand organizations and organizational problems [30]. Birnbaum argues for a cybernetic view of organizations [7]. Bensimon et al. provides eleven principles of cybernetic leadership, which manifest themselves through the incorporation of organizational theory, leadership theory and higher education [5]. These principles help leaders build an integrated perspective of leadership in higher education.

Bolman and Deal also point out that "multiframe thinking is challenging and often counterintuitive" [10] (p. 380). They argue that effective leaders and managers need to reframe until they understand the situation at hand and use a multiframe perspective in leadership. While the emphasis on a cognitively complex viewpoint is certainly well developed, the importance of multiple perspectives is evident in other scholarship [4], [5], [7], [8], [10], [30].

Bolman and Deal and Birnbaum argue that organizations need to be examined from multiple frames and that it is critical for an organizational leader to be able to understand and use frame thinking if they are to be effective [7], [10]. These frames or images of organizations impact how an individual leads and manages. Research has shown that it is difficult to understand and lead complex organizations from a single frame [4], [5], [6], [7], [8], [9], [10], [20], [21], [30], [37], [40], [45].

4. PERSONALITY INVENTORIES

Personality inventories are tools used to report behavioral preferences of individuals. These tests include a host of questions and are designed to offer awareness to individuals about how they would generally respond to situations. These inventories can also be used as a team building activity. The idea is that by understanding your behavior style and the style of others, you will gain a better understanding of each other, which can lead to more effective communication [31].

4.1 Myers-Briggs

The most familiar tool, Myers-Briggs, can be traced back to the early 1920's when a Swiss psychiatrist, Carl Jung, developed his theory of personality types, stating that people are different in the way they process information and make decisions [31].

Jung's theory classified individuals as having a natural preference in all of four dichotomies. The four dichotomies are: introversion/extroversion: how one prefers to get organized, sensing/intuition: how one prefers to take in information, thinking/feeling: how one prefers to make decisions, and judging/perceiving: how one prefers to approach life [31].

It was Jung's theory that led mother, Katherine Briggs, and daughter, Isabel Myers, to create a tool to help others understand themselves better, the Myers-Briggs Type Inventory (MBTI) [11]. The MBTI consists of multiple-choice questions and a discussion about what your personality type means. It is meant to show preferences related to the four dichotomies. It is important to note that we may use each of these eight preferences, but some are more natural for us. There is no right or wrong, and all preferences are equally valuable [12].

For example, someone might be introverted, sensing, thinking and judging (ISTJ). This means they have an attention to detail, appreciate facts, rules and fulfilling obligations. This tendency may conflict with someone else's who may be extroverted, intuitive, and makes decisions based on feelings. The theory behind the MBTI instrument is when individuals are aware of their own styles and those of others, they can hopefully adjust or be more understanding towards each other based on this knowledge [15].

4.2 DiSC

The DiSC assessment is similar to Myers-Briggs in that it is an instrument meant to measure behavior styles. It was built upon the model of behavior by William Marston, a psychologist with a degree from Harvard. His 1928 book, *Emotions of Normal People,* categorized behaviors into four primary types or styles: Dominance (D), Influence (I), Steadiness (S), and Conscientiousness (C) [14].

Walter Clarke, another psychologist, created an assessment instrument around Marston's theory [14]. Similar to Myers-Briggs, the idea with the DiSC instrument is that everyone has a preferred style, and by understanding this, you can learn to adapt your style to work more constructively with others [16].

Back in the early to mid-1900s, when these theories of behavior and instruments were being developed, people were skeptical of the field of psychoanalysis, especially those in the scientific community, and are even skeptical to this day [12].

But in the last 20 years, administering these instruments to those in corporate America has become a big business. The idea that it can lead to more productive teams has grown. A large selling point for both Myers-Briggs and DiSC is that no behavior is better or worse than the others, and can only lead to better understanding. This positive approach to understanding behaviors is helping continue to sell these instruments to corporate America.

5. PRACTICAL APPLICATION IN IT ORGANIZATIONS

Winona State University (a mid-sized university located in southeast Minnesota of 9,000 students) IT support is provided by Information Technology Services (ITS) which is organized into four units: User Services, Development and Web Support Services, Infrastructure Services, and Teaching, Learning, and Technology Services. The ITS leadership team consists of the Chief Information Officer and the Directors of User Services, Development and Web Support Services, Infrastructure Service, and Teaching, Learning, and Technology Services. This leadership team began using the research base of cognitive frames and personality inventories to enhance organizational performance.

5.1 Leveraging the Power of Cognitive Frames as an Information Technology Leadership Team

The ITS leadership team at Winona State University tries to set aside one meeting a month for the purposes of professional development. Over a period of six months the group read and discussed "Reframing Organizations" by Bolman and Deal and also discussed important elements of "How Colleges Work" by Birnbaum. Each month a different frame was discussed. Real work issues were examined using the frames. Several problems were discussed on how people within the organization use a

different organization frame could perceive the same issue very differently.

This professional development activity was shorted and then presented to the technical lead group made up of project managers, the chief security officer, lead developers and system administrators. Again the process was used to examine real world work issues using the multiple perspectives of cognitive frames.

This activity was done over two years ago, but the directors still will use the cognitive frames to describe issues at the University. It has provided a common tool/language for the leadership team to discuss organizational issues. At the same time cognitive frames were being discussed at the leadership level, one director was involved in an initiative to use personality inventories to assist members of her team to better understand the personal dynamics of the unit.

5.2 Leveraging the Power of Personality Inventories to better manage/lead IT staff

At Winona State, the Development and Web Support Services Team, a team of fourteen people, used the DiSC assessment as a tool to increase each team member's understanding of one another and improve communication. The team hired an outside facilitator to administer the DiSC to each individual, analyze the results and schedule a two-day session to review and discuss results. The session agenda included the following:
- Developing an understanding of the different individual behavioral styles;
- Identifying my own style;
- Identifying the styles of our team and others;
- Modifying our styles for improved communication.

The most aggressive of the behavior styles is (D)ominant. Individuals who score high in the D category tend to be decisive, tough and competitive. Under pressure these individuals can appear to be self-centered and not concerned about others. This style can be more concerned about results than people, and can be impulsive. It would be important to utilize someone with a D personality when decisions need to be made and to keep processes and projects moving ahead [47].

The most social style would be (I)nfluence. Individuals who have a high I tend to be very talkative, enthusiastic and persuasive. They do not focus on details, so under pressure these individuals can appear disorganized. These individuals are good with people, yet like to see results also, and would be called upon to help align others towards a common goal [47].

The most patient style would be (S)teadiness. These individuals are also social, good listeners, yet very careful before making decisions. These individuals appear laid back yet like consensus before moving forward with an action. This can also cause them to appear indecisive; as they want to make sure everyone is heard before a decision is made. It would be important to call upon those with an S style when needing to make an important, high impact, decision that involved many viable options [47].

The last of the four styles is (C)onscientiousness. Someone with this style is a rule-follower, very logical, precise and careful. These individuals can appear impersonal, as they tend to be more concerned with details than people. It would be important to call upon someone with this style when details are important [47].

During the two-day session, each individual evaluated their own results and did a few exercises around how their preferred style is typically seen by others. They discussed motivators and de-motivators for each style, and were asked to bring up real-life examples from their job. They were also presented with the team's results and asked to pair up with an individual with a different preferred style. During this exercise, individuals explored ways they can adjust their style based on various circumstances. They learned to recognize their comfort zone and areas of discomfort, and when they may need to work outside of their comfort zone. Finally, those with similar styles broke into groups and created the top ten things we want others to know about how to best communicate with us, and presented to the rest of the group.

At the end of the two days, each individual had a better understanding of themselves, each other, and learned to recognize when they needed to adjust their style to better communicate with others. Through this exercise, the group determined that all of the developers are high C's. They are concerned with details and want to ensure their work in precise and error-free. The director, was a high D and I, and was concerned about results. With this realization, the director is able to better build project teams with styles that complement each other. For example, if a project needs quick results, the director will help ensure the project keeps moving. If the project requires careful analysis and attention to detail, the director will call upon her development team to manage the project. Overall, the use of DiSC in the director's area has led to better teamwork, more effective and efficient use of resources, quicker project completion, and overall improved morale department-wide. There is a need to periodically revisit the session to reinforce what the group learned, but overall this has been well received by all team members.

6. RECOMMENDATIONS

From our experiences with managing and leading IT professionals, we can make several recommendations. First, based on the literature and findings in the field, the use of the structural frame is critical in effective management. The chief information officer as an effective manager: thinks very clearly and logically, strongly emphasizes careful planning and clear timelines, uses logical analysis and careful thinking, develops and implements clear, logical procedures, approaches problems with facts and logic, has extraordinary attention to detail, sets goals and holds people accountable for results, and strongly believes in a clear chain of command.

Literature will support that structural framing appears to be a risky, if not untenable, means of leading an information technology division. As such, if the job requirements of a CIO necessitate the exercise of managerial skills (e.g., coordinating the work of others, solving problems, making equipment purchases, scheduling installations, etc.), working from a structuralist perspective is advantageous. However, if the demands of the position are really leadership oriented (e.g., thinking strategically about the development and implementation of an IT plan, visioning the future, reorienting the basic approach to the conduct of work in the area, etc.), a structural framework may lead to difficulty with staff charged to carry out this work. Thus, the CIO needs to carefully assess his organization's needs, his or her

relationship to the institution, and engage those frameworks needed to be successful. Metaphorically, the CIO needs to be chameleon-like, able to be flexible enough to adapt to the environmental circumstances as they are presented.

The chief information officer needs to be aware that various stakeholders, internal and external to their unit, weigh in on how effective they perceive the CIO to be in their work. In the CIOs managerial capacities, perceptions are driven by how the chief information officer integrates the political with the structural frames into their daily practice. In the environment of higher education, the chief information officer is not the owner of the information they store, protect, and report but is responsible for this information that is actually controlled by a variety of departments with competing priorities. It is in this surrounding, that to be managerially effective, the chief information officer must create the appropriate structures needed to maintain the IT enterprise while also having the requisite political sensitivities to the larger environment. Both of these frames provide the tools, or perspectives, for the chief information officer to be an effective manager. Yet, once again, though, the CIO needs to be sensitive to the use of structural approaches to problems when the needs are more strategic and require the exercise of leadership. Additionally, he/she need to be aware that a human resource perspective does not necessarily advantage them in either domain.

Today most information technology services are treated like a public utility (e.g., phone, gas, and electric company); people expect 100% performance all of the time. It is hard to create an environment that supports innovation when stability has become the main focus. When stability of the network or other information technology services is important, the structural frame is emphasized. This use of the structural frame to create stability negatively impacts the need and desire of other campus constituents for innovation, which in turn negatively impacts the overall leadership effectiveness of the chief information officer, as perceived by others. While this concept may be riddled with inconsistencies, it is the nature of leading a complex loosely coupled system. The CIO is constantly assessing and reassessing the issues and reframing his or her actions. One could use the analogy of a teeter-totter with the chief information officer balancing the conflicting needs of stakeholders.

Given the increasingly visible role of CIOs, combined with the enormous resource investment dedicated to information technology, the CIO must use multi-frame thinking to be effective as the role of information technology management has expanded to include both leadership and management responsibilities. It is important to remember that frames are viewpoints from which organizational leaders process events and determine actions.

Where understanding the different frames can help a leader achieve a better understanding of one's environment, personality inventories enable leaders to better understand their people. Theories, by such psychiatrists as Carl Jung and William Marston, which started to dig into the behaviors of people and how understanding these behaviors can lead to more productivity. These theories have proven successful through the creation of instruments such as Myers-Briggs and DiSC. These same environments that require the use of multiple frames also require individuals to understand each other in order to work in harmony and produce results. As information technology leaders at Winona State, we have implemented the use of these tools successfully, and through continued review of the literature and work with our teams, we strive towards continuous improvement.

7. REFERENCES

[1] Becker, N. J. (1999). Implementing Technology in Higher Education: The Leadership Role and Perspective of the Chief Information Officer. *Dissertation Abstracts International,* (UMI No. 9939460)

[2] Benjamin, R. I., Dickinson, Jr., C. & Rockart, J. F. (1985). Changing role of the corporate information systems officer. *MIS Quarterly, 4* (1). 21–34.

[3] Bensimon, E. M. (1989). The meaning of "good presidential leadership": A frame analysis. *The Review of Higher Education*, 12, 107–123.

[4] Bensimon, E. M. (1990). Viewing the presidency: Perceptual congruence between presidents and leaders on their campuses. *The Leadership Quarterly, 1*, 71–90.

[5] Bensimon, E. M., Neumann, A. N. & Birnbaum, R. (1989). *Making sense of administrative leadership: The "L" word in higher education.* Washington, DC: ERIC.

[6] Bergquist, W. H. & Pawlak, K. (2008). *Engaging the Six Cultures of the Academy.* San Francisco: Jossey-Bass.

[7] Birnbaum, R. (1988). *How Colleges Work.* San Francisco: Jossey-Bass.

[8] Birnbaum, R. (1992). *How Academic Leadership Works: Understanding Success and Failure in the College Presidency.* San Francisco: Jossey-Bass.

[9] Bolman, L. C. & Deal, T. E. (1991). Leadership and management effectiveness: A multiframe, multisector analysis. *Human Resource Management, 30*(4), 509–534.

[10] Bolman, L. C. & Deal, T. E. (1997). *Reframing Organizations* (2nd ed.). Boston: Pearson Publishing.

[11] Center for Applications of Psychological Type. (2012). The story of Isabel Briggs Myers. http://www.capt.org/mbti-assessment/isabel-myers.htm

[12] Cunningham, L. (2012). Myers-Briggs test not all psychologists' type. *Sydney Morning Herald.* http://www.smh.com.au/world/myersbriggs-test-not-all-psychologists-type-20121217-2bigg.html

[13] Datz, T. (2003). 6 habits of highly effective CIOs. *CIO,* http://www.cio.com.au/pp.php?id=1232468866&fp=512&fpid=88482248

[14] DiSC Indra Research Report. (2003). Inscape Publishing. http://www.discprofile.com/what-is-disc/history.htm

[15] Drenth, A. J. (2013). The functional stack and Myers-Briggs theory. Personality Junkie. http://personalityjunkie.com/functional-stack-myers-briggs-theory/

[16] Inscape Publishing. What is DiSC? http://www.discprofile.com/whatisdisc.htm

[17] Frenzel, C. W. (1992). *Management of Information Technology.* Boston: Boyd and Fraser Publishing Company.

[18] Green, K. C. (2002). *Campus Computing 2002: The 13th National Survey of Computing and Information Technology in American Higher Education.* Encino, CA: The Campus Computing Project.

[19] Hayley, K. J., & Bolek, R. W. (1989, December). CIO survival. *CIO,* (3:3) p. 10.

[20] Heimovics, R. D., Herman, R. D., & Jurkiewicz Coughlin, C. L. (1993). Executive leadership and resource dependence in nonprofit organization: A frame analysis. *Public Administration Review, 53*(3), 419–427.

[21] Heimovics, R. D., Herman, R. D., & Jurkiewicz, C. L (1995). The political dimension of effective nonprofit executive leadership. *Nonprofit Management and Leadership, 5*(3), 233–248.

[22] Hurley, M. A., & Ko, C. N. (1991). *The IT Organization and the Role of the Information Technology Executive.* Canada: Nolan Norton and Company.

[23] Kwak, M. (2001). Technical skills, people skills: It's not either/or. *MIT Sloan Management Review, 42*(3), 16.

[24] Lattimer, D. A. (1999). National survey of chief information officers in U.S. higher education. Retrieved August 14, 2001 from http://ciosurvey.utk.edu.

[25] Maslow, A. H. (1968). *Toward a Psychology of Being.* New York: Van Nostrand.

[26] McClure, D. L. (2001). *Maximizing the Success of Chief Information Officers.* GAO-01-376G CIO Executive Guide. Diane Publishing Co.

[27] McClure, P. A. (2003). Managing the complexity of campus information resources. In P. A. McClure (Ed.), *Organizing and managing information resources on your campus.* San Francisco: Jossey-Bass

[28] McGregor, D. (1960). *The Human Side of Enterprise.* New York: McGraw-Hill.

[29] Mintzberg, H. *Structure in Fives: Designing Effective Organizations.* Engleweek Cliffs, N.J., Prentice-Hall.

[30] Morgan, G. (1997). *Images of Organization* (2nd ed.). Thousand Oaks, CA: Sage.

[31] Myers, Briggs, I & Myers, P. B. (1980, 1995). *Gifts Differing: Understanding Personality Type.* Mountain View, CA: Davies-Black Publishing.

[32] Penrod, J. I., Dolence, M. G., & Douglas, J. V. (1990). *The Chief Information Officer in Higher Education.* (Professional Paper Series No. 4) Boulder, CO: CAUSE.

[33] Penrod, J. I. (2003). Building an effective governance and decision-making structure for information technology. In P. A. McClure (Ed.), *Organizing and Managing Information Resources on your Campus.* (pp. 15-28). San Francisco: Jossey-Bass.

[34] Personality Desk (2013). ISTJ: The Inspector. http://www.personalitydesk.com/istj

[35] Pitkin, G. M. (1994). Leadership and the changing role of the chief information officer in higher education. Paper presented at the 1993 CAUSE Annual Conference held in San Diego, CA. http://www.educause.edu/ir/library/text/CNC9305.txt

[36] Potter, R. E. (2003). How CIOs manage their superiors' expectations. *Communications of the ACM, 46*(8), 74–79.

[37] Quinn, R. E. (1988). *Beyond Rational Management.* San Francisco: Jossey-Bass.

[38] Rockart, J. F., Ball, L. & Bullen, C. V. (1982). Future role of the information systems executive. *MIS Quarterly*, 6, 1-14.

[39] Rockart, J. F. (1988). The line takes the leadership: IS management in a wired society. *Sloan Management Review,* 29, 457–64.

[40] Slater, R. O. (1995). The sociology of leadership and educational administration. *Educational Administration Quarterly 31*(3), 449–472.

[41] Stephens, C. S. (1995). *The Nature of Information Technology Managerial Work.* Westport, CN: Quorum Books.

[42] Synnott, W. R. & Gruber, W. H. (1981). *Information Resource Management: Opportunities and Strategies for the 1980s.* New York: John Wiley & Sons.

[43] Taylor, F. W. (1911). *Principles of Scientific Management.* New York: Harper & Row.

[44] Weber, M. (1947). *The Theory of Social and Economic Organizations.* London: Oxford University Press.

[45] Weick, K. E., & Bougon, M. G. (1986). Organizations as cause maps. In H. P. Sims Jr. & D. A. Gioia (Eds.) *Social Cognition in Organizations.* San Francisco: Jossey-Bass.

[46] Zastrocky, M. R., & Schlier, F. (2000). The higher education CIO in the 21st century. *EDUCAUSE Quarterly*, 23 (1), 53–59.

[47] Extended DISC (2013) http://www.extendeddisc-na.com/

Parallel Reporting: The Future of Support

Gursimran S. Koonjul
Carnegie Mellon University
5000 Forbes Ave
Pittsburgh, PA, 15213
(412) 268-4448
gskoonju@andrew.cmu.edu

Kimberly A. Hennessey
Carnegie Mellon University
5000 Forbes Ave
Pittsburgh, PA, 15213
(412) 268-9559
sport883@andrew.cmu.edu

ABSTRACT

Academic environments are evolving and require more cross-disciplinary relationships and cross-functional support. Collaborative learning spaces are more difficult to support with isolated single-department employees. As more and more institutions are compelled to do more with less, a niche for IT professionals with varying interests and skills sets could be multi-disciplinary and cross-departmental support. Moving forward, parallel-reporting employees may indeed play a vital role in supporting technology for teaching and learning environments.

The parallel-reporting structure is often associated with the "matrix" management structure of the 1980's (employees with analogous skills from separate groups assembled for assignments). The matrix model is considered difficult and outdated by most organizations due to the numerous structural and strategic traps. In a parallel-reporting model, there are several requirements from both management and the employee to ensure efficient success.

At Carnegie Mellon University, the collaboration of Computing Services and the College of Fine Arts requires a unique support model for technology services and academic technology spaces available to faculty, staff and students. The foundation of this model includes a parallel-reporting staff consultant cross-disciplined in both the arts and technology: a Multimedia Clusters Support Specialist. This position has a dual-reporting relationship with both Computing Services' Clusters Support Services team and the College of Fine Arts Dean's Office.

Categories and Subject Descriptors

K.6.1 [**Management of Computing and Information Systems**]: Project and People Management– *Management techniques, Staffing,*

General Terms

Management, Documentation, Performance, Design, Human Factors, Standardization, Theory.

Keywords

Support, academic technology, computers, Carnegie Mellon University, parallel-reporting, management.

1. INTRODUCTION

Today, "doing more with less" has become the mantra for most educational institutions all over the nation as budgets have become smaller while demand for services and support has increased. Universities are no longer able to be stagnant in the type of amenities and facilities that they provide – students, faculty, and staff are continuously looking for ways to keep up with rapidly evolving technologies that enhance teaching and learning both in and outside the classroom. One effective approach to managing these needs is collaboration – partnering with other departments or groups can provide multiple advantages, including increased support for teaching and learning technologies and shared or decrease in costs. As the number of cross-departmental services increases, the nature of this support has to change. University technology support groups can no longer get by with the typical "techie in the shadows" mentality of one expert in a single field supporting one service and another person supporting another. IT consultants must now be cross-trained and versatile if the potential for success is to be truly developed.

The objectives of this paper are threefold. The first is to highlight the fact that academic technology environments are evolving, and require more cross-disciplinary relationships and cross-functional support. The second is to demonstrate that as institutions are compelled to do more with less, parallel reporting via a liaison is an effective way to support multiple departments and improve collaboration. The third objective is to point out the important conditions required, both from the management and the employee, for parallel-reporting to be successful. These conditions are related to the flexibility, agility, and collaboration of all parties involved.

To meet these objectives, the IT support group and structure at Carnegie Mellon University will be described along with the type of services it provides, in particular, some of the cross-disciplinary services that require more multi-faceted support. Next, specific ways that parallel reporting has contributed to this group's success, in particular, projects and goals will be examined. Finally, many of the lessons learned from the existence of this position and its impact on the ability to support the university will be identified.

2. ABOUT THE ORGANIZATION

2.1 Computing Services

Carnegie Mellon University is world-renowned as a leader in the use of technology in education and research. Carnegie Mellon University's Computing Services is composed of multiple departments that support the computing infrastructure within the university, both on the local Pittsburgh campus and abroad.

Clusters Services (Clusters) is a sub-division of Computing Services with a special focus on supporting the academic mission of the university by providing and maintaining reliable and usable environments for teaching, learning, research, and collaborative activities. Some of the services provided include:

- Technology environments for academic spaces

- Access to academic software applications and equipment

- Support for academic leadership, faculty and students in their use of technology for teaching and learning

Public computer labs or "clusters" provide technology-rich teaching and learning spaces to faculty and students, as well as access to multimedia and various types of peripherals. These spaces support over 3,000 class sessions each academic year in over 18 different locations across campus. Clusters provide access to more than 70 Windows, 70 Linux, and 50 Macintosh Application Packages on over 400 physical machines, Web Stations, and virtual workstations. Over 30 printers are available across campus using a centralized system.

2.2 Academic Partnerships

Academic and administrative departments everywhere have discovered that collaborating by integrating technology both inside and outside the classroom can greatly enhance teaching and learning. Computing Services works with partners to extend core infrastructure on campus. By leveraging supported technologies, partners are guided through the development of technology-rich collaborative spaces and distance education facilities, deployment of printers and computer labs, and upgrades to departmental classrooms based on classroom technology standards.

But the work doesn't stop with the creation of a space or the installation of new technology. What has become increasingly important is the support of those spaces and services; new technology means there will always be a learning curve for users. Another major challenge that institutions face is just as one class becomes accustomed to and trained to use the technology in a space, the semester ends and a new batch of students and faculty roll in. The support cycle never ends, and it has become increasingly important to improve and streamline workflows and training. Nevertheless, it is even more vital to have staff members who are able to not only provide direct support for multifaceted technology from the computing backend, but serve as advocates for faculty and students on the frontlines.

2.3 The College of Fine Arts

Clusters Services has multiple support partnerships with many different groups on campus, including the College of Fine Arts (CFA) at Carnegie Mellon University. The CFA is composed of a community of internationally recognized artists and professionals organized into five schools-Architecture, Art, Design, Drama, Music, and associated centers and programs.

In 2012, the CFA was ranked #1 for best graduate schools in Multimedia and Visual Communications last year, and ranked #7 in Fine Arts (U.S. News & World Report Rankings, 2012). Both the graduate and undergraduate programs at the CFA are known to be excellent, offering a vigorous curriculum and world-renowned artists, designers, and musicians as instructors for the school's course offerings. Another major factor in the College's high ranking is the services and technology provided to students.

The five schools provide students with a vast array of resources including photo labs, computer numerical controlled shaping machines, laser printers, 3D printers, large-format plotters, woodshops, and multiple departmental clusters that assist with digital design, programming, and other media. One of the major facilities offered by the college is the CFA Multimedia Studio.

2.4 The CFA Multimedia Studio

Located in the north wing on the 3rd floor of the CFA main building, the CFA Multimedia Studio is a joint venture between Computing Services and the College of Fine Arts. The studio serves an essential role in many of the curricula offered by the university. It includes three regularly updated and upgraded computer labs, a multitude of lendable equipment for video, photography, and voice recording, and a fully functional sound room that allows users to record audio in an isolated booth. Among the numerous public clusters across the university, the CFA Multimedia Studio provides the most comprehensive range of hardware and software for electronic and time-based media. It is managed jointly by Computing Services and all five schools in the college.

The studio is composed of four rooms that house over 50 computers, black & white and color printers, two web stations (kiosks that allow streamlined internet access and printing), a vast array of peripheral hardware including MiniDV decks, external monitors, scanners, and Blu-ray players, and state of the art lecterns that assist faculty in teaching multimedia based courses. It accommodates multiple courses, workshops, and seminars every week and is open 24/7 to users.

Figure 1. CFA 317 PC/Windows Cluster

2.4.1 Clusters Services Multimedia Lending

Clusters Services provides equipment for lending at the CFA Multimedia Studio to all members of the campus community. Any individual with a valid CMU ID may borrow equipment. Equipment for lending includes: Canon Rebel T2i & T3i Digital Single-Reflex Cameras, Sony High-Definition Video miniDV and digital-data camcorders, Zoom audio recorders, a variety of Audio-Technica and AKG microphones, GOPRO Hero2's, Wacom Intuos tablets, Optoma pico pocket projectors, tripods, and a multitude of other equipment and cables.

2.4.2 CFA 321 Sound Room

The CFA 321 Sound Room is also available to anyone with a valid CMU ID. The room provides a main work area with an Onyx mixer, Novation midi keyboard, table-top microphone, and

Rocket speakers, while the booth chamber houses a Blue Yeti Pro microphone allowing for isolated recording.

Figure 2. CFA 321 Sound Room (Main Area)

2.4.3 CFA Multimedia Studio Software Package

The CFA Multimedia Studio provides a variety of specialized software that is not available anywhere else on campus. The computers in the space are equipped with Adobe Master Collection, the entire Autodesk Suite including 3D programs like Maya and 3dsMax, Final Cut Pro 7 and Final Cut Pro X, Logic Pro, Pro-Tools, Rhino & Grasshopper, Finale, and a variety of programming tools and other programs.

Now that these resources have been described, the complex and multilayered question needs to be answered – how is a facility like this supported? How is this model sustainable? How are faculty and students getting everything they need in an efficient way? How are users prevented from being overwhelmed and bogged down by the learning curve of the technology?

3. MULTI-LAYERED SUPPORT

It is clear that the CFA Multimedia Studio requires a different kind of support than regular IT support. It is difficult for support consultants with a general background in IT troubleshooting to adapt to environments that require more specialized expertise, in this case, multimedia. Here are some of the typical questions that both faculty and users ask at the CFA Multimedia Studio:

- I'm trying to film a commercial for a project in my class. What type of camera should I use and how can I put my footage on the computer?

- I have an old Hi8 tape that I want to put onto a DVD. Can you show me how to digitize and burn it?

- I want to send audio from my laptop to the room speakers while displaying the screen of the DSLRs to the projector for my students. Is there a way to do this?

As one can see, these questions require a different type of expertise than just IT knowledge. However, this isn't to say that typical software-based IT questions don't come up:

- I'm trying to run Adobe Photoshop but it's just not launching. Also, everything on my computer is running slowly. What should I do?

- I tried saving this file to my network space, but now it's not there. Can we get it back?

These last two problems don't necessarily warrant a multimedia expert. Someone well-versed in the IT architecture of the systems supported by the university computing support would be able to handle these types of questions – provided they are directly related to the infrastructure afforded by the institution.

3.1 Blended Support

It can be discerned that there are two distinct realms of knowledge that are required to support a space like the CFA Multimedia Studio. One might easily suggest using a blended-support model and hiring two staff members – one well versed in the multimedia aspects of technology, and one well versed in the sub-level system architecture. But there are some difficulties with this model. For one, it isn't cost effective. Assuming institutions are spending their budgets to create collaborative and innovative spaces that enhance teaching and learning, it is difficult to state they will have plenty of funding to acquire staff to support all aspects of the space.

Additionally, each staff member is at a disadvantage – since they have no expertise overlap they cannot promote transparency in the work that they do. This model slowly devolves into the realm of "I don't know how to do this/this isn't my specialty, go ask the other guy." Not only does this mindset not help users, it also doesn't help IT staff with their own professional development. It's too easy to defer and deflect questions and not progress one's own skills when there is an expert to direct problems to.

There is a final overarching problem with the blended-support model – who do these staff members report to? In the case of the CFA Multimedia Studio, there are two entities that have a hand in the operation and management of the space. The College of Fine Arts provides the space for the studio and salary for a single support staff member, and Computing Services provides the hardware, software, and equipment. Although there are many classes that are managed by other departments, the majority of courses at the space are taught by CFA faculty. The two entities have different needs and different goals, which all need to be represented and advocated for in some way in the support that is provided at the space. When making upgrade and update decisions, both groups need to have a say in the decision-making process, and in order for this to be successful they need to be in the loop for any support issues or problems that come up. For a staff member supporting this kind of space, there needs to be some reporting links to all the departments involved in the management of the space.

3.2 Matrix Management and Reporting

Matrix management is a type of organizational management in which staff members who have similar skill sets are assembled together for work tasks. This type of management was very popular in the 1970's and early 80's, when businesses recognized the need for cross-functional expertise. The typical vertical hierarchy was not enough to get tasks done, and there was a large movement among companies to pool groups of people together to get tasks done. Individual employees would often have multiple managers – in most cases an operational manager, who oversees the overall project area, and a functional manger, who directly assigns the individual work-related tasks.

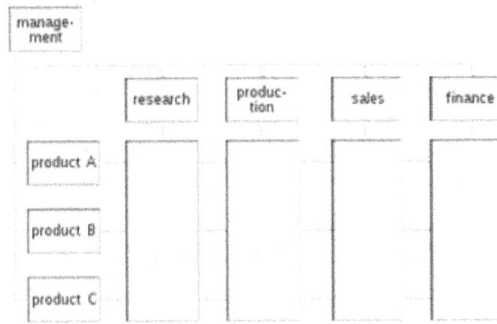

Figure 3. A Matrix Organization (Wikipedia)

The matrix style of management was considered, in theory, to be more efficient. This is because individual workloads would be decreased and the reporting overlays to each department would dissipate, since the individual was communicating with both sides at the same time.

However, there were many problems with this type of management, and it has long since become outdated in today's organizations. Many problems stem from the relationships the individual has with each reporting department or manager. Often loyalty would come into question that would lead to conflicts of interest between the groups – trapping the employee right in the middle. Employees would get overwhelmed with the number of tasks assigned to them from their supervising groups as there was no communication flow between them. It was hard to weight the demands between one group and the other, and ultimately matrix management led to poor employee morale, frustration, and isolation.

As discussed, there are important lessons that can be learned about the nature of blended-support and matrix management. How can a model that can better support the needs of future technology teaching and learning spaces and other academic environments be constructed? Each model has its own advantages and disadvantages, but both rely on something very important – good relationships and clear communication. There is a huge human factor at work here.

3.3 Dual or Parallel Reporting

At Carnegie Mellon University, an atypical model has been developed for the support of the CFA Multimedia Studio. The foundation of this model includes a unique staff position that reports in parallel to both the CFA and Clusters Services. In general, the Multimedia Clusters Support Specialist (MCSS) provides first-level support for Clusters Services especially to faculty and students, appropriately escalating issues, and assisting faculty & students using specialty equipment, software and hardware. Additionally, this position maintains and administers the Clusters Services Multimedia Lending collection as well as the CFA 321 Sound Room. The Multimedia Clusters Support Specialist position is in essence, a versatile and multi-faceted consultant position.

This position and its reporting structure will be broken down to demonstrate how it works, and why it is an effective method of supporting this unique environment. The human factors associated with this position will also be examined – the necessary qualities in managers and an employee, as well as the type of relationship required, to make this model effective and successful.

4. PARALLEL-REPORTING MODEL

4.1 Structure

The organizational composition of the Multimedia Clusters Support Specialist is unique when compared to other typical IT consultant positions. At the base level, the MCSS position is affiliated with both Computing Services and the College of Fine Arts. This position is sponsored by the CFA Dean's Office, but is a member of the Clusters Services Support Team. In this way, it reports to two different direct supervisors, the CFA Assistant Dean for Business Affairs (CADBA), and the Clusters Support Services Manager (CSSM).

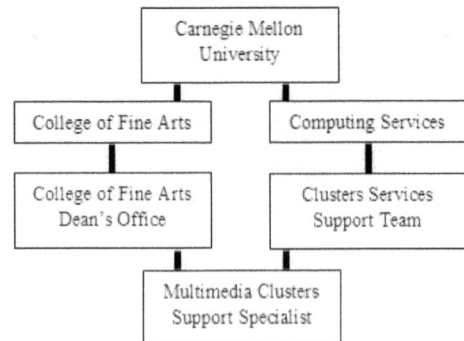

Figure 4. MCSS Managerial Hierarchy

The CSSM acts as the direct functional manager of the MCSS. The MCSS is delegated tasks, project work, and general day-to-day work by the CSSM. The MCSS meets with the CSSM bi-weekly and funnels all communication related to the direct support of the CFA Multimedia Studio through the CSSM. If there are support issues that require escalation to another group or department, the CSSM acts as the main proponent for accelerating a response, and catalyzing action and follow-up. This manager-employee relationship is structured typically the same way one as an IT manager-consultant relationship.

On the CFA end of things, the MCSS has a dotted-line reporting relationship with the CADBA. The CADBA serves in a secondary supervisory and advisory role to the MCSS, serving as the line of contact for aspects related to Human Resources, building facility maintenance, and CFA staff and faculty updates. This third attribute is extremely important as the MCSS serves as the main CFA proponent and representative to Computing Services.

4.2 Networks

The MCSS is poised in a distinct position in comparison to typical IT consultants due to the managerial hierarchy and the relationships with members on each "end of the table." The networks formed by these connections are incredibly important for advocating and promoting the interests of each side to the other. The MCSS is part diplomat and part harmonizer.

At the Computing Services end, the MCSS serves as the primary agent for the College of Fine Arts community. The MCSS receives direct news and information about CFA programs and members from the CADBA and other members of the CFA Dean's Office. Because the MCSS is out in the field, the CFA faculty members are able to communicate directly with the MCSS about software/hardware requests, recommendations, and issue or problem reports. Additionally, the MCSS interacts with students directly – assisting them with not only troubleshooting issues in the CFA Multimedia Studio, but also aiding with and providing suggestions on course project work related to multimedia and computing. In this way, the MCSS is the main conduit for CFA staff, students, and faculty needs, delivering information to and advocating needs to Computing Services.

At the other end of the spectrum, the MCSS serves as the face of Clusters Services at the CFA Multimedia Studio. The MCSS relays update information, project developments, and computing news to the CFA community. The MCSS works closely with the entire Clusters Services team, and may also be involved with other groups within Computing Services, including Media Technology, Systems & Applications Integration Services, and the Information Security Office. Additionally, the MCSS serves a secondary supervisory role to student Cluster Consultants (CCons), student IT assistants that staff many of the cluster locations on campus, including an office at the CFA Multimedia Studio office. The MCSS provides training and guidance to CCons working at CFA to increase support effectiveness and provide extended-hours of assistance to evening courses and students.

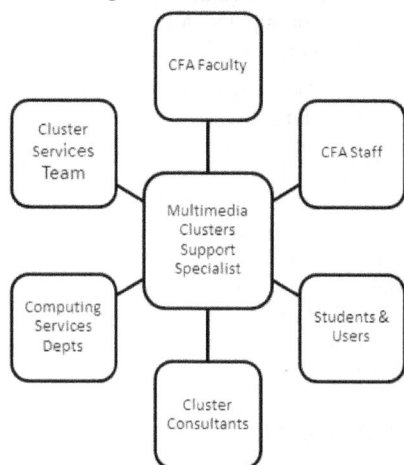

Figure 5. MCSS Networks

4.3 Job Functions

To give a better depiction of the exact responsibilities of the Multimedia Clusters Support Specialist, here is a list of the current job responsibilities:

Table 1. MCSS Job Responsibilities with Time Percentages

Responsibility
25% - Cluster User Support. Immediate 1st level and technical support for faculty and students; provide assistance, information, and instruction as necessary; Actively participate in meetings with faculty users; relay and respond appropriately.
20% - General Cluster Support. Supervise student assistants (cluster managers and cluster consultants), monitor supplies, report facility issues and problems, participate in monthly rotation of Computing Services Staff Hotline for after hour emergencies, and coordinate with CFA users and Computing Services.
20% - Equipment Lending Library. Coordinate equipment lending library, set and implement guidelines for lending and use of equipment. Track, maintain and improve database. Maintain statistics on lending and prepare statistical reports for Computing Services and CFA.
20% - Multimedia Support: Troubleshoot and maintain a variety of hardware and software including DV decks, printers, sound

room, etc. Maintain inventory. Perform preventive maintenance on hardware as required and follow-up on related Remedy tickets

10% - Training and Documentation. Train cluster consultants on CFA cluster-specific hardware and software. Develop and maintain up-to-date, relevant trainings, workshops, tutorials and documentation. Cross-train Clusters Services staff on multimedia hardware and software.

5% - Special projects and general administration. Attend meetings: supervisors in each unit, staff meetings, departmental meetings, and divisional meetings. Participate in special projects and teams as needed.

5. SUCCESS STORIES

Now that the position has been described in its entirety, to better demonstrate the potential and impact a parallel-reporting staff member can have, below are a list of successful projects that have relied heavily on the relationship, networking, and job function of the Multimedia Clusters Support Specialist. Key factors required for the parallel model to work will be highlighted.

5.1 CFA 321 Sound Room Discovery

In the fall 2011 semester, Clusters Services and CFA initiated a Discovery Project to understand the current uses and future requirements for the CFA 321 Sound Room. Faculty and students had long described multiple issues with the space and equipment – particularly the large learning curve that existed in order to use the tools provided. The equipment was outdated, very complicated to use, and it was difficult for faculty to use the space for teaching and learning. The goal of the Discovery Project was to explore how this facility was used, its value as a service, and potential improvements or adjustments to accommodate teaching and learning needs.

CFA and Clusters Services members contributed to the project, utilizing the MCSS as a lead and conduit for the exchange of information. As part of the project, data and statistics of users of the space were collected, such as the departments they were from and how they used the room. Next, a feedback form was distributed by the MCSS to sound room users to determine benefits and needs of the space. Finally the MCSS interviewed CFA faculty and staff directly during walkabouts in the space.

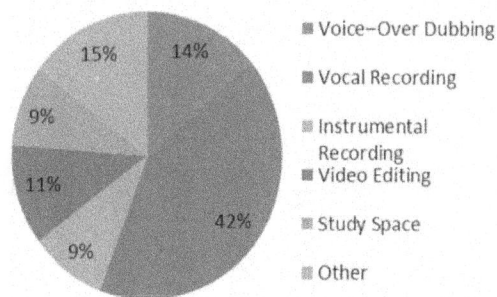

Most Common Purposes

- Voice–Over Dubbing
- Vocal Recording
- Instrumental Recording
- Video Editing
- Study Space
- Other

Figure 6. Sample survey question: For what purpose(s) did you use the 321 Sound Room this semester?

As a result of these efforts, a recommendations report was produced to address the value of the space, provide lessons learned and suggested next steps. The ultimate outcome of this discovery project was a revamping of the space, upgrading the equipment to increase usability and quality, adding sound dampening, acquiring and piloting new software, and utilizing a new power distribution system.

While this project had a direct impact on what students and faculty could accomplish in the space, there were enormous subtle effects as well. The faculty felt very involved with the project. Due to the nature of the interviews they felt more like they were assisting in improving the space collaboratively rather than acting as third party consultants. The MCSS served as the direct liaison for recommendations and suggestions for the space. The student community was also very invested in the process – offering walk-in feedback and discussions with the MCSS about how the space could be improved.

5.2 Facility, Software, and Lending Refresh

Every year, Clusters Services evaluates the hardware, software, and the massive multimedia lending collection offered at the CFA Multimedia Studio. Each category falls under a different refresh cycle, and like other institutions offering hardware and services, refreshing old facilities efficiently is important. New purchases have to be justified with teaching and learning needs in mind, and frivolous spending must be completely avoided. In that regard, optimum decisions must be made with regards to longevity.

To facilitate the needs of all cluster locations on campus, Clusters Services organizes annual faculty meetings in February to discuss summer refresh plans that impact upcoming fall classes. For CFA, Clusters Services specifically meets with the Art and Architecture schools. The MCSS serves as the point person for following up on issues discussed at these meetings, and communicates with faculty and staff about the decisions points and next steps.

The MCSS is well-equipped for this task as the position is deeply engaged with students and faculty throughout the semester. If an issue pops up during an Art or Architecture class in one of the clusters at CFA, the MCSS is on hand to troubleshoot or escalate, and perform follow-up afterwards.

Demand for equipment is high, as students and faculty rely heavily on the multimedia equipment offered to complete coursework and projects. Therefore, it is important that suitable equipment for these tasks is provided and maintained.

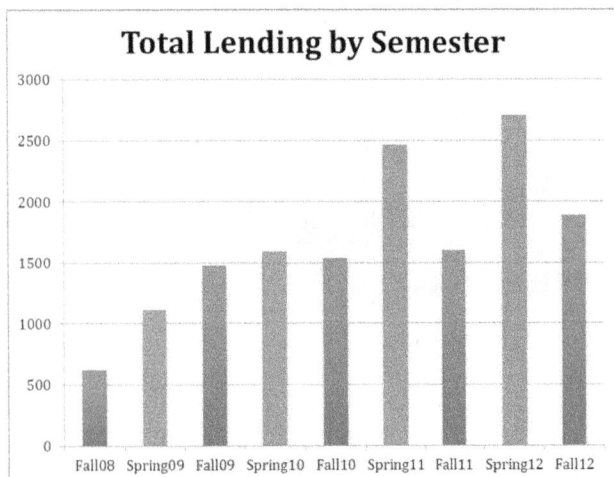

Figure 7. Total Lending by Semester over the last few years

Due to evolving technology, the MCSS must keep in close contact with faculty about needs and recommendations over hardware and software refresh. Occasionally an innovative multimedia item is released that provides a number of teaching and learning

opportunities and with which the community is interested in testing. It is important for a staff member to coordinate the research and evaluation of the equipment, purchase it, deploy it out into the field, and collect feedback on its usefulness.

5.3 Support and Learning Enhancement

From the information presented above, it is clear the MCSS position has enhanced teaching and learning for students through networking. If a class experiences a technical or multimedia-related issue, the MCSS troubleshoots the problem and resolves the issue for the faculty, and the course is able to continue. Often because of the close relationship the MCSS maintains with faculty and students, the MCSS has the opportunity to positively impact learning in the spaces.

Many faculty members often request the MCSS to provide one-on-one consultation with themselves or students to learn about specific processes, troubleshooting techniques, or effective technology use. One may consider this part of an IT consultant's job, but there are more dynamics at play. These interactions are based on a trust relationship the MCSS has developed with individuals inside the environment.

In numerous situations, faculty have requested the MCSS to spend portions of their course time discussing multimedia equipment or computing procedures with the entire class. Topics such as "what equipment is available," "different types of cameras," "how does lending work," and "how to manage files on cluster machines," are all special mini-workshops that have been integrated into many course curricula and are led by the MCSS. This is very popular as it allows the students to receive correct and full information directly from the agent responsible for the support of this equipment. Faculty testimonials continue to rave about the benefits of this position.

6. FACTORS TO SUCCESS

So far, the services that Carnegie Mellon University provides and the role the Multimedia Clusters Support Specialist have been discussed, as well as examples of successes in the parallel-reporting structure. One might be led to believe that the quality of service provided is only related to the employee's personality and characteristics – if you have a bad egg, no amount of management or organizational support will improve the work performed. This is true only to an extent. While the ideal parallel-reporting employee should possess certain characteristics, many factors contributing to success rely on the relationship of the manager with the employee, the relationships the managers have with each other, and the relationship the employee has with the organization and the environment.

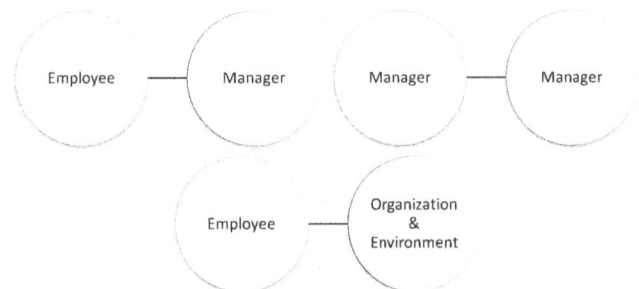

Figure 8. Important Relationships in the Parallel-Reporting Model

6.1 The Law of Propinquity

The law of propinquity, in social psychology, refers to the physical proximity between two people. Greater "closeness" between people demonstrates greater propinquity, or greater interpersonal attraction. In essence, the law means that people who are physically or psychologically closer to each other interact more often. In this regard, if you have a team of people and would like to increase the amount of team interaction, you should keep all of the team members in closer proximity to each other.

Businesses and institutions don't often realize the importance of the physical location of their employees. Employees working in the same area interact more than employees working on the same floor but in different areas. Those working on the same floor but in different areas interact more than people working in the same building but different floors. These people in turn interact more than people at the same site but in different buildings, who interact more than people in different cities, countries, or continents. Even though the law of propinquity seems rather obvious, it has extraordinary effects that aren't always measurable or recognized.

What does the law of propinquity tell us about IT support? Keeping consultants together in the same office location is conducive to the teamwork aspect that is enhanced by higher propinquity. If your employees are close together, they interact more. This doesn't mean that they are guaranteed to become great collaborators automatically; it just means they have greater opportunities to grow their relationships. Therefore, one might consider that the 'techie in the shadow' model is great for teamwork because all of the consultants are together somewhere. But what about the relationship between the support members and the people they serve? The law of propinquity demonstrates that if you place an IT consultant away from the students, faculty, and staff you support, you prevent the opportunity for more interactions and deeper relationships between your group and your user base. Therefore, it is highly important that consultants spend time in the field.

Of course, one might suggest that this will be a detriment to the group dynamics of the field consultant and the rest of the team. Isolation of employees in the field needs to be avoided; else they are likely to feel abandoned or outcast from the rest of the team. Therefore, providing field consultants multiple opportunities to interact with the support team is highly important as well. For the MCSS position, a dedicated work area is allocated in the same location as the rest of the Clusters Services team in the Cyert building, which is about 200 meters away from CFA. In this way, when the MCSS needs to work with the rest of the Clusters Services team there is a welcoming environment in proximity of the other members.

6.2 Manager Relationship

6.2.1 Manager – Employee

The relationship between each manager and employee in the parallel-reporting model is critical to its success. This can be related back to matrix management failures in the 1980's, when the strains on the relationship in the organization model resulted in decreased employee morale and performance. In the parallel-reporting model, the employee must be given some independence when compared to a typical IT employee. Should any of the two managers apply pressure to or micromanage the employee, the employee will recede in the opposite direction.

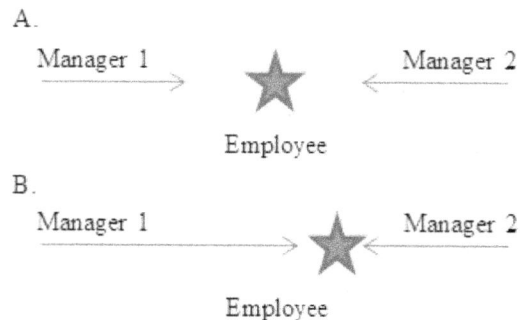

Figure 9. Employee shift during managerial pressure

In the figure, it can be demonstrated that a close to equal amount of correspondence from both managers is ideal. The employee will feel valued by both departments and feel loyalty to both departments. If one manager makes overreaching demands or stresses the relationship with the employee, this causes the employee to start valuing the individual characteristics of the managers, and results in the same loyalty-questioning failures experienced by matrix management employees.

Ideally, each manager should meet with the employee bi-weekly (alternating weeks). This allows the employee equal opportunity to report face-to-face with each manager, while still receiving ample supervision and advisory information.

6.2.2 Manager – Manager

As demonstrated in the above situation, managers have to be careful about how much they demand from dual-reporting employees. It is imperative the two managers communicate with each other about the employee's tasks, projects, professional development, and human resources matters, especially performance reviews. This relationship should be consistent rather than be frequent. It is important for the two managers to meet at least a few times a year to discuss the employee's progress and any updates to job functions, special project work, or other important matters that should be decided jointly.

The relationship between the two managers also sets the basis for the employee's perception of the relationship between the two departments. This is also critical as it reinforces the employee's commitment to both groups, rather than feeling like they are only part of one team.

6.3 Employee

Perhaps the most significant component that one would consider in a parallel-reporting model is the employee. Although it has been demonstrated that there are other contributing factors to the success of this organizational model, it is important to be able to identify the right kind of employee for this type of position. Not everyone who works in IT may be equipped to handle the types of situations that a cross-disciplinary employee will encounter.

6.3.1 Harmony

Ideally, the most important skills to look for in a parallel-reporting employee are communication and diplomacy. In international politics, diplomats are often the people who are responsible for acting as liaisons between nations and have big impacts on promoting international cooperation. In the same regard, the parallel-reporting employee acts as a liaison between two departments that may not necessarily have the same values, expectations, or needs. Therefore, it is important to identify an employee who is adept at resolving conflict and encouraging others, but more importantly creating *harmony* among people.

6.3.2 Affiliation

Parallel-reporting employees constantly work with departments and communicate with multiple people. They are the conduits between two groups and lie in the middle of a huge network. It is important for these employees to easily create relationships with other people. Therefore, identify employees who are highly *affiliative* – who constantly seek to align themselves with other people and have a need to create relationships or connected links. This isn't necessarily the person with the greatest social ability, but a person who has a high need for liking and forming networks with others.

6.3.3 Interest and Learning

Employees who are curious, value increasing their knowledge and education, and acquiring information make great parallel-reporting employees. Parallel-reporting employees are involved in multiple fields, and people who enjoy learning new things will be very comfortable in those types of environments. These employees will be much more interested in applying their knowledge of one area of expertise to the other, looking for synergy between the two fields, and enhancing their environment.

6.3.4 Achievement

In any high technology teaching and learning environment, the employees who are star performers are the ones who have high ambition and a need for achievement. These are the aces whom many support groups have and others long for – the ones who have no lack of energy and are willing to constantly accomplish tasks. These are employees with pronounced work ethic and place great value in the job they perform. They will work tirelessly for the sake of the institution and its members. Star performers are more likely to succeed in parallel-reporting positions than typical workers due to the nature of the work required.

6.3.5 Experience

Similar to typical IT consultants, parallel-reporting employees are always better equipped to succeed if they already have some experience not only in the field(s) they are working in, but also the organizational models of each department. Originally serving as a student cluster consultant as an undergrad student, our MCSS was able to obtain working organizational and service knowledge of Computing Services. Our MCSS additionally attended many electronic, time- based media studio courses, consistently working in the CFA Multimedia Studio and forming relationships with faculty. Although this was very favorable in our case, other organizations may not have employees with this kind of dual-experience. It will therefore be important to prepare potential employees who have the right skill-set with development opportunities and training.

6.3.6 Talent Expression and Opportunity

One might be led to believe that not just the ideal parallel-reporting employee is being discussed, but the ideal employee in general. All of the factors previously discussed are not absolutely required strengths. These factors are talents that all employees possess, and some are able to express in more ways or more explicitly than others.

Another aspect to keep in mind is the professional development opportunity that parallel reporting allows for employees. These employees experience a completely different type of managerial and organization structural experience than any other employee in a department due to their cross-disciplinary relationships. Parallel reporting is not for everyone, but it is a wonderful prospect for able employees looking to receive a different kind of learning and education.

7. CONCLUSION

In evolving teaching and learning environments, campus technology groups and departments have a unique opportunity to collaborate and create academic partnerships through technology support. Carnegie Mellon University's Computing Services and College of Fine Arts provide a model for a parallel-reporting support structure that fosters both cross functional and cross-disciplinary campus connections. These connections are becoming more and more valuable every day.

As organizations continue to have a need to "do more with less", utilizing parallel-reporting could be an effective way to harmonize multiple departments, improve support, and encourage collaboration. With the right management and employee relationships, a proper set of rules about the working environment, and a dedicated, dynamic group of employees, a parallel-reporting model can greatly benefit technology support within the community. Parallel reporting and cross-functional employees will play a major role in the future of support.

ACKNOWLEDGMENTS

Special thanks to Patricia Pavlus at the CFA Dean's Office, Connie Deighan Eaton Cheryl Koester,and the entire Clusters Services team at Computing Services.

8. REFERENCES

[1] Diers, Melissa, and Ziskovsky, J. C 2002. Integrating educational technology with a limited support staff. *Proceedings of the 30th annual ACM SIGUCCS conference on User services.* (New York, NY, USA, 2002).

[2] Faulks, Joelle. 2004. Outsource this! Broaden support and reduce staff burnout. *Proceedings of the 32nd annual ACM SIGUCCS fall conference.* (New York, NY, USA, 2004).

[3] Ramsden, Paul. *Student Learning and perceptions of the academic environment.* Institute for Research and Development in Post-Compulsory Education, University of Lancaster, Lancaster, UK. Higher Education. Volume 8, Issue 4, 1997.

[4] Galbraith, J.R. (1971). "Matrix Organization Designs: How to combine functional and project forms". *In: Business Horizons,* February, 1971, 29-40.

[5] Kelly, Melissa. *Creating an Academic Environment: High Expectations and the Classroom.* About.Com Education. http://712educators.about.com/cs/discipline/a/environment.htm

[6] Reh, F. John. *Matrix Management.* About.com Management. http://management.about.com/od/projectmanagement/g/MatrixManagemen.htm

[7] Corkindale, Gill. *Lost in Matrix Management.* HBR Blog Network, 2008. http://blogs.hbr.org/corkindale/2008/06/lost_in_matrix_management.htm

Social Media: Multiple Channels to Capture Multiple Audiences

Katherine L Derby
University of New Hampshire
1 Leavitt Lane
Durham, NH 03824
011.603.862.5064
kathi.derby@unh.edu

ABSTRACT

In this paper, I discuss several social media applications and their use to create a full media campaign to target the correct demographics. Applications such as Facebook, Twitter, Instagram, and more offer unprecedented access to faculty, administrators, students, staff, and other members of a campus community. Social Media has broken down the silos between segments and sections of society and allows communications to occur organically and effectively. Moreover, information is consumed in real time and "just in time." The new communications, public relations, and marketing campaigns have a new arsenal of communication channels to use. The only thing left to do is to know which to choose, how to apply them, and how to measure their effectiveness.

Categories and Subject Descriptors

K.8.1 [**Application Packages**]: Data communications, Freeware/Shareware

General Terms

Management, Documentation, Performance, Design, Human Factors, Theory.

Keywords

Social media, marketing, communications, Twitter, Facebook, Instagram, Vine, Pinterest, Return on Investment, Engagement.

1. INTRODUCTION

In an April, 2013 tweet, Enterasys CMO Vala Afshar likened the phrase, "we use Facebook, we're a social business" to saying, "we use an oven, we're a gourmet restaurant." [Afshar, personal communication, April 2013] His point hits home with those working in communications, marketing, and social media who have often heard similar announcements. The truth is building and maintaining a social presence for a company or entity takes a lot of skill and talent. Creating a Facebook page for your college/university department or group doesn't mean you've effectively leveraged your message across social channels nor does it mean your messages are effective or being received.

SIGUCCS'13, November 3–8, 2013, Chicago, Illinois, USA.
Copyright © 2013 ACM 978-1-4503-2318-5/13/11...$15.00.
http://dx.doi.org/10.1145/2504776.2504799

As much as technology changes, the principles of marketing and psychology remain the same. Applying the Three-Plus Rule to social media campaigns works as well as it did decades ago in print ad campaigns. The tools we use change, but the need to be an insightful marketer doesn't.

1.1 Background

The University of New Hampshire is a public university in the University System of New Hampshire, Founded in 1866. The main campus is located in Durham, New Hampshire, United States. Additional campuses are located in Manchester, NH and Concord, NH. The University of New Hampshire is a land-grant, sea-grant, and space-grant university offering undergraduate and graduate programs. A team of 3,000 faculty and staff support approximately 15,000 undergraduate and graduate students. With students at three separate locations, social media allows UNH the ability to communicate important messages to students, staff, and faculty and to listen to ideas, problems, and information from all in real time.

2. SOCIAL MEDIA VS PRINT ADS

Three-Plus Rule

As far back as fifty years, marketing professionals would cite the three-plus rule when placing print ads. The three-plus rule was simple. It would take the average reader seeing an ad placement three times before recognizing they've seen it once. When placing newspaper ads, marketing executives would make sure to run the ad at least three times that week to achieve the maximum rate of return.

Sending messages using social media is no different. Care must be taken to ensure your important message is broadcast three times in a short period of time in order to maximize the number of people who receive your message.

Let's say you have a need to inform students of a new feature in their email. You've determined you are going to use Twitter to send a message. Make sure to send a minimum of three messages scattered at various times you know are effective. If you know students aren't typically early risers, concentrate efforts during times when they are usually checking messages or on computers (lunch, early evening, late evening.) Have fun with the 140 characters; you can send the same message with slight variations and maximize the reach of your message.

The three-plus rule can also be done with different pairings of social media tools, all with the same wording and message, to span the reach beyond just those using Twitter. A combination of Facebook, Twitter, and Instagram is currently a powerful trio to reach UNH students. If there is a graphic or logo accompanying the message, the continuity will create a stronger impact, as well. Including pictures with faces, especially fellow students, will also yield higher engagement and return on investment(ROI.)

2.2 Don't Rely On One Channel

Social media is much like print ads. Relying on one channel or one post a week is unproductive and should not be thought of as a comprehensive social media plan. Because messages are sent and appear in a stream among other messages, they may not be seen. More importantly, different people use different social media applications - each has it's own unique subset and understanding who is using what is crucial.

Frequent and engaging posts on several social channels/applications allow your message to be seen by people multiple times. Moreover, it allows for different market segments to be targeted. One may be an excellent application to reach parents/faculty/staff while another may have a strong female following. Matching the application to its market segment is similar to your marketing department choosing which television channel and time slot to choose. Of course, because each application is different than the other, this means the message may need to be written for each service in your social media toolbox.

Care should be taken to create a message that maximizes the strength of the application being used. Instagram is very popular with Tweens and beyond and allows for the use of hashtags and tagging pictures. Using Instagram to showcase the most beautiful places on your campus and the faces of current students allows prospective students to see the campus and the type of students they will be joining. It's much easier for someone to picture himself or herself on your campus.

Vine is a popular application (by Twitter) allowing for six-second looping videos to be placed on Twitter, among others. These short video clips create moving images that grab even more attention. Once placed on Twitter, use the same url and post to Facebook.

2.3 Which Channel is the Right Fit?

Each channel is an opportunity to connect with a subset of followers and hopefully they will forward the message on to their followers to extend the reach exponentially. That being said, you don't have to be on all of the channels or using all of the applications. Select several that work for you and focus on doing those well rather than maintaining ghost presences on every channel out there.

Knowing exactly which channels to use, crafting a message which is engaging or is worthy of being shared with others, and understanding how to measure the effectiveness is the art and skill of our craft.

Several resources exist to aid in choosing the right social media application for the market segment. One of the best resources for determining, which one is best, is by asking. The University of New Hampshire regularly surveys its students to determine what forms of communication are used and how to best relay and receive information. Social media is changing quickly, so it's best to survey as often as possible. Over 600 students participated in a web poll to gauge social media use. The results of UNH's survey can be found at: http://www.slideshare.net/UofNH/2013-unh-student-social-media-survey.

Additional information was gathered throughout the 2012-13 academic year. Students were asked to participate on a communication task force. In exchange for their participation in monthly meetings, students were given lunch and the opportunity to meet, discuss social media, and influence university communications. Each month, priceless insight into the preferences and usage was extracted from the group. After meeting with these students, UNH Information Technology had a much stronger sense of which social media channels to use, when, and how.

Students aren't always the market segment the university wants to attract. Parents, Alumni, and Donors are also important groups. Understanding each service demographics can assist in planning a successful campaign. Successfully pairing the right tool and the right message is very important if you want to leverage the full power of social media for each target market.

The University of New Hampshire is fortunate to be located a few miles from Portsmouth, NH, home of many companies on the cutting edge of technology, marketing, and social media. There are regular meetings for anyone who wants to gather to discuss emergent technologies, the latest social media applications and their effectiveness, and tips to create a successful campaign.

Check your area to see if similar meetings are held and then take the time to go! Check for local TweetUps, Meetups, and other similar events. If there are none – start one! Early morning meetings or events after typical work hours during the week have proven popular on the seacoast of New Hampshire. Just one of the regular meetings is the Portsmouth Breakfast Club.

The Portsmouth Breakfast Club (http://portsbkfstclub.com) meets every Wednesday morning at 6:48am in a local coffee shop in downtown Portsmouth, NH. On any given Wednesday, you'll find a dozen or so folks gathering to discuss social media and tech news or sharing tips with others. It's a casual group that allows anyone to drop in and has some of the best and brightest in the field gathered. Those unable to make it can follow the tweets or read the blog posted later in the afternoon.

3. SOCIAL MEDIA CHANNELS AND THEIR AUDENIENCES

The following is a breakdown of several social media applications and current audiences based on the results of the UNH Social Media Survey of Students and additional information available at this time. Social media changes quickly, so it's important to note the information may have changed.

3.1 Facebook

Facebook is still the number one communication tool for engaging with students. However, our polls show students are losing favor with Facebook and instead are going to other applications to engage with other students. While students do use Facebook, they limit their interaction to special or closed groups. As one student said in an interview, "We are on Facebook – but we lurk, we don't comment or like stuff. My parents and grandparents are on Facebook. I have to be careful." Conversely, Facebook is an extremely good tool to choose to reach parents, alumni, staff, and others.

3.2 Twitter

UNH has found students prefer using Twitter to communicate after Texting and Facebook. Hashtags allow for students to create and follow conversations and topics. Direct messages function the same as SMS/text messages and allow for sending pictures, hyperlinks and conversations with multiple people, making it an attractive vehicle for students.

In order to generate a genuine and trusted atmosphere, UNH uses student interns to tweet as @UNHStudents. Students and others want to see a personality through Twitter – not just canned messages. Let your personality shine through! UNH Information Technology makes sure to cover lots of topics while showing our personality. You'll see tweets covering a variety of topics; news, available positions, tech tips, workshops, and many others including humor. We also post lots of pictures from campus that don't necessarily have anything to do with technology, but highlight the natural beauty surrounding us (flowers, horses at the Equine Center, hayfields, unique architecture, piles of snow.)

3.3 Instagram

Tweens and Teens use Instagram heavily. Instagram also uses hashtags, allowing for conversations between users. Create a unique hashtag for followers to use when they take pictures on campus depicting a day in the life of students. UNH uses the hashtag #instaUNH and occasionally runs contests on Instagram. This is a great way to communicate to not only current students, but to bring your message to those interested in attending UNH. It's a strong recruitment tool since younger students are also on Instagram.

Instagram Video has just entered the scene. Now, users can create short videos with the same application and use the same hashtags and send

3.4 LinkedIn

LinkedIn is the professional application of choice and an excellent way to target alumni. Quick searches find professionals who identify UNH as their alma mater. Having a presence on LinkedIn allows us to communicate directly with alumni quickly.

LinkedIn has also proven a strong recruitment tool for staff and faculty. LinkedIn may not be an application students are thinking about in their first year, but becomes more popular as they approach graduation.

3.5 YouTube

Searches on YouTube are second only to Google. Having a YouTube presence is an excellent opportunity to show you campus, services, and more. Having a strong presence on YouTube also helps with your Google ranking. Beyond that, it's just a fun and creative way to send messages. 94 percent of the students questioned in the UNH Social Media Survey 2013, indicated they had a YouTube account and regularly used the application.

3.6 Pinterest

Pinterest is heavily used by women, making it an excellent choice to target this population. People are pinning more than recipes and decorating tips. It's a great place to store your InfoGraphs, cartoons and graphics, and to create "Boards" of information for all of your services, departments, and more. One Board could be a campus tour with beautiful pictures of your campus with the script under each slide. The entire Board can be sent out by Twitter, Facebook, email, and more.

3.7 Vine

Vine is an emerging application for iOS and Android phones founded in June of 2012 and acquired by Twitter in October of 2012[2]. Vine allows the user to create short, looping, six-second videos that can be shared through Twitter or Facebook and can be embedded on websites. Vine users like the ability to create very quick videos that can be posted in seconds. Vine's potential to emerge as a major player remains to be seen but the application's acquisition by Twitter places it in the forefront.

4. DON'T JUST TALK – LISTEN!

Once target markets are identified, social media channels chosen, and messages for the campaigns crafted and sent, the hard part comes in to play. You must listen. It's not enough to talk to students. Social media is different than running a print ad, or a television commercial. It's social because they are allowed to engage in a conversation. Be prepared to receive messages and acknowledge their receipt. Engagement is key, so when it happens know how to recognize it. It may be someone sending a direct message through Facebook or twitter. It may be someone talking about your institution or service by using hashtags to start a conversation. It may be someone following your channel or liking a picture, comment, or post. When this happens, make sure to acknowledge you've heard them.

4.1 Engagement

Social Media Engagement is a term to describe when a customer/client has responded to your message. This can mean they 'liked' your Facebook page, or 'favorited' or retweeted your tweet, or liked your Pinterest, or Instagram photo. Sharing is the ultimate goal of engagement, which makes your post suddenly accessible to another group of people and is seen as an endorsement for the content. Engagement furthers your message reach and creates an opportunity to capture more followers. Engagement is viewed as an indicator of your campaign's effectiveness. Measuring engagement for each channel helps to determine which social media applications are most effective for your campus.

4.2 Analytics

Understanding analytics and reach is crucial to setting benchmarks and making decisions on future campaigns. Employing analytics is an essential step in all marketing.

Some social media tools have built in analytics. Facebook allows managers of Pages to view recent analytics. These include the number of posts/day, the reach, number of engaged users, the number talking about the post, and the virality.

The application HootSuite is useful for managing multiple social media channels. The pro version also offers analytics and reporting. UNH is currently using HootSuite University to allow the key offices/departments to send messages, assign communications, and create reports to each other.

5. CONCLUSION

Social media is changing the way we communicate whether it's our personal life or our professional life. The lines are becoming blurred and it's important for those in higher education to join in the conversations happening outside the classroom. The University of New Hampshire has embraced the social media culture, breaking down silos that previously existed, and offered unprecedented access between faculty, students, administration, support staff, alumni, and our surrounding communities. Conversations are happening in real-time and allowing information to be exchanged as never before.

Understanding the applications available, the demographics of their users, and the strengths for each contribute to a sound, effective, organic, and cost-effective communications and marketing plan. Modern communications campaigns are limited only by the creativity of the team. Departments, services, and higher ed. professionals also participate in social media and enrich the vibrancy of campus life.

6. ACKNOWLEDGMENTS

My thanks to ACM SIGCHI for allowing me to present on this topic. Thanks also to my Special thanks also to the University of New Hampshire, Durham, NH.

7. REFERENCES

[1] University of New Hampshire Social Media Survey of Students 2013 April, 2013 http://www.slideshare.net/UofNH/2013-unh-student-social-media-survey.

[2] Kafka, P 2012. *Twitter Buys Vane, a Videop Cilp Company Thatn Never Launched.* *http://allthingsd.com/20121009/twitter-buys-vine-a-video-clip-company-that-never-launched/*

Raising the Bar on Training at Valparaiso University

Kevin M. Steele, Ed.S.
Valparaiso University
1410 Chapel Drive
1-219-464-6930
kevin.steele@valpo.edu

Matthew Smith
Valparaiso University
1700 Chapel Drive
1-219-464-5773
matt.smith@valpo.edu

ABSTRACT

We have recently overhauled our IT training program that we offer our students, faculty and staff. In the past, the training program consisted of sessions about changes to campus systems or sessions related to very specific software uses such as mail merge or tables. Users can now expect that training will be more than software use and how-to's. We have started looking at ways to enhance our clients overall use of campus technology. As we examined ways to better serve our campus community, we engaged in qualitative observations in many areas. We examined how our graduate students were using technology to collaborate. The faculty were observed by our training staff to see how they were employing campus technology in courses and integrating technology into their assignments given to students. We interviewed our Help Desk Student Consultants to see what they observed as major training goals throughout the campus based on their interactions with clients.

Upon completion of our observations, we outline our course development plans for increasing technology integration and full use of our campus technology offerings to further our mission of enhancing learning, teaching and job function through technology. Our goal is to reach beyond the software functionality and take our clients to the apex of relevance and application.

Categories and Subject Descriptors

K.6.1 [**Management of Computing and Information Systems**]: Project and People Management – *training.*

General Terms

Management, Measurement, Documentation, Performance, Design, Human Factors, Standardization.

Keywords

training, development, qualitative observations, case study, use case, help desk, client services, course development, software, end-user interaction

1. INTRODUCTION

Valparaiso University is a selective, independent Lutheran institution consisting of over 3,000 undergraduate and 1,100 graduate students. The university employs just over 1,000 administration, faculty and staff.

Valparaiso University offers training to community of end-users through the Office of Information Technology. This service is provided as an extension of our Help Desk in the division of Client Services. Our Client Services staff, consisting of 7 fulltime employees, works with university students and employees to determine need based on formal and informal means. This past year, we restructured our IT Client Services division to match up staffs' skill sets more closely with their position. In this change, the training area was looked at as an outreach arm of the Help Desk. In the past, one person from the Client Services was responsible for the planning and delivery of all training initiatives. In our change, one person leads the team and 5 individuals from the Client Services division assist in the rollout and delivery of the training initiatives.

We really began to explore need informally by observing how students were using technology in class, how staff were using technology in their roles and how faculty were using technology to teach. As Loerzel [2] points out, "Given its importance to the success of any technology implementation, it is imperative to understand the merits of training and how the value of training stands on its own."

2. THE HISTORY

As previously mentioned, training and development in the IT arena has always had focus at Valparaiso University. The program was focused on providing needs-based training for specific software. In this section, we will explore the previous training program, which by standards was running smoothly and met the training needs of most on campus with regard to software.

Classes, or workshops, were only offered via face-to-face delivery methods in a typical computer lab environment. University constituents could also request a one-on-one training to address specific issues. As some members of the team put it, the training program had become "stale." The need for improvements and change were evident in declining numbers of attendees and the course offerings remaining the same for a great amount of time.

3. QUALITATIVE OBSERVATIONS

To focus our efforts on improving the training offerings on our campus for our end users, we required a needs analysis. This could have been done using a survey metric, but we realized that the development of the metric was going to be time consuming and we were examining metric delivery options for future projects. This would not be a feasible option for our current semester.

We had two options: (1) deliver the former model of software based training whereby we had workshops on a specified Microsoft product, Gmail, etc; or (2) find a new method for measuring what our students, faculty and staff could use. At a training meeting which is comprised of several Client Services staff, we decided to make observations about how students were using the technology and what improvements we could make to learning, teaching and job function. These observations came from several sources outlined below:

3.1 Graduate Case Study

In a recent graduate capstone class, students were assigned a business to prepare a proposal for growth and acquisition of new markets. The students were working in a group of five students. They were preparing a PowerPoint presentation to support their oral presentation to the Board of Directors in attendance that night. The arrived to the class about 2 hours before the start. They were busy going over the presentation and correcting errors.

The students prepared their presentations by emailing the presentation from one person to the other. They spent hours preparing data, but even more time was spent correcting the errors in versions, layout consistency and other variations that arose. Productivity suffered, frustration soared and in the end the grade was impacted.

The issue was related to the way they had incorrectly collaborated using email. In the end the presentation still had major errors when they were presenting. When asked later, the group counted that they had on average 55 emails between them. That is 275 emails and version of the PowerPoint file! A simple online collaboration tool would have eliminated all the different versions that existed and cut down their email count to 3 emails to get started.

This posed an interesting question for future course development. The students were versed in setting up PowerPoint, but they needed assistance working with collaboration tools to make this run smoother for them. They also needed some soft skills training on workflow and project management. Just a couple of suggestions and a good tool to work with.

3.2 Technology Room Use

Throughout campus there are several classrooms that were setup and designed with technology at the center of the design. One room in particular caught our attention in our College of Arts and Sciences. The room is setup using the concept created by Steelcase in a 360° seating arrangement with SMART boards on three walls that can be controlled from the professor workstation or can be used in small collaboration groups with laptops.

We setup some informal observations with professors. When we were called to the room to change settings, we would observe what was happening in the room and how the technology was being employed in the lesson. In many cases, it was not being used to its classroom technology potential. Several professors from the English department were using the room for the large tables for discussion. Even the low-tech features, such as huddle boards, were not being used.

Through discussion with known users in casual conversation, we found that some professors were requesting room changes when they were assigned to this room. Upon further inquiry, we found that it was truly a training issue. The professors were uncomfortable with the new Smart software and the boards. They were never informed about the layout and design of the room.

3.3 Faculty Teaching Observation

All of our training staff have other responsibilities in the Office of Information Technology (IT). Through these responsibilities, we have the opportunity to provide live support in classrooms. This has been a great opportunity for discussion about how faculty are employing the use of technology in classrooms. In contrast, it has proven advantageous in observing classes in which technology could be employed and supported in the classroom.

For example, we have been able to identify ways to streamline uses of YouTube in our Social Work department to eliminate disk media and the codec issues that come from DVD creation. This has also allowed us to create relationships within departments where we can offer small, customized trainings for classes that may benefit and relieve the stress from the professor that is not proficient with the technology.

3.4 Help Desk Interaction

As part of the evaluation process, we met with the Help Desk Student Consultants and overviewed the common issues they face when supporting users. This allowed us to do three things; (1) identify training opportunities, (2) cross-market our training offerings with Web Help Desk, and (3) bring in students to begin training users.

In the initial meeting, we found that the Help Desk was getting questions related to software that was offered by the Career Center. In discussions with the Career Center, we found they were happy to have the training collaborative to reduce their need to support the software.

We also found that users needed basic introduction and overview instructions for IT offerings when they start on our campus. So, at the time of this publication, we are working on an IT welcome video to walk users through the steps of getting started.

The Help Desk is also encouraged to find relevant training offerings for end-users when they are interacting with them and make the gentle suggestion that they might find the benefit in attending the seminars. We are also looking at ways to link this with our campus-wide knowledgebase and our Web Help Desk knowledgebase.

One unexpected outcome during our collaboration with the students was that they were interested in conducting some of the trainings. We found that this would have two advantages; (1) marketing to students and having the Help Desk buy-in to assist in marketing and (2) educational benefits in developing student trainers. Students working at the Help Desk certainly have input in our training program and offerings. They interact with our users more regularly than most of the full-time IT staff.

4. ANALYSIS

After our evaluation process, we noted that several things needed to be done differently. It was clear that we were going to develop an ever-changing, yet high-quality experience for our end-users. We noted that we were working in a team, where others before had been working alone. This was a welcome change. We also noted that there needed to be a process for course development. While it didn't need to be long and tedious, we did need some common threads that all members of the team would be expected to carry out. We needed a shift in thinking and a point of focus. We also needed to work collaboratively with other colleges and universities, because even in a team our ideas would be limited by our history.

4.1 Focus on Need – Not Software

In the past, Valparaiso University's training programs have focused on software rollouts and on software packages. The shift in focus during the development phase to skill needs and practical use needs has proven to be a paradigm shift in delivering high-quality, in-demand training programs.

We focus on the best use of software and train from a perspective of lighting the fire of continued learning and experimentation with technology. We know that software will continually change, especially with the shift to cloud-based software services. This shift will be less about the software itself; but more about the usability and the skills in continued learning and skill building as the software and delivery methods continue to evolve.

This shift in thinking requires trainers to be ready to answer questions related to applicability and to cater a standup training immediately on the spot. Trainers must be dynamic speakers, quick thinkers, and stakeholders in the university. They must understand many of the job functions and learning functions throughout the university. All trainings are offered, free of charge, to the entire university community of students, faculty, staff and alumni. Understanding each role and program in the university is key to the success of the trainer.

4.2 Course Development

Prior to the evaluation of our training program, our Director made a choice to restructure our department based on the match of skills. As a result, our training program inherited an individual with teaching experience and pedagogical training. This was critical in developing the process by which courses would be developed.

Each course requires a few items which are outlined below:

4.2.1 Learning Objectives

Learning objectives are developed using the revised Bloom's Taxonomy Verbs developed in the 1990's for educational practices of the 21st century[1]. All objectives start with a measurable outcome that users should be able to perform if asked. Of course, we don't assess our users after the training, but we do ask them to evaluate the training itself against the objectives and other measures.

4.2.2 Overview/Course Description

The overview is used as the course description that should give a summary of what the users should expect. This is the marketing piece, but also informative about what users can expect to learn at the seminar.

4.2.3 Handout

Each participant can expect to receive a branded, full-color handout that has important information about the training. This is designed so that the users can get back to their residence halls or offices and replicate the training procedures. This sometimes has step-by-step instructions about common or obscure procedures, or it has underpinning observations about how to overcome issue using the particular topics training steps. It may also host a variable myriad of both.

4.2.4 Content Outline

The content outline provides the speaking topics of what the training will cover. This serves to standardize our practices between trainers. This is a working document that can vary a little between trainers and presentations; but serves to make sure that the content is presented using the same topics and methods.

4.2.5 Reference to Other Trainings and Lynda.com

We cross-market our programs and refer others to do follow-up work with lynda.com. We also encourage the attendees to continue to explore other related or similar topics that are being offered.

4.3 Collaboration with Duke University

Prior to rollout and after the initial evaluation, we reached out and did a video conference call to Christine Vucinich and one of her student trainers, Patrick Royal, at Duke University. They walked us through their experiences as trainers and allowed us to ask questions of their experiences. This was a critical step that allowed us to move forward more quickly to learn from the experiences of others. During this meeting, we began to put our pre-conceived concepts to the test. We learned that email marketing of the program was and proved to be the most cost-effective and beneficial way to market the program. We also took away some great advice for increasing attendance through an online reservation system. We are so grateful for the opportunity to collaborate with others. We look forward to growing such relationships.

5. ROLLOUT

Rollout of the program continues. We started in the Spring 2013 semester with face-to-face, classroom style trainings. However, we are continuing adding other training options that we will discuss in section 5.6.

5.1 Summary of Results

In our initial rollout, in the Spring 2013 semester, we hosted 21 pre-scheduled, hour-long technology training seminars. We had a total of 130 registrations for all events listed on our booking web site at bookwhen.com/Valpo. As a result, we received 4 requests for one-on-one trainings. We were also invited to offer an evening event to our Greek Life organization officers on collaboration tools. We experienced the highest attendance from our staff on campus with faculty in second place. Students were in the lowest attendance, so our shift has been to entice more students by diversifying our offerings and the times we offer these events. We are working with our Integrated Marketing and Communications (IMC) division to assist in bolstering the student attendance.

We have used the trainings to further market our lynda.com training program and have seen an increase in the usability of this offering. We are finding that the training seminars spark interest and that the users find more details on specific functions utilizing the lynda.com Online Training Library®.

5.2 Marketing the Program

Marketing the program has been grassroots style. We have several methods that we attempted. By far, our most successful marketing comes from email blasts to our users. This delivers a link to the registration system where they can sign up. We reach out to departments and cross-market through many other means. We poster the campus, place cards in the dining halls, and we schedule overviews with our constituents in the international office and admissions. We work throughout new student orientations to get the word out.

We work with our marketing department to create different means of reaching our users.

5.3 Initial Offerings

Our initial offerings are listed below with their course descriptions:

5.3.1 Unlocking the Potential of YouTube

Need to host a video to share with only a few friends, only those you share the link, or the general public? YouTube is a great way to get the message out! YouTube is full of features for creating embedded videos on your own websites, creating your own channel for subscribers, or just hosting your video. Did you know that YouTube has lifted the 15-minute restriction on videos? Attend this session to look, in-depth, at the many learning and project options you can use in your classes (faculty, student and staff, alike) to communicate using video.

5.3.2 Online Collaborative Workspaces

Collaborative work is not going away anytime soon. Attend this training session to learn about many of the tools that allow you to work within a team using things like Google Docs, wikis, blogs and other apps to share information in the cloud and work together at a distance and on your own time. Asynchronous, cloud-based tasks are becoming the norm. Get a jump on the competition today!

5.3.3 Getting Started with Google Sites

Come to this session to learn how to get started creating a personal web site using your Valpo account on Google Sites. Your online presence is important! What do you want future teammates, colleagues and employers to know about your work and skills? This training session will focus on developing a personal online identity and brand for you. Bring some sample work and digital pictures with you to be able to work alongside others on your sites.

5.3.4 Quick & Easy Promotional Materials with Microsoft Publisher

Planning an event? Need to create a brochure or flier and just don't know where to get started? This seminar will review the basics to get you started creating publications including exploring and modifying available templates, modifying themes, colors and more...

5.3.5 Navigating Excel (Secrets & Formulas) – Intermediate to Advanced Users

You know the basics of Excel but might need a quick review. This session will review the basics, special formatting (autofill, paste special, etc.) as well as printing. We'll then cover more advanced topics: conditional formatting, freeze panes, autofilter, v-lookups, pivot tables and more.

5.3.6 Creating Better Presentations

Public speaking and presentation skills are a critical component of success. Audiences have become accustomed to visual representations through multimedia tools. This session will be broken into two parts. The first part will be the skills related to giving a great presentation. This will give way to the second half of the session related to the technology tools. Topics include: body language, verbal communication, and multimedia tools to include fonts and colors, master pages, fill effects, drawing diagrams, appropriate animation and some tricks for running shows smoothly. This session will also review several of the presentation software available today including PowerPoint, Keynote and Prezi.

5.3.7 Introduction to Prezi

Prezi puts a new spin on your presentation. It deviates from the traditional PowerPoint (slideshow) model and focuses a lot on design. If you are new to Prezi or want to know more about creating more visually appealing presentations using Prezi, this is the workshop for you!

5.3.8 Using the lynda.com Training Library (Self-training using video lessons)

Learn about the lynda.com Online Training Library® as a campus wide resource. This training will provide an overview of Lynda Campus: Using the Home Page, Advanced search & time stamped search of transcripts, content curation, Teaching and training methodologies, Player options, Sharing your "favorites", plus accessibility, usability, queues, certificate of completions, and mobile devices. Time will be available for Q&A.

5.3.9 Optimal Resume

Are you looking for that first job? Internship? Summer job? Have you developed your resume? This workshop will maximize your potential for locating and landing the interview. The session will focus on the use of the Optimum Resume tool offered through the Career Center. This should be the first step in preparing yourself to get the interview.

5.3.10 Cleaning Up Your Digital Footprint

Did you know that two-fifths of all employers will Google your name before even calling for an interview? How do you improve your chances of having your profiles show? Have you cleaned up all of your old profiles? This workshop will focus on helping you consider all these and more! Attend to make sure that your best digital foot is forward when seeking employment.

5.3.11 Web Security & Privacy: What we should watch for when we use the Web

We will go over some typical attacks and tricks that hackers use to compromise your computer redirecting you to malicious websites. And we will talk about ways to protect ourselves from those attacks.

5.4 QR Code Trainings

In our previous example in 3.2 on Technology Room use, we could have designed a traditional training about the room and taken 30-60 minutes to go over the features, this would have been overwhelming. So we created a small card of five 5-minute videos with QR codes that users could view at their leisure. The videos took a day to create over the winter break and have been gaining popularity based on viewing statistics on YouTube. The videos are listed below for convenience:

Getting Started - This tutorial video will cover the basic operations of starting the SMART Boards in the Arts & Sciences Building (ASB) room 234n and Valparaiso University.

Duration: 3 min. 15 sec. - http://youtu.be/t0YfwsDqS3k

Basic Software Training - This tutorial video will cover the basic operations of projecting and using PowerPoint presentations on the SMART Boards in the Arts & Sciences Building (ASB) room 234n and Valparaiso University. Duration: 2 min. 22 sec. - http://youtu.be/JBLj7swMPSc

SMART Meeting Software Training - This tutorial video will cover more advanced features embedded in the SMART Meeting software on the SMART Boards in the Arts & Sciences Building (ASB) room 234n and Valparaiso University. Duration: 3 min. 2 sec. - http://youtu.be/4QieXcqDK24

Collaborative Room Space and Technology Setups - This tutorial will cover the use of laptop computers to work in independent groups using the SMART Boards in the Arts & Sciences Building (ASB) room 234 at Valparaiso University. The tutorial also covers the use of the low-tech huddle boards found in the room. Duration: 4 min. 10 sec. - http://youtu.be/B46euT2mMZI

Room layout concept - This video overviews the design concepts behind ASB 234, and how the classroom can be used to enhance students' learning experience. Duration: 4 min. 1 sec. - http://youtu.be/r2rwBjarMSs

5.5 Eyes to the Future
One of the first things we noted when we started evaluating our program was that this could be very overwhelming. So, we started simple and knew that we would keep innovating and changing based on feedback from our end users. We end our meetings with the development of the "percolator" where we discuss future endeavors. Some of our ideas and rollouts in progress are outlined below:

5.5.1 Microsoft IT Academy
For the 2013-2014 school year, we will be doing a soft rollout of the Microsoft IT Academy online teaching program. We are working to simplify the process of assigning learning plans through the system for the testing on which our users will want to focus their studies. We are also working with Prometric to become a testing center so that our participants have a one-stop shop for Microsoft certification.

5.5.2 INdorsed Indiana General Studies Courses
We have courses in software proficiency that we will be offering for elective credit. We have combined a great deal of our courses and matched them with the Indorsed Indiana objectives for career development for our students to be able to get credit for their offerings. Our first course will be "Software Survival Toolkit" which focuses transition software use from academic to professional use. This will be a one-credit, seven week class that will allow students to get credit for our IT training offerings.

5.5.3 Training Library Integrated with Knowledgebase
We are working to tie our training library to our knowledgebase and Web Help Desk ticketing system. Combining efforts and working with other divisions simplifies the end-user experience and raises the potential for all stakeholders.

5.5.4 Video Training in Addition to lynda.com
We are working with our Human Resources Services and Faculty Development Office to combine our training efforts into one place where students, faculty and staff can go for online, on-demand training. We envision one place that would house all of our training tapes that we could have linked handouts and supplemental materials for all of users.

6. SUMMARY
Our IT training staff is making great strides to reach our end-users and enhance their technology experience. This has led to a rough development of our mission statement for the training division. While it is a work in progress, it is a start in developing our core values for training. In the rough draft it reads, "The mission of the IT Training Department is to provide timely and structured learning experiences, operational training and career development programs to the entire Valparaiso University community to improve learning, teaching and job performance with regard to technology and its function to an individual's role within the university."

7. REFERENCES
[1] Faculty Development and Instructional Design Center. 2009. Teaching with the revised bloom's taxonomy. Northern Illinois University. http://www.niu.edu/facdev/programs/handouts/blooms.shtml

[2] Loerzel, T. 2002. Effective training provides knowledge and comfort. *Infotech Update*. 11.6. p. 5-7.

Gulliver's Toss: Google's Chronic Big Load to University Mail Server and Its Sudden Resolution

Yoshiaki Kasahara
Kyushu University
6-10-1 Hakozaki, Higashi-ku
Fukuoka 812-8581, Japan
+81 92 642 2297
kasahara.yoshiaki.820@m.kyus
hu-u.ac.jp

Eisuke Ito
Kyushu University
6-10-1 Hakozaki, Higashi-ku
Fukuoka 812-8581, Japan
+81 92 642 4037
ito.eisuke.523@m.kyushu-
u.ac.jp

Naomi Fujimura
Kyushu University
4-9-1 Shiobaru, Minami-ku
Fukuoka, Japan
+81 92 553 4434
fujimura.naomi.274@m.kyushu-
u.ac.jp

ABSTRACT

Traditionally, Kyushu University has been providing email service internally using its own domain name for staff members and students of the university. Around January 2012, we noticed that the high load of the university authentication server, and we realized that one of causes was the access from the mail server for students (called Student Primary Mail Service). Detailed analysis showed that there was chronic big load produced by Gmail's Mail Fetcher, especially toward nonexistent accounts removed due to graduation. In this paper, we explain the situation and reasons of the big load induced by Google, its possible countermeasures, and its sudden resolution by Google's silent change.

Categories and Subject Descriptors

H.4.3 [**Information Systems Applications**]: Communication Applications – *Electronic mail*

Keywords

University mail service; On-premises service; Deleted accounts; User authentication.

1. INTRODUCTION

Information and communication service is indispensable for education and research activities in universities. Among various services, electronic mail is one of the fundamental services even before the Internet had been widely available in the world. From the perspective of equipment, mail service offered by a university can be categorized into two kinds. One is an in-house (on-premises) service operated by the university itself, and the other is SaaS (Software as a Service) type service operated by other parties. SaaS-type email services such as Google's Gmail, Yahoo! Mail, and Windows Live@edu (now known as Office365) became popular around 2007.

We aren't going to discuss which is superior here, but for various reasons, Kyushu University has been providing on-premises email services using its own domain name for our university staff members and students for several years. Email service for students was started in 1995 (the current incarnation is called "Kyushu University Student Primary Mail System") [1][2], and another service for university staff members was started in July 2009 (called "Kyushu University Primary Mail Service") [3].

Various network services (including these email services) inside our university utilize the university-wide authentication service, and we have been analyzing the load of the authentication servers [4]. We realized that requests from the university-wide wireless LAN service and the student email service was enormous and dominated more than 95% of the whole requests to the authentication servers. In this paper, we describe more detailed analysis of the student email server which revealed that there were a lot of POP3 accesses from Google's network ranges to the email server. In fact, 57% out of all the POP3/IMAP4 requests to the student mail server came from Google. In addition to that, 65% of Google's accesses were toward non-existent accounts (mostly removed by graduation).

In this paper, we describe the analysis of the heavy load induced by Google to the student email server and its consequence. The rest of this paper is organized as follows. In Section 2 we describe email services in Kyushu University. In Section 3 we describe the situation of the student email server's load by analyzing log files of the student email server. In Section 4 we discuss possible countermeasures against Google's accesses. In Section 5, we report the sudden resolution of the problem. Finally, we present our conclusions in Section 6.

2. PRIMARY MAIL SERVICES

First of all, we explain about university-wide mail services provided by Kyushu University Information Infrastructure Initiative.

2.1 Number of Users

The main members of our university are students, faculty, and staff members. Most of students are undergraduate and graduate curricular students. There are also some non-curricular students such as research students and special register students. In addition to students, faculty, and staff members, there are other members with various roles such as research fellows, temporary staff,

Table 1. The number of IDs in Kyushu University (Mar 2012)

Role	Total No. of IDs (approx..)
Curricular students	19,000
Non-curricular students	500
Faculty and staff members	9,000
Temporary staff etc.	800
Total	29,300

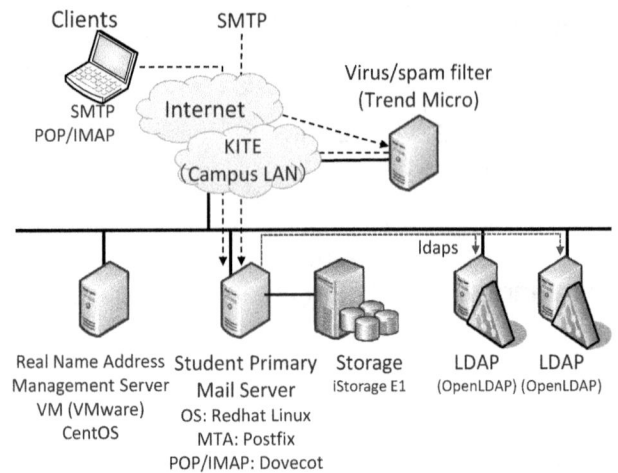

Figure 1. Overview of Student Primary Mail Service

visiting researchers, and so on. Table 1 shows the approximate number of IDs issued for the university-wide authentication service. The number also represents how many people can use both "Primary Mail Services".

The approximate number of ID turnover per year is 6,000 for students. It includes about 3,000 undergraduate students and 3,000 graduate students. In other words, every year 6,000 accounts are both created and deleted on Student Primary Mail Service.

On the other hand, turnover of faculty and staff members is about 1,000 per year and mostly happen in March and April (1,000 retired or moved out of the university in March and 1,000 added in April). Due to that, every year 1,000 accounts are both created and deleted on Primary Mail Service.

2.2 System Overview

Because Primary Mail Service (for faculty and staff members) have been using separated authentication servers (due to some service requirements) and irrelevant to the discussion in this paper, we only explain the system overview of Student Primary Mail Service.

Figure 1 shows the system overview of Student Primary Mail Service. The system employs user authentication through SMTP-AUTH for email submission to avoid third party relaying of spam messages. Users retrieve their email messages through standard POP3/IMAP4 over SSL/TLS with user authentication. Users won't do shell login to the server directly.

The system had been built using open source software such as

Postfix and Dovecot on top of general purpose IA servers to reduce the system cost. To support relatively large number of students, we needed to concentrate budgets to the spool storage.

3. SYSTEM LOAD INDUCED BY GOOGLE

In this section, we will explain how we noticed chronic load induced by Google, and its analysis in details. Actually the discussion from here to Section 4 was applicable as of September 2012 and already resolved now as described in Section 5, but we want to present them here for references.

3.1 Outline

The university-wide authentication system included LDAP servers for processing user authentication and account information retrieval. They were used by not only "Primary" email services but also various information services in our university. From around January 2012, intermittent outage of authentication service started to be observed, causing user authentication failures of various services. We investigated the reason and realized that the LDAP servers were simply overloaded by too many requests and failed to process them.

Table 2. Access statistics of Student Primary Mail (June 2012)

	POP/IMAP accesses per day (ave.)		Unique IDs accessed per day (ave.)	
Total	234,843	(100.0%)	19,996	(100.0%)
Authentication successful	113,491	(48.3%)	6,435	(32.2%)
from Google	33,835	(14.4%)	2,732	(13.7%)
from campus LAN	19,081	(8.1%)	3,432	(17.2%)
Authentication failure by incorrect password	29,824	(12.7%)	1,761	(8.8%)
from Google	12,422	(5.3%)	542	(2.7%)
from campus LAN	6,483	(2.8%)	689	(3.4%)
Accesses to non-existent IDs	90,773	(38.7%)	3,989	-
from Google	86,495	(36.8%)	3,567	-
from campus LAN	1,266	(0.5%)	190	-
Other errors (no ID provided etc.)	755	(0.3%)	-	-

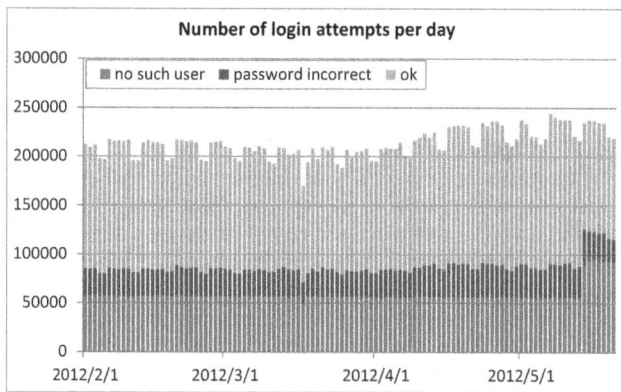

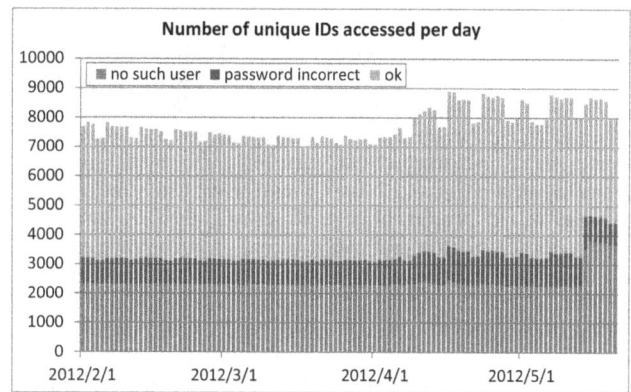

Figure 2. The number of login attempts and unique IDs per day

The two largest users of these LDAP servers were university-wide wireless LAN service using 802.1x authentication, and Student Primary Mail Service (Primary Mail Service for staff members had already migrated to their own LDAP servers). Especially, Student Primary Mail Service employed the LDAP bind operation to authenticate users so we considered that it must be more demanding to the LDAP servers.

By investigating the log files of the mail server, we found that there was unexpectedly large number of POP3 authentication requests from Google's network addresses. Actually we also realized during investigation that these LDAP servers were not properly tuned because initially they were prepared for web services and not expected to serve such a huge number of requests. If the LDAP servers had been optimized enough, probably we wouldn't notice the load from Google.

3.2 Analysis

To understand what was going on, first we investigated log files of the mail server from Dovecot POP3/IMAP4 software and PAM system used for user authentication backend of Postfix SMTP software for one month (June 2012). We gathered the number of login attempts and number of unique IDs used. We didn't distinguish POP3 and IMAP4 accesses because the authentication process of them was the same (using PAM). During analysis, we noticed that there seemed to be many accesses from Google's network addresses, so we also distinguished accesses from Google and campus LAN to compare each other. Table 2 shows the results.

From Table 2, about one-third of total users (6,435 out of 19,996) accessed the mail server using POP3/IMAP4 during the period, and about 42% (2,732 out of 6,435) of users were from Google's network addresses, probably retrieving messages through Gmail. Also it was notable that most of accesses toward non-existent accounts were also from Google. By the access counts, 39% (90,773 out of 234,843) of accesses were toward non-existent, invalid accounts, and its 95% were from Google. That means that if these invalid accesses from Google disappeared, about 37% of the total load of login authentication processes is gone. In total, 57% (132,752 out of 234,843) of all POP3/IMAP4 accesses were from Google, and 65% (86,495 out of 132,752) of all accesses from Google were toward non-existent accounts. Actually we didn't expect this large number of accesses toward non-existent accounts from Google at all. Google's accesses toward non-existent accounts seemed irregular compared to accesses from campus LAN.

Next, we analyzed chronological trends of POP3/IMAP4 accesses from February 2011 to May 2012. Figure 2 shows the number of login attempts via POP3/IMAP4 and the number of unique IDs used per day during the time period. These graphs show both the number of accesses toward non-existent accounts and the number of unique (non-existent) accounts were almost stable during the time period, and there was a sudden gap in the middle of May 2012. The gap represented the deletion of graduated students' accounts, and about 1,200 (out of 6,000 deleted) of now-invalid accounts were added as invalid accesses. The graduation happened in the end of March, but the account deletion was committed in the middle of May due to operational reasons. As mentioned before, most of these accesses were from Google. It seemed that many graduated students didn't change their Gmail settings, and Google didn't care about authentication failures too.

3.3 Google's Mail Fetcher Service

We couldn't tell exactly what software was used to generate these accesses from Google by our log files, but we believe that Google's Mail Fetcher service was used. Google's help document says that Mail Fetcher can be used "to centralize all your email from different accounts into one Gmail account." Mail Fetcher uses POP3 protocol to collect email messages from other (possibly multiple) email servers and stores them in the mailbox of Gmail.

We guessed some possible reasons why many students were using Mail Fetcher. One reason was that we explicitly informed students how to move their messages from our service to another email service. Until 2009, we provided webmail as a part of student email service, but it was abolished when the entire educational system was replaced in 2009 due to budget restriction. The vendor support of the previous webmail software had already ended, and we couldn't prepare a good alternative with sufficient server power to support all the students within our limited budget. Actually, the previous webmail was under-powered and there were a lot of complaints. So we considered that we should provide alternative methods to access their messages conveniently. Especially for Gmail, we also provided how to fetch their messages through Mail Fetcher. In addition to that, in some departments, there was a hands-on session of obtaining Google account and configuring Mail Fetcher during introductory lecture of information technology. So basically we encouraged students to use Mail Fetcher (without realizing the consequences).

Usually using Mail Fetcher is believed to be preferable over simple email forwarding, because email forwarding has bad effects to spam filtering. For example, when a user configures to forward all the messages to another mail system, spam messages are also forwarded. If a lot of users do the same thing, the origin of forwarded messages may be mistakenly flagged as a spam source (it depends on the way of spam detection, though) and causes lower reputation and even in some blacklists. Also announcement messages from the university to all the students may be treated as spam because of sending the same content to many accounts of the destination server. It is common to share blacklists and reputation of servers/domains among anti-spam servers, so these bad effect may be amplified. In addition to that, it is known that SPF (Sender Policy Framework) doesn't work well when email forwarding is involved [8]. To avoid these bad effects, it is better to use a mechanism like Mail Fetcher instead of mail forwarding.

We took these issues into consideration and encouraged students to use Mail Fetcher, but we didn't realize what would happen when many students configured Mail Fetcher and then these accounts were deleted from our mail system after their graduation.

3.4 Frequency of Mail Fetcher's Accesses

Details of access frequency from Mail Fetcher weren't disclosed by Google. The help document only mentions "Google will check your other accounts on a regular basis, and new mail will appear automatically in Gmail. Gmail checks each account at different rates, which are based on previous attempts to fetch new messages; you can't choose the frequency." To guess how the frequency was decided, we collected the number of successful accesses from Google to each accounts and failed accesses to each non-existent accounts per day. The duration was from July 1st to 7th, 2012. Figure 3 shows the cumulative distribution function of accesses per day from Google against successfully accessed accounts and non-existent accounts.

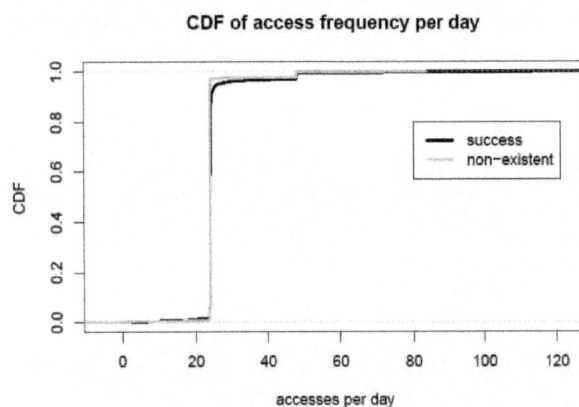

Figure 3. CDF of access frequency per day from Google

The graph shows that the access pattern seemed almost irrelevant to whether the account was accessible or not. More than 90% of accounts were accessed once per hour (24 times in a day) and most of other accounts had frequency of a multiple of 24 (such as 48 and 72). That means that Google controlled the access frequency in number per hour. Also, there were some non-existent accounts with higher access frequency. That means that even an account was inaccessible, Google continued to determine its access frequency by using the last record of message arrival rate when the account had been still accessible.

4. IMPACT AND COUNTERMEASURE

In this section, we discuss the impact of accesses from Google, and possible ways to circumvent it.

4.1 Impact of Accesses from Google

By discussion in Section 2.1 and 3.2, we realized that about 6,000 accounts were replaced every year and about 1,200 (~one-fifth of 6,000) accounts were accessed continuously even after removed. The current incarnation of Student Primary Mail Service began its service in 2011, but it had inherited the previous server's FQDN for mail client migration from the previous system (in service from 2009). From 2009 these invalid accesses to deleted account were accumulated, resulting about 3,600 (~ 3 years' worth) deleted accounts still accessed by Google.

To estimate the scale of the impact of accesses from Google, we checked the total number of university students in Japan. According to the School Basic Survey of the Ministry of Education, Culture, Sports, Science and Technology (in fiscal year 2010), there were 2.9M university students including national, public and private universities in Japan [6]. If all the students had email accounts provided by their universities, and one-third of students were replaced every year, then about 1M accounts are replaced every year. In Kyushu University, about 20% of them were considered using Google's Mail Fetcher, but it must be over the average. Let's assume 10%, and every year about 100,000 accounts were accumulated as invalid accesses to deleted accounts from Google. The total number of Gmail accounts was 350M in 2012 [7], so only 100,000 invalid accounts per year should be negligible for Google.

Such accesses from Google continue to give useless loads over various mail services all over the world. Especially mail services in universities have higher rate of account turnover than in enterprises, so adverse effect must be greater. Also, when designing services for students, it is usually assumed that the number of students is mostly constant and the budget is limited, so it is likely that constant increase of such load interfere the normal operation of the system.

4.2 Possible Countermeasures

We discuss the following methods as countermeasures for increasing access from Google.

1) Filter out POP accesses from Google

2) Ask users of Mail Fetcher to change their configuration

3) Optimize mail system to reduce load

4) Ask Google to change its access policy

4.2.1 Filter out POP accesses from Google

This is the most instantaneous and effective measure to remove the load induced by Google. It is pretty easy to implement such a filter, but it also greatly reduces users' convenience, so it should be considered a last resort. There was one case of this method actually implemented in Hokkaido University of Education because the load from Google was high enough to hinder ordinary users' accesses.

4.2.2 Ask users to change their configuration

This is a method which tries to remove loads by reducing the number of Mail Fetcher users. When users, whose Mail Fetcher setting has problems, are still enrolled in the university, we can

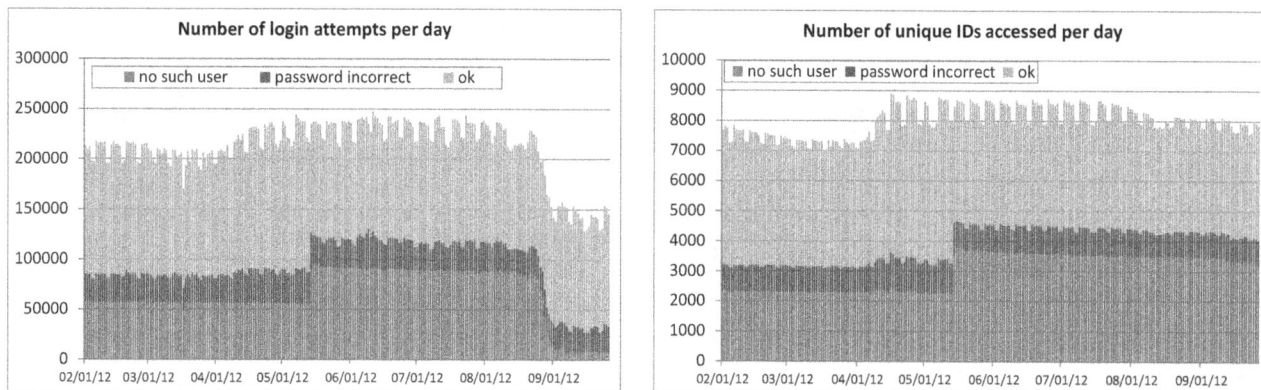

Figure 4. The number of login attempts and unique IDs per day (including Google's change)

contact them (via email or bulletin boards) and make them fix their configuration. But actually most of the load we want to reduce is caused by deleted accounts of graduated students, and it is hard to contact them already. Also we cannot contact the original Gmail account because no information is provided from Mail Fetcher to the destination server who is using the Mail Fetcher.

One possibility is to revive invalid accounts temporarily and put a message into the mailboxes which directs the users to remove Mail Fetcher setting, and let Mail Fetcher fetch the message to the corresponding Gmail account. It is not a trivial task, and also it has limited effects because some users might abandon Gmail accounts and don't read messages anymore.

4.2.3 Optimize mail system
Another way is to reduce the overall system load itself by changing configuration of servers. For example Dovecot has an ability to cache authentication information (such as IDs and passwords) to reduce load of the authentication server. But enabling it should be carefully considered because such a cache always has a problem of cache inconsistencies and synchronization, especially when a user changes his/her password. Another method is to route accesses from Google into other servers using a load balancer. But the load from Google will accumulate every year, so these methods may have limited effects. It is hard to continue investing in system for deleted accounts.

4.2.4 Ask Google to change its policy
The fundamental problem is that Google doesn't care about unsuccessful logins and continues the accesses indefinitely. It should be easy for Google to improve Mail Fetcher to solve the problem. For example, it is common to implement back-off (extends intervals between failed logins) and time-out (gives up accessing inaccessible accounts after several trials) processing in case of login failures. When time-out occurred and Mail Fetcher was disabled, the event should be reported to the original Gmail account by putting a message into the mailbox. If the user is actively using the account, he/she will notice the warning and change the configuration. If the account has been abandoned, it is also fine because Mail Fetcher stays disabled anyway.

A problem is that there is no clear way to inform Google about such a problem. Feature requests to Google supposed to be posted into Google Product Forums. We found that there was an article

in the forum about a similar request posted in August 2010, but there was no response and no improvement as of September 2012.

5. RESOLUTION
After we realized about the problem with Google's Mail Fetcher, we decided to present the issue in a domestic workshop to gather information [5]. We also considered to bring it to an international conference such as ACM SIGUCCS to draw attention and gather information about the status in other organizations outside Japan. But Google actually took the initiative.

Just one day before the session of the domestic workshop in September 2012, we realized that the number of authentication failures had suddenly decreased in the beginning of September. Figure 4 shows the number of login attempts and accessed unique IDs per day from February 2012 to September 2012.

The graphs show that the number of login attempts suddenly decreased to about one-tenth, while the number of unique accounts is not changed. It seemed that Google silently decided to stop accessing inaccessible accounts every hour and only tried once or twice in a day. By this change, the authentication failure from Google became almost negligible and the issue was resolved by Google's own discretion. We couldn't find any announcement or blog entries by Google about that change.

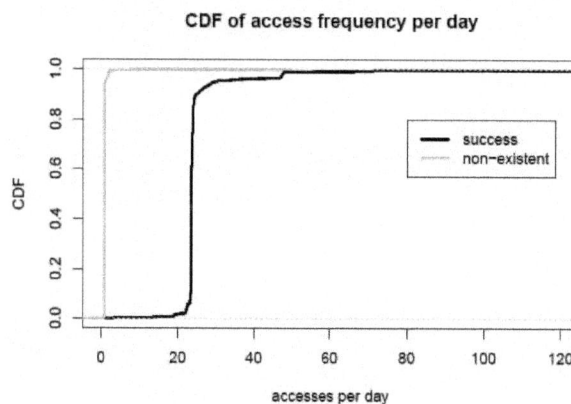

Figure 5. CDF of access frequency per day from Google (after Google's change)

Figure 5 is the same graph as Figure 3 after Google's change (from September 11th to 17th, 2012). It clearly shows that Google started to treat inaccessible accounts differently from accessible accounts. More than 95% of non-existent accounts were accessed only once a day, but some accounts were still accessed twice to several times a day.

6. CONCLUSION

In this paper, we described details of a chronic load induced by Google's Mail Fetcher, its possible countermeasures, and its sudden resolution. We analyzed log files of Student Primary Mail service to show the load status of these servers. As a result, we realized that Google caused a chronic load to our university mail server. We also discussed about the impact of Google's access and possible ways to mitigate it.

This particular issue presented in this paper has been resolved by itself without our actual intervention. That means that such an issue may happen again when these giant service providers such as Google, Microsoft, and Amazon decided to introduce a new service or modify their existing services. It must be done by their own goodness, but it is like a DoS (denial of service) attack for our small installment of services when their pinkie finger comes toward us. It is hard to predict and prepare for such an event, but at least we should take them into consideration when designing our system, and be observable to the status of our own system. Sometimes we should act quickly against their moves to protect our own services and our users.

7. ACKNOWLEDGMENTS

Our thanks to all students who are using our services, and staff members of the Primary Mail Service working group and the Authentication Infrastructure working group to develop and maintain these systems in Information Infrastructure Initiative of Kyushu University.

8. REFERENCES

[1] Fujimura, N., Togawa, T., Kasahara, Y., and Ito, E. 2011. Primary Mail Service for students based on their names. *IPSJ SIG Technical Report*, Vol. 2011-IOT-14, No. 10, 1-6.

[2] Fujimura, N., Togawa, T., Kasahara, Y., and Ito, E. 2012. Introduction and experience with the Primary Mail Service based on their names for students. In *Proceedings of the SIGUCCS 2012* (Memphis, TN, October 17 - 19, 2012). ACM, New York, NY, 11-14. DOI= http://dx.doi.org/10.1145/2382456.2382460.

[3] Ito, E., Kasahara. Y., and Fujimura, N. 2009. The current status of e-mail services for staff members in Kyushu University. In *Proceedings of ECIP 2009*, D3-4.

[4] Ito, E., Kasahara. Y., and Fujimura, N. 2012. A study of LDAP load balancing for University ICT services. *IPSJ SIG Technical Report*, Vol. 2012-CSEC-57/2012-IOT-17, No. 11, 51-56.

[5] Kasahara. Y., Ito. E., Hori. Y., and Fujimura, N. 2012. Google makes a chronic big load to university mail server. *IPSJ SIG Technical Report*, Vol. 2012-EVA-39, No. 5, 1-6.

[6] MEXT in Japan. 2010. School Basic Survey (in fiscal year 2012). http://www.mext.go.jp/b_menu/toukei/chousa01/kihon/kekka/k_detail/__icsFiles/afieldfile/2010/12/21/1300352_2.pdf.

[7] Page. L. 2012. 2012 Update from the CEO. http://investor.google.com/corporate/2012/ceo-letter.html.

[8] Yamamoto. K. 2006. A Proposal to fix the "SPF vs forwarding" problem. http://salt.iajapan.org/wpmu/anti_spam/admin/operation/suggestion/a-proposal-to-fix-the-spf-vs-forwarding-problem/.

Motivating Skill-Based Promotion with Badges

Peter Wallis
University of Washington
Box 353080
Seattle, WA 98195-3080
+1.206.221.7648
pwallis@uw.edu

Michelle S. Martinez
University of Washington
Box 353080
Seattle, WA 98195
+1.206.616.1778
solangel@uw.edu

ABSTRACT

In response to a state-wide freeze on pay increases beginning in 2009, the Learning Technologies (LT) unit at the University of Washington moved from a seniority-based to a skill-based promotion system for student employees in the unit. We almost immediately encountered a problem of motivation, as busy students did not take action to develop necessary skills. In 2013, we are piloting a badges program to encourage skill development. We have already seen early success and will provide an overview of the current badge landscape, details of our implementation, and valuable lessons learned. Though our focus is on student staff, our findings are applicable to professional development at all levels.

Categories and Subject Descriptors

K.6.1 [**Management of Computing and Information Systems**]: Project and People Management – *Training.*

Keywords

Badges, Training, Skill Development, Motivation, Human Resources, Student Staff, Gamification, Promotions, Documentation, Recognition

1. INTRODUCTION

The University of Washington (UW), a world-renowned tier one research university, has three campuses, with its main campus located in Seattle, Washington. With nearly 40,000 students on the Seattle campus alone, those in positions supporting the university mission must be prepared to work with and support a very diverse population. It is on this campus that the Learning Technologies unit of UW Information Technology carries out its mission: to improve the student experience through technology.

In the center of campus is Odegaard Undergraduate Library where Learning Technologies has set up and oversees a computer lab of over 450 computers with a changing landscape of operating systems and hardware.

Currently the lab contains approximately 50% Dell Windows, 50% Mac, but will be shifting to 96% Apple with virtualized OS choices over Summer 2013.

Student staff members are critical to the daily operations of the lab and many other services provided by LT. With only six full-time staff and a director making high-level decisions about the direction of the unit, LT relies heavily on its student staff for tasks ranging from maintaining lab computers, supporting customer use of lab computers, and helping clients with problems on their personal computers, to answering callers' questions about campus learning management software such as Catalyst and Canvas and supporting the use of the Tegrity lecture capture tool. Student staff members also help run our video conferencing services and teach our technology workshops provided for free to University-affiliated clients. LT's student staff is its most valuable asset.

Without student staff, LT and its many services would suffer greatly.

2. WAGES AND PROMOTION

On February 18, 2009, the Washington State Legislature implemented a freeze on salaries paid to state workers in response to the economic crisis that began in 2008. In 2011, the freeze was further extended through June 30th, 2013. This freeze on any sort of wage increases included many people in diverse jobs across the state, and most impactful for LT, included student workers both on work study or on simple hourly pay at all of the state universities, including the University of Washington. This resulted in only one option for increasing one's pay - moving into another job title with different and increased responsibilities.

Because of the state wage freeze, for nearly four years, student workers at the University of Washington, who may have begun working in a campus position in their freshman year, have received no raises in their positions without having changed jobs. The Seattle Times quoted President Michael Young as saying that "he believes the UW is the only major research university in the country that has not given raises for four years in a row" [1].

Those who manage student staff recognize that keeping students motivated and engaged is vital to retaining quality employees, especially once the honeymoon phase of a new position has worn off. One way of doing this in the past has been to increase pay dependent on seniority (duration of employment). With that option no longer available, skill-based and responsibility-based changes in job titles were required.

Although the state of Washington has one of the highest minimum wages of the country at $9.04/hour, because the UW must compete for student employees at the going market rate for the area, this high minimum wage does not benefit those seeking to hire student employees, especially in technology fields. While things appear to be looking up for 2013 as the UW "has put in place a two percent increase this year and next year for academic student employees working as teaching assistants and research assistants" [1], a two percent increase on minimum wage dollars is only approximately 18 cents per hour.

In response to this, the Learning Technologies unit of University of Washington Information Technology has created several tiers in their various student staff support teams. Each level indicates a higher degree of skill along with increased duties and responsibilities. Separate job descriptions were required for each new level. All promotions must be justified with documented evidence that the change in job title is appropriate and necessary. In some cases, certain job titles have had to become particularly competitive, although we have several tiers for which there is no limit to the number of staff who can be employed at that level.

The state wage freeze has forced us to transition from a seniority-based promotion environment to one based on skill and knowledge acquisition. Ultimately, we feel this may be a better approach in terms of keeping staff driven to learn more and achieve greater results.

3. DIFFICULTIES OF SKILL-BASED PROMOTION

In addition to justifying promotion to the university, skill-based promotions allow us to guide and direct our student employee development. This development requires tracking, evidence, and consideration. We began by assigning projects to students pursuing promotion. However, these projects were often time-consuming, uneven, and presented an unclear path to the students toward the skills we were attempting to encourage. Students were understandably discouraged when projects, through no intent of the assigners, could vary from 2 to 10 hours.

To attempt to resolve these issues, we have begun to explore digital badges. We hope that digital badges can make our expectations of student knowledge and growth clear. We want digital badges to not only offer rewards for specific activities, but to define how a collection of skills is an expertise within our team. For example, a student may receive a badge for writing a graphics documentation article, another for editing a Photoshop lasso tools article, and a third for passing a test on Photoshop. Together, these and other badges would represent an expertise, a readiness to answer questions and train clients and other staff in image editing.

Several other institutions have begun experimenting with digital badges in order to resolve the issues of informal learning and fine-grained skill certification. Partnering with the current badge landscape has presented a major challenge to our skill-based promotion process.

4. PURPOSE AND FRAMEWORK OF BADGES

Throughout the world, people are learning things. Some people are learning HTML and others are learning French. Some are learning to appreciate the taste of leek and onion oyaki. While learning happens throughout life, not all learning is recognized in formal ways [2]. Degrees and certificates do not adequately represent all of our learning.

While an encyclopedic record of all of an individual's learning and achievements is likely not feasible, digital badge systems attempt to recognize more fine-grained and informal learning than diplomas or degrees can. Badges also provide students with a way to display their skills and achievements. The Mozilla Open Badge

Infrastructure (OBI, http://openbadges.org/) [3] offers a new industry-standard framework for badge delivery and infrastructure. Mozilla's structure provides software developers and entrepreneurs with a standard for what information a digital badge should include, along with guidelines on how to develop these badges.

5. POTENTIAL OF BADGES IN OUR SITUATION

In the Learning Technology group of UW-IT, we have a couple of very specific problems to solve. We employ a large group (50+) of student employees, who each come to our teams with certain technology skills, and learn a number of skills on the job. We have started to investigate badges primarily as a way of measuring and documenting their skills, and encouraging them to continue to improve their skills. Simultaneously, our technology workshop team, which teaches basic technology skills to students, faculty, and staff, is looking for ways to more deeply engage attendees in the workshops, and provide those attendees with some evidence and summary of the skills they gained.

In addition to documenting skills, we hope that badges will help guide students through skill development. Badges, being small and inexpensive digital objects, provide the opportunity to be more specific than recognizing expertise in "technology" the way a traditional degree does. Badges can be awarded for something as fine-grained as using the layer tool in Photoshop properly, or creating a basic HTML document. This high-resolution view of expertise will help us to guide student employee, and possibly workshop attendee, development.

While we see tremendous potential in badges, there are a number of complicating factors in the field. Current badge creation, delivery, and authentication tools are all fairly new to the web. Code-bases are young and not well established, and a number of existing tools leverage existing systems we did not want to rely on. This document, in providing recommendations for our badge experiment, provides a brief overview of the details of these challenges.

In order to deal with these challenges and develop strategies, we launched a badge pilot in January of 2013. This badge pilot has so far consisted of product and system evaluations, focus groups with students, and collaboration with Sean Fullerton, a Ph.D. student in the UW Information School, who is doing doctoral work on badge systems.

6. COMPLICATIONS AND THE BADGES LANDSCAPE

The Mozilla Open Badge Framework allows for any interested software company or organization to participate in the delivery of badges, sparking a large crop of recent entries into the field. We recommend that those interested in an overview refer to the Google Spreadsheet here:
https://docs.google.com/a/uw.edu/spreadsheet/ccc?key=0AsHml-k4XnX7dHJQSDBrdUphYlprc1N0N09KMzFzckE#gid=0 [4] for a full overview of badge systems existing and those under development and review.

We can broadly divide these systems into two fields, Open Source/Creative Commons and commercial. The decision between these two options seems to be a consistent decision point in many projects in both Academic and Commercial fields.

Though many of the pros and cons of each approach are have been stated elsewhere [5] [6] [7] [8].

6.1 Open Source Solutions

Open Source solutions (badg.us, BadgeOS) must be self-hosted and self-maintained. Especially in the context of a large university with a number of existing tools, developer time will be required to enable authentication through the university's standard. The benefits of these systems include flexibility and lower direct cost. So long as there is good foundational code, developers, including student developers, can expand on that code to offer tools and features in the system not present in other systems. Finally, on-site developers allow for a certain measure of responsibility and ownership to remain with the university as direct contact with developers generally improves support, increases up-time, and adds flexibility in the creation of new features.

6.2 Commercial Badge Systems

Commercial badge systems (for example, Credly) by and large do not currently have set pricing or income models. This leaves open opportunities for commercial systems to become unaffordable or unsustainable and makes the low direct costs of open badge systems attractive. A commercial system which shuts down may cause many hours of staff work spent creating and administering badges to disappear, while open systems often allow for a more graceful transition.

Commercial systems, however, come with several benefits. Responsibilities and roles can be clearly defined in contracts, and commercial systems often are willing to work toward integration with existing identity management. As will be discussed later, code may be of a higher quality, and support can be integrated across several institutions and businesses, avoiding the silos created by branching Open Systems.

However, this may not make the badge system as fully integrated into other systems as we would desire. One particular aspect arising from our focus groups, discussed in more detail below, is the desire of students to have badge systems integrated with other tools they use. While commercial badge systems are likely to help integrate their system into one of our tools, integration into the whole toolset or development for easy integration with several of our tools is unlikely at best.

7. REVIEWING OPEN SOURCE CODE

The difficulties with open source code appeared quickly in our review of Seton Hall's badge code. Seton Hall has not yet released their code for consumption, but through a web-conference contact, they graciously allowed us to look at their code. While we appreciate this opportunity, we were forewarned that the code needs some updating before it is ready to be released to GitHub, the standard location for group and open coding projects, and we agree with this assessment.

As an example of the quality issues of open source code, our developers found that there was limited abstraction of the authentication code – several parts of the code authenticated individually, rather than all authenticating through a single piece of code. As a result, when authentication and identity configurations were changed, they had to be updated in as many as six places individually. Seton Hall's code was built in PHP, without a standardized framework, which tends to make it particularly difficult for our developers to collaborate on the abstraction process.

In contrast, badg.us is built in the Python language with the Django framework. This is attractive to our developers, as they are attempting to standardize the languages they use, and Python is a current primary and preferred language. Badg.us exists currently on GitHub, with a fair bit of activity and several existing branches, indicating code ready for use. Our developers also have existing standard authentication modules ready for the Python/Django set.

Badg.us, however, lacks a fair number of features we want to provide. While the fine-grained aspect of badges is attractive, it is far more attractive if badges can be rolled up into "meta-badges," badges which represent only that the recipient has achieved a number of other badges. For example a meta-badge for Photoshop might represent several badges for layers, color palettes, and drawing tools, among others. Likewise, badg.us currently lacks features for private or limited views of badge backpacks, which would allow administrators to see what badges have been awarded. Seton Hall's code allows for both of these currently.

8. A WAY FORWARD

When we began the planning process of this report, we were hoping for a clear answer – a way forward, or a sign to stop. It seems, however, that there is no clear way forward except to continue to explore. While we have been exploring badges, interest has been expressed from experiential learning programs and the department of English in participating in badge experiments. Several of our students enjoyed the opportunity to earn badges using Code Academy's online tutorials, and gave us positive feedback on those.

In addition to consulting developers, we have partnered with a graduate student in the UW Information School "iSchool" to run focus groups with the student employees. The graduate student, Sean Fullerton, has been a great help in running these focus groups. Several findings have emerged from the focus groups.

One of the primary concerns we had entering into the badge process was a lack of flexibility among students. As managers, we see it as preferable that, sometimes, if an employee displays skills in informal ways, or outside of regularly set tracks, we can recognize that employee's work. Within a badge system, this would lead us to tend to give administrators within the badge system the power to assign badges on an ad-hoc basis. We were concerned students would see this power as unfair, opening up possibilities for resentment and feelings of neglect. We heard from students, however, that they would prefer to treat badges as flexible systems, each badge being low enough in value that assignment outside of the traditional "earning" would not be seen as unfair.

Students' attitude towards badges exemplified flexibility in many other ways. Few cared deeply whether or not badges were immediately published to public "Badge Backpacks" for example, or whether or not leaderboards and internal-team points pages increased the game system of the badges. Of course, a focus group can only say so much, and students who attend our focus groups tend to be those willing to spend extra time at work to begin with. As such, in a rollout, badge systems with these features may see significantly more push-back, and we intend our badge system to be rolled out with our concerns as a guide.

One concern we did hear from the engaged and motivated student employees in these focus groups was that of tool proliferation.

Several factors, including changing institutional expectations on several levels of the organization, rapidly changing software fields, and an aging intranet within our team has led to a recent proliferation both in internal and external tools. Students showed deep concern about this proliferation, and the increasing difficulty of referring to any point as a single source of truth, or knowing where to refer for particular processes and documentation.

As such, any time a new technology tool introduction is planned, we advise that the current landscape of the institution is reviewed. This is especially vital when working with student employees, who have additional demands placed upon them by the academy to learn and interact with academic tools for discussion boards, library articles, assignment submissions, and other similarly scholarly activities. This large number of tools becomes particularly difficult to manage when work assignments and school assignments must each be submitted in deeply different systems.

Our student employees are already expected to interact with a large number of tools in their work. Our lab includes video editing sections, graphics and design software, a sound studio, and much more. Recent changes include the adoption of the Canvas LMS as an institution and are moving our website and documentation to WordPress from Plone. Our lab is moving from being approximately half Windows, half Mac, to almost completely Apple, with virtualized options for other operating systems.

One possible solution to the difficulties presented is to integrate our Badge system into these existing tools. Several badge systems under development integrate into WordPress, including BadgeOS [9] and Open Badger [10]. In investigating these tools, however, we found that they lacked several key items, especially skill trees and easy "meta-badges". Several badge systems also have an integration with the Canvas LMS, including BadgeStack and Open Badges. BadgeStack is an add-on to BadgeOS [9] and Open Badges simply signs in the student to their Mozilla Open Badges backpack, not providing any badge assigning functionality [11]. BadgeStack allows the WordPress installation of BadgeOS to be displayed within an iFrame within the Canvas LMS, after signing the student in. We do not consider this to be a particularly useful integration, however, if the WordPress installation could be stripped down significantly, it could operate. We plan to continue to look to at this quickly growing part of the field, and plan a future badge system around integration with one of these tools. Both BadgeStack and Open Badges are simple to write LTI integrations, and we may be able to contribute a similar integration into Canvas to the existing code on another Open Source system.

Our current recommendation is that we continue dedicating time to investigating badge systems. We need to focus on badge systems that will integrate with our current tools. Through this learning process, we now know that we will need to extend our badge project and its timeline to take the best advantage of the opportunities available.

While we move forward with these systems, we want to keep a few important points about the psychology of motivation in mind. We want to be cautious that badges do not become a completely extrinsic motivator, and we want to be cautious about the authority structures that badges can create.

Extrinsic motivators are motivators that exist outside the subject (as opposed to intrinsic motivators, which are inside the subject or learner.) Obviously, badges exist outside the motivated person, and rely upon rewards (even if the reward is a badge) to motivate those badge earners. Intrinsically motivated people will pursue good work in the presence or absence of external reward, and there are two reasons intrinsic motivation is vital to student employee motivation. The first reason is that students are smart, and no badge system can outsmart them. If they are motivated only to receive badges, rather than to achieve and express expertise, they will find ways to game the system. The second reason is that there will remain for some time a set of expertise that is outside of the measure of badges, expertise which will benefit students throughout their lives.

Though it is not equivalent to intrinsic motivation, Self-Determination theory as laid out by Ryan and Deci [12] posits three factors for high-quality motivation, factors which most conceptual badge systems fulfill. The three factors are autonomy, competence, and relatedness. A well administered badge system would motivate learners well by encouraging these three factors: Allowing autonomy as they choose their next expertise and their next path of expertise. Allowing learners to express and display competence as they earn badges. Finally, allowing learners to relate themselves with other learners as they compare badges and competences, and hopefully share tips, tricks, and lessons they learned.

Alexander Halavais [13] wrote a "genealogy of badges," describing two different origins and purposes of badge systems, one to describe and represent expertise or experience, and the other to represent authority or power. This historical overview has not been explored further by the practical applications found in our research, but it is a worthwhile line of questioning, especially insofar as Halavais' delineation may explain the success and failure of different badge structures.

9. EARLY SUCCESSESS

While our work so far has largely uncovered a number of challenges in this maturing field, we have also encountered a number of early successes that encourage us to continue pursuing badges as a solution not only for motivation, but for several other ongoing issues.

While we were considering and experimenting early with badges, we assigned students who did not know the basics of HTML and CSS, fundamental pieces of knowledge on a team that consistently receives questions about basic blogging and web publishing, to learn from CodeAcademy, which offers a number of badges for its basic web development curriculum. CodeAcademy validators check the code automatically, making this assignment especially low in administrative overhead, automatically check these badges.

Students reported being both motivated and involved by this process, and especially appreciating the clear goals set by the curriculum. This reinforced for us that one of the primary intrinsic motivating factors in a badge system is the clarification of progressive skills, and the ease of setting achievable goals.

As such, and in planning to release a badge system, we asked senior students to begin laying out curriculum for the skills they would expect a junior colleague to display in the various programs we support. This process alone has been motivating and engaging for the students involved. Beginning students have appreciated already having necessary skills mapped out to a greater level of detail. Our experience has demonstrated that the technology for a badge system need not be in place before the team begins working on understanding its skills in terms of the fine-grained and scaffolded view offered by badges.

10. ACKNOWLEDGMENTS
Our thanks to the programming team at Seton Hall University for letting us review their code before release, Sean Fullerton, Ph.D. student in the University of Washington iSchool, for partnering with us to understand our student's needs better Craig Stimmel, Web Master in Academic and Collaborative Applications at the University of Washington for his work in helping us to understand code, and Jacob Morris, Interim Director of Learning Technologies, for his encouragement and support in the planning and writing process.

11. REFERENCES

[1] Long, K. (2012, November 7). *UW wants state to lift freeze on salaries*. Retrieved from http://seattletimes.com/html/localnews/2019631381_salaries08m.html

[2] Stevens, R. Bransford, J. & Stevens, A. LIFE Center Lifelong and Lifewide Learning Diagram. Retrieved from http://life-slc.org/about/citationdetails.html

[3] "Open Badges." *Mozilla Open Badges*. Mozilla Foundation. Retrieved from http://www.openbadges.org

[4] Goligoski, Emily. *Platforms for Issuing Open Badges.* Retrieved from https://docs.google.com/a/uw.edu/spreadsheet/ccc?key=0AsHml-k4XnX7dHJQSDBrdUphYlprc1N0N09KMzFzckE#gid=0

Stable copy available at: https://docs.google.com/spreadsheet/ccc?key=0AjLct53V0IzTdEVHMThqTTlkZ1BGMFZQMmhsY21SWWc&usp=sharing

[5] "Open Source Vs Commercial Apps: The Differences That Matter II | ZDNet." *ZDNet*. Web. 24 May 2013. Retrieved from http://www.zdnet.com/open-source-vs-commercial-apps-the-differences-that-matter-ii-2039195509/

[6] "Open Source Vs. Proprietary Software | PCWorld." *PCWorld*. 3 Nov. 2011. Web. 24 May 2013. Retrieved from http://www.pcworld.com/article/243136/open_source_vs_proprietary_software.html

[7] "Open Source Vs Proprietary CMS." Web. 24 May 2013. Retrieved from http://www.bloomtools.com/articles/open-source-vs-proprietary-cms.html

[8] "Open Source V. Proprietary Software." Web. 24 May 2013. Retrieved from http://www.academia.edu/777383/Open_Source_v._Proprietary_Software

[9] BadgeOS. *BadgeOS*. Retrieved from http://badgeos.org/

[10] GitHub. Mozilla/openbadger. Retrieved from https://github.com/mozilla/openbadger

[11] Machajewski, Szymon. *Open Badges*. Retrieved from: https://lti-examples.heroku.com/index.html?tool=dataiiOB

[12] http://www.selfdeterminationtheory.org/theory#overview

[13] Halavais, A. M. C. (April 01, 2012). A genealogy of badges: Inherited meaning and monstrous moral hybrids. *Information Communication and Society, 15,* 3, 354-373.

The Art of Productive Meetings

Laurie Fox
SUNY Geneseo
1 College Circle
Geneseo, NY 14454
(585) 245-5577
fox@geneseo.edu

Lucas Friedrichsen
Oregon State University
121 Valley Library
Corvallis, OR 97331
1 (541) 737-8244
Lucas.friedrichsen@oregonstate.edu

Mo Nishiyama
Oregon Health & Science University
3505 SW Veterans Hospital Road
Portland, OR 97239
1 (503) 494-1406
nishiyam@ohsu.edu

ABSTRACT

Meetings are a necessary part of working in higher education. This presentation will cover the fine points of planning, preparing, and participating in effective meetings. We will also discuss remote attendance, scheduling, formal vs. informal meetings, and etiquette.

Categories and Subject Descriptors

K.6.1 [**Management of Computing and Information Systems**]: Project and People Management – *Management techniques.*

Keywords

Meeting, project management, productivity, team leadership.

1. INTRODUCTION

Our panel consists of professionals who lead, participate in, and suffer through meetings on a regular basis. In the exploration of what defines a productive meeting, we reached an agreement on the basics. A productive meeting is one where preparation is thorough, execution is satisfactory, and action items are clear and objective. Participants in these meetings understand why they are invited and have an opportunity to participate in an open and honest manner. There is also a social element to meetings that can have a positive impact on your department's culture.

Meetings are a fantastic opportunity for decision making, communication, collaboration, and team building. They can also be an effective management tool for tracking the progress of a project or implementation.

Characteristics of an awful meeting are also easy to define. Lack of planning or an agenda may lead to an unfocused and unproductive meeting. Project meetings falter when a leader does not step forward. Meetings that are too long, too frequent, or have too many attendees may also be unsuccessful.

Some departments have a culture of regular meetings at a set date and time. These meetings have the highest chance of being nonproductive. One way to prevent this is to have a plan for

SIGUCCS '13, November 03 - 08 2013, Chicago, IL, USA
Copyright 2013 ACM 978-1-4503-2318-5/13/11…$15.00.
http://dx.doi.org/10.1145/2504776.2504783

cancelling a recurring meeting if there are no agenda items 24 hours before the scheduled meeting time. This shows respect for the participants' time. "One of the greatest blocks to organization productivity is the lack of decision by a senior person about the necessity of a meeting, and with whom, to move an important issue forward." [1]

2. PLANNING
2.1 Input

The meeting organizer should solicit input from participants for collaborative meetings. This ensures that the agenda is accurate and complete. There may also be a miscellaneous section of the meeting, where participants can raise issues that were not included in the original agenda.

2.2 Agenda

Agenda items should be sent to participants in advance. This gives them opportunity to prepare ahead as necessary, and avoids any nasty surprises at the meeting. If there is sensitive information to be presented at the meeting, it may be help to be semi-transparent in the agenda to avoid rumors.

2.3 Goals

Meetings must have a clear purpose. Is the meeting for apprising participants of each others' work status updates, or a one-way dissemination of information? Can this information be disseminated via email or through a collaborative environment? How will attendees benefit from information discussed at the meeting?

Project meetings can be scheduled at milestones to measure progress, kick off the next portion of the project, and make necessary corrections or decisions.

2.4 Location

Select an appropriate venue with minimal distractions. Possible locations include someone's office, a conference room, a different area on campus, or an off-site location. Each of these has varying degrees of benefits and disadvantages depending on the size and purpose of the meeting.

2.5 Format

When scheduling a meeting, consider starting a few minutes past the hour (or half-hour) and ending a few minutes before the next hour so attendees can get to other commitments on time. Meetings can also be held in a Standing Meeting format. "Lengthy, pointless meetings are less likely to happen when everyone is standing and gradually getting weak in the knees." [2]

Meetings can also be held remotely. Popular video collaboration software includes: Google Hangout, Skype, Adobe Connect, and Big Blue Button. Project teams can also use persistent group chat software like HipChat.

3. PREPARING

3.1 Agenda Items and Handouts

Provide handouts and other visual aids before the meeting. Ensure such items are relevant but do not distract attendees during the meeting.

3.2 Communication

Send out meeting invitations in a timely manner. This allows options for rescheduling meetings if key participants have scheduling conflicts. Let invitees know what the meeting is about and send discussion items beforehand. "Planning with lots of lead time goes a long way towards finding suitable time for all parties. Start early." [3]

3.3 Invitations

Determining whom to invite is important. A larger attendee list can lead to a greater chance for scheduling conflicts. Decide on who the key participants are and schedule according to their availability. Non-key attendees may be able to send delegates in their place. When possible, do not schedule meetings adjacent to others' conflicts unless all meetings occur in the same physical space. Respect attendees' need for time to process items from their previous meetings and also to prepare for subsequent meetings.

4. PARTICIPATING

Clear expectations for meeting participation can help the attendees avoid conflicts, encourage active conversations, and produce positive results.

4.1 Expectations

One preferred method to get buy-in from the group is to develop a set of shared values and expectations to help the team produce the best results possible. Some examples of expectations include:

4.1.1 The Golden Rule
Treat others as you expect to be treated.

4.1.2 Active listening, engage in the conversation
Give your full attention to the speaker.

4.1.3 Respect
Everyone has ideas that deserve your attention and respect.

4.1.4 No interruptions
Give the speaker the opportunity to finish his or her ideas and statements. Interruptions cause unnecessary tension and could cause the speaker to feel less valued.

4.1.5 Avoid personal attacks
Some topics do reach an emotional level, but personal attacks should never be part of a meeting.

4.1.6 Time per item
If the topic has an allotted amount of time, respect that time. Create some action items, table the discussion for later, and move on to the next topic.

4.1.7 Don't hold back
If you have an idea or information that goes against the grain, share it with the group. That knowledge could change the course of action for the better.

4.1.8 Assume the best
If you assume people have the best intentions, personal conflict can be reduced.

4.2 Action Items

Action items that linger from meeting to meeting can demotivate attendees, create tension, and cause people to dread future meetings. Stamp that behavior out by ensuring every action item is assigned clearly to an attendee with clear information and a deadline. Work with supervisors and managers to ensure deliverables are completed on time.

Utilize task management software to track tasks. Action items can also be tracked in an existing ticketing system. A shared task management system will help the group's momentum and reduce time spent rehashing past items.

Action items should also be included in all meeting minutes.

4.3 Roles

Clear and specific roles help move meetings forward and produce results. These roles can include: facilitator/moderator, timekeeper, note taker, and meeting leader/sponsor. Roles are most important in large size meetings.

To allow effective participation from all, roles should be split amongst attendees. Otherwise, too much cognitive load is placed on attendees performing administrative meeting tasks and decreases if not negates their participation in the discussion.

4.4 Meeting Notes / Minutes

Minutes or notes from a meeting can be invaluable to reflect on discussion and action items. Minutes can also communicate effectively to supervisors and peers about specific decisions, initiatives or projects. Complex meetings or topics may require more formal notes after the meeting.

Store minutes in a format and location where they can be easily referenced. Avoid having attendees store notes on their own computer where no one else can refer to them as needed.

4.5 Decisions / Consensus

Every meeting benefits from some leadership and facilitation. The leader will set the tone of the meeting and can settle tense discussions. In many cases, the leader or facilitator will also have the authority to decide when the group cannot reach a decision effectively.

Some groups – particularly cross-functional management teams – utilize consensus to reach decisions. If consensus is not possible, it is useful to leverage a concept known as "consensus with qualification." When a group cannot reach consensus or make a decision, the person with the most knowledge of the subject makes the decision based on the input of the group. The group trusts that person to make the best decision for the organization and their customers.

Decisions should also be clearly indicated in the meeting minutes to ensure they are recorded properly for future planning.

5. MAKING MEETINGS FUN

How many meetings do you look forward to attending? Ideally, you appreciate meetings and benefit from your attendance. If that is not the case, how can you and your colleagues make the gathering more fun?

5.1 Icebreakers

Icebreaker activities can be cheesy, but if done correctly, the bond between attendees can be strengthened by learning about non-work interests of your colleagues. Some examples include asking the group about their weekend, favorite hobbies, and their next vacation.

5.2 Off-site Meetings

Do meetings happen in the same place and at the same time? Break up the monotony and suggest an off-site meeting location to bring a breath of fresh air. Capitalize on the energy from a new location to strengthen the team, power through the agenda, and relax, reenergize and enjoy the company.

5.3 Food

Food can also be a fun addition to group meetings. Elect one person to bring something to each meeting and rotate the responsibility amongst attendees. Nothing diffuses tension like a sweet treat! Hold a lunch meeting with a potluck style gathering. Take time to enjoy lunch and then breeze through the agenda.

5.4 Remote Attendance

Remote attendance to meetings can be an excellent opportunity to include colleagues who are not located close together. Attendees can also continue to be productive in their offices while keeping an eye and ear on meetings that they may not need to be actively participating in. Ensure all attendees have the necessary technology to participate and provide input.

6. ACKNOWLEDGMENTS

Thanks to the various SIGUCCS volunteers that make the community an amazing place to be involved!

7. REFERENCES

[1] Allen, D. 2002. *Getting Things Done: The Art of Stress-Free Productivity*. Penguin Group. New York, NY.

[2] Belsky, S. 2010. *Making Ideas Happen*. Penguin Group. New York, NY.

[3] Petz, J. 2011. *Boring Meetings Suck*. John Wiley & Sons. Hoboken, NJ.

The Path to Google: Selling Ice to Eskimos

Christopher H. King
NC State University
Box 7109 – NCSU
Raleigh, NC 27695-7109
(919) 515-5431

chking@ncsu.edu

ABSTRACT

Higher education conferences over the past few years have been full of presentations, papers and panels on the processes involved in migrating a campus and its people to Google Apps for Education. While it is useful to hear about marketing tchotchkes, data validation, and the pros and cons of web clients, what seems to get ignored is the process that led to the decision to move to Google Apps in the first place. At North Carolina State University, where students were already using Google Apps, the decision to move employees involved almost as much time, effort and heartache as the technical migration. As the users saw it, they had a working system, even if that system only worked because of huge expenditures of time and money both on the backend server maintenance and the client need to implement terribly complex workarounds for simple functionality. The end result: a 94-page white paper and the realization that it's hard to sell ice to Eskimos[1], even if you show them that their ice has already melted. This paper and presentation will discuss the information gathering and needs assessment done by NC State prior to the decision to move employees to Google Apps, and the successes and difficulties involved.

Categories and Subject Descriptors

K.4.3 **[Organizational Impacts]**: Computer-supported collaborative work, Reengineering

General Terms

Management, Measurement, Documentation, Design, Economics, Reliability, Experimentation, Security, Human Factors, Standardization, Legal Aspects.

---

[1] Eskimo is considered by some to be a pejorative, preferring Inuit as the preferred generalization. I merely use it out of respect for the old saying, and not in any negative context.

SIGUCCS'13, November 3–8, 2013, Chicago, Illinois, USA.
Copyright © 2013 ACM 978-1-4503-2318-5/13/11…$15.00.
http://dx.doi.org/10.1145/2504776.2504778

Keywords

Google, Email, Calendaring, Implementation, Cooperation, Cat Herding

1. INTRODUCTION

My father has quite a way with people. He has a demeanor and friendly attitude that draws people to him, but he is also forceful enough in will to get his way. Once, we drove past a house that was for sale. We stopped and, after an hour or so of talking to the man selling the house, my father purchased it. In addition, he'd convinced the man to sell us HIS house next door – a house that wasn't for sale.

I grew up in that house hearing how my father could "sell ice to Eskimos," meaning that he could sell someone something that they already had and didn't need. As we began the process to move employees at NC State over to Google Apps, I did not think that the saying applied. Instead, we were selling ice to Floridians in July. We had an obviously necessary commodity that we were selling to its target demographic. Or so we thought.

2. BACKGROUND

NC State has traditionally had disparate email and calendaring systems, in addition to all of the other computing resources surrounding them. These tended to be split into three groups: the administrative staff who tended towards business and ERP-type systems, academic units who used more open and simple technologies, and the departments who used a mixture of the first two plus whatever additional resources they could build in-house to supplement their constituents. Specifically, email and calendaring tended along two lines.

2.1 Academic computing

Academic computing at NC State came from the Office of the Provost, and was targeted at not only the academic employees (faculty, general staff, and whomever else wanted to use them) but the students as well. These accounts, called Unity, were provisioned to everyone affiliated with the university, although some users elected to keep these accounts mostly dormant in favor of departmental or other resources.

Email was handled with a combination of Cyrus mail servers and sendmail-based relays. Users accessed their email via thick clients such as Thunderbird and Mac Mail or via a web-based client running SquirrelMail.

Calendaring was slightly different. An Oracle Calendar system was run for employees, but access was limited and offered by request only.

2.2 Administrative computing

Administrative computing was offered via the Office of Finance and Business, and was targeted at administrative officers and supporting staff. These systems had a much smaller customer base, which allowed for a tighter control of data and the ability to more easily maintain the system for more specific needs.

Email and calendaring were handled via Novell's GroupWise product. Access was via the GroupWise client, and services were granted with a combination of Novell and third-party software offerings.

2.3 College and departmental computing

Some colleges and departments also ran their own local computing environments, offering email, calendaring, and other services only to their customers using a wide range of software services.

2.4 CCEI

Besides the more obvious issues of duplication and cost, the primary motivation for changing the status quo was simple: none of these systems talked to each other. Email was sent between GroupWise and Cyrus, but that broke the ties that GroupWise used for some of its received notifications and message retraction. Calendaring was even worse, and most administrative support staff on campus survived by having both a GroupWise and an Oracle account and booking meetings on both simultaneously. Several attempts to rectify this had occurred, and they were known by many names including the CCEI (Campus Calendaring and Email Initiatives). These groups tended to fall into the same cycle: representatives from both warring factions gathered in conference rooms, flanked by the neutral parties from the departments. After a few meetings with no clear consensus, things would remain as they were until the next iteration.

2.5 WolfWise

You can lead a horse to water, and if you take away all of its remaining sources of hydration, you might get it to drink. The final push towards unity came with the WolfWise project – an attempt to make the GroupWise system an enterprise resource. WolfWise started under the auspices of unified calendaring, and coincided with the death of the Oracle calendaring system. Over time, when newly-converted people saw that they now had two email accounts and administrators saw that same duplication writ large, the push came to move employees fully over to WolfWise. This met with a large amount of pushback and resistance as Cyrus users lost a lot of key functionality in GroupWise (such as a reliable web client, non-Windows platform support, and VPN-free access).

This was the state of affairs as of 2010. Campus professionals waged war over which system was better, but since both sides had differing needs, neither could convince the other.

2.6 The student Google migration

Students had not been much better off when it came to email (which was poor) and calendaring (which was nonexistent). For years, they had been complaining about the Cyrus system and its outdated web interface and low mailbox quotas (which had recently been upgraded to an indulgent 50Mb default quota per student). The WolfWise project had drawn resources away from Cyrus development and maintenance, and that, coupled with feedback from students that they primarily forwarded their mail to off-campus providers, put Cyrus improvements lower on the priority list than was tenable. In 2008, the decision was made to form a Student Email Task Force "to review and evaluate student email services offered by the Office of Information Technology and determine the best path forward to support current and future student needs." (Hoit) This task force was asked to look at four options:

- Keep (and enhance) our current system,
- Outsource
- Move to a forward-only system
- Option Not-Appearing-On-This-List

The task force quickly came to the determination that outsourcing was the way to proceed, and after a fairly exhaustive vetting process, it was narrowed to two finalists: Microsoft's Live@EDU and Google Apps Education Edition.[2] Ultimately, the decision was made to move to GAEE and, starting in the fall of 2010, all new students were provisioned with Google Apps accounts.

3. NEXGEN

As beta testing began for the student migration to Google Apps, hundreds of applications had to be refused – because the applicants weren't students. As employees followed along from the sidelines, they saw the potential that Google Apps had for curing many of their ills when it came to functionality and interoperability. When you consider it from the angle of a faculty member wanting to collaborate with their students, the draw was even more palpable – and legitimate. Those hundreds of refusals led to some interesting backdoor methods – some staff members registered for classes as students, and others went so far as to threaten to remove their employee status in the various systems of record for a day to trick the validation scripts. When these actions led to increased pressure for further review, it became apparent that the idea of having one system on campus for students and staff was not as onerous as it was originally believed.

In April 2010, the NexGen Task Force was formed to explore the next generation (thus "NexGen") of email and calendaring services for faculty and staff. The task force was co-chaired by the director of IT for the university's department of Electrical and Computer Engineering and an assistant director of tech support in the central IT unit on campus[3], and also contained various representatives of the employee population on campus.

---

[2] As those products were known by in 2009-2010

[3] aka "the author of this paper"

3.1 Charge

One critical difference between NexGen and previous email/calendaring teams was the specificity of the charge. The task force wasn't supposed to go out and find a product or evaluate a preselected group of them. The charge was clear, and that was to answer one question: "Can Google Apps meet the needs of the faculty and staff?" Surprisingly, in most of the initial correspondence and focus groups, that had to be spelled out in great detail.

One other advantage that the task force had was in the ability to say with certainty that the WolfWise system currently in place was going away. Even if it was determined that Google was not the answer, the consensus amongst management was that something else needed to be done. This policy decision mitigated (but never fully stopped) the flood of protests for keeping WolfWise. The arguments based on the massive resource drains involved (both in money and in employee time) in maintaining WolfWise in its current state fell on deaf ears – whatever kept the lights on was worth the expenditure.

3.2 Information Gathering

The task force used three methods to gather information on employee needs for a new system:

- Consulting with other colleges and universities that had elected to move to GAEE, or to not move,
- Surveying the task force members themselves and working through feature needs and issues based on the constituencies that they represented, and
- Gathering data from focus groups and inserting task force members into existing meetings for directed conversations.

These methods gave the task force a large amount of data in many different areas, and allowed for a much more broad sense of what campus wanted, what they thought that they wanted, and what was necessary to sustain life on campus.

3.3 Timeline

These information gathering methods were streamlined because the task force itself was on a very tight schedule. Three months separated the task force announcement and the publishing deadline for the final report.

3.4 In the End

After three months of information gathering, weekly task force meetings, and copious amounts of wordsmithing, the task force produced a final report:

http://go.ncsu.edu/nexgenreport

This 94-page report outlined all of the data gathered, the process behind that gathering, and the analysis done by the task force to come up with the conclusion that Google Apps could meet the needs of the employees of NC State University. Mostly.

4. LESSONS LEARNED

The previous section outlined, in a nutshell, how the process went. What bears further discussion are the lessons learned from this process, and how future generations of task forces should learn from these lessons – either as models to follow, or dark examples to avoid at all costs.

4.1 Ask the right questions

As any Google consumer knows, the one constant of their feature set is its inconstancy. Features changed on a regular basis, and as a result, the task force could not come up with a straightforward matrix of desires vs. features. Because of this, the focus groups and polls conducted largely focused on asking people what they used and how they used it. The glaring issue with this is that any decent technology obfuscates the very features that a task force wants to discover. The concept of "shared contacts" was a good example of this. As far as a user is concerned, they wanted the ability to send email to one address or group, and have it go to the same group no matter which user sent the message. In one light, Google Groups could handle this, but digging deeper showed that Groups only handled the group mailing aspect, ignoring the shared administration as well as the ability to share that Group out to a more limited group of users. It is almost impossible to get this amount of detail strictly by asking someone directly as opposed to observing behavior and discovering the processes in the background behind that activity.

4.2 Don't paint yourself into a corner

One huge obstacle to overcome in this process was trying to break bad habits that had been reinforced by system tweaks over the years. One major hurdle was the idea of maximum message size. Many users reported the need to send huge files via email, and then said that major business processes relied on this ability. Maximum message size is non-negotiable with Google, but in our old system, a combination of unlimited attachment and message size, unlimited mailbox size, and no cross-departmental shared storage led people to use their mail system as a file system. Google Docs (now Drive) would have been an easy (and more sustainable) replacement, but it took (and still takes) a lot of convincing to get users to see the logic behind the newer philosophies. What seemed like a customer-focused decision years ago caused massive headaches in the future, and those unintended consequences should always be avoided whenever possible.

(As an aside to this, one of those unintended consequences was an inability to directly migrate email to Google, which happily and without prejudice rejected messages over its size limit.)

4.3 When "Yes" or "No" isn't enough

The task force was charged with a simple question that could not be simply answered. This debate could not be boiled down to yes or no – there were dozens of areas in which yes vs. no was determined by continued training, hard and fast policy decisions, and the whims of administration. Even when asked "yes" or "no", the task force answered with "kind of", which generated a lot of stress amongst the task force members who wanted more consensus and certainty.

4.4 A little dissention now and then can be a good thing

The NexGen Final Report wasn't as final as its name implies. Three members of the task force felt that their particular needs weren't addressed (or were intentionally ignored), and chose to write what boiled down to a dissenting opinion. The so-called "minority report" was sent to the CIO directly, stating that some of the task force felt marginalized by the process and worried that their outstanding issues should have been more heavily considered in the final report. While tempers flared and professional tensions rose as a result of this report and its delivery (the task force did not know of the report until the CIO had already read it and publicized its existence to the group), that situation is highlighted here for one simple reason. No member of a team should be denied an equal share of consideration. On the flip side, no member of a team should allow a decision to move forward without speaking and ensuring that they are being heard.

4.5 When culture becomes religion

The hardest part of this process was convincing users that change is not inherently a bad thing. More importantly, a process is not good just because it has been in place for a significant amount of time. However, many users wailed and gnashed their teeth when the prospect of a post-WolfWise campus was mentioned. It was not the feature sets, cost, or any other factor that caused this consternation – it was the fact that the status quo was becoming the status quo ante[4]. Processes that had been in place for years were being challenged, and more emphasis was being put on the users changing instead of all of the work getting done by the administrators. What user wants that?

5. CONCLUSION

Now I know that "selling ice to Eskimos" can mean different things in different situations. The expression can also mean selling someone something that they only THINK that they have. The diehard WolfWise users were convinced that their system was more than adequate to do what needed to get done, and their expansive set of workarounds only testified to its flexibility. They ignored (or just did not appreciate) the accounts of the hundreds of thousands of dollars that went into additional storage, mail servers (there were over 30 post office servers for less than 9,000 users at the end), third-party applications, and employee time and training every year just to maintain that "flexibility". The need to change just never entered their minds, and as long as the tail is allowed to wag the dog, situations like this will continue to exist. Does this mean that the needs of the service consumer are outweighed by the needs of the service owner? Not at all, but it behooves any service provider to ensure that they are making the best decision that balances the demands from every direction, even if it means painful change on either side.

6. REFERENCES

[1] Hoit, Marc. Memo to various campus employees: Student Email Task Force, NC State University, Raleigh, NC. 21 October 2008.

---

[4] "status quo" translates to "the state in which", and "Status quo ante" means "the state that existed previously"

Sustainable Automated Software Deployment Practices

Dan R. Herrick
Colorado State University
Engineering Network Services
Fort Collins, CO 80523-1301
970-491-3131
Dan.Herrick@Colostate.edu

John B. Tyndall
The Pennsylvania State University
Information Technology Services
University Park, PA 16802
814-865-2886
jbt8@psu.edu

ABSTRACT

Many organizations follow the same error-prone, time-consuming, and redundant procedures to install software manually, whether as part of a master image or on individual computers. Usually this involves visiting a system, executing some sort of interface, selecting a subset of modules or configuring certain options, and waiting for the installer to complete. There is another way: automated software deployment, which affords greater efficiency, consistency, and ultimately, service.

This paper discusses the organization and detailed implementation of automating software installations and updates using silent and unattended methods, with various levels of administrative intervention, from help desk to systems administrator. We also describe different approaches to creating such an environment for both "mass" devices (e.g., public computer lab systems) and individual devices (e.g., faculty/staff desktop systems).

Key concepts include leveraging management software and resources you may already have (i.e., the "zero budget" approach) versus efficiency gains from third-party resources, high-level administrative toolkits along with low-level control methods, and developing a workflow for automated and semi-automated software installations.

Categories and Subject Descriptors

C.5.3 [**Computer System Implementation**]: Microcomputers—*personal computers, portable devices, workstations*; D.0 [**Software**]: General

General Terms

Design, Documentation, Performance, Standardization, Theory.

Keywords

Baseline, best practice, EASI, EASI Make, installation, process, software, software deployment, software distribution, software installation, software packing, thin imaging, UPDATER

1. INTRODUCTION

This paper discusses automated software deployment scenarios

that have been tested and used in production environments at both the College of Engineering at Colorado State University (CSU) and Penn State University (PSU).

Collectively, both universities provide regular, managed installation support for 300-400 automated software packages.

1.1 Colorado State University

Within the College of Engineering at CSU, an IT group of 8 FTEs and 25 part-time student employees supports about 4,000 users (545 of which are faculty/staff with at least one university-supported computer) and about 1,650 computers (350 of which are centrally managed computers, e.g., computer lab PCs, servers, virtual desktops connected via thin clients).

1.2 Penn State University

University Services, a sub-department in Information Technology Services, manages approximately 7,500 lab and classroom computers state-wide and offers a systems management service for an additional cooperative administration of 21,000 faculty/staff computers throughout the University. Instead of using traditional *thick* images with pre-installed software, computers are provisioned with a *thin* image with software deployed in the background. Originally, Group Policy software installations [3] were used; however, since 2008 PSU has been employing IBM Endpoint Manager [2].

2. PROCESS OVERVIEW

The process of automated software deployment breaks down into three phases: software packaging, software distribution and integration, and systems management. This paper will primarily focus on software distribution and integration, although an understanding of key elements from the other two areas is important to this process.

Software must be distributed, either using automated or manual methods (or a hybrid of both), after it has been packaged and before it can be managed. Software distribution is the actual process of installing the prepared software package onto client computers. Once the software is installed, it may need some integration to accommodate the specific computer, the needs of the user(s), and/or the network environment.

3. SOFTWARE PACKAGING

When automating installation of software, the installers that we receive from the Original Equipment Manufacturer (OEM) generally do not work for our needs; that is, they require user intervention: to select a destination folder, to select install-time options, and to select the appropriate components of a program. We find situations where we need to modify the OEM installation packages to allow for silent and unattended installation.

3.1 Silent and Unattended Installations

A *silent* installation is one that does not display to the user any windows or messages while it runs. An *unattended* installation is one that requires no user interaction and does not always imply a silent installation (e.g., a progress bar may show the status of an installation as it automatically completes each step); however, a silent installation typically is also unattended.

This non-interactive nature lends itself easily to deploying software to large numbers of computers, in particular without interrupting users' sessions. A software installer may have a command line parameter that enables it to run silently; several common applications are built with these capabilities [5]; however, not all are, nor are they always easy to find.

The best way to find a command line parameter for a silent installation is usually an Internet search. Websites dedicated to software deployment [1] may be helpful, and vendors may list silent capabilities in their documentation for the product. If a silent mechanism does not exist, repackaging the application into a deployable format (e.g., **.msi**) may be necessary; however, this should be avoided, if possible, for reasons beyond the scope of this paper. Additionally, command line parameters often allow the ability to specify options (in the form of switches/properties or "response"/configuration files) that typically are entered at install-time.

Proper testing is also an important component and ensures that software installations and deployments work correctly [5].

3.2 Managing Software Installation Packages

Key to managing automated software installers, even in a relatively unmanaged environment, are common software management factors like file organization, version control, and administrative access. In fact, it is a good idea to treat a system of automated installers like a software development project. Some type of revision control system is helpful (and necessary if several administrators contribute to the resource). The assumption is that these automated installers will be re-used frequently and used by more than one technician.

As a baseline, a central repository for software installation files should be used, and the automated installer support files either stored either those installation files or in an organizational system that parallels the software installation files.

Note that in Figure 1, the file structure for the automated installer support files parallels the file structure for the software repository that contains the source (i.e., original) install files. In Figure 2's structure, the automated installer support files can be integrated with the source install files. Either method can be used, although for EASI Make (see Section 3.2.1) and EASI, the file structure presented in Figure 1 must be used.

Having a neat, tightly organized file structure for installation files is good practice in any case, particularly when sharing with multiple administrators or groups as discussed in Section 3.4.

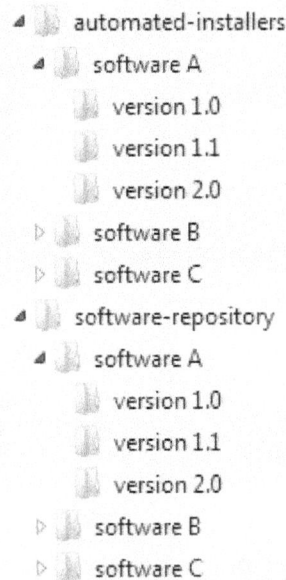

Figure 1. Parallel File Structure.

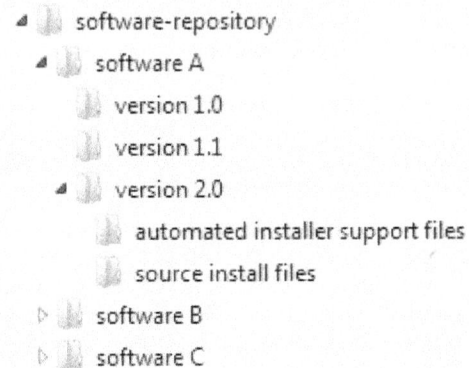

Figure 2. Integrated File Structure.

3.2.1 EASI Make

While there exist several commercial solutions for automated software deployment, an organization may not have the budget for one of these solutions. Accordingly, CSU created a tool to more easily manage the process of creating unattended installers (also called automated installers) called EASI Make. This tool takes as inputs the name of the program, the version, and optionally, components of the program, and outputs a batch script to a central store of automated installers. This script contains template code for running the automated installer, plus the specific information asked for in the EASI Make tool. The code to run the automated installers is simple; however, the administrative management of an automated installer infrastructure can be complex, particularly when multiple administrators are involved, and this helps reduce that complexity. One of the advantages of this tool is that it keeps the automated installer support files organized and consistent.

Figure 3. The EASI Make utility.

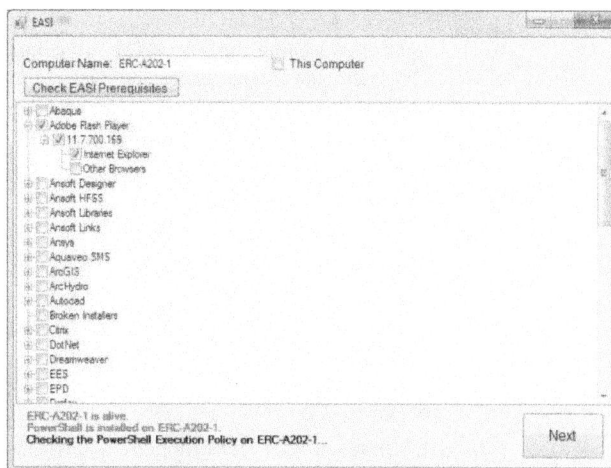

Figure 4. The EASI utility.

3.3 Bundling Software Packages

When packaging software installation files for custom distribution, it is convenient to re-package multiple installers as one single installer. There are multiple methods to accomplish this. The simplest is to use batch scripting (via Windows PowerShell, for example) and create a "wrapper" script that installs the desired software packages consecutively. Alternately, individual software installers can be re-packaged into new installer packages after changing installation options, and these new installer packages can be combined into one single installer package that installs multiple software packages from different original sources.

A commercial example of this type of service is Ninite [4], which allows users to select multiple common (and free) software installers into one installer package. The user then runs the combined Ninite installer, which downloads the specified software packages and installs them silently and automatically with Ninite-specified custom options. These options include using the default installation location, skipping up-to-date applications, skipping reboot requests from installers, and de-selecting toolbars and "add-on" programs. Such interfaces perform the functionality mentioned in Section 3.1 with the advantage of a convenient GUI.

CSU has developed a program called Engineering Automated Silent Installer (EASI) to perform a similar service. The technician selects from a list of available automated installers, and EASI builds a software package to install each selected software package. EASI creates a custom, on-the-fly PowerShell script from a template to run each selected installer consecutively. It is important to an error-free execution of this process that the installers are not run *concurrently*, since they may modify the same files on the computer. This "master" script simply calls each individual installer script, which can be a PowerShell or Windows Batch script.

Rather than download the software provider's own installer packages, EASI uses automated installer packages that have been prepared by in-house technicians, so these installer packages are already customized to our environment. It should be noted that communication between technical team members is key for consistent operation of these scripts. In many cases, multiple automated installers exist for the same software packages, but with different options which suit different user groups or use cases. One example is a 32-bit version of the program versus a 64-bit version.

3.4 Sharing Packages

While most universities have a central IT organization, IT departments are generally decentralized for practical (e.g., regulatory concerns, specializations) or political reasons. With that said, almost all of these different organizations eventually install the same packages on their users' systems, potentially even with the same settings and options.

One way to prevent this duplication is to share installer packages. For simple applications, this is for convenience; however, for more complicated installs, this helps save resources as well as time. An example is explained below.

A centralized "install" share (e.g., install.university.edu) is accessible to any staff member who is considered an IT employee. The root of this share has folders denoting units or departments (referred to as division), e.g., UNI, COE, HBG. In this case, the UNI division is the abbreviation of the university that contains freeware and/or site-licensed "university" packages; the COE division is "College of Engineering" and may have additional subfolder division (e.g., EE for Electrical Engineering, CE for Computer Engineering); similarly, the HBG division is for the Harrisburg campus (typically only one division unless it has multiple IT departments). Creating separate divisions/folders for each IT unit gives the ability to granularly allow access to certain packages; there are several options (1 is always assumed).

1. Allow read-access to the UNI division for all IT staff.

    a. Since these are considered packages installable to all university-owned machines (e.g., Microsoft Office, Firefox), all IT staff should be able to use them.

    b. An alternative is to allow both read and write access so that other IT staff can contribute to this share; however, it may be more beneficial to have them submit the package to the department hosting the share. This way, that department can quality-check the package to ensure it works correctly (and is properly licensed) before releasing it to the rest of the community.

2. Allow read-access to all other divisions for all IT staff.

   a. This option allows IT staff to see what packages other units have already created. For example, the Harrisburg campus may need to package SolidWorks (typically an engineering application); instead of packaging a duplicate, they could see and use COE's SolidWorks package.

   b. One problem with this method, obviously, is that the HBG might not be licensed to use COE's package (it also could be the case that COE's package has license server information embedded in the package and would not work on HBG's machines anyway).

3. Allow read-access to top-level division folders and write-access to sub-level division folders for members of a division.

   a. For example, only IT staff members who are part of COE (regardless of whether or not they are EE, CE, etc.) have read access to the COE division but not the HBG division. Packages in the COE division (e.g., MiKTeX, MathType) would be common and installable for anyone in CE or EE. The only IT staff having write-permissions to COE would be central COE IT staff.

   b. CE staff would have read-access to COE (i.e., common engineering) applications as well as write-access to their CE division (but not EE) for their own CE-specific packages (e.g., ActiveHDL).

   c. It is assumed that anyone having write-access to COE would also have write-access to CE, EE, etc.; however, this does not necessarily have to be the case if it is not desired.

Such granularity is relatively straightforward to set up if a centralized directory service (e.g., Microsoft Active Directory) is used in the university. Permissions to the divisions are best handled by assigning permissions to groups rather than individual users.

Finally, it may be helpful to have two primary shares (e.g., Deploy and Source) on the package file server. That is, \\install.university.edu\source and \\install.university.edu\deploy. Both have the same divisional structure (e.g., UNI, COE, HBG); however, the unmodified, original installer is placed in Source, while the modified, deployable version is in Deploy.

4. SOFTWARE DISTRIBUTION

The ultimate goal of creating silent and unattended installations is to deploy them via some mechanism, usually to automate the software installation process. In this section, we discuss two types of methods for doing so: unmanaged and managed.

The terms "managed" and "unmanaged", when applied to deployment methods, is different from a "managed" versus "unmanaged" computer. With regard to the operating system and software, there are various levels of managed computers: a public lab computer, for example, is at the high end of the management spectrum, while a laptop belonging to a faculty member might be at the low end, depending on each organization's policies. Every level of computer can benefit from the unmanaged deployment methods described here, but typically only highly managed computers can benefit from the managed deployment methods. That is because most of the managed deployment factors are dependent upon a number of conditions being met (other system software at the correct level and version, remote and administrative access enabled for the computer, etc.)

4.1 Unmanaged Deployment

In order to accommodate a wide variety of use cases, the automated installers are made as modular as possible. Thus, if a technician needs to simply install a program on a unique computer and not have to guide the installation manually, he or she may start the automated installer manually, then come back to the computer when it is finished. This alone improves the technician's efficiency.

A typical automated installer is a Windows PowerShell or batch script. The script can set environment variables and perform error checks (such as a check to see if the program is already installed) before triggering the silent unattended installer. The unattended installer is normally a **.msi** file containing the vendor's software installation package, along with command-line arguments [5]. One example is a silent, unattended installer for Adobe Flash Player:

```
msiexec /i "install_flash_player_11_plugin.msi" /qn
```

In a desktop support scenario, unmanaged deployment methods work well with both technicians in the field and at the bench. Unmanaged deployment methods may be used with any level of computer, from a tightly controlled public lab computer to a relatively uncontrolled laptop. For this type of method to achieve maximum potential, it is helpful to bundle software application installers (see Section 3.3).

4.2 Managed Deployment Components

Managed deployment, in this case, refers to some centralized mechanism of which end user computers are a part. This could simply be by joining a computer to the organization's domain or by installing a systems management agent on all University-owned computers. The goal is to automatically install (in this case) software without physically or remotely visiting an end user's workstation.

Since software installations occur automatically either when the machine starts or as a background process, this is why determining how to silently install applications via the command line is important. This command can then be added to a script or systems management application, which will then remotely run on the computer without interrupting their sessions (and without IT intervention).

Determining which software is applicable to a machine, i.e. "can be installed" is an important concept for implementing a truly automatic deployment process.

4.2.1 Systems Management Utilities

Systems management is the enterprise-wide administration of (often) distributed systems, typically from a single, centralized software interface. In most platforms a small software agent is installed on managed endpoints and communicates with the central server. Administrators of the central system can execute remote commands on client endpoints without having to physically or remotely visit the endpoint.

Several utilities exist, with varying levels of complexity, scalability, and cost. Common features may include built-in inventory, software and/or image deployment capabilities, patch management, and even power management.

IBM Endpoint Manager (IEM) is a commercial systems management tool compatible with multiple platforms (e.g., Windows, Mac, Linux). All managed endpoints are displayed in a single console regardless of whether or not they are members of the same (or any) domain, which is helpful.

IEM can be used to automatically and silently deploy software either immediately or at a scheduled time to managed endpoints. Besides having the ability to install software without interrupting users' sessions, an added benefit is not having to restart the computer to initiate an installation. If a software installation is optional, it can be deployed as an offer, which displays a window on the screen with a list of offered applications (a user can choose to accept or reject an offer; a user can also postpone an offer but then eventually have to accept it after a pre-determined time period). A tiered server structure conserves network resources, and installations occur locally on endpoints. IEM can typically perform any task that can be executed from the command line and also has built-in capabilities to determine whether or not an application has installed and then to retry the installation if it has not.

4.2.2 Group Policy

While purchasing a systems management tool certainly makes administration of large deployments easier and more organized, there is typically a large cost involved as well as significant learning curves and back end infrastructure to maintain. Such tools can be overkill or just simply not realistic for smaller organizations.

Organizations in a Microsoft Active Directory environment typically also use Group Policy Objects to centralize management of user settings (e.g., password policies, folder redirection, firewall management). Group Policy is a familiar interface that can also be used to deploy software in a managed fashion.

4.2.2.1 Software Installations

Software installations are a quick and easy way to deploy Windows Installers (.**msi** files). An application deployed via group policy automatically determines whether or not it needs to install on a system, and Windows Installers also provide a mechanism to determine if they are performing a new installation or simply updating an older version.

Typically, installing applications on lab computers (where installations are mandatory) is a computer-based policy with an assigned deployment type. For faculty/staff systems, optional packages can be user-based policies that "publish" an application; this allows the end user to decide whether or not he or she wants to install the application by using Add/Remove Programs.

To uninstall an application, simply remove the application from the software installation group policy.

One caveat to using group policy software installations is that the package must be in Windows Installer format. While many applications are in this format, many are not. Repackaging software installers as **.msi** packages can be time-consuming and error-prone. For installers that are not Windows Installers, a startup script can be used.

4.2.2.2 Startup Scripts

A startup script is a Windows script (e.g., **.bat** file) that runs when the computer starts (similarly, a logon script runs in the user context when a user first logs in to a computer). Startup scripts can be used to execute command-line installations for non-Windows Installer applications, though startup scripts can be used to install those, too.

Something to keep in mind when using startup scripts is that there are not any built-in mechanisms to determine whether or not an application needs installed. Thus, one will have to be written. One benefit of using a startup script, however, is that post-installation configuration can be built in to a single location.

For example, creating a startup script that installs Notepad++ might consist of the following. First, the silent installer command is needed; in this case, it is simply **/S**. The best way to determine whether or not Notepad++ is installed on a system is to see if its Uninstall Registry key exists; when Notepad++ is installed on a system, Windows creates the following registry key:

```
HKLM\Software\[WOW6432NODE]\Microsoft\Windows\CurrentVers
ion\Uninstall\Notepad++
```

Note that the WOW6432NODE is only if Notepad++ is installed on a 64-bit system (since the application is 32-bit).

Using this information and considering the deployment share described in Section 3.4, the complete deployment package and script can be created as follows:

1. Since this is a university-wide application, create the following folder:

   \\install.university.edu\deploy\UNI\NotepadPPxx, where xx is the version.

2. Put the installer in the NotepadPPxx folder, and then create a text file called installNotepadPPxx.bat. This will be the full deployment script that the software installation startup script points to.

3. To determine whether or not Notepad++ is installed, use the DOS **reg** command:

   ```
   reg query HKLM\SOFTWARE\Microsoft\Windows\
   CurrentVersion\Uninstall\Notepad++
   ```

4. If the above command returns 0, then Notepad++ is already on the system; if it returns something else, Notepad++ is not installed. Use the following command to check if Notepad++ is *not* installed:

   ```
   if %errorlevel%==1
   ```

5. The following command starts the silent installation of Notepad++ from the deployment location and waits for the installer to complete.

   ```
   start "" /wait "\\install.university.edu\
   deploy\UNI\NotepadPPxx\npp.Installer.exe
   /S
   ```

6. An additional check using the **reg** command to see if the application installed is optional, but might be helpful.

7. Post-installation processing of moving the Start Menu shortcuts can be used with the **mkdir** command (to create the new Start Menu category folder) and the **move** command (to move the shortcuts).

Make sure that the script works correctly. Additional scripting may be desirable to ensure that it eventually stops processing if there is a problem. Otherwise, the computer could hang at startup.

4.2.2.3 Permissions

One thing to keep in mind is that, natively, installations and scripts execute from a server location. One benefit to this is that adding or editing files and/or scripts is organized since they are in a centralized location. This location must be shared so that managed endpoints can access it, but it may not be a good idea to give open (or even authenticated) read-access to all objects in a domain.

Computer-based software installations and startup scripts execute using the built-in SYSTEM account, which is an operating system account used for background processes.

Using the folder structure discussed in Section 3.4, assume an organization places deployable software installers in a deployment share located at \\install.university.edu\deploy. The deploy folder should be shared read-only with *Domain Admins* and *Domain Computers*. Security permissions for the folder should let *SYSTEM* and the *Administrators* group of the local machine have full control, and only let *Domain Computers* have general read access (e.g., Read & execute, List folder contents, Read). Users will see that a *Deploy* folder is shared on \\install.university.edu; however, they will not be able to view its contents. Yet, because *Domain Computers* has read access, group policy software installations and startup scripts will execute correctly.

4.2.3 Client Scheduling

Another way to manage automated software deployment is for the client computer to initiate the process through a scheduled task. The advantage is that you can fine-tune each client and select when it should update based on a number of factors. For example, if you wish to have a classroom computer automatically install software when it is not in use, you may find it practical to only perform an update when it is guaranteed that no classes are scheduled in the room.

Like with group policy-based installations, you may also schedule a client to attempt automated updates on each reboot. The key is to set the computer to always perform this check, but leave the list of programs to install blank until you manually add it. This is especially useful for a scenario when a client user needs a software update urgently, but cannot leave the computer at the time the technician is available. (See Section 6.3.) In this case, the technician can remotely edit a control file on the client computer containing the list of programs to automatically install, then ask the client user to reboot the computer at his or her convenience. The computer will reboot, triggering the task which checks for a list of software to install automatically. Finding this list non-empty, it will perform the required software updates automatically, silently, and without any user or administrative intervention.

4.2.4 Control Files

A control file is often useful to manage and guide installations as well as to manage exclusions. The control file is normally a static text file placed in a designated location on the client hard drive.

This file can include useful information such as the build version, build date, and a list of software that should be excluded from automatic updates. It may also include environment variables, such as the location to check for an automated update script.

For example, instead of relying on checking the registry for whether or an application is installed, writing a control file if the installation was successful is another way to know if the application was installed. Also, additional pertinent information pertaining to the installation, including a log of events, could be stored in the control file.

A control file can also be used to help determine flow. Group policies typically execute in an ordered fashion; however, if an earlier component failed, it might not be desirable to install another component later on. If the installer does not check for this dependency, a control file might be a good way to ensure that second component installs only if the first component is installed (i.e., the second component looks for the first components control file).

4.2.5 Master Script

An alternative to the control file is a master script which processes and redirects clients to the appropriate "master script" by a variable passed to the master script, such as IP address or computer name. The master script resides on a server, rather than the client, so that changes to the list of software to update, or even the installation process itself, can be made globally.

CSU has developed a series of modular scripts called "Unified Process for Distributing Automated Tasks and Executables Remotely," or UPDATER. UPDATER has evolved from a simple wrapper script to an optimized series of modular steps that include several error-checking components (learned from trial and error). UPDATER detects when an installation fails and, preventing the computer from ending up in an infinite installation loop, integrates with other timed events (such as Scheduled Tasks), differentiates between different OS builds, and provides detailed logging for troubleshooting purposes.

UPDATER's logic works like this:

1. Match the computer name (passed to the UPDATER script) to the correct group, so it can run the appropriate automated installers associated with that predefined group (e.g., "the GIS computer classroom").

For each software package:

2. Check to see if the program is installed; if it is, skip the installation of that program.

3. Switch to the alternate Windows logon screen (see Section 4.2.6).

4. Check the log for a previously "broken" installation of the same package (see Section 5.2).

5. Begin logging the installation attempt.

6. Call the individual software package's automated installer script.

7. Check for successful installation attempt and log appropriately.

8. Repeat steps 2-7 until it reaches the end of the list of software packages to install.

9. Re-enable the normal Windows logon screen, and re-enable logons.

4.2.6 *Visible Status to the User*

Typically, silent and unattended installations should not display information to the user. In certain cases, however, this may be desirable. One instance is during a series of several sequential installations (e.g., during initial provisioning or major updates), particularly when initiated remotely or via a managed deployment. During this time, computer performance may be impacted, and a user may not want to use the computer because of it.

Changing the Windows logon wallpaper [5] is one helpful way to indicate to users that a machine either is not ready to be logged into yet, or that updates are currently in progress and performance may be slower than normal. In some cases, we may not want users to log on to the computer at all until the installation finishes. In such cases, we temporarily disable logons to the computer. At the end of the installation process, logons are re-enabled, and the logon wallpaper is restored to the normal one.

5. SOFTWARE INTEGRATION

5.1 Post-Installation Scripting

Most of us will still use a "thin" or "thick" master image, deploy it to multiple computers, and use automated software deployment as a secondary method of distributing software (of course, automated software deployment can be used as the primary software distribution method, and that requires much more planning and testing). Typically, a script is run after the master image is deployed and a new hard drive has been cloned, to set variables such as the computer name.

Such a post-installation script is an ideal place to deploy an automated software installation script. The automated software installation script can install software based on certain variables (e.g., computer name, which may indicate which lab it belongs in), and can also be configured to install updates to software that may have occurred after the master image was made. This can result in a substantial decrease in the manual intervention of a technician to each computer.

5.2 Synchronization and Error-Checking

It will quickly become apparent that a complex script or set of scripts requires comprehensive logging features, to trace when there are problems. One problem we resolved via logging was when in this subset of the UPDATER workflow:

1. Check to see if the program is installed. It is not, so call the installer.

2. Switch to the alternate Windows logon screen and disable logons (see Section 4.2.6).

3. Call the individual software package's automated installer script.

4. The automated installation fails.

5. Go back to step 1. The UPDATER script is now in an infinite loop and the computer is unavailable to users because logons are disabled.

To solve this problem, we enabled detailed logging and error checks (see Section 4.2.5). In addition, when a software installation fails on a computer, that failure is logged centrally, that computer is flagged, and an administrator is notified so he or she can follow up.

5.3 Coexistence with Other Automated Processes

All computers have regularly-scheduled events and automated processes, some built into the operating system (such as operating system updates), and some created by third-party software (such as an update checker). In addition, administrators may have created other automated processes or externally-triggered events. For example, CSU public lab computers have a scheduled task which powers the computer down after it has been idle for a certain time, after a certain time of day. This feature saves power use and increases the longevity of the computer, so it has merit and cannot be discarded in favor of an automated software installation process. Yet, we found that our automated software update service was not being triggered when the computers were powered down, and we did not want the updates to run when the computer was powered on, because it would interfere with class time. Thus, we had to carefully orchestrate the order and timing of various automated processes on the same computer. This should be taken into account when planning an automated software deployment infrastructure.

6. MANAGING SYSTEMS

Managing systems (i.e., computers and the networks of which they are a part) is not a homogenous or even mutually exclusive experience, even if the systems are the "same" at a lower level. Faculty/staff systems versus computer lab systems is also not even a standardized battle.

Besides determining what software should install on what systems, there are several other factors to consider at a higher level than the system itself.

6.1 Consideration of Administrators' Needs

Waiting to make the occasional mouse click or answer a rhetorical question from an installation program is wasteful. Clearly, the efficiency gains from automated software deployment systems have the most direct effect on the productivity of the administrators and technicians for the computers involved. Automating any process results in greater efficiency, and software installation is no exception.

Consider, however, that efficiency gains to the technician who must install the software may have indirect effects on other IT administrators, such as the network administrator. Consider staggering computer updates so that the network is not overwhelmed with multiple, concurrent software installations from a single network share (See Section 6.2).

6.2 Consideration of Users' Needs

Computers should be separated into groups carefully; a one-size-fits-all automatic software deployment clearly does not make sense. Even for very common programs, such as a Java client, we have found that there is always at least one exception to the "everyone should update" rule. A granular approach to organizing groups of managed computers can require more time up front, but pay off over time.

One clear example is classroom computers. Of course, we do not wish to schedule software installations to conflict with a class. We also discovered that we did not wish to schedule software installations at the time the computer starts up, because it may have been turned off for the night (and often are, to save power), and they may be turned on just in time for the 8 a.m. class. A software installation that takes 20 minutes and makes the computer unavailable during that time is inappropriate.

In public computer labs, it is disheartening for a user to walk in and find all of the computers updating their software at the same time, and no seat available. Thus, good practice is to stagger the automated software installations. This can be easily accomplished with the random delay feature of the Windows Task Scheduler.

In many cases, users are not able to surrender their computer when a technician is available. Normally, the needs of the software installation for the user will eventually trump the inconvenience to the user of not having their computer available for the time it takes for the installation, but this can be difficult to schedule for the user and the technician. With good automated software practices, this conflict is avoidable.

6.3 Service Desk Workflow

Many software installations or updates are initiated at the request of a user, often to solve an immediate problem. When a user contacts the service desk to request a software installation, the technician can determine if it is a managed or unmanaged computer. If manual intervention is required, the technician may log in to the client computer (remotely or in-person) and initiate the automated software installer. Alternately, the technician may configure the client computer remotely with the requested software installation packages, and ask the user to reboot the computer at his or her convenience, which will automatically initiate the software installation. (See Section 4.2.3.) If the computer in question belongs to a group of managed computers, the service desk technician passes the request to the managed computer's administrator, who schedules the automated update through the normal managed deployment. (See Section 4.2.) In all cases, the modularity of the automated installer process works to the service desk's advantage, because even in the least case, they have gained efficiency.

7. CONCLUSION

The goal of automated software deployment is to reduce the effort (and inconsistencies) involved when installing the same application on multiple computers. This paper demonstrated and detailed workflows and recommendations for converting traditional GUI-based installations to scripted, semi-scripted, or managed automated installations.

As discussed, automating software installations is an involved process; however, it greatly benefits computer provisioning and maintenance whether it is used as a supplement to traditional methods or as the only method. This benefit not only extends to IT administrators (who spend less time servicing installs) but end users (who receive faster service) as well as the organization in general (which receives more consistent builds and updates).

8. REFERENCES

[1] Dell Inc., "ITNinja (AppDeploy)," [Online]. Available: http://www.itninja.com.

[2] IBM, "IBM Endpoint Manager," [Online]. Available: http://www.ibm.com/tivoli/endpoint.

[3] Microsoft Corporation, "Group Policy Software Installation Overview," [Online]. Available: http://technet.microsoft.com/en-us/library/cc738858(v=WS.10).aspx

[4] Secure By Design Inc., "Ninite: Install and Update All Your Programs at Once," [Online]. Available: http://www.ninite.com.

[5] J. B. Tyndall, "Building an Effective Software Deployment Process," in *Proceedings of the 40th Annual ACM SIGUCCS Conference (SIGUCCS '12)*, New York, NY, 2012.

Education goes the Distance with IPTV

Robert Sobczak
Telecommunications Transmission Engineer II
University of Maine System, ITS
Augusta, Maine 04330
207-621-3326
sobczak@maine.edu

ABSTRACT

The University of Maine System was looking for a way to increase the number of high school students going to college by offering a live, distance education solution that would keep the student in their hometown. Through the years, UMS Distance Education has continued to grow from over the air television courses to offering live IP delivered instruction. This paper will focus more on the history of the UMS system, while the presentation will discuss the current setup.

Categories and Subject Descriptors

H.5.1 [Information Interfaces and Presentation]: Multimedia Information Systems - *video*

General Terms

Management, Performance, Design, Economics, Reliability, Experimentation.

Keywords

Distance Education, Streaming Video; Delayed Viewing; Federal Communications Commission (FCC); Video Capture, Broadcast; Television; Copyright; Instructional Television Fixed Service (ITFS); Internet Protocal Television (IPTV); Panopto; Polycom

1. INTRODUCTION

The University of Maine System consists of seven campuses. In 1986, Distance Education began as a regional system of Point to Point Television Microwave Transmitters between only a few locations. A more economical way was developed to blanket the state with televised classes. The Education Network of Maine began offering Live, Interactive TV classes statewide beginning the fall of 1989. Online courses were developed and better ways of distributing the TV signal also came to the forefront as technology improved.

2. HISTORY

In 1985, a study showed Maine being ranked 48th in the nation with high school students continuing to higher education. And Maine was ranked 50th for adults participating in any form of higher education. The major stumbling block was the distance from a student's home vs. the distance to a nearby college campus. Being a rural state, many students and parents could not fund both tuition and residence at the campus. Travel was also a deterrent due to the lack of four lane roads and long winters in Maine. Add to that, traditional manufacturing jobs were disappearing. Non-traditional, laid-off workers (the parents of these same students) were now using retraining funds to go to college, but needed to be able to stay at home with their family.

In September 1989, the University of Maine System began using ITFS (Instructional Television Fixed Service-utilizing 2.5 GHz Microwave) to reach the entire state, and to help close the distance gap between the student and campus locations.

The Education Network of Maine started with over forty High School sites and ten remote Campus Centers scattered throughout the state. With thirty broadcast towers and two television channels statewide, live interactive classes were presented from 7am to 10pm Monday thru Friday, and 8am-2pm on Saturday. Classroom instruction originated from twelve Broadcast classrooms at the seven Campuses of the UMS.

2.1 Video Distribution

The original ITV network was breaking ground in the state as the first fiber optic network to go statewide. When the network signed on the air in September 1989, the final connection for all UMS fiber optics was still fifteen months from completion. The final connection was a handoff between New England Telephone and GTE Telephone. This handoff was in the middle of the northern Maine woods, between the towns of Portage and Eagle Lake. Three miles outside Portage, you can watch the utility poles with electric and telephone soon turn to just our fiber optic line. This ran for five miles until the handoff. At that point, GTE took the fiber and buried it for the remainder of the trip, until it finally reached the city of Fort Kent, ME, 35 miles away. It was because of the UMS fiber optic installation that subscribers in the GTE service area finally had a choice for long distance phone service. (Remember the battles between AT&T, MCI, Sprint and 10-10 Long Distance Carriers)

In addition to building and maintaining all the transmit and receive locations, the four ITV engineers would monitor the New Telephone portion of the fiber in this densely wooded area. Many calls were made to the Presque Isle Central Office to let NET workers know that trees were weighing down the fiber. There were three breaks in the line in the early years which took days to repair.

When the network was built to full capacity, there were thirty-three DS3 circuits carrying the video into Master Control in Augusta for statewide distribution. (See Figure 1)

The Education Network of Maine

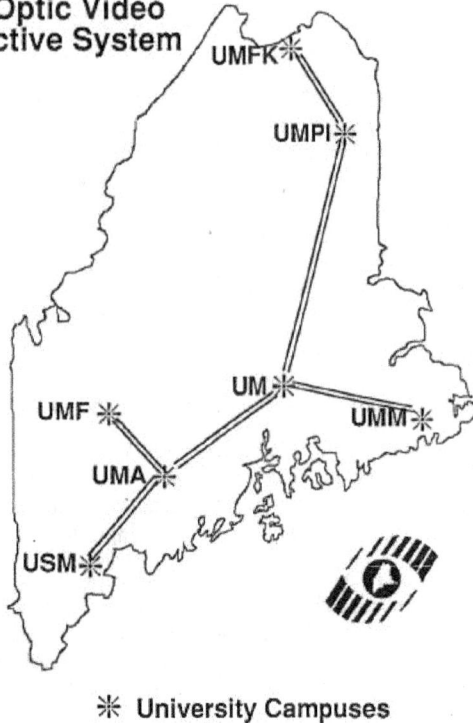

Figure 1 ITV Fiber Optic Connections

There was a fiber node at each of the seven campuses. The node output went into a Bosch Video Router then outside to a Microwave Radio Corp 23 or 18 Ghz video microwave radio, then to a tower.

At the receive tower, the microwave receiver down-converted the signal to composite video, which fed a Catel or Scientific Atlanta modulator. The modulated IF (intermediate frequency) signal was then fed to the 2.5 Ghz Comwave and Emcee ITFS transmitter. The combined signals of the transmitters fed into a Quadraplexer (four transmitters combined into one antenna). That output then went up the tower to the Bogner and Shively ITFS/MMDS antenna.

Most transmitters fed a repeater transmitter. The average region was three repeating transmitters. The Orono region had seven transmitters.

At the final receive location, an antenna on the roof fed into a Conifer or California Amplifier down converter, taking the 2.5 Ghz signal down to CATV channels, starting at channel 24. At six locations, 100ft towers were constructed to clear the trees and receive the signal. Due to terrain issues, four locations required

contracts with local cable companies to get the classes to the schools.

Inside local schools, we built a small CATV distribution network throughout the facility and set up as many receive classrooms as we had channels. Cable ready TVs had just become the norm, so there was no need for set top boxes at this time.

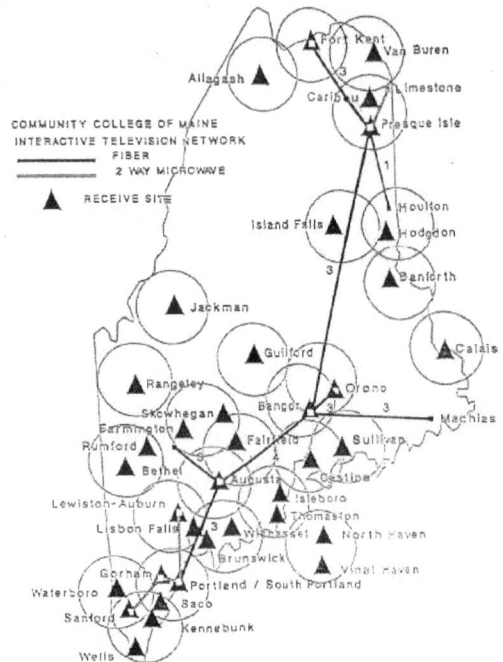

Figure 2 ITV Network, circa Sept. 1989

2.2 Control Rooms

Broadcast Origination rooms were built like traditional TV control rooms with Grass Valley Switchers, three Sony Broadcast Cameras with remote control Pan/Tilt controls for each camera, Shure gated audio mixers, Phone hybrid units, Chyron Character Generators, video disc players, and VHS recorders and players. As we grew, so did the technology. ScanDo units were installed with Macintosh and Windows computers giving direct computer scan converted output into the television stream, Chroma-Key (green screen) was also added, giving instructors the ability be on the screen and point out a subject on a graphic from any source - similar to your TV weatherman. Additional audio and video inputs were included for presenting more than the typical class. Bands could perform live in the classroom for music classes. Satellite or conference connections could be used for backhauls to bring in a remote presenter (similar to a TV reporter talking to someone across the country.)

2.3 "How ya'll doin'?"

Not all course material originated from within the borders of Maine. Classes also came from Massachusetts and South Carolina. When we began sharing material with Massachusetts, they wanted our video to come back to them, so they purchased a KU satellite uplink for our use.

A Master of Library Sciences degree was not offered in the state, but through satellite, we sent South Carolina ETV signals through our ITV network to offer something that wasn't available in

Maine. This went on for many years, but it was a little odd to hear a professor with a southern accent call on a student in Bangor, Maine at first.

2.4 Master Control

In the beginning, Master Control was the operations center. MC operators were responsible for all class recordings, switching of TV video signals and taking trouble calls. As the system improved and was more stable, MC started taking calls to deal with these newfangled things called personal computers. Remote sites were equipped with 80286 PC's and 9600 baud modems to gain access to UMS data. Research could be accomplished with system-wide resources from the mainframe and local 3B2 servers. In 1992, Master Control changed its name to the Technical Support Center.

Today, TSC serves as the system-wide Help Desk serving all the locations that ITV has served since the beginning, in addition to dealing with system wide staff and student login issues and network system software like Blackboard, Panopto, Adobe Connect, UMS PeopleSoft, Google mail, etc.

2.5 "Ooh, Ooh, Mister Kotter!"

Each receive classroom was equipped with cordless telephones. The electronic equivalent of raising your hand to ask questions was to dial the phone number to the classroom you were viewing. (The number was on the bottom of the screen and phones were preprogrammed with one-touch memory dial numbers). When the phone rang in the control room, the ITV technician would answer the phone and place you into the classroom queue. When the professor saw the onscreen cue "caller on the line", they would recognize the caller and ask them to comment. Up to four callers could be on the air at one time. The students in the live classroom would hear the callers, as well as everyone out in TV land.

2.6 The dog ate my Homework and Handouts

Class assignments, exams, handouts were handled by site coordinators at each receive location. The central Augusta office tracked all incoming and outgoing mail and directed papers to and from each professor. Very few assignments were lost in transit and complaints of "but, I turned it in" were nipped right at the student's local site by the log.

2.7 Maine Department of Education

The ITV system carried more than just University of Maine System instruction. The State of Maine Department of Education was allotted twenty hours/week for instruction to K-12 schools. It was utilized for instructing grade school personnel and students in Athletics and Teams/Coaching, Food Handling/Safety for food service personnel, and resume building for High School students.

Air time also included a monthly program hosted by Maine's Governor, highlighting jobs available in Maine. "Maine Works" was a program to encourage High School students to look into education for jobs already available in Maine with openings, which lacked enough qualified workers to fill those jobs. This also encouraged young graduates to stay in Maine, rather than leave the state for work. Each Maine Works program included

guests with a fifty-person studio audience, plus split screen remote two-way sites with students at other broadcast origination rooms. Arnold Schwarzenegger, who served as the Chairman of the Presidential Council on Physical Fitness and Sports under George H. W. Bush, was also a guest when the program featured Physical Fitness jobs in Maine.

2.8 Lobstah and Buttah

UMS held a yearly on-site Distance Education Conference, which attracted participants worldwide, hosting over 150 participants learning about the Maine model, plus what other presenters were doing at their campuses with distance education. It was capped off with an all-you-can-eat DownEast Maine Lobster Bake. Steak was also all-you-can-eat for land-lovers!

2.9 But I'm Not Really Alone

The Phone Bridge was a twenty-five-line phone conference controller. This allowed classrooms across the state with only one student to call into the bridge and join small groups over the phone with others for discussion of topics in class. Within the bridge, we controlled the size of each group, typically 4-6 students per group. Incoming WATS lines were used. Groups could be recorded upon request. Off time was sold to businesses, nonprofits, and other groups upon request. Due to aging equipment, maintenance cost and the upcoming conversion to VoIP for campus phones, the Phone Bridge was taken out of service and UMS began using InterCall to handle call conferencing in 2011.

3. SYSTEM GROWTH

By 1994, 250 hours of class content was produced each week and sixty-five courses were offered each semester. The system was offering classes on four channels at over 100 locations statewide. Receive sites included businesses who signed on to offer on-premises classes and a project called "Classroom to the Home" over a few cable companies. With live, interactive classes originating from all over the state, businesses benefitted by offering tuition discounts to workers, allowing workers to take classes and who now didn't have to lose time traveling back and forth for classes at a campus.

Signal Path analysis was conducted to investigate the feasibility of offering courses in New Brunswick, Canada and New Hampshire. Results were favorable, but contracts were never completed.

3.1 Teleconferencing

In 1996, Video Teleconferencing was introduced to the system. Eleven British Telecom units were spread to each campus, with distribution over spare T1 lines on the DS3 circuits. This expanded our capacity for small classes that couldn't be accommodated on the ITFS network. A BT T1 bridge was utilized for connections between one and other.

Thirteen BT units were in place when Polycom came into our system in 2003. The ability to use IP greatly opened our teleconferencing footprint, allowing us to install units at campus centers. With seven campuses and thirteen remote campus centers, we could now offer upwards of ten live interactive classes at any one time. Due to the 56kb bandwidth limitation of the Maine State Library Network, high school sites were never able to get on the teleconference connection.

3.2 FCC does the splits

In 2004, the FCC split the ITFS spectrum into three sections. Twelve 5.5 MHz channels on each outside portion and eight 6 MHz inner channels. The middle section was intended for video/data. The two outside sections for data were considered "excess capacity". This allowed for license holders to lease to outside parties or keep it for expanding our own use. In 2006, the Portland region was converted to Digital ITFS (four standard definition, 256 QAM, video channels occupying one 6 MHz channel). Per FCC rules, Sprint paid for the conversion, this to help clear the UMS signal out the Boston Market. Each ITFS transmitter had a thirty-five mile protection radius. Our most southern transmitter at York, ME, had its protection radius on the southern side of Haverhill, MA.

While not as high as some mountains, it helped that the Mount Agamenticus transmitter in York, had an elevation of 692 feet above sea level. On a clear day, you could see the skyscrapers in Boston.

3.3 Is it live or is it Memorex?

Initial class recordings were done on VHS tape. Our tape inventory was an order for 14,000 VHS tapes yearly. Master Control recorded four standard tapes and one S-VHS tape of each class. These tapes were sent by request if a student missed the class or if there were technical problems that kept students from watching the live class. Classes were also recorded at the receive site to eliminate the need for mailing. Tapes were recycled and recorded over at the end of each semester. Tapes were replaced approximately every four to five years with fifteen record passes on them.

VHS changed to DVD recording which dropped the cost of media. UMS was still purchasing 14K DVD's, only paying .30 cents each vs. $1.04 for VHS.

3.4 Online delayed viewing

When we began offering online and delayed viewing, Echo 360 recording systems were used to capture video. UMS had five units to record the four channels of ITFS video and one used for testing and backup. Streams were available through Blackboard. Unfortunately, the original Echo 360 software was not compatible with Macintosh.

3.5 Analog Video to Digital compression

On the original DS3 network, we had to switch each and every class from its origination location, bring the signal to Augusta, then send it out to each campus before it could hit the wireless.

1999 began the conversion to Asynchronous Transfer Mode (ATM). The ATM data stream was connected to General DataCom MAC 500 to bring out the video at each campus location, reducing the need from thirty-three DS3 point-to-point circuits down to one for each campus. The ATM stream also was connected to the Campus Centers to increase data capacity. While cheaper than DS3, IP quickly became inexpensive to connect and

offered more bandwidth. Within a few years, we were converting all the ATM circuits to IP. We continued to utilize the MAC 500 units for video, but in the IP mode. By doing this changeover, our distribution operating costs were cut by almost two thirds.

Even the Maine Department of Education had started abandoning the ATM service they had built statewide because of cost and lack of use of the systems they had installed at approximately thirty schools around the state. The biggest user was the Baxter School for the Deaf, teaching American Sign Language to remote locations. Wanting to expand beyond where the DOE ATM network delivered services, UMS utilized ALL the Baxter classroom equipment, installed a two-way point-to-point 23 GHz microwave system and offered their classes to all ITV receive locations, including both college and high school students.

3.6 Panopto

Panopto is used two ways in our system. The primary use is of the Panopto system; recording broadcast classes, Compressed Video (Polycom) Classes and routed sources. Eight CPU's with USB composite video dongles take in video from a video router. Panopto Scheduler is programmed to talk with each CPU. Classes are marked using Course Registration Numbers (CRN). Content is record at 250 KB/second.

Following the recording of the class, the MPEG4 video file is transferred to the Panopto server. Each class is queued to the server and takes about 15 minutes EACH before they are available to stream. Blackboard receives the link back to the Panopto server.

The second Panopto usage is locally controlled camera, microphone, graphic captures on a local CPU. Recording control is started and stopped by the local operator. The operator can edit recorded content, but often doesn't. With the CRN, the same process posts a link on Blackboard for playback.

The 4 Tb Panopto server is cleared of current content during the middle of the next semester.

3.7 IP Video Streaming

Initial trials of stand alone MPEG video following the MAC 500, included a combination of HaiVision Tasman H264 encoders with Amino and Nighthawk decoders. While the Tasman units seemed to work well, the decoders were difficult to use. Manufacturers were slow to allow us access to customize the decoder setup for operation within our network and decode units also required a daily reboot to eliminate audio/video sync issues. Motorola and General Instruments decode units were looked at but dropped when Video Furnace became the choice for distribution.

3.8 Live Streaming

Because of copyright and security issues with classes, UMS does not offer live streams available outside the statewide network on a regular basis. Special events like hearings and presentations are the only live programming offered outside UMS.

3.9 Cut, Cut, Cut

Due to budget cuts and an FCC mandate to transition into the middle 6 MHz band in Fall 2010, ITFS was switched over to

IPTV (Internet Protocol Television). Using Standard Definition, digital TV signals now stream to a limited number of locations statewide. UMS chose the Haivision Video Furnace system for live content distribution. At the time, HD was available, but cost prohibitive for UMS. Since then, the cost has come down and we have tested HD units on the network, but have no plans at this time to change until the origination rooms are upgraded to HD.

Standard definition set top boxes have been discontinued by Haivision, so new STBs are HD. We're fortunate that only two STB died since being installed and I've repaired the others that have malfunctioned.

Furnace is currently set up to encode at a bitrate of 3 meg/channel. STBs can only be used on the UMS IP network. There is no scheduling system. Thirteen encoded channels are always available. Four channels still originate at any one time. We could do all thirteen, except for the lack of equipment and space at the receive locations.

The Video Furnace server, encoders and STBs have encrypted, multicast signals and all can be controlled remotely. Updates can be pushed at our will.

A desktop viewer allows the same stream to be viewed without the STB. UMS limits access to the viewer to control network traffic load.

4. THE FUTURE (Gaze into my crystal ball)

In the spring of 2013, talk of what is being termed "ITV 2.0" began to come up. What does ITV 2.0 mean? Good question. Even today, UMS is still working on a definition. The main idea is to enhance existing ITV programing and expand the reach beyond the UMS IP network.

The first descriptions involve live streaming outside of the Video Furnace, with authentication through Blackboard. Video streams would be more Panopto looking, with separate video, graphics and chat windows. Rather than scan converted VGA graphics within a video window, original graphics would be in a separate window for better resolution.

Distribution would be Unicast instead of Multicast streams. The live stream would be captured and playback would be available as a Blackboard link.

Testing began in May, as this paper was being written. At present time, the live capture is hampered due to the location of the capturing machines. Each control room uses a Haivision encoder to send the class to the capture machine in Augusta. In order to accomplish the initial plan, those capture machines would need to be moved to each broadcast origination site making management more difficult. Plus, the capture machine would have to originate the graphics used, as to maintain the higher quality of the graphic presentation. Most graphics are currently created and shown on Macintosh computers and would still have to been seen full screen on the televised class.

The pilot, due to begin in June 2013, wants to experiment with IM chat or video such as Google Hangouts or Skype. These chat areas are not meant to be received by the professor during class instruction.

Privacy concerns and the fact that students MUST supply their own computers to participate are major stumbling blocks.

4.1 What about the FCC Licensed Spectrum?

The spectrum that the ITFS/EBS occupied was converted to WiMAX in 2011. Through an agreement with a statewide cellular reseller, our EBS bands are currently being used as a licensed WIFI operation. Currently, the UMS is the only user of the WiMAX.

The transmitters are located on University campuses, hooked to our statewide internal network, and offer Line of Sight (LOS) or Near Line of Sight data to registered dongles and stand-alone units with wireless speeds up to 20 Mbps. Most locations are good for 2 miles LOS. The farther the distance, the lower the bandwidth is, but still carries a respectable 2Meg signal. High gain point-to-point antennas are also available to longer hauls. The reseller is under contract and must provide service to the university when this system becomes fully developed, which is regulated by the FCC. The Spectrum is still licensed to the University of Maine System Board of Trustees.

5. ACKNOWLEDGMENTS

Without the push of my intelligent and gorgeous wife Carol to include me in these conferences, this opportunity would not have been realized.

The network is run by the UMS Information Technology Services System Engineering Staff; Former Network Transmission Supervisor Brian King; Senior Systems and Design Engineer John Tiner; Systems Engineering Specialist Ryan Gagnon; and UMS Chief Information Officer Richard Thompson, Jr.

You Can't Do It All! Using Student Leaders to Manage the Team

Karen McRitchie
SIGUCCS Board
South Amana, IA 52334
1-319-538-1459

Karen.mcritchie@gmail.com

ABSTRACT

Most student staffing models in Information Technology (IT) services departments are managed by one staff member who coordinates schedules, training, payroll, team-building and all other things relating to a student staff team. Often this IT staff member has other responsibilities in addition to managing the students employed by his/her department, which limits the time that can be invested in the student staff.

At Grinnell College, I had a team of 75-100 students who worked for the Information Technology Services department. They provided services to the Audio-Visual Center, library, computer labs, help desk and other technology areas. In order to manage such a large group effectively, I created a student leadership team to help in the management and daily operations of the student staff team.

By utilizing a student leadership team, not only have some of the operational tasks been offloaded, but this has also given the students the opportunity to be mentored in a management position, which gives them experience in a supervisory role for future career opportunities. The student staff in IT provides service to the campus in supporting technology, but they are also given many opportunities which will contribute to the foundation that they have started in their career journey. Student leaders are a large part of this strategy.

Categories and Subject Descriptors

K.6.1 [**Management of Computing and Information Systems**]: Project and People Management – *staffing, training.*

General Terms

Management, Measurement, Performance, Human Factors

Keywords

Management, Student Staff, Teams, Leadership

1. INTRODUCTION

The higher education experience focuses on academics, but can also be a time for students to gain experiences and skills that will help them as post-graduates. Those students who participate in employment, organizations, and other learning opportunities will benefit from these experiences after their tenure in higher education is over. "Helping students develop the integrity and strength of character that prepare them for leadership may be one of the most challenging and important goals of higher education." [1]

Keeping this in mind, student staff working for the Information Technology Services (ITS) department were an optimum resource for a leadership program.

There were two reasons for creating the leadership program and team within the student staff group in ITS. First, one person cannot do it all. There were all of the operational supervisory tasks as well as hiring, training, and daily crisis management that were difficult for one full-time staff member to manage. The second reason was to provide a safe environment for students to learn some supervisory and leadership skills that would contribute to their post-graduate success.

2. VISION

"The Student Technology Consultant (TC) Program is a one designed to employ students who assist Information Technology Services in supporting technology on campus. It gives students real work experience and training in various technologies used on campus that will benefit them in their post-graduation employment. To assist in the supervision and professional development of the student staff, a leadership team of student coordinators and ITS staff manage the daily operations of the program. The coordinators of the TC program are hired because of special skills and their desire to work in a leadership position. This is a team of students who will work together on projects and duties that directly benefit the TC program. They will each have projects or tasks that they will be responsible for coordinating. They will manage and delegate tasks to other members of the team or other TCs as needed. This is a learning experience as well as a job. This role on the leadership team will provide experience in supervising others while allowing you to learn and develop some management skills. The coordinators will work with Karen on developing their own skills, while supervising the operations of the TC Program." [2]

It was the opportunity to give students who demonstrated leadership qualities a mentored environment where they could learn and practice skills that would help them in their future. It was also an opportunity for the students to specialize in an area that they enjoyed. There are many different roles in technology and most often when a career in technology is considered, programming seems to be the focus. The implementation of student leaders and categorizing the tasks gave students a first-hand look at other technology career areas. For example, an Audio-Visual Coordinator position was created and made part of the leadership team; the person in the position mainly supervised the students working in the Audio-Visual department.

3. INITIAL DESIGN OF THE LEADERSHIP TEAM

It was important to satisfy two objectives in determining the model to be used for a leadership team. The student leaders had to be productive and relieve some of the tasks from the full time staff, while also providing the experience and mentoring to benefit their own career experience. Over the years, there have been a few leadership roles designed that did not fit the objectives or meet the needs of the IT department. Each role developed is evaluated after one semester and sometimes they are discontinued. The needs and objectives of each IT department are unique and it may take some attempts before finding the perfect team roles.

3.1 Administrative Coordinator

This position was the most important for daily operations. The Administrative (Admin) Coordinator would work closely on a daily basis with the ITS Administrator for the student staff. Their role was determined by tasks that they could do - for example, making sure staff attended their work shifts - but not things that were the responsibility of the ITS staff, like payroll.

The TC Administrator performed the daily supervisory tasks that were necessary for the TC program operations. He/she maintained personnel records for the active employees and coordinated any disciplinary efforts. This person coordinated the hiring process and was responsible for the evaluation process of current staff. The Admin TCC supervised the Systems Developers, Lab Services Coordinator, and Wiki Administrator. Responsibilities included:

- Check email daily or assign to another TCC if unavailable.
- Maintain the data within TC database (TCDB), updating individual records as necessary.
- Approval and verification of timesheet records prior to processing by payroll staff.
- Maintain the certification data within TC database, updating as necessary.
- Coordinate advertisement and hiring of new staff.
- Maintain database of application and interview scores for each hiring process.
- Coordinate the interview process.
- Coordinate TC scheduling and daily subs.
- Coordinate evaluation of staff.

- Bring any disciplinary concerns to the TCC team and Karen for resolution.
- Resolve any problems or concerns with TCs, reporting on the resolution at the weekly team meeting. Recommend actions to the leadership team for discussion.

- Conduct any disciplinary meetings (non-trainees) regarding attendance or other issues; include other members of the team as necessary.
- Prepare and post the weekly meeting agenda for the leadership team
- Coordinate the semester scheduling
- Work with Karen to resolve any payroll issues.
- Approve hours for TCs and send reminders for payroll.

3.2 Education Coordinators

The education of the Student Technology Consultants had two parts: initial training/mentoring and ongoing training. The responsibilities were too much for just one student leader, so two roles were created. One of the coordinators would supervise the training program and the other would assist with the training, but mainly coordinate the outreach sessions for all students as well as continued training for the student staff. The responsibilities of this position included:

- Obtain a list of new hires from the Admin TCC, and contact them with information about the orientation session.
- At the Orientation session, present an overview of the training program with a complete schedule of all sessions.
- Coordinate placement of the new hires with a mentor
- Supervise the Mentor Program. Provide mentors with instructions, checklist of tasks and schedule.
- Maintain records on the progress of each new hire, communicate with each trainee about their progress and report progress of trainees at the weekly leadership meeting.
- Conduct meetings with any trainee about attendance issues, inviting the Administrative Coordinator attend the meetings.
- Communicate and maintain email for the training class.
- Assign projects and coordinate grading efforts for each project.
- Advertise and obtain trainers for each workshop from the entire TC body.
- Meet with each trainer to discuss the presentation and details of the workshop.
- Maintain a folder on storage server with a sub-folder for each training session. Each training folder will contain copies of the presentation, documentation and training outline.
- Develop the training sessions by setting objectives and creating activities for the session. Document each training session.

- Update each training workshop yearly with the TC trainer assigned.

- Update the TC Administrator upon any completion of training, so tcdb records are updated.

- Coordinate the Technology Consultant training in August.

- Coordinate the general student training throughout the year as well as educational materials used around campus.

- Work with Karen to train TCs to be certified facilitators.

3.3 Help Desk Coordinator

This role was an important one as the help desk was the first point of contact for the ITS department. The students who staffed the help desk were our top support staff and this coordinator had to provide the guidance that would maintain the excellent level of service that we wanted to give the campus. The main responsibilities of this coordinator were:

- Direct supervision of all help desk staff.

- Monitor the Help desk schedule to ensure adequate staffing.

- Maintain high customer service standards.

- Coordinate certification process for new help desk staff

- Coordinate training of new help desk staff, using a mentor program.

- Maintenance of resources for help desk.

- Communications to all help desk staff on current issues.

- Handle any escalated support issues or send them to the ITS staff.

- Schedule and coordinate agenda items for semester meetings.

- Work with Karen on performance evaluations of all Help desk staff each year to determine if they maintain certification.

- Analysis of weekly/monthly reports of Kbox (service database) calls.

- Coordinate the help desk operations of New Student Orientation

3.4 Audio-Visual Coordinator

In 2006, the campus' Audio-Visual (AV) Center became a part of the ITS department. Since AV technology was becoming more digital and computer-centered, this became another facility that was supported by the ITS student staff along with the full time

AV staff. Many students enjoyed working with audio and video, assisting with editing tools, and assisting with student projects. This has become an easy schedule to fill, due to the experience and interests of our student staff. It was the job of the coordinator to assist the AV Director and full time AV support assistant with the students who worked in the center. The responsibilities included:

- Direct supervision of all AV student staff.

- Monitor the AV schedule to ensure adequate staffing.

- Work with AV Manager on staffing and support issues.

- Maintain high customer service standards.

- Coordinate training and testing for AV certification.

- Maintenance of the checkouts in the webcheckout database.

- Communication to all AV staff of current issues.

- Handle any escalated support issues or send them to the AV Manager.

- Work with Karen on performance evaluations of all AV staff each year to determine if they maintain certification.

- Ability to run the AV database reports and follow up on delinquent assets.

4. HIRING THE RIGHT LEADERS!

The challenge has always been, "who are the right students to put into a leadership role?" Often student leaders would stand out during the training process, which would help gain some insight as to their leadership ability. Experience was not expected, as for some students, this was their first job. Each of the coordinator roles required a specific personality type and this information was sought out during the interview process. For example, the Administrative Coordinator needed to be detail-oriented, have good communication skills and organized, while an Education Coordinator would tend to be a more creative person with great communication and presentation skills.

Each role had its own application where the students were given a situation and then they could describe how they would handle it. The application would give insight into the specific skills that were required by each of the roles. The interviews were performed by the ITS advisor (Karen McRitchie) and then discussed with the current leadership team.

It was important to look at the group dynamic as well as the individual characteristics of the applicants. The new coordinators needed to "fit" into the team and be able to work well with the existing leaders. It was also important to hire from various graduation years, so that we were not recreating the team each year and that experienced students would coach the newer coordinators.

5. MENTORING

Mentoring is a large part of our new ITS student staff training program and it was also important to the student leadership team. The leadership team met weekly with the ITS Manager (Karen) and often met with some individually. For example, when the summer training sessions were being planned, the education coordinators met to design the sessions and put together the training schedules.

The environment was one that could allow a safe place to practice skills or try something new. When a new Administrative coordinator had to discuss tardiness with one of the student staff, he/she first met with Karen to go over the process as well as discuss what would be said to the student. Karen was involved in the first meetings, until the Administrative coordinator felt comfortable with this task. The Education coordinators were instructed and then provided guidance in designing workshops, which included the content as well as the evaluation of each session.

6. BASIC SUPERVISORY SKILLS

On-going mentoring was important to the success of the leadership team, and also was teaching basic skills for supervisors as most of the student leaders had no experience in this area.

6.1 Communication

It was important for the student leaders to practice their communication skills, both verbal and written. Guidance was provided for email messages and for discussing performance issues with the other student staff. This could be a difficult task, as the student leaders needed to supervise their peers and friends. One of the tools that were used for the student leaders was the "I Message." This is a statement that can be used to make sure that communication is about the behavior and not the person. The guide is:

- When _____ (describe behavior only)
- The effect on _____ is _____. (quality, quantity, time, cost, safety, honesty, etc.)
- I feel _____ (concerned, frustrated, etc.)
- I hope/would prefer that in the future _____. (list the behavior that you would like to see in place of this behavior)

6.2 Problem Performance

One of the conversations that no supervisor likes to have with a team member is one about a performance problem. If the student leaders were given some training about this, then it may not cause stress in a future position. The more knowledge/skills that each student leader obtained would be beneficial for the success of the leadership team. The student leaders were provided with some training on identifying the problem, analyzing the cause and then determining if it is due to a deficiency in knowledge/skill or a deficiency in execution/attitude. In other words, "Could the employee do the task if he/she wanted to, or do they need the experience/skills/training to complete the task successfully?"

6.3 Time Management/Meetings

Time management was an important skill for the student leaders to have mastered. Many of them already juggled school, work, and other activities successfully and by giving some time to discussing/training would reinforce good habits and identify bad ones.

One of the focus areas that were important was meetings. There are too many unnecessary meetings and so our team meetings were a guide to how to do it correctly. The meeting had to have an agenda with time assigned to each topic. The agenda was posted as a Google doc, and then all of the leadership team could contribute. If Karen or one of the other leaders wanted an update, it was put on the agenda, if there was a disciplinary issue to discuss, it was put on the agenda. If there was an empty agenda, there was no meeting. Project meetings were similar, with each of the leaders or Karen creating the agenda and then those participating would be sent the agenda and supporting materials prior to the meeting. For example, when a new training was being developed, a work team was established, lead by the Education coordinator, and the objectives and activities were established prior to the training design. This allowed others who were interested in that project, to be involved in the planning without making the commitment of being a coordinator.

6.4 Accountability

One of the main reasons that performance problems exist is due to the misunderstanding or lack of expectations. It is important to learn that team members need to have clear objectives and expectations for the tasks and responsibilities that they are assigned. They are then accountable for communicating their understanding and completing the tasks. If the expectations are not clear, then it is the job of the supervisor to provide additional information until they are understood.

6.5 Other Types of Skills/Knowledge

There are many opportunities for various skills/knowledge training or information that will benefit the student leaders. Often a topic was added to a weekly meeting agenda for a 15 minute session regarding a new skill or leadership topic discussion. Some of the past sessions:

- team building
- civility
- presentation skills/facilitation
- mentoring
- creativity
- problem solving
- failure, stress and other depressing things
- conflicts
- planning/goal setting
- project management
- leadership styles/personality styles

7. STUDENT MIDDLE MANAGERS

One of the benefits of off-loading some of the work to the student leadership team is that there is more time to work on some other aspects of the employment program, enhancing the overall structure and services provided. In order to do this successfully, about 4 years ago, a middle level group of student leaders was created based on special projects and services. This was an opportunity given to students to be more like project managers who organized and supervised a project rather than supervising people. There were several opportunities created which ended up enhancing the employment program for the department.

- Application Development Team leader—2 years ago, a team of student developers was created to develop apps for mobile devices. There was not any plans to have app development as part of the ITS department and with ITS management, this gave 6 students an opportunity to do some "real time" development in iOS, Android and the Windows mobile environments.

- Wiki Librarian—all of the internal and external documentation was organized in a wiki. This position was the manager of the wiki, updating content, soliciting content from the student staff and generally managing all of the wiki functions.

- TCDB System Administrator—since we maintained our own database system on a linux system, a computer science student was hired as the system administrator. System administration experience is very good to have on a resume'.

- Volunteer Coordinator—the local school system had only one IT staff member, so we asked the student staff to give 1-two hour shift per semester to assist him with the K-12 schools computers. They assisted with images, software installs, hardware installs and even some teacher training. One person coordinated this and was the liaison to the local schools.

- Assistive Technology Assistants—to work with the students using technology tools for accommodations.

- Women in Tech leader—led the Women in Tech group, organized meetings and communications.

- Social Coordinator—planned and organized all social events, from Origami Sumo Wrestling to picnics.

8. SUCCESS STORIES

Not only was the student leadership team successful in that they provided assistance to off load tasks from the ITS Manager, but these positions also provided a great environment for gaining some management experience that would be beneficial for future careers. Over the past 15 years, many students have reported that their tenure as a student leader led them to be successful in their post- graduate career. With all things being equal for graduates, applying for jobs, having management experience is a great advantage. Several statements from graduates can show the benefits of working in a leadership role during college:

"I want to thank you for all that the TC program has given me. It is not often that you find a work experience as engaging and fun as the one you helped create. I have used many of the skills learned in my job at Amazon."

"I thought that because being a TC Coordinator was an important job, it would be an awful work environment but it has been AMAZING! Thank you so much for creating that space in which I could grow and realize that I can have fun while getting the job done too. I will try to keep the values you taught us going as I begin my new job."

"My experience working as the Help desk coordinator helped me get a job working at the help desk in the Pentagon. There were three college graduates being considered and I had three additional years of experience at a help desk and as a supervisor."

At first, the idea of having a student leadership team was mainly to offload some of the daily operational work, however, when I realized how beneficial it would be for the students as well, it evolved into a way for students to gain valuable experience for their future careers. It was a way, through work experience, to provide those skills and knowledge that would aid in their success after graduation. College is the transition from childhood to adulthood and not only are students being prepared academically, they are also able to gain those things needed to encourage their post-graduate success when they are given opportunities for leadership.

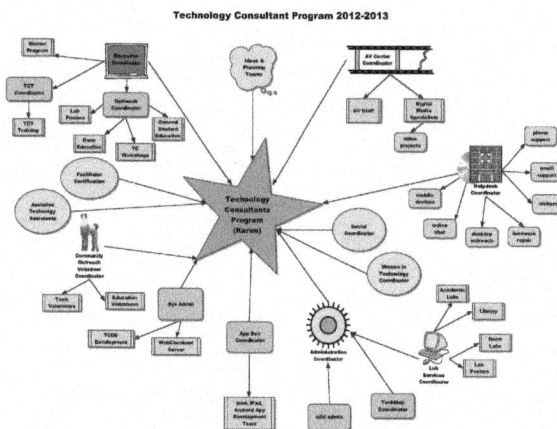

Figure 1: Student Staff Model

9. REFERENCES

[1] King, P.M. (1997) Character and civic education: What does it take? *Educational Record*, 78 (3,4), 87-90.

[2] McRitchie, Karen (2009) *TCC Roles and Responsibilities,* 1.

Minimal Computing-Minimizing Technology to Maximize Work/Life Balance

Scott J. Saluga
Oberlin College
Center for Information Technology
148 W. College St., Oberlin, Oh 44107
ssaluga@oberlin.edu

ABSTRACT

I have been in Higher Ed IT for almost 20 years. I believe in the "KISS" principle. Keep it Simple, Stupid has been my mantra for some time.

It is easy in our modern world to throw money at a technology to do that one thing that helps us in our work. The problem is that those "one things" tend to accumulate over time to become an unwieldy mess.

Over the last few years I have noticed that I use less and less individual software, tools and techniques than I have in the past and have honed my computing to a minimal level to get more and more completed. I have pruned my work life down to the bare essentials. In doing so, I have gained control of my workday. I now have the opportunity to pursue other skills and duties that I would not have otherwise had time to attempt

Whether it is via laptop, tablet or phone, I find myself using the tools and skills that allow me to get what I need done with minimal effort and then focus on other duties.

I find that other aspects of my work life have adapted as well. This paper or discussion will expand on my mantra of minimal computing to maximize work/life balance.

Categories and Subject Descriptors

C.5.3 [**Microcomputers**]: Portable devices (e.g., laptops, personal digital assistants, tablets, phones.)

H.3.5 [**Online Information Services**]: Commercial Services, Data Sharing, Web-based Services.

H.4.3 [**Communications Applications**]: Electronic Mail, Information Browsers.

H.5.2 [**User Interfaces**]: Input Devices and Strategies, User-centered design.

K.4.4 [**Electronic Commerce**]: Payment schemes.

Keywords

Cloud Computing, Mobile Computing, Apple, iOS, iPad, iPhone, Google, Android, tablet, Square, GPS, Twitter, Facebook, Instant Messaging.

SIGUCCS'13, November 3-8, 2013, Chicago, Illinois, USA.
Copyright © 2013 ACM 978-1-4503-2318-5/13/11...$15.00
http://dx.doi.org/10.1145/2504776.2504807

1. INTRODUCTION

I have used computers for over 30 years. Just thinking about that floored me. I have been a professional for almost 20 years, but the 30 years really got me thinking.

I started out on Apple II+ and a TRS-80. Those days were like magic. Magic because it was a whole new world. Painful because it was so difficult to do the most basic of things. I remember typing in programs and writing them to cassette tape or 5.25" floppy discs. Tonight, I ordered and paid for a customized Chipotle burrito from my iPhone. Unbelievable.

I used desktops until 1999. My former supervisor was a proponent of using a laptop as his primary computer. At that time, a fully loaded PowerBook was $6500. He would get a new laptop and then I had would get his hand me down. My first laptop was a PowerBook 3400C. I went from an iMac that cost $1200 to carrying around a $6500 laptop. I treated that like a rare gem.

But it made me realize the power of mobility. Being able to do anything from anywhere was a real eye opener. The desk in my office was no longer an issue. I preferred the freedom that it allowed me. I have never looked back. Laptops have been my primary computing device for the last 14 years.

2. PERSONAL

My wife and I are the children of parents that were born during the Depression and grew up rationing during World War II. Therefore our parents were something on the level of hoarders. Not in the crazy, unlivable homes that you see on television today, but those who never threw something away in the event that you may need it in the future.

As we moved out of our homes and started our lives, we accumulated a lot of stuff and were always given more. We noticed that instead of using the stuff we had, at best we dusted and moved it around.

Our stuff owned us. It was terrible. This was the time when we started looking at the causes of why we were continuing what our parents were doing and realized that much of this type of behavior was based on some level of fear. Fear of losing what you had or fear of never having this stuff again. It was a real eye opener and understanding the cause made it much easier to begin to correct it.

"Living a minimal life doesn't have to mean not owning things. It can mean, and I choose it to mean, owning only the things that matter." [1]

3. MOORE'S LAW

For many years the race after Moore's Law meant that every few months, computer vendors were bringing out faster and faster processors and computers. With the rise of the usability of the web and feature creep of ever bloating software, it was mandatory to be on a constant upgrade path. It was like an arms race that appeared without end.

As a technical professional, I felt that if I did not keep up, I was going to get left behind.

Trying to keep up with every little hardware and software update was an impossible task. I began to see that users were tired of the upgrade cycle and the ever-growing feature set of software that they neither wanted nor needed.

It took us tech types a few more years to get the hint.

4. APPLE ASCENDANT

t. The first two major changes that I started to really notice a difference in attitudes were the introduction of Apple's iMac in 1998 and Apple's Airport in 1999.

The introduction of the iMac was the first real change in how computing was accomplished and packaged in more than ten years. All legacy ports were removed and there was no floppy drive.

Everyone thought that Apple was crazy for not having a floppy drive, but in reality, we rarely used them for years before the iMac's introduction.

The second major change was the introduction of Apple's Airport Wireless card and Airport Base Station. This was the technology that allowed us to take our computers wherever we wanted.

With Airport, this is the point that I realized that I wanted a different way to use technology and live. With the ability to no longer be tied to a desk and a desktop computer, my work quality of life was about to be radically different. That was thirteen years ago.

5. iOS

The last and most major changes that contribute to this era of Minimal Computing are the release of iOS, iPhone and iPad. [2] This was the game-changer that so many were waiting for.
The mobile industry is split into two eras, before the iPhone and after the iPhone.

Before the iPhone, mobile phone vendors had all kinds of phones with differing operating systems. Nothing was similar and user interface was difficult to use at best. With the iPhone, ease of use and power had arrived.. It was like using Microsoft's Disk Operating System and moving to Mac OSX; Night and day difference. Because the ease of use was one of the driving needs of a mobile device, Apple designed a clean and easy to manipulate interface. Apple knew that early adopters, fans of the Apple brand, would snap up the iPhone the day it was released. Now Apple needed a way to convince non-technical users to purchase the iPhone Luckily, with iTunes, they already had a built-in market. iTunes is Apple's online music and movie store. Most people that already had an iPod also had an account with iTunes. This was Apple's Trojan horse.

The iPhone replaced the ubiquitous iPod very quickly. Now people only needed to carry one device instead of two or three. One device replaced the phone, Internet communications device, iPod, still camera, video camera, contacts and datebook.

Its introduction was a clutter killer by design.

The creative agency, W&CIE, took this photo demonstrating what the iPhone meant. [3] Now, this is 1993 versus 2007. But the point is clear.

5.1 iPAD

The iPad takes everything learned from the iPhone and makes it a little bigger. It was designed and thought of as a media consumption device, but everyone knew from the iPhone that the iPad would be an incredible media creation device.

6. ME AND iOS

The iPhone and the iPad have really changed not only how I do my job, but also how I interact with people and the larger world. I find more often than not I grab my iPad or iPhone before I would ever think of using my laptop to work. From email, to Twitter, to most of my daily work, I find that my iPhone and iPad can do 80-90% of what I need to do, without using a laptop or desktop.

I prefer clean and uncluttered rooms as well as computers. Nothing bothers me more than a desktop full of papers and folders. That goes for the physical and well as the virtual.

I find that if my computer desktop is cluttered, so am I. The iPhone/iPad user can only see and manipulate one application at a time. This single-minded approach helps me concentrate on the task at hand. I find it easier to accomplish tasks this way.

Even if the iOS apps have a MacOS counterpart, I still prefer the simplicity of the iOS apps. I simply get more done and in a more efficient manner on iOS.

After almost 20 years of primarily supporting Apple's product line in higher Education, I was, frankly, getting bored with computing and support. Had iOS not come along, I am not sure what I would be doing today.

6.1 New Routine

Let's talk about a usual day. My iPhone is with me all the time. I use it as my alarm clock beside my bed. It wakes me with a gentle strumming of a harp. What a nice way to wake up. I turn on my SiriusXM app or my WKSU NPR app to listen to news, music or entertainment to get me started. I check the weather, radar and calendar to see what the day holds and Twitter for any traffic alerts for my commute.

Using this method is much more efficient than turning off a regular alarm clock, finding the radio and turning on the TV. I get what I need, exactly the way I want it, in a minute or two.

I check email once before I start commuting to see if there is anything that requires an immediate response.

I usually stop for coffee at Starbucks on the way to work and pay for it with the Starbucks app. I can reload my virtual gift card from my credit card or PayPal right within the app. Readers at the register scan my virtual Starbucks card and I am on my way. I check email once more and finish my commute to work.

Once I arrive at work and get settled, I text my wife that I am safe at work. Next, I use my iPad or iPad mini and check email, Twitter, Facebook and App.net. Even if I decide to use my desktop or laptop, my iPhone is always with me and my iPad is open.

I rarely take anything more than my iPhone and iPad to meetings. I have any documents that I need either in Google Drive, Dropbox or Good Reader. My Notes and Pages documents are synced through iCloud so I always have them with me. I attempt to keep paper to a minimum. It is just clutter to me and I tend not to use something if I feel it is clutter.

Since my handwriting is not very legible anymore due to non-use, I take all my notes in the "Notes" app.

I also tend to use the camera to take still images and video to describe problems or issues instead of typed notes; A picture is worth a thousand words. For example, one of our labs was in a terrible state of cleanliness and upkeep. I wrote numerous emails to the responsible parties with no real action taken. I took a couple of pictures and a short video, sent it off to all parties and the problem was handled within 24 hours.

I can do all of this with one silent, lightweight device that is fun to use; Brilliant.

6.2 Personal and Professional

Aside from giving me something that makes work fun and exciting again, iOS is the catalyst that has brought change to my professional and personal life. Since the iOS devices are communication devices, I am able to communicate to friends, colleagues and strangers at all hours of the day and in all sorts of locations. With Twitter, Facebook, App.net, Instagram, Vine and Meetup, I can network and communicate with experts all over the globe. Nothing is more exciting than conversing with someone you look up to and get near instantaneous feedback from them. I was talking to Patrick Rhone of Minimalmac.com about this paper and he expressed interest in reading it; I was shocked. Patrick is someone that I admire and I read his writing often. For him to be interested in what I have to say is a new experience for meThis is just one example of the positive aspects of minimal computing. All of the unnecessary junk gets out of the way. Computing gets out of the way. You get to a pure essence of communication.

One of my co-workers said it best, "Less computing and more communicating." [4] I could not agree more. I tend to be someone who prefers to do things myself. Being an only child brings out that type of behavior. It is not that I think that I can do things better than anybody, it is just my comfort zone. Now, I get excited and search out more ideas, comments and help that I have ever done before.

I regularly chat with a Computerworld writer. His writing was something that connected with me and I thanked him on Twitter. A few seconds later, he and I were having a deep discussion about Apple.

My wife and I text all the time. It lets me know that she is fine and vice versa. We can talk in very specific bursts and spend the rest of the time making each other laugh. It has really strengthened our relationship. We know that friendly ear is a text away. It can be so much more efficient than talking on a phone conversation. We can also chat when it is not convenient or practical to have a phone conversation. She will ask me a question and I can Google it and give her the answer right away.

My devices are navigation guides using GPS technology to help me get to where I need to go. The Chipotle App is the greatest thing since sliced bread. I can type in my order, pay for it and select the time I want to pick it up. I stroll right past the line and straight to the register. After about 5:30, the wait time in line can be 20-30 minutes depending. That free app saves time and my sanity.

The Nike Running App gives me a specific GPS map of my run, the elapsed time of my current run and how it compares to all the previous runs that were recorded into it. It also allows me to send updates to Facebook and Twitter and people can cheer me on. There is nothing like hearing a cheer from a friend at 7:15am. Using these tools to communicate has really opened up life in ways that I could have not foreseen.

Square Register is another app that I use in my personal life. I am a ceramic potter, I create ceramic pottery pieces on a pottery wheel, and sometimes sell work that I do. With Square Register, I can take credit and debit cards like any store. I even use it when we go to lunch and the staff does not separate the bill. I will pay the total and then I take payments from everyone else; many of the small stores in my neighborhood use the Square register. It is fast, convenient and paperless. A receipt can be emailed to you desired.

I keep the manual to many of my devices, my automobiles and anything else I need in Books or Dropbox. I use Keyring to scan in all of the store loyalty cards that people would normally fill up their keyring with. Those cards end up fraying, getting filthy and fall apart. My cards are brand-new and I do not have to hand out my keys all the time. I keep copies of all my pertinent medical and personal information as pictures in case I lose my wallet. All of these things save time and remove stress from my life. They make me more productive because all of those nagging things that keep you up at night, or not allow you to focus are taken care of, backed up and secure.

If my iPhone is stolen, I can track it and remotely wipe it with, Find My iPhone, a free app from Apple. Peace of mind is priceless.

7. OTHER

For those of you wondering when I was going to touch on Android, BlackBerry or Windows Mobile, well don't worry. I am not going to. I have used every mobile operating system to come out since Newton OS. I just don't find them to be as useful or easy to use as iOS. This is a personal preference for sure. There is a lot to like about all of them, but when I look at them in the totality of what they offer, they just do not do it for me. There are over 800,000 iOS apps with over 300,000 of those iPad only and there are more apps every day. Anyone can find the handful of programs they need to make their own life easy and simple and fun to use.

REFERENCES

[1] http://whowritesforyou.com/2013/03/18/pick-one/

[2] http://minimalmac.com

[3] https://www.facebook.com/agencewcie

[4] Linda Iroff Oberlin College, 2013, comment to me

Front Line Help Desk at Rice University

Rick Roberts
Support Specialist II
6100 Main Street, MS 119
Houston, Texas 77005
1-713-348-4887
rroberts@rice.edu

Diane Yee
Asst.Director, IT Customer Service
6100 Main Street, MS 119
Houston, Texas 77005
1-713-348-4887
diane.yee@rice.edu

Al Grazis
Client Services Manager
6100 Main Street, MS 119
Houston, Texas 77005
1-713-348-3132
agrazis@rice.edu

ABSTRACT

This paper is a description of work at the Rice University Help Desk, from the perspective of a staffer working in the cubicles. It includes a description of the range of Help Desk customers, individuals and organizations, at Rice and their needs. I discuss how the interaction with the customer is critical to the work and about my methods of customer interactions by telephone and text. This paper includes a limited discussion of volume and ticket processing statistics (my workload). This paper discusses recent evolution of services offered and changes we anticipate. This paper discusses the tools we use, and the planning stages of implementing at Rice. I talk about the practical work at the phones and the keyboard. A slide presentation will accompany the paper.

Categories and Subject Descriptors

C.5.m [Computer System Implementation] - Miscellaneous

General Terms

Management, Measurement, Documentation, Performance, Design, Reliability, Security, Standardization, Verification

Keywords '

Help Desk, Automated Call Distribution. Account Management, Email, Password, Data, Hardware, Printing, Remote, Reset, Mobile Devices, Printing, Repair, SPAM, ACD

1. INTRODUCTION

This paper is a description of work at the Rice University Help Desk, from the perspective of a staffer working in the cubicles. It includes a description of the range of Help Desk customers, individuals and organizations, at Rice and their needs. I discuss how the interaction with the customer is critical to the work and about my methods of customer interactions by telephone and text. The paper includes a limited discussion of volume and ticket processing statistics (my workload). The paper discusses recent evolution of services offered and changes we anticipate. The paper discusses the tools we use, and in are in the planning stages of implementing at Rice. I talk about the practical work at the phones and the keyboard. A slide presentation will accompany the paper.

2. TOOLS

2.1 Contact Center Manager, Avaya Inc.

The first tool of a call center is the Automatic Call Distribution (ACD). This, in our case, is software that runs on our Nortel Telephone switch that does what the name implies, distributes the calls among the staff. The usual configuration is to give the next incoming call to the phone that is idle, or, in the case of multiple idle phones, the phone that has been idle the longest. Our configuration starts the day for us by enabling the phones at the start of the business day. Callers that come in prior to the start of business, get a recording informing of our business hours and an emergency extension they can call. The system also shuts down at the close of business, no new calls are distributed after closing and the after-hours announcement resumes. During business hours, callers get a greeting and are routed to a call queue with music on hold, in the event that all of us are busy. We can modify that recording at times when call volume spikes, in the event of a service outage on campus. The software provides management with service data, the number of calls, customer wait times, length of calls, the data you would expect a manager would need to understand the service level the department is providing.

2.2 Request Tracker, Best Practical Solutions

Request Tracker is the heartbeat of the Help Desk at Rice. Usually referred to as the "ticketing system" or "RT", it's, essentially, a web-based database. We use it to record customer service requests and service outages. The database has ties to the university's LDAP directory. If a ticket is created with the customer's Rice email address, the ticket fields are populated with his directory information. It is not tied to our phone system. The program is customizable by customers. I see all new tickets that are not yet assigned to a person of division of IT. Once a ticket is assigned, I no longer see it on my screen -- unless it's assigned to me. Tickets are numbered and time-stamped. Email notification is turned on. Customers receive email notification upon the creation of a ticket which includes the links to the ticket. Customers and IT communicate by responding to the ticket. Only comments are not communicated to the customer. Comments are used internal IT communication of the ticket.

2.3 Confluence, Atlassian

Confluence is a team collaboration tool, mainly used by the Help Desk to offer our customer's online tutorials and documentation on services offered by IT. The Help Desk staff usually refers to it as the "wiki". If a customer is unable to call us, we can usually send a link to a tutorial article. We also use it for our internal documentation of policies and procedures. The tool allows us to control access to pages, so we can use it for internal data, such as staff contact information.

2.4 Bomgar™, Bomgar Corporation™

Bomgar™ is a web-based remote support tool. We can direct a customer to our Bomgar™ web address, talk them through downloading a small application and make a connection to their computer that provides us with a visual of their desktop, along with keyboard and mouse access. Bomgar™ makes the Help Desk more than just a dispatch service. When we get a call from a customer with a problem that might be difficult to talk him through, frequently we can make a connection with Bomgar™, take control of his computer and resolve the problem. Email is a good example. When new staff arrives, one of the most anxiety producing issues for them is getting access to email. With Bomgar™, I can help the customer initialize his account and configure his mail client for him. I can help him with his spam filtering and I can demonstrate the use of the mail client's features. I can make his connections to storage shares and networked printers. I can help him install our VPN client, or configure the native Mac VPN client. Using Bomgar™ I can frequently resolve issues that would normally require a visit by an IT Desktop Support staffer. Even if a Bomgar™ session can't entirely resolve an issue; it can frequently reduce the workload of the staffer that might still need to visit the customer. The significance of this comes down to time to resolution. The median time of resolution of tickets that need to go out to the field is 1.88 days. Median time for tickets handled by the Help Desk is .25 days.

2.5 Account Management: apply.rice.edu

The Rice University Online Account Management System (OAMS) is usually called simply "Apply". Apply (really, no one calls it "OAMS") is a web interface to Rice accounts. The Help Desk has limited powers over accounts. Apply creates accounts based on a nightly data feed from the Registrar and Human Resources, who are the sole arbiters of who gets and keeps Rice accounts. We can, when instructed, lock and unlock accounts, but we cannot create them and we cannot bring them back after HR or the Registrar has marked them as inactive. This policy removes IT from the discussion when a customer has lost, or is about to lose, account access.

The most common use of Apply, at the Help Desk, is to help customer set new passwords and help new faculty, staff and students to register their accounts.

Our email administrators have recently added a tool that will allow customers to receive a reset token. In order to use this tool, the customer must have an alternate email or cell phone registered with the Rice University Emergency System. The customer gets a link by email or phone to reset their password.

3. MY DESKTOP

The Help Desk workstations are Macs, running Mountain Lion. I have a virtual Windows install, but I rarely use it. Most of my network tools are either web-based or available at the Terminal. The Bomgar™ tool keeps my Windows chops in good order, so I can help our Windows using customers.

4. ISSUES

4.1 Email

As I write this our most recent data shows that 47% of issues handled by our Help Desk are email related. The data shows 27% of our tickets are spam-related and 20% are Email, but since spam is email, I'm going to say 47% or our workload is email. Our email technology is Cyrus, offering customer IMAP or POP mail service. There is no standardized mail client. We support the full gamut of mail clients, including Pine, Eudora, Apple Mail, Thunderbird and Outlook.

4.1.1 Mail client configuration
Usually a changed password, but sometimes a mail client will do unexpected things to account configurations. Bomgar™ is particularly useful for troubleshooting mail clients.

4.1.2 Service Differences
Undergraduates get email hosted by Google. Staff and faculty get university hosted UNIX mailboxes. The exception is our business school and some departments, who have their email hosted on a Microsoft Exchange server, which IT manages and the business school sponsors. Email accounts expire with the customers' active relationship to the university. May graduates are purged every November. Departing staff and faculty are locked out by their Human Resources termination code. The only customers who get lifetime email are retirees.

4.1.3 SPAM or Phishing
This is typically a report of phishing, or a complaint that the customer is getting more spam than they feel is reasonable. We can help these customers by guiding them through the process of training the SPAM filter we use at the server.

4.2 Account Management

Another category we track is Account Management, which weighs in at 24%, and in my experience those issues are mostly "I can't login to my email". This is usually a password issue or the account has not been created through the automated process after Human Resources processes a new hire. Human Resources processing can sometimes take a day, or even two or three, after the first day of employment and frequently results in a call to the Help Desk. New customer calls can be long. We talk the customer through registration of their accounts and, typically, spend time with the customer getting their email client configured

4.2.1 Password Management
Lost passwords and new customers make up the bulk of these calls. Password resets can be a problem over the phone. For security reasons, we must do our best to verify a caller's identity over the phone before we help a caller set a new password. Our customers have found the password tool to be extremely reliable.

4.2.2 Inactive Accounts
It often falls to the Help Desk to inform former staff and students that their university email accounts are no longer available after their departure from employment or active student status (graduation -- we hope). Undergraduate and graduate students keep their email until the next November, when we purge old accounts. Departing staff are often surprised when they find out that their email service ends with their Rice employment. Fortunately, IT is not the arbiter of active accounts. At Rice that decision is made by departments, in consultation with Human Resources, and the Help Desk is spared the discussion.

4.3 Mobile Device Management

This issue doesn't hit us as hard as you might think. 1% of our issues this year have been related to mobile devices. This could be something the customers are handling themselves or they're just waiting to ambush their local IT staffer in a hallway, rather than calling the Help Desk. When we do get calls, generally they are from new smart phone and tablet or pad customers. Typically, those calls take 30 minutes to resolve, when we can handle them without sending the request to field staff.

4.4 Mailman

The Help Desk is responsible for creation and troubleshooting Mailman mailing lists. We can fulfill a typical request for a Mailman list quickly, but service requests frequently take longer. Mailman service request can be time-consuming, often requiring time spent with the customer to analyze their needs and then research to determine how best to configure the list to meet the customer's needs. The Mailman administrator web interface can be challenging to interpret and changes often require testing.

4.5 Off-Campus

We get calls from Rice University customers experiencing trouble accessing the network from off-campus. This is becoming more common as staff start to telecommute. Remote Desktop Connection customers require prior configuration of their office computer by field staff. We will not dispatch field staff off-campus. We will help with accounts, mail client configuration and VPN connections -- just about anything else we limit to a best effort.

4.6 Student Computer Consultants (SCCs) Repair Center

The Repair Center was established to centralize help for undergraduate and graduate student personal computers. The service is staffed by undergraduates. Service is limited, but, we don't charge a fee. We can handle malware infections, system reinstalls, software upgrades and hard drive failures. The Repair Center also handles other troubleshooting tasks such as network connections and software installation problems. Previously, that work was handled by student workers in the colleges (dormitories). The change resulted in a timelier and consistent service to the students, but the fallout was a new set of customers. Shortly after opening the repair center we started seeing staff and faculty who did not want to wait for field staff and retired staff and faculty started bringing in their personal computers from their homes. Usually, the requests are simple -- email client configurations, account help, smart phone and mobile device configurations. The result is that, along with helping students, the customer base has expanded to cover current and retired staff and faculty who walk-in. We've tried turning these customers away and restricting service to account level help, but that conversation is often a non-starter.

4.7 Hardware

When a graduate and undergraduate student brings us his computer for hardware failures, he signs a release that holds us harmless for any data loss. For hardware failures, our staff will pull a hard drive that's having trouble and attempt to recover the data for restoration to a replacement hard drive that the customer provides. Data recovery from notebook hard drives is both a common trouble and one that consumes a large portion of our Student Computing Consultant time.

Most computer repair businesses and warranty service centers will replace a dying hard drive and re-install an Operating System. Data recovery is too time consuming and is, typically, not covered under warranty. For our students, that data is too precious to lose and, frequently, there is no backup. While we can't recover data from a dead hard drive, the students have gotten good at working with drives that are failing with commercially available software recovery tools. The failing drive is connected to a Mac recovery station with a USB to SATA connection and the data is simply copied over to our local storage. It is not uncommon for us to recover the hard drive's data and return the notebook to the customer, who then sends it off for warranty.

4.8 Data Management, Drobo, Inc.

Storage for data at the Repair Center has proven to be a challenge. Our solution has evolved over time from one DROBO consumer backup device to a network of four DROBO units with about 10 terabytes of redundant storage. Since the standardization in configurations of the DROBO units, they have been extremely reliable. A team of student consultants designed the backup network and wrote an application in python for Linux. That application is tied to our Request Tracker application. Each customer's data is tied to a Request Tracker ticket. Data is stored for 10 days after the ticket is closed, unless it is flagged. The software will delete data two weeks after the ticket is closed, unless the directory is flagged for "hold".

4.9 Printing

Each semester the School of Architecture hosts printing Charrette generates over 200 plotter posters in a period of 4 days. In order to meet poster printing assignments deadlines, our Student Computer Consultants assist customers with prepping print jobs for our 5 color plotters. IT does charge students for printing. Printing refunds are fairly easy, bad prints that are our fault we refund -- usually ink and paper related problems. SCCs will take the requests, enter the information in Request Tracker which automatically generates an RT ticket and placed in the Printing Refund queue. The full-time staffers will approve and process refunds. Bad print jobs that are the result of customer error by the student are not refunded.

5. WORK SHIFTS

No shifts. We don't offer after hours support. We're open Monday through Friday, 9:00 a.m. to 5:00 p.m. -- that's it. We don't run shifts at night and we don't cover weekends. It's OK, close your jaw, that's right, we have banker's hours and it works for us. We have experimented with longer hours, but the Rice campus tends to shut down at 4:00 p.m. due to the lack of student activity in the early evening hours. We've found it to be a wasted effort. For after hour emergencies, we have an Operations Desk and On-Call admins. You don't end up with a staffing emergency when the night shift staffer gets sick, or just when someone working nights or weekends wants to take vacation. To my knowledge, there is no clamor for extended hours from our customers.

6. CUSTOMER FEEDBACK

In a recent campus-wide survey, the feedback was positive. Our client services were rated 4.2 out of 5. In addition to this survey, customers have the opportunity to send commends to our Bravo Board by completing the form: http://it.rice.edu/bravo.aspx. The Bravos are posted in the lobby of the Mudd Building which houses our IT department.

7. REFERENCES

[1] Avaya Inc., 4655 Great America Pkwy, Santa Clara, CA 95054-1233

[2] Best Practical Solutions, LLC □PO Box 441333 □Somerville, MA 02144

[3] Atlassian, 1098 Harrision St., San Francisco, California 94103

[4] Bomgar, 578 Highland Colony Parkway, Paragon Centre, Ridgeland, Mississippi, 39157.

[5] Rice University, Online Account Management System, © 2004 Rice University

[6] Drobo, 2460 North First Street, Suite 100, San Jose, CA 95131

Author Index

www.ingramcontent.com/pod-product-compliance
Lightning Source LLC
Chambersburg PA
CBHW061414210326
41598CB00035B/6212